Žižek

Žižek

A Reader's Guide

Kelsey Wood

A John Wiley & Sons, Ltd., Publication

This edition first published 2012
© 2012 John Wiley & Sons, Inc.

Wiley-Blackwell is an imprint of John Wiley & Sons, formed by the merger of
Wiley's global Scientific, Technical and Medical business with Blackwell Publishing.

Registered Office
John Wiley & Sons Ltd, The Atrium, Southern Gate, Chichester, West Sussex,
PO19 8SQ, UK

Editorial Offices
350 Main Street, Malden, MA 02148-5020, USA
9600 Garsington Road, Oxford, OX4 2DQ, UK
The Atrium, Southern Gate, Chichester, West Sussex, PO19 8SQ, UK

For details of our global editorial offices, for customer services, and for information
about how to apply for permission to reuse the copyright material in this book please
see our website at www.wiley.com/wiley-blackwell.

The right of Kelsey Wood to be identified as the authors of this work has been
asserted in accordance with the UK Copyright, Designs and Patents Act 1988.

Library of Congress Cataloging-in-Publication Data
Wood, Kelsey, 1960–
  Žižek : a reader's guide / by Kelsey Wood.
    p. cm.
  Includes bibliographical references and index.
  ISBN 978-0-470-67475-8 (hardcover : alk. paper) – ISBN 978-0-470-67476-5
(pbk. : alk. paper)
  1. Žižek, Slavoj. I. Title.
  B4870.Z594W66 2012
  199′.4973–dc23

                                        2011052162
A catalogue record for this book is available from the British Library.

Set in 10/12.5pt Plantin by SPi Publisher Services, Pondicherry, India
Printed in Malaysia by Ho Printing (M) Sdn Bhd

1   2012

for John Brennon Wood

Contents

Epigraphs   ix
Acknowledgments   x

1   Introduction   1
2   *The Sublime Object of Ideology*   46
3   *For They Know Not What They Do: Enjoyment
    as a Political Factor*   55
4   *Looking Awry: An Introduction to Jacques Lacan
    through Popular Culture*   66
5   *Enjoy Your Symptom! Jacques Lacan in
    Hollywood and Out*   75
6   *Tarrying with the Negative: Kant, Hegel,
    and the Critique of Ideology*   94
7   *The Metastases of Enjoyment: On Women
    and Causality*   108
8   *The Indivisible Remainder: On Schelling
    and Related Matters*   115
9   *The Plague of Fantasies*   125
10 *The Ticklish Subject: The Absent Centre of
    Political Ontology*   136
11 *The Art of the Ridiculous Sublime: On David Lynch's
    Lost Highway*   146
12 *The Fragile Absolute: or, Why is the Christian Legacy
    Worth Fighting For?*   155
13 *On Belief*   163

Contents

14 *The Fright of Real Tears: Krzysztof Kieślowski between Theory and Post-Theory* — 171

15 *Did Somebody Say Totalitarianism? Five Interventions in the (Mis)use of a Notion* — 180

16 *Welcome to the Desert of the Real* — 193

17 *The Puppet and the Dwarf: The Perverse Core of Christianity* — 201

18 *Organs without Bodies: On Deleuze and Consequences* — 212

19 *Iraq: The Borrowed Kettle* — 220

20 *How to Read Lacan* — 227

21 *The Parallax View* — 237

22 *In Defense of Lost Causes* — 249

23 *Violence* — 257

24 *First as Tragedy, then as Farce* — 267

25 *Living in the End Times* — 278

26 Conclusion — 295

Further Reading — 315

Index — 322

Epigraphs

As a general rule, disciples have been won over for the wrong reasons, are faithful to a misinterpretation, overdogmatic in their exposition, and too liberal in debate. They almost always end up by betraying us.
—Alain Badiou, *Deleuze: The Clamor of Being*, p. 96

Lacan's scandal, the dimension of his work which resists incorporation into the academic machinery, can be ultimately pinned down to the fact that he openly and shamelessly posited himself as an authority, i.e., that he repeated the Kierkegaardian gesture in relationship to his followers: what he demanded of them was not fidelity to some general theoretical propositions, but precisely fidelity to his person – which is why, in the circular letter announcing the foundation of La Cause freudienne, *he addresses them as "those who love me." This unbreakable link connecting the doctrine to the contingent person of the teacher, i.e., to the teacher qua material surplus that sticks out from the neutral edifice of knowledge, is the scandal everybody who considers himself Lacanian has to assume: Lacan was not a Socratic master obliterating himself in front of the attained knowledge, his theory sustains itself only through the transferential relationship to its founder.*
—Slavoj Žižek, *Enjoy Your Symptom! Jacques Lacan in Hollywood and Out*, p. 100

Acknowledgments

Thanks go to Slavoj Žižek and to Clayton Crockett. John Brennon Wood read every chapter, offered constructive criticism, and suggested many improvements to the text. Our frequent conversations were a source of inspiration, and his knowledge of computer media showed me that dialectical materialism is alive and well in unexpected places. We are grateful to Stan Wakefield, and to Jeff Dean, Executive Editor at Wiley-Blackwell. And to Jana Wood, Margaret, Jacqueline, Raymond, and Bruce: we are close to each other by way of being close to the third thing.

1

Introduction

*Today, one often mentions how the reference to psychoanalysis in cultural
studies and the psychoanalytic clinic supplement each other: cultural
studies lack the real of clinical experience, while the clinic lacks the
broader critico-historical perspective (say, of the historic specificity of the
categories of psychoanalysis, Oedipal complex, castration, or paternal
authority). The answer to this should be that each of the approaches
should work on its limitation from within its horizon – not by relying on
the other to fill up its lack. If cultural studies cannot account for the real
of the clinical experience, this signals the insufficiency of its theoretical
framework itself; if the clinic cannot reflect its historical presuppositions, it
is a bad clinic.*

　　　　　　　—Slavoj Žižek, "Jacques Lacan's Four Discourses"

Who is Slavoj Žižek?

Slavoj Žižek is widely regarded as the most significant and provocative
thinker of our age. As the above quotation indicates, Žižek deploys concepts
from the psychoanalytic theory of Jacques Lacan in order to reactualize a
dialectical method in philosophy.[1] The result is a radically new vision of

---

[1]　Jacques Lacan (1901–1981) is the most important psychoanalytic theorist after Freud,
and his ideas transformed psychoanalysis; however, his theories are notoriously difficult.

Žižek: A Reader's Guide, First Edition. Kelsey Wood.
© 2012 John Wiley & Sons, Inc. Published 2012 by John Wiley & Sons, Inc.

human nature and human society. In addition to Jacques Lacan, Žižek has been strongly influenced by the work of G. W. F. Hegel, F. W. J. Schelling, Karl Marx, Sigmund Freud, Martin Heidegger, Jacques Derrida, Louis Althusser, and Alain Badiou. In his public lectures, Žižek has concisely introduced his own thinking as Hegelian in philosophy, Lacanian in psychology, "Christian-materialist" in religion, and communist in politics.[2]

But why has Slavoj Žižek become so well known in the two decades since his first publications in English? What is so captivating and so revolutionary about his fusion of philosophy and psychoanalysis? Why is Professor Žižek widely regarded as one of the most important thinkers in the world today? A preliminary answer to these questions is that he is a charismatic speaker with an extraordinary ability to engage his audience. Žižek regularly draws large crowds and packs auditoriums across whatever continent he visits, and consistently fills lecture halls beyond their normal capacity. But anyone who has also sat in his classroom will be impressed by Žižek's ability to make difficult ideas comprehensible; he is an extremely effective *teacher*. Moreover, a look into any of his books reveals immediately that Žižek is an enormously accomplished scholar. He is the sole author of more than 20 books in English (and counting), and these innovative and theoretically substantial works have established him as one of today's preeminent thinkers.

Žižek has written – with humor, lucidity, and extraordinary erudition – on the philosophical problem of identity, ontology, globalization, post-modernism, political philosophy, literature, film, ecology, religion, the French Revolution, Lenin, the philosophy of language, the philosophy of mind, and numerous other topics. Without question the work of Slavoj

---

Because Žižek's remarks are often addressed to an audience that is already familiar with Lacanian psychoanalysis, the reader new to Lacanian theory may need to consult an introductory text as well. One of the best short introductions to Lacan is Sean Homer's *Jacques Lacan* (London: Routledge, 2005). A more in-depth (but still non-philosophical) introduction to Lacan is *The Lacanian Subject: Between Language and Jouissance* by Bruce Fink (Princeton: Princeton University Press, 1995). The best essays on Lacan and philosophy are Alenka Zupancic's *Ethics of the Real* (London: Verso, 2000), and Joan Copjec's *Read My Desire* (Cambridge, MA: MIT Press, 1994). For additional essays on Lacan and philosophy, see the website *The International Journal of Žižek Studies*, at http://www.zizekstudies.org/. Readers should regularly explore the wealth of resources available from the website lacan.com, run in New York by Josefina Ayerza. Newcomers to Lacanian theory might want to consult Dylan Evans' *An Introductory Dictionary of Lacanian Psychoanalysis* (London: Routledge, 1996).

[2] For an online biography of Žižek, see the faculty page of the website for the European Graduate School at http://www.egs.edu/faculty/slavoj-zizek/biography/. Another online biography is available at http://www.notablebiographies.com/supp/Supplement-Sp-Z/Zizek-Slavoj.html.

Žižek will continue to inform philosophical, psychological, political, and cultural discourses well into the future. In an effort to explain the Žižek phenomenon, Ian Parker writes:

> Žižek burst onto the world academic stage with commentaries and interventions in politics and psychoanalysis, with powerful examples of the way an understanding of these two domains could be dialectically intertwined and powered through a close reading of German philosophy. Žižek's academic performance has also drawn attention from a wider intellectual audience, and this has given him the opportunity to elaborate some complex conceptual machinery that can be applied to music, theology, virtual reality, and, it would seem, virtually any other cultural phenomenon. His writing appeared at an opportune moment, offering a new vocabulary for thinking through how ideology grips its subjects.[3]

But Ian Parker's remarks do not indicate the fundamental reasons why Žižek's work has become so prominent (and so controversial) since the publication in 1989 of *The Sublime Object of Ideology*. Žižek is not only a charismatic speaker and a brilliant cultural theorist who, at an opportune moment, captivated the public with elaborate and innovative theories. Significantly, Parker (who is a practicing psychoanalyst) neglects the *philosophical* implications of Žižek's work. According to Marek Wieczorek, "The originality of Žižek's contribution to Western intellectual history lies in his extraordinary fusion of Lacanian psychoanalytic theory, continental philosophy (in particular his anti-essentialist readings of Hegel), and Marxist political theory."[4] Žižek utilizes Lacanian psychoanalytic concepts *in order to reinvent Hegelian dialectics*; he puts Lacanian theory to work in order to reactualize German Idealism for the twenty-first century.

---

[3] Ian Parker, *Slavoj Žižek: A Critical Introduction* (London: Pluto Press, 2004), pp. 2–3. Parker's interpretation of Žižek's work lapses repeatedly into circumstantial ad hominem fallacies. For example, in an attempt to formulate a critique of Žižek's politics, Parker offers a lengthy digression intended to demonstrate Žižek's alleged "over-identification" with his Slovenian origins and affiliations. In fact, Parker's entire chapter 1 is devoted to the formation, operation, and decomposition of the Yugoslav state. Parker rehashes this caricature of Žižek in his contribution to the stunningly misnamed book, *The Truth of Žižek*, edited by Paul Bowman and Richard Stamp (London: Continuum, 2007). Significantly, Žižek's afterward to *The Truth of Žižek* is titled "With Defenders like These, Who Needs Attackers." This afterward is by far the most valuable contribution to the work. Žižek responds to Parker's efforts to discredit him on pages 231–2 of *The Truth of Žižek*, and succinctly refutes Parker's claims.

[4] See Marek Wieczorek, "Introduction," in Žižek, *The Art of the Ridiculous Sublime: On David Lynch's Lost Highway* (Seattle: The Walter Chapin Simpson Center for the Humanities, University of Washington, 2000), p. viii.

This being said, it must be added that Žižek is also a psychoanalyst, and it is thus no accident that his discourse provokes what Lacanian psychoanalysts call *jouissance*. As students of the history of philosophy know, many philosophers lack a sense of humor. The prime example of this is Martin Heidegger, whose only documented joke was a jibe directed at Lacan: "Significantly, the ONLY joke – or, if not joke then, at least, moment of irony – in Heidegger occurs in his rather bad taste quip about Lacan as 'that psychiatrist who is himself in the need of a psychiatrist' (in a letter to Medard Boss)."[5] Žižek is one of the few philosophers since Socrates who is able to inspire the love of learning and also to make his students and interlocutors laugh. And like Socrates Žižek continuously engages in self-critique, usually by ironically indicating the obscene underside of acceptable liberal-tolerant discourse. Žižek's students immediately recognize when he ironically criticizes himself. If, for example, Žižek jokingly calls himself a racist, it is in the context of his criticism of those who indulge in obscene racist fantasies. But his endearing and self-deprecating sense of humor is another fundamental reason for Žižek's success. In fact, many of his fans find his books and his lectures so enjoyable as to be almost addictive, and *enjoyment* is at the origin of the Žižek phenomenon.

"Enjoyment" is the accepted translation of the Lacanian term *jouissance*, and in his work, Žižek reveals the vital role of enjoyment in social life. But in order to understand Žižek, it is necessary to keep in mind that enjoyment is not pleasure: *jouissance* is surplus enjoyment that manifests as a strange fascination accompanied by uneasiness or discomfort (e.g., gawking at a car crash). Enjoyment is a kind of excessive stimulation, an unbearable pleasure *in* pain, an incalculable "something more" that can induce human beings to act against their own self-interest. Žižek shows that even though subjects are not usually aware of *jouissance*, all politics relies upon and manipulates an economy of enjoyment. However it is not merely Žižek's *understanding* of enjoyment, but more importantly, his ability to *produce* enjoyment that has led to his large following. The *jouissance* engendered by his discourse is one of the primary reasons why Žižek has been the eye of a storm of cultural, political, and philosophical controversy for decades.[6]

---

[5] Slavoj Žižek, "Religion between Knowledge and *Jouissance*," available online at http://www.lacan.com/zizsmokeonthewater.html#_ftn8.

[6] In an interview in 2007, Paul A. Taylor described how Žižek constantly questions further and revises his own thinking. Taylor points out that the uncategorizable aspect of Žižek's writing is indicated by the geographical and disciplinary spread of his readers. But perhaps the primary feature of all his work is its ethical quality: such as his exposure of hypocrisy

Along these lines, because Žižek is a psychoanalyst, it is no coincidence that he is so successful at engendering *transference*. Although transference may manifest as hate, it more often manifests as love.[7] And moreover – as Lacan showed – transference is primarily related to knowledge and the love of learning. Žižek's depth of psychoanalytic insight makes him one of those rare philosophers who very effectively engender transference as the love of truth. He thrives on this transference relationship with his audience and, because of his own love of learning, he pushes himself to the limit in testing and revising his analyses, and induces his readers to actively engage in this struggle for truth. Žižek's aim is always the further development of previous analyses.

Unfortunately, at the time of this writing, Žižek's major work on Hegel is not yet available. This book does not pretend to be a comprehensive study; it merely provides an introductory-level focus for the approach to 24 of Žižek's monographs.[8] What follows is not intended as an encyclopedic synopsis of the meaning of Žižek's work, much less as a narrative account of Žižek's development and significance. This guide simply attempts to facilitate – for general readers – the engagement in Žižek's philosophical struggle for the truth. The following essays simply try to let Žižek speak for himself (as much as possible) about certain fundamental problems of philosophy. Along the way, we hope to indicate why philosophy after Žižek, if it is not to regress, must build on his methodology. What follows is intended as an aid for readers who are simultaneously reading the texts that are being discussed.

---

and lazy thinking. Another appeal of Žižek's theorizing is its practical usefulness; his unabashed speculative approach nevertheless uncovers the issues behind actual events better than so-called "pragmatic" works. The full interview is online at http://zizekstudies.org/index.php/ijzs/article/viewFile/3/9.

[7] Žižek sometimes discusses love with reference to the song "In Praise of the Third Thing" (*Lob der dritten Sache*) from Brecht's *Mother*: "The mother keeps (or rather, regains) her son in the very act of losing him 'through the third thing'; they are close to each other by way of being close to the third thing (in this case, of course, their common struggle for communism)." See Slavoj Žižek, *Opera's Second Death* (New York: Routledge, 2002), p. 195.

[8] The following essays are arranged in (approximately) the order in which Žižek published the books, but have been written in such a way that they may be read *either* sequentially *or* individually (i.e. in any order). There are some minor inconsistencies, due to the fact that Žižek himself is inconsistent. For example, in some texts, he uses the term "non-all," whereas in other texts he uses "not-All." In the following commentary, I have tried to preserve Žižek's variants. This explains why certain terms are capitalized or spelt differently depending on which book is under discussion. In addition, the chapter titles (except for this "Introduction" and also my "Conclusion") correspond *exactly* to Žižek's book titles, except for standardizing Žižek's idiosyncratic capitalization.

What Does Žižek Mean by "Dialectic"?

In addition to the *jouissance* he provokes, and in addition to his ability to engender transference as the love of knowledge, there is another reason for Žižek's profound impact. He is not just a theorist; he is also a theoretical activist and revolutionary. He does not simply write books and give talks: every book and every talk is an *intervention*. He intentionally provokes us, his listeners and readers, to overcome our complacency and to confront our own relation to fantasy, enjoyment, and the dialectic of desire. Žižek's discourse engages us to the point that we actively participate as both analyst and analysand. Because of the level of engagement his thinking demands and induces, theory for Žižek is much more than what Ian Parker refers to as "conceptual machinery." Žižek's dialectical materialism does not merely describe the world; on the contrary, it is already changing the world. In fact, his work has already led to the reinvention of the basic theoretical coordinates of an astonishing variety of disciplines and discourses. So on the one hand, his theory involves intervention, and the inducement to the Lacanian act, which ruptures symbolic reality, and opens the possibility of new possibilities. But, on the other hand, Žižek also reveals the extent to which intervention and struggle always rely (at least implicitly) on theory.

A close reading of Žižek's books will reveal that his dialectical materialism offers a new approach to most of the traditional problems of philosophy. Consider the ancient controversy between nominalism and realism. *Nominalism* (derived from the Greek *onoma*, meaning "name"), is the doctrine that universal, abstract ideas, have no real existence, but are simply general names invented by humans to indicate individual entities. According to nominalism, the locus of truth and reality are these individual entities. By contrast, *realism* is the doctrine that (at least some) universal ideas transcend our identification and naming of them: these universal natures or essences (allegedly) inform all intelligible experience. Neither of these doctrines achieves the subtlety or clarity of Žižek's ontology; but the very antagonism between them is an example of the moment of incommensurability that Žižek evokes in his investigations into what we mean when we say that something is "true." Žižek shows how both realism and nominalism fail to recognize that what is universal is the Lacanian Real as the incommensurability or parallax gap that provokes the struggle for truth. Philosophical realism errs in conceiving the truth as some enduring content that serves as an infallible standard of correctness for all possible disclosures or human actions. Nominalism errs by reducing all conflicts to the different particular definitions of some term. For the nominalist, there is really no conflict; the problem is simply that the two parties in the disagreement use the term (e.g., justice, freedom, etc.) in two different senses. Both realism and nominalism are wrong in presuming that we have access to some unambiguous ground or thing-in-itself (conceived either as universal ideal or as individual entities). But as we will see, Žižek points out again and again that the true universal is the Real as antagonism itself, the struggle for hegemony is itself the only sameness that permeates any possible symbolic "reality." The price for our access to what we experience as reality is that something must remain unthought.[9]

But if any one – any whole or totality – is inherently inconsistent, then how does a name refer to the objects it denotes? Descriptivists (such as John Searle) argue that names refer to objects because of the meaning implicit to the name. According to descriptivism, a name is like a cluster of positive properties, descriptive features that comprise the meaning of the word. For example, the *intensional* meaning of the term "mouse" consists of the properties connoted by the word: being a small furry rodent, having large ears and a long thin tail, squeaking, nibbling holes in cheeses, etc. The *extensional* meaning of the word "mouse" is all of the entities in the universe denoted by this term. Intension has logical priority over extension insofar as the set of universal properties connoted by the word "mouse" determines whether or not an object belongs to the set of mice.

In contrast to this approach, antidescriptivists (such as Saul Kripke) argue that a name refers to an object because of an act of "primal baptism." Kripke argues that a name functions as a "rigid designator" that refers to the same object in any possible worlds. Kripke's most famous example involves the claim that "Hesperus is identical to Phosphorus." "Hesperus" is an old name for an object that was formerly described as the evening star, and "Phosphorus" is an old name for an object that was described as the morning star. But unknown to the users of these names, both referred to the same object, the planet Venus. Therefore, the claim "Hesperus is identical to Phosphorus" must be necessarily true, because Hesperus and Phosphorus are proper names for the identical object. Each name refers to its object (and to no other object) in all possible worlds, because the object that both names designate is Venus, and Venus is self-identical: Venus is identical to Venus. Kripke argues that these names, like other names, are rigid designators.

Žižek's account of how names refer to objects develops the philosophical implications of Lacanian theory, and departs from both descriptivism

---

[9] Cf. Slavoj Žižek, *Tarrying with the Negative: Kant, Hegel, and the Critique of Ideology* (Durham, NC: Duke University Press, 1993), p. 44.

and antidescriptivism.[10] Because language cannot be private, meaning is always intersubjective; it exists in the symbolic order, the Lacanian big Other. But the symbolic space of language and discourse is made up of signifiers that are ambiguous: their literal meaning is "overdetermined" by metaphorical surplus meaning. This ambiguity in the field of meaning is tied down, or fixed in place through naming. Žižek argues that both descriptivists and antidescriptivists overlook the radical contingency implicit to naming.[11] Žižek's account shows a sense in which, not only proper names, but every name in any common language, implies a circular, self-referential moment: "Here we encounter the dogmatic stupidity proper to a signifier as such, the stupidity which assumes the shape of a tautology: a name refers to an object *because this object is called that* – this impersonal form ('it is called') announces the dimension of the 'big Other' beyond other subjects."[12] This tautological moment, which is a constituent of every use of names in language, is the Lacanian Master-Signifier. The Master-Signifier is an empty signifier which has no signified content, and which unifies a field of meaning precisely through this very lack or inconsistency:

> each master-signifier works not because it is some pre-existing fullness that already contains all of the meanings attributed to it, but because it is empty, just that place from which to see the "equivalence" of other signifiers. It is not some original reserve that holds all of its significations in advance, but only what is retrospectively recognized as what is being referred to. Thus, to take the example of "democracy," it is not some concept common to the liberal notion of democracy, which asserts the autonomy of the individual over the State, and the socialist notion of democracy, which can only be guaranteed by a Party representing the interests of the People. It is not a proper solution to argue either that the socialist definition travesties true democracy or that the socialist alternative is the only authentic form of democracy. Rather, the only adequate way to define "democracy" is to include all political movements and orientations that legitimate themselves by reference to "democracy" – and which are ultimately defined only by their differential relationship to "non-democracy."[13]

[10] One of the clearest and most accessible accounts of the philosophical implications of Lacanian psychoanalytic theory is in chapter 3 of Slavoj Žižek's *The Sublime Object of Ideology* (London and New York: Verso, 1989), pp. 87–129.

[11] Slavoj Žižek, *The Sublime Object of Ideology* (London and New York: Verso, 1989), p. 92.

[12] Slavoj Žižek, *The Sublime Object of Ideology* (London and New York: Verso, 1989), p. 93.

[13] See Rex Butler, "Slavoj Žižek: What is a Master-Signifier," online at http://www.lacan. com/zizek-signifier.htm. See also chapter 2 of Butler's excellent book, *Slavoj Žižek: Live Theory* (London: Continuum, 2005).

This means that "beneath" the alleged unity of the field of meaning, there is only a tautological, self-referential, *performative* gesture. In other words, it is not some pre-existing, substantial fullness of meaning to which all of the particulars refer. The Master-Signifier is an empty signifier that is – only retrospectively – seen as that to which the field of meaning refers. Every use of the term (e.g., "Democracy") is defined through relations of difference toward others. In sum, the Master-Signifier is pure difference *misperceived* as pure identity.

The fundamental problem for antidescriptivism is to explain what makes an object identical to itself even if all of its positive properties change over time. In other words, even if antidescriptivism is correct and names function as rigid designators, how are we to conceive the "objective correlate" to the rigid designator? Žižek points out that the standard version of antidescriptivism overlooks the *retroactive* effect of naming: "That 'surplus' in the object which stays the same in all possible worlds is 'something in it more than itself,' that is to say the Lacanian *objet petit a*: we search in vain for it in positive reality because it has no positive consistency – because it is just an objectification of a void, of a discontinuity opened in reality by the emergence of the signifier."[14] This implies that antidescriptivism is misguided in its emphasis on the external causal chain that (allegedly) transmits the reference of a name to its object. Naming is radically contingent insofar as it is the act of naming itself that constitutes its own reference, in a retroactive way. There is a "necessary" (noncontingent) dimension of naming, but this necessity is only constituted *after the fact*, once we are already involved in the process of dialectical differentiation.

While reading Žižek's books, it is important to keep in mind that he continuously refines his own earlier insights; he is perhaps his own best critic. This is an example of Žižek's dialectical method. Methodology is the analysis of method itself, and Žižek continuously refines his own method. For example, in *For They Know Not What They Do: Enjoyment as a Political Factor* (his second book in English), he criticizes his remarkably successful previous book, *The Sublime Object of Ideology*:

> *The Sublime Object* fails to deploy the complex interconnections within the triad Real–Imaginary–Symbolic: the entire triad is reflected within each of its three elements. [...] The Real is thus, in effect, all three dimensions at the same time: the abyssal vortex which ruins every consistent structure; the mathematized consistent structure of reality; the fragile pure appearance. And in a strictly homologous way, there are three modalities

[14] Slavoj Žižek, *The Sublime Object of Ideology* (London and New York: Verso, 1989), p. 95.

of the Symbolic (the real – the signifier reduced to a senseless formula; the imaginary – the Jungian "symbols"; and the symbolic – speech, meaningful language); and three modalities of the Imaginary (the real – fantasy, which is precisely an imaginary scenario occupying the place of the Real; the imaginary – image as such in its fundamental function of a decoy; and the symbolic – again, the Jungian "symbols" or New Age archetypes).[15]

Žižek is as ruthless a critic of himself as he is of others. But he is famous for intervening in contemporary intellectual debates and then showing precisely in what sense *both* sides are wrong: he exposes fallacies and vanities in a way that few thinkers have ever done. But Žižek is no cynic, and he supplements his devastating reductions to absurdity with startling new insights. Contemporary philosophy, psychology, cultural studies, sociology, political science, esthetics, literary theory, film theory, and theology simply cannot be evaluated without reference to the terrain-shifting innovations of Žižek's thinking.

For example, Žižek's dialectical materialism reveals the extent to which both post-analytic philosophy and contemporary continental philosophy are haunted by the specter of German Idealism. But in order to grasp the profundity of Žižek's impact, it is crucial to remember that his central concern involves the reactualization of dialectical thinking. In approaching Žižek's texts for the first time, it is important to realize that there is an insight that must be achieved regarding the dialectical aspect of Žižek's thought. Once the dialectical insight is apprehended, afterwards everything begins to make sense, and Žižek appears in a whole new light. This insight is not a factoid or a bit of information that can simply be poured into the mind of the beginning reader like liquid from one jar to another. In order to attain this insight, the reader must *actively engage* in the struggle to understand Žižek's texts. Žižek's Lacanian reactualization of the German Idealist tradition – particularly Hegel – emphasizes the radical finitude of consciousness, knowledge, and, significantly, *reality itself*. But how can reality be finite or incomplete? In order to begin to understand this, we need to first consider the meaning of "dialectical" thinking.

In what follows, the reader must bear in mind that whenever Žižek discusses film, literature, or popular culture, he is not offering psychoanalytic interpretations of the books and films that he discusses. Popular culture in his books is never the whole point; the point is to introduce dialectical thinking to people who have already been

---

[15] Slavoj Žižek, *For They Know Not What They Do: Enjoyment as a Political Factor* (London and New York: Verso, 2002), p. xii.

indoctrinated into nondialectical so-called "thinking" (e.g., many professional philosophers in the USA, myself included). In short, Žižek discusses familiar examples from cinema and literature in order to make a dialectical point about philosophical-psychoanalytic theory. When he occasionally gets details wrong in referring to an example from a film or text, this is because *his primary aim is always the explication of a theoretical point.* As Sheila Kunkle puts it: "Žižek's examples, if we understand them in their connection to his theory, are meant to change our orientation to the reality we think surrounds us and they open up a space for a critique of universals that emerge out of the particular cases themselves."[16]

Whatever he is discussing – even if he is making a joke – Žižek's primary aim is the development of dialectical materialist theory. Sometimes he articulates an insight for those who already grasp the basics of dialectics, as when he argues that Hegelian dialectic involves negativity, and that therefore, "synthesis" – properly understood – posits the difference as such. If the reader initially finds this confusing, but then suddenly notices that Žižek is repeating the same old joke for the umpteenth time (e.g., "Coffee or tea? Yes, please!"), the reader should not make the mistake of some hasty critics and jump to the conclusion that there is no logic or argumentation in Žižek's texts. The point is never simply the joke: in this case, the relevant point is that the response "Yes, please!" refers to both coffee and tea without effacing *the disjunction* between them. The "yes" functions in a homologous way to Žižek's reading of Hegelian synthesis as *not effacing, but instead preserving difference.* Along these lines, how can Žižek call himself a "Christian-materialist" when he also asserts that "Only an atheist can believe"? The answer to this apparent contradiction is easy to grasp if you just remember the coffee versus tea joke: "Christianity or dialectical materialism? Yes, please." Is Žižek (along with other materialist theologians) audaciously trying to reinvent Christianity? Or instead, does he reveal radical-emancipatory potential in Christianity in such a way so that – retroactively – it is as if this potential was always already "there"? Once again, a provocative but accurate dialectical response to this kind of false dichotomy could be simply "Yes." This use of a joke to undermine a dichotomy – by affirming both a conjunction and a disjunction – gives some indication of Žižek's provocative and amusing (but ultimately rigorous) dialectical procedure.

With this in mind, here is an initial working definition of the sense in which Žižek's thought is dialectical: there is no way to isolate "things" or

---

[16] Cf. Sheila Kunkle, "Embracing the Paradox: Žižek's Illogical Logic," in *International Journal of Žižek Studies*, vol. 2, number 4 (2008), p. 4.

"facts" from our symbolic representations of things or facts. In other words, we cannot formulate any comprehensive and consistent way to separate "reality" from its symbolization. As Rex Butler puts it:

> Our descriptions do not naturally and immutably refer to things, but – this is the defining feature of the symbolic order – things in retrospect begin to resemble their description. Thus, in the analysis of ideology, it is not simply a matter of seeing which account of reality best matches the "facts," with the one that is closest being the least biased and therefore the best. As soon as the facts are determined, we have already – whether we know it or not – made our choice; we are already within one ideological system or another. The real dispute has already taken place over what is to count as the facts, which facts are relevant, and so on.[17]

In other words, it is not just our understanding that is dialectical; "reality" is also dialectical, and ultimately there is no unambiguous way to separate our understanding *of* reality from reality. As Žižek and Markus Gabriel write: "Otherwise put, the whole domain of the representation of the world (call it mind, spirit, language, consciousness, or whatever medium you prefer) needs to be understood as an event within and of the world itself. Thought is not at all opposed to being, it is rather being's replication within itself."[18]

Another way to articulate this insight into the dialectical character of reality is to say that no element or term from Lacanian theory or Hegelian theory may be defined in isolation. For example, a clearing in the forest is not simply the open ground; without the surrounding trees, this ground would just be an indistinguishable bit of land. What a clearing in the forest *is* involves both openness and enclosure. Terms only signify in relation to one another, and, moreover, *in the particular context of their use*.

Furthermore, when we isolate two meaningful approaches to the same entity or event, and there is no way to unify these two approaches into one all-encompassing perspective, we must bear in mind that each approach is inherently incomplete. And each approach must work on its own inherent limitation – from within its own universe of discourse – without relying on the other approach to complete it or fill in its lack. The reason for this is that there is no overarching and complete metalanguage, or discourse of all discourses. This "universal perspectivism"

---

[17] Rex Butler, "Slavoj Žižek: What is a Master-Signifier," online at http://www.lacan.com/zizek-signifier.htm. See also chapter 2 of Butler's *Slavoj Žižek: Live Theory* (London: Continuum, 2005).

[18] See Markus Gabriel and Slavoj Žižek, *Mythology, Madness and Laughter: Subjectivity in German Idealism* (London and New York: Continuum, 2009), p. 3.

characterizes Žižek's dialectical materialist philosophy. It implies that incompleteness and inconsistency are irreducible; in other words, the Real is immanent to any possible symbolic reality. Thus there can be no transcendent perspective of all perspectives. This is another way of saying that the universal must be articulated as a negative a priori:

> The Universal is not the encompassing container of the particular content, the peaceful medium-background of the conflict of particularities; the Universal "as such" is the site of an unbearable antagonism, self-contradiction, and (the multitude of) its particular species are ultimately nothing but so many attempts to obfuscate/reconcile/master this antagonism. In other words, the Universal names the site of a Problem-Deadlock, of a burning Question, and the Particulars are the attempted but failed Answers to this Problem. Say, the concept of State names a certain problem: how to contain the class antagonism of a society? All particular forms of State are so many (failed) attempts to propose a solution for this problem.[19]

Because of this negativity of the universal (as a problem-deadlock, or struggle *for* universality), a dichotomy that presents us with an either/or decision ultimately proves to leave various contingent alternatives out. Žižek's works contain many examples along these lines: he investigates a dichotomous polarity between two alternatives and then shows how both sides fail to consider something, such as a presupposition they both share.

This dialectical method also informs Lacanian theory. For example, in order to come to understand a term like "the Master-Signifier," it is also necessary to think about ideology, *objet petit a*, suture, the *sinthome*, the Real as primordially repressed *jouissance* which is constituted retroactively, etc. A term signifies only in relation to other terms, and in relation to elements that are not terms (for example, a fantasy or an image). Moreover, the relations in question are often negative relations of difference. In sum, reality is dialectical in that there is no pure self-identity: no thing, event, or property simply is what it is; what a thing *is* – its very existence – involves what it is not.

Because of this negativity, opposites are never harmoniously reconciled in any higher "synthesis." Instead, *their difference is posited as such*, in the form of an inconsistent totality. Žižek clarifies this concept of dialectical materialism with a reference to the distinction between subject and object:

> The ultimate *philosophical* example here is that of the subjective versus objective dimension: subjective perception-awareness-activity versus

---

[19] Slavoj Žižek, *The Parallax View* (Cambridge, MA: MIT Press, 2006), pp. 34–5.

objective socio-economic or physiological mechanisms. A dialectical theory intervenes with a double short circuit: objectivity relies on a subjective surplus-gesture; subjectivity relies on *objet petit a*, the paradoxical object which is the subject's counterpoint. [...] On the one hand, we should accept the lesson of Kant's transcendental idealism: out of the confused multitude of impressions, *objective* reality emerges through the intervention of the *subject's* transcendental act. [...] On the other hand, the Lacanian *objet petit a* is the exact opposite of the Master-Signifier: not the subjective supplement which sustains the objective order, but the objective supplement which sustains subjectivity in its contrast to the subjectless objective order: *objet petit a* is that "bone in the throat," that disturbing stain which forever blurs our picture of reality – it is the *object* on account of which "objective reality" is forever inaccessible to the subject.[20]

The above quotation makes some difficult theoretical distinctions, which will be discussed in subsequent chapters. At this point, the most relevant idea is that, although "objective reality" emerges through an act of the subject, this does not imply that truth is "subjective." As Žižek puts it with reference to Badiou: "not only is Truth not 'subjective' in the sense of being subordinated to the subject's whims, but the subject himself is 'serving the Truth' which transcends him; since he is never fully adequate to the infinite order of Truth, the subject always has to operate within a finite multiple of a situation in which he discerns the signs of Truth."[21]

This dialectical problematic, which can be traced back through German Idealism to Plato's Eleatic dialogues (especially *Sophist* and *Parmenides*), implies that there is no consistent and unambiguous way to isolate reality as *given* (e.g., simply observed) from reality as *produced* (as when the very act of observing something changes it). Along these lines, the twentieth-century philosopher J. L. Austin distinguished between a "constative" utterance that *describes* the world, and a performative utterance like a promise or a vow that effectively intervenes in reality. Žižek argues that the symbolic order (the big Other, the intersubjective social network) involves a performative dimension that confers symbolic efficiency. Žižek offers an example to clarify this performative dimension: "the meeting is closed when, by means of the utterance, 'The meeting is closed,' this fact *comes to the big Other's*

[20] See Judith Butler, Ernesto Laclau, and Slavoj Žižek, *Contingency, Hegemony, Universality: Contemporary Dialogues on the Left* (London and New York: Verso, 2000), p. 239.
[21] Slavoj Žižek, "Psychoanalysis and Post-Marxism: The Case of Alain Badiou," *The South Atlantic Quarterly*, vol. 97, issue 2, Spring 1998, pp. 235–61.

knowledge."[22] In several works, Žižek describes how the distinction between the performative and the constative dimensions of meaning cannot simply be dispensed with, but neither can it be maintained in the form of an unambiguous binary opposition. Instead, the constitution of subjectivity implies a kind of conversion or direct coincidence of the opposites, since "the performative production of reality necessarily assumes the form of stating that 'it is so.'"[23]

This is an example of why there is no meaning apart from alienation in the signifier. The only way to define the identity or unity of any object (or entity, or event, or property) is to assert that the identity of the object consists in the fact that "this is the object which is always designated by the same signifier – tied to the same signifier. It is the signifier which constitutes the kernel of the object's 'identity.'"[24] This arbitrary (or contingent) alienation in the signifier informs symbolic identity and reality (any theoretical or ideological "system"). This means that necessity is constituted after the (contingent) fact: in other words, once things happen, they *retroactively* become necessary. The entire field of symbolic reality is reconfigured through encountering the Real and engaging in the Lacanian act. That is to say, through the free act, the subject reinvents a new symbolic reality, and her own identity. But at the moment this new order emerges, it is as if it always already was: in this sense, the free act of a subject restructures the past. And insofar as an act retroactively creates its own possibility, possibility does not simply "precede" actuality; on the contrary, *we have preceded it* once this actuality emerges.

Thus ultimately there can be no fixed or unchanging reality or symbolic signification. The meaning of any signifier arises in the particular context of its use, and through its relations with other terms in a dynamic and historically contingent (not deterministic) system of differences. And through the Lacanian act, a subject reinvents a new symbolic order. In sum, we can never completely and unambiguously isolate the thing from its symbolization, and yet, as Žižek emphasizes throughout his works, this radical contingency does not imply relativism. Why not? For one thing, there could not even be any equivocation without "the One" (the Master-Signifier) around which an equivocation revolves. Along the same lines, without the Lacanian *point de capiton* ("quilting point") – which "stitches

[22] Cf. Slavoj Žižek *Enjoy Your Symptom! Jacques Lacan in Hollywood and Out* (London and New York: Routledge, 1992, revised 2001), p. 98 in the revised edition.

[23] Slavoj Žižek *Enjoy Your Symptom! Jacques Lacan in Hollywood and Out* (London and New York: Routledge, 1992, revised 2001), p. 99 in the revised edition.

[24] Cf. Slavoj Žižek, *The Sublime Object of Ideology* (London and New York: Verso, 1989), p. 98.

together" the signifier and the signified – there would be no reality and no identity. But it is only when the sentence is completed that the (necessary) illusion of fixed meaning arises, in a retroactive way.[25]

These are difficult points, which we will develop more fully in what follows. For now, we should note that dialectical materialism squarely addresses the paradox of self-reference implicit to the claim that "No truth is universal." The paradox is that "No truth is universal" is itself a *universal* claim. A similar paradox of self-reference is implicit to the familiar postmodernist assertion that "All concepts are metaphors." Žižek reveals the limitation of this assertion: "the very reduction of a concept to a bundle of metaphors already has to rely on some implicit *philosophical (conceptual)* determination of the difference between concept and metaphor – that is to say, on the very opposition it tries to undermine."[26]

Žižek discusses the paradox of this "self-referential loop" in numerous texts. On the one hand, he emphatically asserts that subjectivity is dispersed and multiple; moreover, we can never "step onto our own shoulders" and include ourselves in the picture: in this sense, the ethico-political act is "blind." Nonetheless, on the other hand, the unity of the subject is guaranteed in the self-referential symbolic act. The subject is the performative gesture of self-positing, of saying "I":

> This is the mystery of the subject's "self-positing," explored by Fichte: of course, when I say "I," I do not create any new content, I merely designate myself, the person who is uttering the phrase. This self-designation nonetheless gives rise to, ("posits") an X which is not the "real" flesh-and-blood person uttering it, but, precisely and merely, the pure Void of self-referential designation (the Lacanian "subject of the enunciation"): "I" am not directly my body, or even the content of my mind; "I" am, rather, that X which has all these features as its properties.[27]

Thus "what I am" is an X, a Void of self-referential designation; this means that what makes me who I am cannot be located in my genetic formula. Nor can "what I am" be located in the way my genetic predispositions developed due to environmental influences. In fact,

---

[25] See Dylan Evans, *An Introductory Dictionary of Lacanian Psychoanalysis* (London: Routledge, 1996), p. 149. Evans explains that the *diachronic* dimension of the *point de capiton* is a retroactive effect of the production of meaning. The *synchronic* dimension, however, is metaphor: through metaphor the signifier "crosses the bar" into the signified.

[26] See Judith Butler, Ernesto Laclau, and Slavoj Žižek, *Contingency, Hegemony, Universality: Contemporary Dialogues on the Left* (London and New York: Verso, 2000), p. 231.

[27] Slavoj Žižek, *The Parallax View* (Cambridge, MA: MIT Press, 2006), p. 245.

according to properly dialectical procedure, we cannot even speak of an *interaction* between the genes and the environment:

> More precisely, even the word "interaction" is not quite adequate here, in so far as it still implies the mutual influence of two given sets of positive conditions (genes and environment), and thus does not cover the crucial feature of *self-relating*, the self-referential loop due to which, in the way I relate to my environment, I never reach the "zero-level" of being passively influenced by it, but always-already relate to myself in relating to it; that is, I always-already, with a minimum of "freedom," determine in advance the way I will be determined by the environment, up to the most elementary level of sensible perceptions. The way I "see myself," the imaginary and symbolic features which constitute my "self-image," or even fundamentally, the fantasy which provides the ultimate co-ordinates of my being is neither in the genes nor imposed by the environment, but the unique way each subject *relates to him or herself*, "chooses him or herself" in relationship to his or her environs, as well as to (what he or she perceives as) his "nature." We are thus dealing with a kind of "bootstrap" mechanism which cannot be reduced to the interaction of myself as a biological entity with my environment: a third mediating agency emerges (the subject, precisely), which has no positive substantial Being, since, in a way, its status is purely "performative."[28]

In sum, there can be no purely self-identical (nondialectical) mode of discourse, thought, or existence. Symbolic identity and symbolic reality – any "One" – is ruptured by the odd juxtaposition of the parallax gap. This gap (the Real) is the focus of Žižek's dialectical materialism, whether he is talking about German Idealism, Lacanian theory, science, literature, film, religion, or politics.

In the essays that follow, we hope to indicate how properly dialectical procedure leads beyond itself, and culminates in the paradox involved in the encounter with the Lacanian Real. The Real is manifested as the inconsistency and incompleteness of the symbolic, but insofar as it cannot be symbolized, the Lacanian Real cannot be incorporated into reality. In this sense, the Real is "impossible." Regarding the Real, certain ambiguities or paradoxes are ineradicable, so that sometimes all that we can do is to maintain a "parallax view," by holding open both of the two inconsistent perspectives. This fundamental antagonism or paradox of the Real proves to be the only "sameness" that always recurs. This means

---

[28] Slavoj Žižek, "Of Cells and Selves," in *The Žižek Reader*, ed. Elizabeth Wright and Edmund Wright (Malden, MA, and Oxford: 2009), p. 314.

that there can be no universality as an all-encompassing, perspective of all perspectives: every "opening" of signification or meaning is constituted through a covering-over. This insight will help us to understand Žižek's arguments that rationality involves a moment of unreason, and that the symbolic Law implies presymbolic violence.

Regarding political theory, Žižek's dialectical materialist approach facilitates a critique of capitalism that reveals the duplicity of liberal and (allegedly) tolerant multiculturalism:

> Liberal attitudes towards the other are characterized both by respect for otherness, openness to it, and an obsessive fear of harassment. In short, the other is welcomed insofar as its presence is not intrusive, insofar as it is not really the other. Tolerance thus coincides with its opposite. My duty to be tolerant towards the other effectively means that I should not get too close to him or her, not intrude into his space – in short, that I should respect his intolerance towards my over-proximity. This is increasingly emerging as the central human right of advanced capitalist society: the right not to be "harassed," that is, to be kept at a safe distance from others. The same goes for the emergent logic of humanitarian or pacifist militarism. War is acceptable insofar as it seeks to bring about peace, or democracy, or the conditions for distributing humanitarian aid. And does the same not hold even more for democracy and human rights themselves? Human rights are ok if they are "rethought" to include torture and a permanent emergency state. Democracy is ok if it is cleansed of its populist excesses and limited to those mature enough to practise it.[29]

Žižek uses such examples of the "coincidence of opposites" to show how liberalism relies on an imaginary notion of universality as a disengaged, shared and neutral "open space" for compromise. But throughout his works, he demonstrates again and again why there can be no disengaged universality. Here is an example:

> In human society, the political is the englobing structuring principle, so that every neutralization of some partial content as "non-political" is a political gesture *par excellence*. At the same time, however, a certain excess of non-political violence is the necessary supplement to power: power always has to rely on an obscene stain of violence – that is to say, political space is never "pure," it always involves some kind of reliance on "pre-political" violence.[30]

---

[29] Slavoj Žižek, "Against Human Rights," in *New Left Review* 34, July–August 2005. The article is also available online at http://libcom.org/library/against-human-rights-zizek.
[30] Cf. Judith Butler, Ernesto Laclau, and Slavoj Žižek, *Contingency, Hegemony, Universality: Contemporary Dialogues on the Left* (London and New York: Verso, 2000), p. 234.

18

It is crucial to bear in mind that Žižek is primarily a philosopher, and he deploys Lacanian psychoanalytic concepts in order to re-inscribe Hegelian dialectics into contemporary political theory. Žižek elaborates Lacan's analyses of discourse and fantasy, and reformulates Lacanian theory in terms of Hegelian dialectics. The result is a sophisticated critique of postmodern culture and so-called postmodern "thought." Along these lines, he shows why one cannot reinvigorate a Marxist-style critique of political economy without first understanding Hegelian categories. In what follows, we will see how Žižek reactualizes Hegel and Marx for today, and shows how cynical postmodern subjectivity still involves what Marx described as fetishism and alienation.

Žižek analyzes capitalist society, discloses its symptoms, diagnoses its pathology, and, most importantly, reveals its repressed *truth*. In doing so, he has changed the very coordinates of intellectual life under late capitalism, and reinvigorated the philosophical transcendentalism and the ethical-political universalism of the Enlightenment. Again, Žižek does this by elaborating the philosophical implications of Jacques Lacan's linguistic reinvention of psychoanalytic theory.

Žižek's Philosophical Re-inscription of Lacanian Theory

Žižek's writing presupposes basic Lacanian concepts, and in most of his books, he assumes that the reader is already familiar with the "standard" version of Lacanian theory. For readers new to Lacan, this section introduces some basic Lacanian concepts. Žižek elaborates Lacanian psychoanalytic theory in light of the philosophy of German Idealism, particularly Hegelian dialectics, in order to forge a revolutionary new way of interpreting political life and culture. In the process, he revises both Hegel and Lacan. Because Žižek focuses especially on aspects of Lacan's *later* seminars and writings, the essays that follow this introduction will focus on the Real, the limits of symbolization, and the ethico-political implications of the feminine subject position.

Lacan's theory of "the mirror phase" shows that the ego is initially formed when the infant identifies with an external image. Significantly, the entity doing the identifying (the imagination of the infant) is not identical with the entity that is being identified with (the external and reversed image in the mirror). The ego which is formed through the process of the mirror phase is an imaginary object, a fantasy of wholeness. Even before the infant learns to speak and enters the symbolic register, it has formed a nostalgic fantasy image of a lost oneness, a primordial interconnectedness with its mother. In the mirror phase this fantasy image of wholeness (in the form of the ego) unifies the infant's fragmentary and chaotic experiences and in this way serves as a brace or a crutch to help it gain mastery over its own body. As the child complies with the demands of its parents and is weaned and toilet trained, as it acquires language and enters the symbolic order, this phantasmatic image of unity provides an extra dimension of possibility for life. But throughout life the ego involves the identification with an external image, and because of this, the ego is an artificial, external "other." In everyday existence the ego functions as an agent of *falsification*. As a fantasy image of wholeness, the ego effaces its own otherness; the ego masks the very alienation in an image that constitutes it.

After the formation of the ego in the mirror phase, human beings are split from within by the acquisition of language; the human infant is divided or alienated from itself by its entry into the symbolic order. In a sense, the acquisition of the word is the loss of the thing. For example, any animal has biological needs, but a human infant demands food from the mother even when it is not hungry, simply as a *symbol* of her love. In such ways, the subject is irremediably divided by the acquisition of language between the imaginary register (the ego and fantasies of oneness) and the symbolic register (linguistic concepts defined by difference or otherness). Any speaking subject will always be divided into the ignorance of imaginary experience on the one hand, and, on the other, the effects of his words in the intersubjective, symbolic network. Subjectivity as such implies this discord between imaginary experience and the big Other, the symbolic register.[31] This split is constitutive of the subject; it is a division essential to any speaking, thinking animal.

Žižek refers to the game of chess to distinguish the imaginary and the symbolic registers. The symbolic order is homologous to the rules of the game. For example, the rules of chess define the signifier "knight" in terms of the moves this figure is allowed to make, as distinguished from the other pieces.[32] The imaginary dimension in this example involves the size, shape, and color of the pieces, as well as their names. Thus a variety of objects could be used to serve as a queen, as long as the object was

---

[31] The Other refers both to the radical alterity of another subject (whose desire is Real for us), as well as to the intersubjective big Other that mediates relations between subjects. The mother is the child's first Other, and the castration complex arises when the child realizes her incompleteness: she lacks (and desires) the phallus. The Other is also *woman*: the feminine subject position is the Other for both males and females.

[32] Slavoj Žižek, *How to Read Lacan* (New York: W. W. Norton & Company), p. 8.

moved in accordance with the rules that define what the queen is in the reality of the game.

However, once the process of identification develops a symbolic dimension (with the movement beyond imaginary ego to symbolic subject), there is no purely "raw" sense data. As Žižek points out, we literally perceive judgments:

> what we perceive as immediate reality is directly a judgement. Let's take a standard example from a typical cognitivist book: when you enter a room and you see all chairs there are red, and then you move immediately to a second similar room, you think you see exactly the same. But it has been repeatedly demonstrated that our perception is much more fragmentary than it appears – a significant number of the chairs in the second room have different shapes, colours, etc. What is happening is that you see just a couple of fragments and then, based on your previous experience (and this all happens in the immediate moment of perception before proper conscious judgement), you make a judgement – "all the chairs must be red." The point being that what you see is the result of your judgement – you literally see judgements. There is no zero-level sensory perception of reality which is then later coordinated into judgements. What you always already see are judgements.[33]

During the process of acquiring language, the child is situated within the mother's desire but unable to fully satisfy it; the mother's desire extends to something that is beyond the child. The "phallus" indicates that beyond the child to which the mother's desire is directed, and the child (boy *or* girl) initially tries to be the object of desire – the phallus – for the mother. Lacan's term "symbolic castration" refers to the child's renunciation of its attempt to be the phallus for the mother. A neurotic is a subject who has not fully accepted symbolic castration; a neurotic (male or female) still tries to be the object of desire *for the mother*. According to Žižek: "Lacan identifies hysteria with neurosis: the other main form of neurosis, obsessional neurosis, is for him a 'dialect of hysteria.'"[34]

Unlike the imaginary ego, the "subject" does not exist prior to the renunciation of enjoyment that is the entry into the symbolic order. Though the subject emerges through the acquisition of language, nonetheless the subject as such should be distinguished from the process of symbolic "subjectivization." Subjectivization involves the incorporation

---

[33] Slavoj Žižek and Glyn Daly, *Conversations with Žižek* (Cambridge: Polity Press, 2004), p. 55.

[34] See Slavoj Žižek, "Ideology I: No Man is an Island," note 4, available online at http://www.lacan.com/zizwhiteriot.html.

of the hegemonic ideology of society to such an extent that ideology becomes invisible and seems natural. The subject as such, however, is beyond ideological interpellation. Hysteria emerges when a subject questions his or her symbolic identity, and Žižek reveals the extent to which the subject *is* the hysteric's question: "Why am I what you say that I am?" Thus the subject as such (as feminine) involves the incompleteness ("non-all," or "not-All") of subjectivization, and of symbolic representation in general:

> That is to say, what, precisely, is a "subject"? Let us imagine a proposition, a statement – how and when does this statement get "subjectivized"? – when some reflexive feature inscribes into it the subjective attitude. In this precise sense, a signifier "represents the subject for another signifier." The subject is the absent X that has to be supposed in order to account for this reflexive twist, for this distortion. [...] Hume's famous observation that, no matter how close and deep I look into myself, all I will find there are specific ideas, particular mental states, perceptions, emotions, and so on, never a "Self," misses the point: this non-accessibility to itself as an object is constitutive of being a "self."[35]

The essence of symbolic subjectivity is desire, and desire as such is hysterical desire. The hysterical subject is the subject as the *question*. Hysterical questioning of symbolic reality opens up the void of possible Otherness that sustains desire: "this non-acceptance of the ultimate closure, this vain hope that the Other Thing is waiting for us just around the corner."[36]

Desire manifests as the inconsistencies or gaps in the intersubjective, symbolic network. Unlike a want or a wish, desire is unconscious; it is manifested in the big Other of the symbolic order. Desire shows up as inconsistencies in speech, slips of the tongue, and bungled actions. The symbolic network is the "beyond" in which desire is disclosed; consequently, the unconscious is the discourse of the symbolic Other. Desire is constituted through fantasies about the desire of the Other, as well as fantasies of an impossible oneness. The imaginary ego and other fantasies of unity serve as a support for the consistency of experience; thus the register of the imaginary is constitutive of reality. But the imaginary register also offers a pathway to the Real, for the Real of our desire

---

[35] Slavoj Žižek, "An Answer to Two Questions," in Adrian Johnston, *Badiou, Žižek, and Political Transformations: The Cadence of Change* (Evanston: Northwestern University Press, 2009), p. 212.

[36] Slavoj Žižek, *The Plague of Fantasies* (London and New York: Verso, 1997), pp. 29–30.

announces itself in dreams.[37] The subject of desire – the subject of the unconscious – is constituted in relation to signification; this means that desire is manifested as distortions within the symbolic register (e.g., slips of the tongue). The essential life substance is *jouissance*, of which the subject is usually unaware. Enjoyment is Real; it is the price we pay for being symbolic animals, or speaking beings.

All of this indicates why for Lacan and Žižek desire is not a function of biology, but is *decentered* insofar as it involves imaginative projection (the dimension of fantasy) and the attempt to become whatever it is that the Other desires most. This means that humans must learn to desire; desire is constituted by fantasies about the Other's desire, and fantasies of an impossible oneness. The register of the imaginary is not merely a realm of illusion, for fantasy is constitutive of the consistency of experience: "fantasy mediates between the formal symbolic structure and the positivity of the objects we encounter in reality: it provides a 'scheme' according to which certain positive objects in reality can function as objects of desire, filling in the empty places opened up by the formal symbolic structure."[38] In sum, it is an individual's fantasy that first teaches her how to desire. The problem is that "fantasies cannot coexist peacefully."[39] This is why both Lacan and Žižek insist on the need to *traverse the fantasy* and to achieve an ethics of the Real. Succinctly put, the goal is to see through the distortions and inconsistencies of our imaginary-symbolic reality and then refuse to cede or give way on the Real of our desire.

To summarize, the imaginary register involves alienation in the *image* (visual, auditory, tactile, olfactory); the symbolic register involves alienation in the *signifier* (word, symbolic practice); however, the Real – to put it simply – involves alienation as such. The Real is perhaps the most difficult of Lacanian concepts, and in what follows we will move beyond this initial, working characterization. For now it should be noted that the innermost core of "who I am" is inaccessible to me. Along the same lines, if I approach the Real too directly, both my identity and my reality disintegrate. The Real of the subject involves a radical *decentering* of the subject from itself: "I am deprived of even my most intimate 'subjective' experience, the way things 'really seem to me,' that of the fundamental fantasy which constitutes and guarantees the kernel of my being, since

---

[37] Slavoj Žižek, *The Sublime Object of Ideology* (London and New York: Verso, 1989), p. 45.

[38] Slavoj Žižek, *The Parallax View* (Cambridge, MA: MIT Press, 2006), p. 40.

[39] Slavoj Žižek, *Looking Awry: An Introduction to Jacques Lacan through Popular Culture* (Cambridge, MA: MIT Press, 1992), p. 168.

I can never consciously experience it and assume it."[40] The fundamental fantasy provides the elementary coordinates of the subject's capacity to desire, but it "has to remain repressed in order to function."[41]

Žižek elaborates the philosophical implications of Lacanian theory and, in doing so, develops the theory. Regarding the Lacanian Real, Žižek argues that: "a certain fundamental ambiguity pertains to the Real in Lacan: the Real designates a substantial hard kernel that precedes and resists symbolization and, simultaneously, it designates the left-over, which is posited or 'produced' by symbolization itself."[42] Žižek often describes the Real as an "indivisible remainder" that is constituted retroactively, in and through the inconsistencies of symbolization. But, in addition, he argues that although the Real is the inherent limit of the symbolic register, it also indicates what lies "beyond" the symbolic. This implies that the Real is *not* a merely negative category. For example, desire manifests as the inconsistency of the symbolic, but the Real as drive is the "driving force" of desiring.[43] But if we assert that the symbolic arises from the Real, as a reaction to the Real, nonetheless we must also acknowledge that since the Real cannot be symbolized it is, in a sense, impossible: it never "exists" in symbolic reality. This impossibility of the Real – its unbearably paradoxical character – is why proximity to the Real can provoke anxiety.

By engaging with Lacanian theory in light of his reading of German Idealism (especially Hegel and Schelling), Žižek emphasizes the philosophical implications of psychoanalysis. For example, neurosis at its most elementary involves the repression of desires viewed as inappropriate by the sociosymbolic order; thus the neurotic desires that some desire remains unsatisfied.[44] The nonsymbolic life substance is *jouissance*, and this surplus enjoyment is Real. The neurotic is obsessed with the notion that *jouissance* has been stolen from her, and that some Other is illegitimately enjoying in her place. The typical neurotic strategy is to get back at least some of this "lost" enjoyment by transgressing the symbolic prohibitions that regulate desire.[45]

---

[40] Slavoj Žižek, *The Plague of Fantasies* (London and New York: Verso, 1997), p. 121; *The Parallax View* (Cambridge, MA: MIT Press, 2006), p. 171.

[41] Slavoj Žižek, *How to Read Lacan* (New York: Norton, 2007), p. 59.

[42] See Slavoj Žižek, *Tarrying with the Negative: Kant, Hegel, and the Critique of Ideology* (Durham, NC: Duke University Press, 1993), p. 36.

[43] Slavoj Žižek, *The Indivisible Remainder: On Schelling and Related Matters* (London and New York: Verso, 2007), p. 97.

[44] Slavoj Žižek, *The Ticklish Subject: The Absent Centre of Political Ontology* (London and New York: Verso, 2000), pp. 112–13.

[45] Slavoj Žižek, *The Plague of Fantasies* (London and New York: Verso, 1997), p. 33.

How does Žižek offer a way out of this vicious cycle of Law and its transgression? One of the ways involves the well-known Lacanian distinction between four discourses as four forms of social linkage. In *Seminar XVII* (1969–70), Lacan distinguished between four discourses or social links: the master's, the university's, the hysteric's, and the analyst's. These four discourses are four possible symbolic configurations. The four discourses function as social links by regulating the ways that the Master-Signifier represents the subject for all other signifiers.[46] These four forms are derived through different permutations of four terms: the master (S1), knowledge (S2), the split subject ($), and *objet petit a* (designated by the small *a*). In sum, the four discourses configure four different subjects and four kinds of social link.

Throughout his works, as we will see, Žižek articulates – in light of historical contingency – the philosophical and political implications of forms of discourse as forms of social link.[47] It is in light of (historically contingent) permutations of the four discourses that we should approach certain themes that recur in Žižek's books. For example, he argues that Lacan's "discourse of the university" refers, not just to the university as an institution, but more fundamentally, to knowledge itself. The upper level of the algorithm of university discourse is S2 in relation to *objet petit a*; this indicates knowledge in its endeavor to domesticate and integrate the (Real) excess that resists knowledge. This can help us to understand Žižek's arguments that the inherently transgressive nature of desire means that in a society where everything is permitted, enjoyment takes the form of a paradoxical hedonistic asceticism. Medical knowledge today (as S2) is not neutral; it is co-opted into the libidinal economy of capitalism; scientific knowledge about physical health is incorporated into our late capitalist economy of enjoyment. The superego injunction to enjoy is not directly knowledge; rather it functions as the Master-Signifier of knowledge. This is how university discourse today reinforces the capitalist reproduction of symbolic reality. But ironically, because narcissistic self-fulfillment must be combined with its own opposite (jogging, health food, no smoking, safe sex, etc.), access to enjoyment is as "unfree" as it ever was:

---

[46] Insofar as the Master-Signifier represents the subject for all other signifiers, the master's discourse is an attempt at totalization. But because the Master-Signifier is empty, it is the constitutive exception that marks the *failure* of every attempt at totalization.

[47] Žižek's most accessible treatment of Lacan's four discourses is "Four Discourses, Four Subjects," in *Cogito and the Unconscious*, ed. Slavoj Žižek, (Durham, NC: Duke University Press), pp. 74–113.

Superego is thus not directly S2; it is rather the S1 of the S2 itself, the dimension of an unconditional injunction that is inherent to knowledge itself. Recall the information about health we are bombarded with all the time: "Smoking is dangerous! Too much fat may cause a heart attack! Regular exercise leads to a longer life!" etc. etc. – it is impossible not to hear beneath it the unconditional injunction "You should enjoy a long and healthy life!"… What this means is that the discourse of the University is thoroughly mystifying, concealing its true foundation, obfuscating the unfreedom on which it relies.[48]

The quotation indicates how the discourse of the university (S2, knowledge) always conceals its subservience to the Master-Signifier (S1). As an illustration of this, there is nothing rational about the injunction to excessive enjoyment that permeates today's university discourse. *Knowledge* has become one of the ways that capitalism today "interpellates" subjects as consumers, soliciting in us new and perverse, excessive desires. We are constantly offered new products to satisfy ever more excessive modes of enjoyment.

But how is symbolic desire related to *jouissance*? On the one hand, prohibitions incite the desire to transgress; but, on the other hand, prohibitions relieve capitalist subjects of the superego injunction to enjoy. Law regulates pleasures and thereby delivers us from the superego injunction to enjoy, which dominates daily life in capitalist societies. The way beyond the vicious cycle of Law and transgression involves the subject as Real: not a positive, substantial entity but rather a reflexive asymmetry in the world picture. The key insight here is that because the subject as such is split, it always *remains inherently opposed* to the process of ideological subjectivization. In other words, the Real of the subject is the empty place in the symbolic order, the split or antagonism in the midst of the intersubjective social network. By contrast, symbolic subjectivization relies on fantasy as that which covers over trauma or irreducible social antagonism. Insofar as such fantasies are a primary way that the speaking human strives to remedy its constitutive split and to regain a sense of mythic unity, social reality is first made possible by ideological fantasy. Ideology provides a fantasy construction that allows any subject to behave with some degree of consistency, as though she belongs to a society that is unified through symbolic rules (in fact, what unifies today's societies is the transgression of symbolic rules). A fetish involves my refusal-to-know, or rather, my disavowal of something that I really know already. I know it, but because I refuse to subjectively assume

---

[48] Slavoj Žižek, "*Homo Sacer* as the Object of the Discourse of the University," available online at http://www.lacan.com/hsacer.htm.

this knowledge, I do not yet *believe* it. But every such act of "fetishization" covers a void, such as the inability to become the phallus for the mother, or the impossibility of saying the Real. For now, it should be noted that enjoyment (*jouissance*) is Real. And because the original deadlock – of the (m)Other's desire – is Real, the subject's inability to discover any consistent answer to the question of desire exposes the lack in the symbolic register left by the primordially repressed Real.

Because of the irresoluble split or antagonism inherent to subjectivity, what we ordinarily consider to be reality proves ultimately to be a juxtaposition of the symbolic register (speech, sociosymbolic practices, chains of signifiers) and the imaginary register (fantasies of completeness and consistency). The Lacanian Real exceeds what can be imagined or symbolized, but it manifests as antagonism or asymmetry *within* and *between* the imaginary and symbolic registers. One of the ways that Žižek develops this point is by showing that consciousness as such is always integrally linked to an experience of incommensurability, a sense that things are "out of joint" or that something has gone wrong. This lack of fit is the Lacanian Real; the Real is an ineradicable snag or dissymmetry, an impossible limit moment that is "extimate" (inherent but inassimilable) to both the imaginary and the symbolic dimensions of subjectivity. An experience or affect – such as anxiety – may indicate the proximity of the Real, but the Real is *not* any positively existing entity, event, or property that we can simply point out or experience on an everyday basis. The Real tends to be repressed from consciousness, thus it is not simply a component part of "objective" social reality: the repressed Real does not exist, it *insists*.

It is because the repressed Real is thoroughly *immanent* to imaginary-symbolic reality that it cannot be imagined or symbolized. As Žižek puts it, the "impossible" is Real. And yet, as he emphasizes throughout his works, the impossible Real does happen, in the form of miracles like political revolution or love.[49] Whenever the impossible Real happens, it disrupts from within all signification through the symbolic and the imaginary registers:

> The result of all this is that, for Lacan, the Real is not impossible in the sense that it can never happen – a traumatic kernel which forever eludes our grasp. No, the problem with the Real is that it happens and *that's* the trauma. *The point is not that the Real is impossible but rather that the impossible is Real.* A trauma, or an act, is simply the point when the Real happens, and this is difficult to accept. Lacan is not a poet telling us how we always fail

49   Slavoj Žižek, *On Belief* (London and New York: Routledge, 2004), p. 84.

the Real – it's always the opposite with the late Lacan. The point is that you *can* encounter the Real, and that is what is so difficult to accept.[50]

Žižek's engagement with the Real effectively redefines the philosophical problem of knowledge. For Žižek, knowledge is not harmonious synthesis; this is one reason why he frequently refers approvingly to the radical Copenhagen formulation of quantum physics: the formulae *work*, even though there is no way we can imagine the quantum universe.

Žižek does not simply deploy Lacanian concepts; instead he develops them, especially the implications of the Lacanian Real. One of the primary ways (as already indicated), is that he shows how the entire triad of Real, imaginary, and symbolic is reflected within each of its three elements:

> There are three modalities of the Real: the "real Real" (the horrifying Thing, the primordial object, from Irma's throat to the Alien); the "symbolic Real" (the real as consistency: the signifier reduced to a senseless formula, like quantum physics formulas which can no longer be translated back into – or related to – the everyday experience of our life-world); and the "imaginary Real" (the mysterious *je ne sais quoi*, the unfathomable "something" on account of which the sublime dimension shines through an ordinary object).[51]

The Real may be encountered as the intrusive return of some repressed trauma or antagonism. It might be even be surmised – though Žižek himself does not resort to this – that it is his emphasis on the Real that accounts for why, instead of offering considered arguments against his thinking, hasty critics sometimes resort to irrelevant criticisms of his writing style, or lapse into the straw man fallacy by simplifying Žižek's argument and then knocking over this phony dummy. In other words, if a critic hastily dismisses Žižek's thought, this unreflective dismissal may itself be the result of the anxiety produced by approaching the traumatic Real. After all, the Real is not problematic only because it is *difficult to understand* (because it resists symbolization). The Real is also problematic simply because it provokes anxiety. Neurotic symptoms are a defense against the intrusive Real, and it is easier to remain neurotically repressed than to confront Real antagonism or trauma.

---

[50] Slavoj Žižek and Glyn Daly, *Conversations with Žižek* (Cambridge: Polity Press, 2004), pp. 69–70.
[51] Slavoj Žižek, "Foreword to the Second Edition: Enjoyment within the Limits of Reason Alone," in *For They Know Not What They Do: Enjoyment as a Political Factor* (London and New York: Verso, 2002), pp. xi–xii.

Žižek's focus on the Real underlies his numerous arguments that Hegelian "Absolute Knowledge" is not harmonious synthesis, so much as the apprehension of the impossibility of any complete and consistent synthesis. Žižek, like Hegel, asks "the big metaphysical questions," even though the Real prevents us from ever definitively solving them:

> For the last few decades, at least in the humanities, big ontological questions – "What is the nature of the universe?" – were considered too naive. It was meaningless to ask for objective truth. This prohibition on asking the big questions partly accounts for the explosion of popular science books. You read Stephen Hawking's books as a way to ask these fundamental, metaphysical questions. I think that era of relativism, where science was just another product of knowledge, is ending. We philosophers should join scientists asking those big metaphysical questions about quantum physics, about reality. [...] We ask the big metaphysical questions even though we cannot solve them, and as a by-product we come up with wonderful, solid knowledge.[52]

It is Žižek's evocations of the Real that make his work so significant for contemporary philosophy. However, many established academics, particularly in the USA, do not yet recognize this philosophical significance. But anyone familiar with the history of philosophy – if they engage in serious study of Žižek's re-inscription of Hegel in light of Lacan – will recognize that Žižek effectively reinvents traditional metaphysics (theory of reality) and epistemology (theory of knowledge). Because the imaginary and the symbolic registers are bound together with the Real like the three loops of a single knot, any disclosure of "being" or existence is inherently ruptured from within. The Real is inherent to the imaginary register (fantasies of wholeness) as well as to the symbolic order (social reality). Consequently, although the Real is that which is in a sense impossible to say – it resists incorporation into shared, symbolic practices and intersubjective linguistic systems – nonetheless, what is primordially repressed from the symbolic returns in the Real of the symptom.

Žižek focuses on the Real as this fundamental limit moment. His analyses indicate how imaginary identifications and fantasies of unity prevent the confrontation with the Real that disrupts any symbolic order. The Real is not simply that which exists prior to symbolization. The Real has no substantial presence, and we can only conceive it in a limited way; it is constituted retroactively, as that which is left out of symbolic

---

[52] Žižek Interview from Integral Options Cafe, online at: http://integral-options.blogspot. com/2010/11/io9-slavoj-zizek-wake-up-and-smell.html.

signification. And because signification involves the split or division that is constitutive of subjectivity, Žižek's dialectical materialism does not imply the "presence" of the whole signifier in the consciousness of any subject. The subject's alienation in language means that a dimension of subjectivity is externalized. One manifestation of this externalized (alienated) dimension of the subject is the pre-existing, intersubjective network, the symbolic big Other. When the child internalizes the prohibitions of the symbolic father, its superego is formed, and the public Law indicates this symbolic aspect of superego. However, the hidden side of superego is an obscene injunction to transgress the Law. On the one hand, the symbolic superego ("the Name/No! of the Father"), serves to regulate the subject's enjoyment. But on the other hand, the underside of the symbolic superego is an injunction to transgress, to engage in the unrestrained *jouissance* of the (imaginary) primal father. In numerous places throughout his works, Žižek links the superego – as the obscene injunction to enjoy – with capitalism.[53]

The Lacanian *act* belongs to the Real; and only by means of the act do we break the grip of ideology. Insofar as it is located at the point of symbolic undecidability, the act belongs to the Real. The act identifies the Real of social antagonism in the symbolic theater of politics. The act is not a product of anyone's "will." In the act, I do that which I cannot *not* do. Moreover, the act does not propose a new Master-Signifier, because the act involves an encounter with the Real as inconsistency or sociosymbolic contradiction. The act is a mode of identification with what is excluded by the hegemonic, reigning symbolic order. Thus the act is not founded in the symbolic register, in ideology, or in any positive psychological content. Instead, an authentic act is "founded only in itself."[54] The act involves engagement with the Real; by tarrying with the negativity of the Real, the subject undergoes subjective destitution, loses his essence, and passes over into his Other. In the act we traverse the fantasy and encounter the Real. The act is excluded from the symbolic, big Other insofar as an act suspends the signifying power of words: in an act, symbolic mandates and superego imperatives no longer oblige. Žižek describes the act as "*symbolic suicide*: an act of 'losing all,' of withdrawing from symbolic reality, that enables us to begin anew from the 'zero point,'

---

[53] Žižek develops the logic of the capitalist superego (and the injunction to enjoy) at some length in chapter 3 of his *The Fragile Absolute* (London and New York: Verso, 2000).

[54] Slavoj Žižek, *Enjoy Your Symptom: Jacques Lacan in Hollywood and Out*, revised edition (New York: Routledge, 2001), p. 35.

from that point of absolute freedom called by Hegel 'abstract negativity.'"[55]
In the act we renounce all symbolic ties:

> The new (the symbolic reality that emerges as the aftermath of an act) is
> always a "state that is essentially a by-product," never the result of advance
> planning. There are numerous examples of such acts: from de Gaulle's
> "No!" to Pétain and to French capitulation in 1940, Lacan's dissolution of
> the *Ecole freudienne de Paris* in 1979, up to the mythical case of the act of
> transgression, Caesar's crossing of the Rubicon – all of them gestures of a
> masculine leader. However, we shouldn't forget that the paradigmatic case
> of such an act is *feminine*: Antigone's "No!" to Creon, to state power; her
> act is literally suicidal, she excludes herself from the community, whereby
> she offers nothing new, no positive program – she just insists on her
> unconditional demand.[56]

As this quotation indicates, the feminine subject position is only
accidentally related to biological sex; in other words, a biological male
can occupy the feminine subject position. But the act characterizes
feminine subjectivity. The act as symbolic suicide communicates nothing
and expects nothing; in the act, the (feminine) subject renounces any
support in the sociosymbolic, intersubjective network of the big Other.
The act is possible only against the background of the symbolic order;
but in its withdrawal from symbolic reality, the act proper is not symbolic,
but involves an encounter with the Real.

Against deconstructionist critics of Lacan's alleged "logocentrism,"
Žižek argues that a Lacanian approach to the symbolic register reveals
communication to be constituted in and through the *failures* of
communication. All communication essentially involves miscommunication and all recognition is simultaneously also misrecognition. In sum,
Žižek shows that because of Lacan's emphasis on the Real, the charge of
logocentrism is simply mistaken. The Real is no foundation for any
logocentric metalanguage. How could the Real be a foundation, when
the Real is different for every individual? Again, the Real does not "exist":
it is not simply an entity, event, or property. This is a point that Žižek
makes repeatedly: the Real is constituted retroactively, as the lack or
inconsistency which disrupts our "objective" social reality. But at the
moment of its emergence, it is as if the Real always already was.

---

[55] Slavoj Žižek, *Looking Awry: An Introduction to Jacques Lacan through Popular Culture*
(Cambridge, MA: MIT Press, 1991), p. 43.
[56] Ibid., p. 46.

Žižek's Major Contribution (According to Žižek)

In spite of his numerous political treatises, Žižek claims in the documentary film *Žižek!* that his heart is not really in political theory, because many leftists expect answers which he cannot give (answers which no one can give).[57] In interviews he has stressed that his true focus is not ideology critique, not analyses of films, etc. Žižek has repeatedly emphasized that what really matters to him is *theory*, and then explained that by "theory" he refers primarily to the deployment of Lacanian psychoanalytic insights in order to elaborate the notion of self-relating negativity that is articulated in German Idealist philosophy. He has also described his major contribution as simply a way of taking literally Lacan's indication that the subject of psychoanalysis is the Cartesian *cogito ergo sum* ("I think, therefore I exist"). Žižek develops the notion of the Cartesian subject in terms of radical doubt and the confrontation with madness, and articulates the homology between this Cartesian moment of negativity and the self-relating negativity made thematic by Kant, Schelling, Hegel, and Lacan.

By carefully considering Hegel's actual arguments in the light of Lacanian theory, Žižek undermines the standard interpretation of Hegel's "idealism." Žižek shows that Hegel describes how ideals function in human activity. Ideals are cultural phenomena that develop historically; philosophers build theories, testing and refuting ideals in the struggle to attain the truth. Hegel coined the term *Zeitgeist*, "the spirit of the times," and our postmodern *Zeitgeist* involves cynicism regarding progress. We are relativists who believe that everything about thinking is historically *contingent*, in other words, accidental and relative to its time. The problem (from Žižek's Hegelian perspective), is that we have not thought through our own insight into historical contingency. For example, we fail to recognize that relativism too is historically contingent: it is a phase through which thinking passes now and again. Plato, Kant, and (in his own way) Hegel, were all struggling against the relativism that was fashionable in their times, and Žižek argues that it is time for all of us to thoroughly think through the problem of relativism and the historical contingency of thinking.

---

[57] Cf. *Žižek!* (Zeitgeist Films, 2005), directed by Astra Taylor and produced by Lawrence Konner. Some progressives fault Žižek for not providing a blueprint for a post-capitalist world. But as Marx might say, people make history *under conditions they do not choose*; therefore, it is naive to believe that anyone can provide a hard and fast plan for the future.

Significantly, Žižek's antidote to relativism is itself thoroughly *histori-cal*. But against proponents of identity politics and multiculturalism, Žižek argues that there is a kind of universality that is negative. The universal is not an ideal as some positive content that is always implicit to any "system" of thought. On the contrary the universal is a kind of traumatic antagonism around which ever-changing, thoroughly contingent, historical constellations of thought circle and revolve. Along these lines, according to Žižek's reading of Hegel, the dialectic is a process without a subject, a process which revolves around a void or negativity. No agent (no God, humanity, or class as a collective subject) controls and directs the dialectical process. There is no need for any subjective agent to guide the dialectic, since the emergence of "system" (as inconsistent totality or non-All) is correlative to the emergence of the pure (feminine) subject as void.[58] Thus Žižek argues that Hegelian dialectic does not simply advocate "Absolute Knowledge" as a kind of rationalist "panlogicism." The notorious Hegelian Absolute Knowledge involves the recognition that any system of thought is incomplete and inherently contradictory. Systems of thought are internally inconsistent because they are constituted through the repression of some traumatic, Real antagonism (such as class struggle). Thus thinking and truth involve much more than what Richard Rorty refers to as "solidarity of belief."[59] Beneath the level of narrative, there is a dense background of proto-reality, a more elementary level that provides the proper depth of experience. For such reasons, truth is something otherwise than the narratives we tell: our narratives always leave out something crucial, and this "indivisible remainder" is where we should focus our analysis, if we are to discover how and why truth is externalized and alienated from our narratives.

Whether Hegel was always aware of it or not, dialectic exposes the constitutive *lack* inherent to the symbolic order:

> for Hegel himself, his philosophical reconstruction of history in no way pretends to "cover everything," but consciously leaves blanks: the medieval time, for example, is for Hegel one big regression – no wonder that, in his lectures on the history of philosophy, he dismisses the entire medieval thought in a couple of pages, flatly denying any historical greatness to figures like Thomas Aquinas. Not even to mention the destructions of great

[58] Slavoj Žižek, in *Hegel & the Infinite: Religion, Politics, and Dialectic*, ed. Slavoj Žižek, Clayton Crockett, and Creston Davis (NewYork: Columbia University Press, 2011), p. 231.
[59] See Richard Rorty, "Science and Solidarity," in *Rhetoric of the Human Sciences: Language and Arguments in Scholarship and Public Affairs*, ed. John S. Nelson, Allan Megill, and Donald N. McCloskey (Madison: University of Wisconsin Press, 1987).

civilizations like the Mongols' wiping out so much of the Muslim world (the destruction of Baghdad, etc.) in the 13ᵗʰ century – there is no "meaning" in this destruction, the negativity unleashed here did not create the space for a new shape of historical life.)[60]

In such ways, Žižek demonstrates that Hegel himself (even if he did not always know what he was doing) showed that the negativity of the Real makes complete and consistent synthesis impossible.

What is meant here by "negativity"? Suppose that the cognitive brain sciences could explain – in a causally determinate way – every thought and emotion. If cognitivists could account for *every* feature of conscious life by providing a consistent and comprehensive explanation in purely neurobiological-physical terms, mysteries would still remain. How is it that human beings can sometimes act against their own spontaneous inclinations? Why are we obsessed with questions about the meaning of life? Insofar as Hegelian dialectic evokes the moment of madness inherent to rationality, it implies a materialist dimension. Because of this dialectical moment of negativity or inconsistency (any One is non-identical to itself), Hegel cannot be interpreted as an "absolute idealist":

> In what, then, resides Hegel's uniqueness? Hegel's thought stands for the moment of passage between philosophy as Master's discourse, the philosophy of the One that totalizes the multiplicity, and anti-philosophy which asserts the Real that escapes the grasp of the One. On the one hand, he clearly breaks with the metaphysical logic of counting-for-One; on the other hand, he does not allow for any excess external to the field of notional representations. For Hegel, totalization-in-One always fails, the One is always-already in excess with regard to itself, it is itself the subversion of what it purports to achieve, and it is this tension internal to the One, this Two-ness which makes the One One and simultaneously dislocates it, it is this tension which is the movens of the "dialectical process." In other words, Hegel effectively denies that there is no Real external to the network of notional representations (which is why he is regularly misread as "absolute idealist" in the sense of the self-enclosed circle of the totality of the Notion). However, the Real does not disappear here in the global self-relating play of symbolic representations; it returns with a vengeance as the immanent gap, obstacle, on account of which representations cannot ever totalize themselves, on account of which they are "non-all" (*pas tout*).[61]

---

[60]   From the preface to Žižek's forthcoming book on Hegel. The preface is available online at: http://crestondavis.wordpress.com/2010/07/06/zizeks-preface-to-our-hegel-book-with-columbia-university-press/.

[61]   Ibid. If Žižek's "materialist" reading of German Idealism initially seems far-fetched, the reader should be aware that even in English language discussions the materialist

The dialectical process is always ruptured by some nonrational surd, a nonconceptual element that disrupts the complete and consistent understanding of any whole. As Žižek puts it elsewhere, Hegelian dialectic reveals the impossibility of isolating the essential, apart from the inessential:

> One of the postmodern commonplaces about Hegel is the reproach of "restrained economy": in the dialectical process, loss and negativity are contained in advance, accounted for – what gets lost is merely the inessential aspect (and the very fact that a feature has been lost counts as the ultimate proof of its inessential status), whereas one can rest assured that the essential dimension will not only survive, but even be strengthened by the ordeal of negativity. The whole (teleological) point of the process of loss and recuperation is to enable the Absolute to purify itself, to render manifest its essential dimension by getting rid of the inessential, like a snake which, from time to time, has to cast off its skin in order to rejuvenate itself. One can see, now, where this reproach, which imputes to Hegel the obsessional economy of "I can give you everything *but that*," goes wrong and misses its target. The basic premise of Hegel is that every attempt to distinguish the Essential from the Inessential always proves itself false. Whenever I resort to a strategy of renouncing the Inessential in order to save the Essential, sooner or later (but always when it's already too late) I'm bound to discover that I made a fatal mistake as to what is essential, and that the essential dimension has already slipped through my fingers.[62]

Throughout his works, Žižek carefully distinguishes both Lacan's thought and his own from postmodernism. As the following essays show, Žižek argues that postmodern (late capitalist) society involves the loss of symbolic authority. Put simply, personal freedom of choice has taken the place of symbolic order. But according to Žižek, this overemphasis on personal choice is misguided due to the reflexivity and negativity which are inherent to subjectivity. With the postmodern decline in symbolic

---

interpretation of F. W. J. Schelling and G. W. F. Hegel is not new. See, for example, Frederick Beiser, *German Idealism: The Struggle Against Subjectivism – 1781–1801* (Cambridge, MA: Harvard University Press, 2002), Gregg Horowitz, *Sustaining Loss: Art and Mournful Life* (Stanford: Stanford University Press, 2001), Dennis Schmidt, *On Germans and Other Greeks: Tragedy and Ethical Life* (Bloomington: Indiana University Press, 2001), and Richard Velkley, *Being after Rousseau: Philosophy and Culture in Question* (Chicago: University of Chicago Press, 2002). Though these four studies approach German Idealism from diverse orientations (Anglo-American, hermeneutic, Straussian, and Critical Theory), nonetheless, all four formulate *a materialist analysis*.

[62] Slavoj Žižek, *Interrogating the Real*, ed. Rex Butler and Scott Stephens (London: Verso, 2005), p. 199.

efficacy – e.g., doubt about the efficiency of the master-figure, what Eric Santner called the "crisis of investiture" – and in the absence of the prohibitions of the symbolic Father, the subject's inherent reflexivity manifests itself in paranoia, in submission to forms of subjection, and in pathological narcissism. What is the remedy for these symptoms of postmodernism? Here Žižek asserts the necessity for the ethical or political *act*. The Lacanian act reinvents the symbolic register; therefore, through the act we can reinvent the (capitalist) conditions of possibility of postmodern society. We can overcome postmodern ideology by traversing the fantasy through the Lacanian act. Only by means of the act (e.g. a revolution) can we produce a new sociosymbolic order in which a new type of symbolic subjectivity is possible.[63] Žižek argues that the time of postmodern relativism and cynicism has already passed; postmodernism just doesn't yet know that it is dead.

Žižek has written dozens of books in various languages, including Slovene, French, German, and – since 1989 – in English, but he claims in the film *Žižek!* that his four best books are *The Sublime Object of Ideology* (first published 1989), *Tarrying with the Negative: Kant, Hegel, and the Critique of Ideology* (first published 1993), *The Ticklish Subject: The Absent Centre of Political Ontology* (first published 1999), and *The Parallax View* (first published 2006). Since 2005, when the film *Žižek!* was completed, he has written several additional books. But for now, let us take Žižek at his word and briefly indicate the character of his major contribution through a quick look at these four "best" books.

In his first book in English, *The Sublime Object of Ideology*, Žižek departed from the standard "structuralist" interpretation of Lacan that was then predominant. And significantly, he also departed from the orthodox reading of Hegel. The "sublime object of ideology" is the imaginary supplement that would (allegedly) allow complete and harmonious synthesis, or non-alienated identity. In *The Sublime Object of Ideology*, Žižek shows how ideology (e.g. the ideology of postmodern relativism) allows its adherents to behave as if it is possible for subjects to overcome all dissonance, trauma, or antagonism. In this book Žižek makes thematic the Kantian notion of "the sublime" in order to liken ideology to an experience of something that is absolutely vast and forceful beyond all perception and objective intelligibility. Like the Kantian sublime, ideology allows subjects to behave as though they belong to a

---

[63] See Tony Myers' excellent book *Slavoj Žižek* (London: Routledge, 2003), pp. 47–8, 57–8, 104. Also see Myers' article "Slavoj Žižek – Key Ideas," online at http://www.lacan.com/zizekchro1.htm.

harmonious, unified community that transcends particular differences and social discord. Žižek does not simply define ideology as deception; rather, he shows how it serves as a fantasy construction that unifies and makes possible our everyday notion of reality. Ideological fantasy (for example, in cinema) teaches us how to desire; in fact, it *constitutes* our desire by providing its coordinates.

In *Tarrying with the Negative* (1993), Žižek argues – against deconstructionists like Jacques Derrida and Judith Butler – that Hegelian dialectic implies a fundamental moment of negativity that eludes any comprehensive, intelligible synthesis. Žižek develops his unorthodox but rigorous interpretation of Hegel in light of Lacanian theory. In the process, he shows how nationalistic identity is based on this same gap or negativity that lies beneath the illusion of consistency and harmonious synthesis. Nationalist mobilizations are based on a sublime illusion. The mythic point of origin around which nationalism revolves is actually nothing but a gap or void that is positivized through the actions of believers. Fantasy functions so as to camouflage the Real antagonism that ruptures any (allegedly) organic, social unification.

Both Lacanian analysis and philosophy involve a stepping back from relativistic orientations by exposure of the artificial, contingent character of the "Master-Signifier," which is essential to the intersubjective symbolic system and yet indefinable within it. Again, when a term (e.g., God, democracy, human rights, nature, the people, etc.) functions as the Master-Signifier, it introduces a performative dimension that serves as a Lacanian *point de capiton* or "quilting point" to pin down chains of signifiers and thereby fix the social field of symbolic interactions. In ideology, the phallic Master-Signifier is an irreducibly external and indefinable central term that functions to pin down or fix the field of meaning. But considered in itself, this empty and inconsistent "signifier without the signified" (word without definition) implies a point of reference that is outside any possible universe of discourse. As Žižek puts it: "The phallic signifier is, so to speak, an index of its own impossibility. In its very positivity it is the signifier of 'castration' – that is, of its own lack."[64]

Žižek elaborates the Hegelian theme of "tarrying with the negative" (cf. section 32 of Hegel's famous "Preface" to his *Phenomenology of Spirit*) in order to show how ruptures and paradigm shifts in theoretical systems are homologous to the analysand's efforts to come to grips with trauma through psychoanalysis. The problem of the relationship between the social order and the individual is resolved with reference to the negative

---

[64] Slavoj Žižek, *The Sublime Object of Ideology* (London: Verso, 1989), p. 157.

or materialist dimension of Hegel's philosophy: the reconciliation of the universal and the individual is not in some "higher" synthesis that mediates the thesis and the antithesis. Instead, dialectical analysis reveals that what the universal and the individual share is the very split or ontological difference that runs through both of them.[65]

Subsequently, in his book *The Ticklish Subject: The Absent Centre of Political Ontology* (1999), Žižek clarifies his own understanding of personal identity – or the subject – first by defining it through contrasts with the thinking of Martin Heidegger. Next Žižek differentiates his thinking from that of several important, contemporary French political philosophers (including his friend and rival Alain Badiou). And, finally, Žižek defends Lacanian theory against criticisms from the well-known feminist deconstructionist Judith Butler. Echoing Marx, Žižek begins the introduction to the book by claiming that the specter of the Cartesian subject is haunting Western academia.

The central theme of *The Ticklish Subject* is that traditional interpretations of Descartes' *cogito* ignore the functional role of "I think therefore I exist" within the project of methodic doubt. Standard academic readings of Descartes ignore the radical implications of the effort to "start with a clean slate – to erase the entirety of reality in so far as it is *not yet* 'born out of the I' by passing through the 'night of the world.' "[66] A philosophical-psychoanalytic inquiry into madness reveals that the withdrawal into self and the passage through madness is *constitutive* of subjectivity as such.

In *The Parallax View*, Žižek investigates the "parallax gap" that separates modes of thinking between which no harmonious conceptual synthesis is possible. He articulates this parallax gap as it functions between and within philosophical, scientific, and political discourses:

> First, there is the *ontological difference* itself as the ultimate parallax which conditions our very access to reality; then there is the *scientific parallax*, the irreducible gap between the phenomenal experience of reality and its scientific account/explanation, which reaches its apogee in cognitivism, with its endeavor to provide a "third-person" neuro-biological account of our "first-person" experience; last, but not least, there is the *political parallax*, the social antagonism which allows for no common ground between the conflicting agents (once upon a time, it was called "class struggle"), with its two main modes of existence on which the last two chapters of this

---

[65] Slavoj Žižek, *Tarrying with the Negative: Kant, Hegel, and the Critique of Ideology* (Durham, NC: Duke University Press, 1993), p. 30.
[66] Slavoj Žižek, *The Ticklish Subject: The Absent Centre of Political Ontology* (London and New York: Verso, 1999), p. 34.

book focus (the parallax gap between the public Law and its superego obscene supplement; the parallax gap between the "Bartleby" attitude of withdrawal from social engagement and collective social action).[67]

The Parallax View has been called Žižek's magnum opus, but at the time of this writing, his major work on Hegel has not yet been released. Thus it is far too early to attempt to gauge the full impact of Žižek's ground-breaking work on the subsequent history of thought. In the preface to the revised edition of *Enjoy Your Symptom! Jacques Lacan in Hollywood and Out*, Žižek asks: "Is there then, a hope for the breakthrough of Lacanian theory in the United States?"[68] In what follows, we hope to indicate how Žižek's dialectical materialist development of Lacanian theory embodies this hope, especially in conjunction with the ravages of late capitalism.

What is Žižek's Primary Aim?

The Lacanian register of the Real – as the universal dimension of negativity that is constitutive of all thought and experience – is the focus of Žižek's work. Žižek's primary aim is to evoke this void at the heart of subjectivity. Even his books that focus on the critique of ideology and political economy cannot be adequately understood without first coming to grips with Žižek's concept of "the parallax Real." It is now widely known that twentieth-century mathematicians like Kurt Gödel proved that any formal system is inherently incomplete insofar as it implies at least one undecidable proposition. In short, we now have mathematical proof that we can never know that mathematics is noncontradictory. But long before this mathematical proof of incompleteness was developed, the insight behind it was evoked by dialectical philosophers (e.g., Plato, Kant, and the German Idealists). And along the same lines, Žižek too argues that any nondialectical account of truth masks irreducible paradoxes. For example, there is a self-referential absurdity implied by what he sometimes calls "postmodern relativism." It cannot be universally true that every historical period is entirely determined by non-universal practices.

Žižek's dialectical materialism *does* emphasize radical contingency, but in a way that is much more sophisticated than postmodernism. Žižek avoids relativism by showing the universal to be a *negative* a priori. That which always returns as the "same" in any disclosure is the Real as

---

[67] Slavoj Žižek, *The Parallax View* (Cambridge, MA: MIT Press, 2006), p. 10.
[68] Slavoj Žižek, *Enjoy Your Symptom! Jacques Lacan in Hollywood and Out* (New York: Routledge, 2001), p. vii.

ontological difference, the inconsistency or gap that divides any "one" from itself. Žižek shows how the distinction between the three dimensions of experience (imaginary, symbolic, and Real) facilitates a dialectical understanding of the interrelation between universal necessity and particular contingency. Žižek's work demonstrates repeatedly and in a variety of ways how the concept of the Real as a *negative* a priori reconfigures the traditional problems of philosophy. For Žižek, universal truth is the dialectical process of becoming that is manifested as antagonism or struggle. Truth is externalized from consciousness, insofar as it is related to the encounter (or failure to encounter) the traumatic, repressed Real. In sum, necessity is constituted in a retroactive way: although truth is contingent, the illusion of fixed meaning is a *necessary* illusion.

It is in such ways that Žižek re-inscribes the German Idealist theme of self-reflexive negativity in terms of the Freudian concept of the death drive and the traversal of fantasy as an encounter with the Real. Lacan defines "drive," not in terms of biology (as in the so-called "sex drive"), but in terms of the split subject's relation to the demands of the parents. Along these lines, Žižek emphasizes that drive must not be conceived in terms of physiological needs or biological instincts: "the specifically human dimension" involves drive as opposed to instinct. Drive functions as a brake on instinct: "We become 'humans' when we get caught into a closed, self-propelling loop of repeating the same gesture and finding satisfaction in it."[69]

Žižek argues that drive as such is death drive, and links this to the moment of negativity implicit to the dialectical development of subjectivity: "the Freudian death drive has nothing whatsoever to do with the craving for self-annihilation, for the return to the inorganic absence of any life-tension."[70] Whereas symbolic desire aims at attaining its object (and then switching to some other object that comes to signify desire), drive involves an endless circling around the *same* object: "let us imagine an individual trying to perform some simple manual task – say, grab an object which repeatedly eludes him: the moment he changes his attitude, starting to find pleasure in just repeating the failed task, squeezing the object which, again and again, eludes him, he shifts from desire to drive."[71]

Understanding the Real as self-relating negativity is crucial if we are to comprehend why Žižek argues that the death drive is the pivotal concept of psychoanalytic theory of which even Sigmund Freud was not fully

[69] Slavoj Žižek, *The Parallax View* (Cambridge, MA: MIT Press, 2006), p. 63.
[70] Slavoj Žižek, *The Parallax View* (Cambridge, MA: MIT Press, 2006), p. 62.
[71] Slavoj Žižek, *The Parallax View* (Cambridge, MA: MIT Press, 2006), p. 7.

aware: "crucial here is the basic and constitutive discord between drive and body: drive as eternal-'undead' disrupts the instinctual rhythm. For that reason, drive as such is death drive."[72] Unless we understand Žižek's focus on death drive as radical negativity, we will not grasp the significance of his claims in interviews that his greatest achievement is those chapters in his works in which he develops his interpretation of Hegel.[73] Žižek articulates the death drive as the idea that deep within subjectivity – deeper than truth and beyond the pleasure principle – there is a self-sabotaging, non-economic, and non-evolutionary potential for the *autonomy* of the subject. This subjective autonomy is the source both of the Lacanian act as well as of radical evil. The death drive belongs to the Real of subjectivity, and as we will see, Žižek shows the Real to involve a prelinguistic "primordial repression" which entails that the Real returns in all symbolic, linguistic practices.

The Real as irreducible negativity or incommensurability is the focus of Žižek's analyses of contemporary life and culture in all its aspects: economic, political, artistic, religious, social, sexual, and intellectual. However, unlike previous dialectical philosophers (e.g., Plato, Kant, Fichte, Schelling), Žižek delineates this negativity or "parallax gap" without ever lapsing into an imaginary sense of completeness. He shows that all wholeness is imaginary: the universe – reality itself – is incomplete. But imaginary identifications (as fantasies of wholeness or completeness) prevent confrontation with the Real as the irreducible negativity or antagonism that disrupts symbolic practices: "At the most radical level of subjectivity and experience, there is some initial moment of madness: the dimensions of *jouissance*, of negativity, of death drive and so on, but *not* the dimension of truth."[74] Žižek shows how any symbolization depends on a more originary closing over: any symbolic reality implies primordial repression of the Real. The Real is never directly present as such, because in the encounter with the Real, both identity and reality disintegrate. Although we may approach the Real of desire in dreams, it is homologous to an insurmountable gap between two linked but irreconcilable aspects of symbolic reality. And though it is that which both informs and constitutes symbolic reality, nonetheless the Real qua Real cannot be adequately imagined or consistently symbolized.

[72] Slavoj Žižek, *The Plague of Fantasies* (London and New York: Verso, 1997), p. 31.

[73] For example, see Žižek's interview with Rosanna Greenstreet, published in *The Guardian*, August 9, 2008, and available online at http://www.guardian.co.uk/lifeandstyle/2008/aug/09/slavoj.zizek.

[74] Slavoj Žižek and Glyn Daly, *Conversations with Žižek* (Cambridge: Polity Press, 2004), p. 64.

But insofar as it is the inconsistency (or parallax gap) inherent to any symbolic system, the Real functions as a negative kind of universality. Again, to express the paradox of the Real succinctly, the only consistency/ sameness that always returns in language or reasoning is the Real, and the Real involves fundamental inconsistency/difference. This is why what is universal cannot be some all-encompassing neutral "space" or generic category that grounds each and every possible particular content. That which is universal is not a neutral medium or background to which we can appeal in order to resolve the conflicts between particularities. What is repeated as the same (as universal) in any possible symbolic reality is nothing but inconsistency, antagonism, and non-identity. This means that the universal "as such" involves the negativity of the Real. As a kind of negative a priori, the universal in this sense is never fully "present" either for perception or for thought; it is not an experience, an object, or a property of experiences or objects. How then do we discern it? It is manifested as that irreducible antagonism that the multitude of particular species attempt to occlude or domesticate or resolve. This is why the Real can be discerned only by "looking awry."

In sum, only if we first conceive universality in terms of the Real as a negative a priori will we then grasp Žižek's radical philosophical innovation into the nature of truth. And unless we achieve insight into the Real, we will not comprehend Žižek's claims that we are free to overcome ideology:

> My speculation here is that what Freud calls death drive – if we read it with regard to its most radical philosophical dimension – is something that has to be already operative to open up, as it were, the space for truth. Let's take Heidegger quite literally here: truth is always a certain openness, in the sense of an opening of horizons, an opening of the world, disclosure through speech and so on. But a condition of possibility for the opening of such a space is precisely what, in psychoanalysis, we would call the primordial repression: some original withdrawal, which is again already signalled by radical negativity. And the point I would emphasize here is that, in philosophical terms, psychoanalysis is extremely ambitious. Psychoanalysis is not a simple story of basic instinctual problems; it is concerned, rather, with a formulation of what had to happen in order for the world to open itself to us as an experience of meaning.[75]

The above passage gives some indication of the breadth and depth of Žižek's dialectical materialist methodology (his analyses of method

---

[75] Slavoj Žižek and Glyn Daly, *Conversations with Žižek* (Cambridge: Polity Press, 2004), p. 64.

itself). To express his philosophical significance succinctly, Žižek's dialectical-psychoanalytic approach reveals the inadequacy of the notion of truth held by virtually all other philosophers. As we will see, Žižek's inquiries into freedom as death drive, and his analyses of the relation between this Real spontaneity and truth reveal the vacuity of the liberal-democratic notion of the universal.

Again, in liberal-democratic ideology, universality is conceived as a neutral medium for compromise, and for the expression of self-interest or group identity. Against this, Žižek argues that this sterile notion of universality serves the interests of global capitalism. But how can leftists oppose nationalism without sliding into the vacuous, liberal-democratic notion of universality as a neutral framework for compromise? Žižek answers by reviving the Hegelian notion of "concrete universality," a form of universality that is realized only through the partisan, properly *political* act of taking sides. Žižek argues that at this juncture in history, what is called for is the identification with the disenfranchised "excremental remainder" of society. The universal truth of an event or situation is *not* revealed in the big Other, the intersubjective, sociosymbolic network. On the contrary, the truth of a situation is accessible only to those who occupy the position of the abject, excluded other. Any ideology excludes and makes abject some Other, some particular group, and if this exclusion is symptomatic of a wider problem, the excluded ones experience the pathology of the entire society. This is why Žižek argues that the universal (partisan) truth of the entire social field is disclosed only through the experiences of those who are disenfranchised by the hegemonic ideology.

Žižek reveals the philosophical import of twentieth-century developments in psychoanalysis by articulating Lacanian theory in light of Hegelian dialectics. In the process Žižek illuminates the primary accomplishments (as well as the blind spots) of recent continental philosophers such as Martin Heidegger, Jacques Derrida, Gilles Deleuze, Louis Althusser, and even his friend – today's preeminent French thinker – Alain Badiou. Žižek's dialectical materialist fusion of psychoanalysis and philosophy also promises to bridge the gap between the Anglo-American (post-analytic) and continental approaches to philosophy. As indicated above, Žižek's Lacanian deployment of Hegelian categories casts new light on traditional philosophical paradoxes relating to universality and specific difference. To put the point succinctly, Žižek shows why the reference of a name to its object cannot be understood as a set of predicates or properties designated by that name. Žižek's analyses indicate that no positive ontology successfully avoids ambiguities and implicit paradoxes of singularity and universality (see chapter 10 below). In what follows, we will see how Žižek's version of dialectical materialism casts new light on conceptual impasses relating to universality and specific difference.

For example, one of the basic problems in the theory of knowledge involves the distinction between how things seem, as opposed to how things really are. Žižek refines this question to such an extent that the original distinction becomes virtually useless. According to Žižek's dialectical materialism, there is no "how things really are." It is not just our knowledge of reality that is incomplete; reality itself is incomplete. Moreover, my existence as a subject is characterized by the difference between how things seem to me, as opposed to how things *really* seem to me. Again, Žižek's philosophical elaboration of Lacan shows why I can never access the way things really seem to me: I have no access to my most intimate subjective experience. I can never consciously experience the fundamental fantasy that forms and sustains the core of my existence:

> At its most radical, the Unconscious is the inaccessible phenomenon, not the objective mechanism that regulates my phenomenal experience. So, in contrast to the commonplace that we are dealing with a subject the moment an entity displays signs of "inner life," that is, of a fantasmatic self-experience that cannot be reduced to external behavior, we should claim that what characterizes human subjectivity proper is, rather, the gap that separates the two: the fact that fantasy, at its most elementary, becomes inaccessible to the subject; it is this inaccessibility that makes the subject "empty." We thus obtain a relationship that totally subverts the standard notion of the subject who directly experiences himself, his "inner states": an "impossible" relationship between the empty, nonphenomenal subject and the phenomena that remain inaccessible to the subject.[76]

Anyone who is at all familiar with some of the basic problems of philosophy should by now have some intimation that Žižek's dialectical materialism facilitates a novel approach to questions about truth, existence, identification, ethics, and justice. Žižek's Lacanian reactualization of Hegelian dialectic allows us to discern the externalized truth of contemporary intellectual life. The following essays investigate the ways that Žižek's dialectical-psychoanalytic methodology evokes not only the disavowed truth of traditional philosophy, but also the reasons for this

---

[76] Slavoj Žižek, *The Parallax View* (Cambridge, MA: MIT Press, 2006), pp. 171–2.

disavowal: in particular, the hidden connections between the discourse of the university and the Real power of capital.[77]

If (as Žižek claims) Heidegger is the twentieth-century philosopher that all other serious philosophers today are still obliged to confront critically, then Žižek may be the twenty-first century's definitive philosopher, insofar as his philosophy "connects us in the sense that, in a way, almost every other orientation of any serious weight defines itself through some sort of critical relation" towards Žižek's dialectical materialist ontology.[78]

[77] Tony Myers goes so far as to claim that "Marx's critique of capitalism is the very reason why he writes at all." See Myers' *Slavoj Žižek* (London: Routledge, 2003), p. 18. Myers' book is one of the best introductory books on Žižek currently available in English. Also highly recommended is Rex Butler's *Slavoj Žižek: Live Theory* (London: Continuum, 2005). Like Myers, Butler also has a good grasp of both dialectical philosophy and Lacanian psychoanalysis. The final chapter of Butler's book is an excellent interview with Žižek.

[78] Slavoj Žižek and Glyn Daly, *Conversations with Žižek* (Cambridge: Polity Press, 2004), p. 28.

2

The Sublime Object
of Ideology

Žižek demonstrates that ideology provides a sense of coherence by way of the Master-Signifier, which is an empty indicator of symbolic authority that unifies a discourse by imparting to it a performative dimension. The "mythic wholeness" around which ideologies revolve involves fantasy, which camouflages Real antagonism and lack within any system. Ideological symbolizations and narratives offer an illusion of societal unity by masking the constitutive splitting of the intersubjective symbolic register. Once the Real – as fundamental gap or negativity – has been occluded by some ideological fantasy of societal identity, individuals who have incorporated the hegemonic ideology of their society are then able to interact with some degree of consistency. Žižek analyzes this functioning of ideological fantasy as the imaginary unity that conceals irreducible antagonism and inconsistency. In the process, he revises the standard interpretation of Hegel by showing how Hegel's dialectic is implicitly ruptured by negativity that prevents the full realization of dialectical synthesis. Žižek's account of Hegelian dialectic emphasizes that which ruptures any attempted unification or synthesis, making reality (and our understanding of it) incomplete. In tandem with this dialectical materialist ontology, Žižek also revives a leftist critique of ideology. He refutes the claim that today our world is "post-ideological" by developing a new, unorthodox interpretation of Marx. These analyses show that even our cynical and disengaged, postmodern social activity involves what Marx referred to as alienation and fetishism.

The most elementary definition of ideology is probably the well-known phrase from Marx's Capital: "Sie wissen das nicht, aber sie tun es" –

Žižek: A Reader's Guide, First Edition. Kelsey Wood.
© 2012 John Wiley & Sons, Inc. Published 2012 by John Wiley & Sons, Inc.

"they do not know it, but they are doing it." The very concept of ideology implies a kind of basic, constitutive naïveté: *the misrecognition of its own presuppositions, of its own effective conditions, a distance, a divergence between so-called social reality and our distorted representation, our false consciousness of it. That is why such a "naive consciousness" can be submitted to a critical-ideological procedure. The aim of this procedure is to lead the naïve ideological consciousness to a point at which it can recognize its own effective conditions, the social reality that it is distorting, and through this very act dissolve itself. In the more sophisticated versions of the critics of ideology – that developed by the Frankfurt School, for example – it is not just a question of seeing things (that is, social reality) as they "really are," of throwing away the distorting spectacles of ideology; the main point is to see how the reality itself cannot reproduce itself without this so-called ideological mystification. The mask is not simply hiding the real state of things; the ideological distortion is written into its very essence.*

—Žižek, *The Sublime Object of Ideology*, p. 28

In his introduction to *The Sublime Object of Ideology* (1989; abbreviated *Sublime* below),[1] Žižek states the threefold aim of the book: to introduce some fundamental concepts of Lacanian psychoanalysis, to revitalize Hegelian dialectics by way of a Lacanian reading of Hegel, and to develop the theory of ideology by clarifying correspondences between Marxism and Lacanian psychoanalysis. Žižek writes:

> It is my belief that these three aims are deeply connected: the only way to "save Hegel" is through Lacan, and this Lacanian reading of Hegel and the Hegelian heritage opens up a new approach to ideology, allowing us to grasp contemporary ideological phenomena (cynicism, "totalitarianism," the fragile status of democracy) without falling prey to any kind of "post-modernist" traps (such as the illusion that we live in a "post-ideological" condition). (*Sublime*, p. 7)

Regarding the first of his three aims, Žižek develops his account of ideology through continuous references to, and examples from, the works of Jacques Lacan. He shows how Lacan (like Kant, Marx, and Hegel) reevaluates unexamined assumptions, uncritical beliefs, and

---

[1] Unless otherwise stated, page references for this work are to the following edition: *The Sublime Object of Ideology* (London and New York: Verso, 1989).

unreflective sociosymbolic practices. Žižek accomplishes this by showing how the functioning of the sublime object in social interrelations brings with it an irresolvable problem. Again, the "sublime object of ideology" is the imaginary supplement that would (allegedly) allow complete and harmonious synthesis, or non-alienated identity. But Lacan already showed how the Real is that which is impossible to say; it resists symbolization and incorporation into the big Other of linguistic systems and shared, symbolic practices. Žižek (like Lacan) avoids relativism by way of a radical distancing from the contingent and artificial character of the ideological Master-Signifier. The Master-Signifier is an empty signifier of symbolic authority that pins down or totalizes a discourse by giving it a performative dimension: "It is so because I say it is so." Žižek demonstrates that because the Master-Signifier proves to be indefinable according to *any* possible intelligible criteria, the sense of wholeness offered by ideologies is possible only on the basis of an empty "signifier with no signified." This signifier with no signified pins down the field of meaning, and yet is indefinable within the very field which it pins down. Analysis reveals that the phantasmatic unity or wholeness around which ideologies revolve proves finally to be nothing but a hole or rupture that is positivized in a way that camouflages Real antagonism within any system.

Regarding the second of his three aims, Žižek's *Sublime* redeems Hegel by revealing the inadequacies of the hackneyed interpretation of Hegelian dialectic that still predominates in some circles. According to this standard, dismissive interpretation, Hegel presumed to overcome all differences in a system of complete rational synthesis, or "Absolute Knowledge." Žižek exposes the error of this trite interpretation by demonstrating that Hegelian dialectic always discloses a gap or schism that disrupts any whole or totality. Hegelian dialectic points toward the Real by emphasizing negativity: any conceptual synthesis is disrupted from within by an indefinable negativity that proves to be essential to the very concept in question. Thus Žižek interprets the famous (or infamous) Hegelian Absolute Knowledge as implicitly anticipating the Lacanian Real. In other words, Hegelian Absolute Knowledge involves the insight that any formal-symbolic system is inherently inconsistent, any totality is inconsistent. Žižek supports his interpretation of Hegelian dialectic by astutely observing that Kant had already realized that being is not a predicate; that is, that *existence* cannot be reduced to the conceptual properties of entities. Thus, not only Hegel, but also his predecessor Kant, recognized the futility of any attempt to completely define what it *is* that any concept signifies. Any possible account of the wholeness or unity of "whatness" always discloses an incomplete and inconsistent totality. This implies that belief is symbolic, but knowledge is Real: knowledge involves recognition of the incompleteness and inconsistency of any dialectical synthesis.

Regarding the third of his three aims, Žižek develops a new reading of Marx in order to refute the postmodern claim that because individuals are generally too cynical to believe in ideologies anymore, we now live in a post-ideological world. Marx's account of "commodity fetishism" discloses how, in our social exchanges, the commodity assumes the status of a magical object that seems to have uncanny powers. A fetish is an object that fills in the constitutive lack or void around which the symbolic order revolves. If through labor, an individual produces an item to be exchanged, nonetheless, in the process of social interactions and exchanges, the product takes on an abstract value that is divorced both from the amount of labor involved in its production and the usefulness of the product. As an example of this abstract value, a diamond (even if it is found accidentally) might be exchanged for a house that is both more useful and required much labor to produce. This abstract exchange value transforms the products of labor into *commodities*, and the fetish is the process of abstraction itself, through which the diamond as commodity is capable in the first place of appearing to be "naturally" more valuable than the house. With reference to the work of Alfred Sohn-Rethel, Žižek explains this process of abstraction, and indicates how the economy functions in a way that is homologous to a Kantian "transcendental" category of the understanding:

> Before thought could arrive at pure *abstraction*, the abstraction was already at work in the social effectivity of the market. The exchange of commodities implies a double abstraction: the abstraction from the changeable character of the commodity during the act of exchange and the abstraction from the concrete, empirical, sensual, particular character of the commodity (in the act of exchange, the distinct, particular qualitative determination of a commodity is not taken into account; a commodity is reduced to an abstract entity which – irrespective of its particular nature, of its "use-value" – possesses "the same value" as another commodity for which it is being exchanged. (*Sublime*, p. 17)

As a result of social indoctrination (or ideological subjectivization), judgments about exchange value become habitual and unreflective. However, this illusory appearance of "naturalness" in the exchange values between things masks the social relations and activities that *constitute* the exchange value. Thus social relations are obscured behind a fetish, a phantasmatic, imaginary power of material things to determine values themselves in the marketplace.

It cannot be emphasized too strongly that in order to understand any of Žižek's works, it is crucial not to confuse his thinking with postmodernism. In *Sublime*, Žižek argues that our cynical and disengaged postmodern social activity involves fetishism and alienation. But significantly, Žižek re-inscribes Marx for today's postmodern societies. We should briefly consider the meaning of Žižek's "repetition" of Marx. If B repeats A, what makes it a "true" repetition? Repetition in Žižek's sense involves – not some identity or even similarity of positive content – but rather, the shared struggle (of both B and A) to represent the same unrepresentable X. This shows that repetition does not simply involve recognizing the "openness" of the text, its flexibility or productive ambiguity (its potential to generate a multitude of interpretations). Repetition is not the recontextualization of any positive content; it is the repetition of a Real antagonism or negativity that is left out of (repressed from) the symbolic order. Because that which is repressed always returns, we should try to do today what Marx tried – but failed – to do in his time, and this time we should fail better. In sum, to "repeat" the thought of any thinker is to reactualize the struggle to repeat the same unrepeatable X. Thus Žižek's repetition of Marx involves *reinventing* Marx's struggle for truth, but in relation to our postmodern symbolic order.

As part of his refutation of the naive view that we live in a post-ideological world, Žižek reveals a homology between the Freudian notion of the unconscious and Marx's analysis of commodity fetishism. Žižek's account draws on the work of Alfred Sohn-Rethel in order to show a sense in which *both* the Freudian notion of the unconscious *and* the Marxian notion of commodity exchange essentially involve an irreducible dimension of abstraction of which neither Marx nor Freud was aware. Žižek elaborates this homology between Marx and Freud in order to draw attention to the role of abstract form in their theories. Regarding Freud, Žižek urges that we should not look for the hidden significance behind the dream; rather we need to inquire into why and how fears and desires first take the form of the dream. Regarding Marx, consider what Žižek writes on p. 18:

> Here we have touched a problem unsolved by Marx, that of the *material* character of money: not of the empirical, material stuff money is made of, but of the *sublime* material, of that other "indestructible and immutable" body which persists beyond the corruption of the body physical – this other body of money is like the corpse of the Sadeian victim which endures all torments and survives with its beauty immaculate.

In order to understand Žižek's point here, it is crucial to recognize that Žižek establishes a new way to read the Marxian definition of ideology. Instead of Marx's "they do not know it, but they are doing it," Žižek's reading shows how social reality is guided by a fetishistic inversion. This means that it is not reality that subjects misrecognize, but rather *the fantasy that structures their reality*. This explains why, even if subjects do know how things are, they still behave as if they did not know (*Sublime*, p. 32). Žižek's analysis reveals the efficacy of fantasy within social reality itself by showing how and why belief itself is radically exterior, or alienated. Put simply, metaphysical depth and subtlety is *not* buried in some spiritual essence of the subject, but is "out there," externalized in the exchanges of commodities (*Sublime*, p. 34).

Marx showed very well how the capitalist belief that subjects are rationally guided by their own selfish interests overlooks something crucial. It is not simply the case that individual persons "have" beliefs, whereas commodities (mere things) are exchanged by individuals. In capitalism (because of commodity fetishism), it is the commodities that believe in place of the subjects involved in exchanges. What this means is that the supposedly rational capitalist "personality" is not some inner depth of selfhood, mind, or "soul." Instead the capitalist personality is constituted by external social relations such as the exchange of commodities. Žižek develops Marx's concept of commodity fetishism in terms of Lacanian theory, in order to demonstrate why belief cannot ever be verified externally. Put succinctly, symbolic beliefs rely on an imaginary foundation. Beliefs are radically externalized from consciousness, in unreflective social practices, as in the apparently "natural" exchange of commodities such as a diamond for a house. However, knowledge – as opposed to belief – is Real, and it involves recognition of the inconsistency of the symbolic, and how this inconsistency is masked by fantasy. Thus for Žižek, ideological fantasy is constitutive of sociosymbolic, "objective" reality.

The big Other is the locus of belief. Belief is externalized; belief is inscribed into the symbolic order insofar as it is always belief *through* the Other. Even for cynical postmodern subjects, belief is the assurance that someone else, somewhere, still believes. But whereas for Marx the fetishism of commodities conceals the *positive* network of social relations, for Žižek, a fetish conceals the phantasmatic *void* around which symbolic networks revolve. This indicates a difference between orthodox Marxism and Lacanian theory: in the predominant interpretation of Marx, "the ideological gaze is a *partial* gaze overlooking the *totality* of social relations," but from Žižek's Lacanian perspective ideology "designates *a totality set on effacing the traces of its own impossibility"* (*Sublime*, p. 49). This indicates how Žižek utilizes Lacanian theory to reactualize the Hegelian theme of negativity. Social reality itself is the product of an effort to come to grips with Real trauma or antagonism: "The function of ideology is not to offer us a point of escape from our reality but to offer us the social reality itself as an escape from some traumatic, real kernel" (p. 45). Put simply, symbolic reality is a fiction constituted through ideological fantasy, which shields us from the Real.

A successful ideology allows its adherents to behave as though the Master-Signifier is not just an irreducibly external and indefinable term, but actually names some transcendent thing. Fantasy tries to complete the circuit of signification by reference to something "beyond" signification. The paradox is that although no sublime object (e.g., God, Freedom, Democracy, etc.) is ever "there" in any subject's experience, nonetheless this indefinable central term is taken by the subject to be that which gives coherence to the entire field of all possible experiences. Although any ideology is incomplete and inconsistent, the very indefinability of the Master-Signifier is assumed by believers to prove the validity of the system. The Master-Signifier involves a performative dimension that signifies nothing at the level of *constative*, or theoretical, knowledge. Because this difference is irreducible, the Master-Signifier is pure difference misperceived as pure identity; thus the notion that the Master-Signifier has "meaning" in itself relies on fantasy. In other words, the Master-Signifier is not some pre-existing, substantial fullness of meaning to which all of the particulars refer. The Master-Signifier functions so as to unify a field of meaning precisely because it is an empty, internally inconsistent signifier. Its emptiness is retrospectively mis-taken as that fullness to which any field of meaning refers.

Consequently, postmodernist claims that we live in a post-ideological condition are not only false but dangerously misguided. On the contrary, as Žižek's substantial analyses of contemporary culture demonstrate, if anything, we postmodern subjects today believe more than ever; however, our belief takes the form of imagining that someone else believes. Our cynicism still involves the belief that someone else believes; there is some Other who desires and is envious of our unfathomable X (Freedom, Democracy, etc.). Thus the anti-Enlightenment, Nietzschean tendencies of postmodernism (cynicism, indirections and distantiations, idiosyncratic and mutually exclusive interpretations of the same text) are in fact symptomatic of the contemporary subject's inability to overcome alienation. These postmodernist gestures are modes of reproducing late capitalist symbolic reality; they are ways of domesticating the Real by inscribing it into the intersubjective symbolic network. Postmodernism is not "radical" at all; on the contrary, it exemplifies the elementary operation of ideology. In spite of our postmodern cynicism, today subjects believe more than ever. Again, the key point is that our belief is *externalized*: we believe that there is some Other who believes. Even though we in the USA all know that our so-called "democracy" is dysfunctional, somewhere there is someone who still believes in our democracy. In sum, today's postmodern cynicism does *not* distance us from ideology; on the contrary, it allows us to be immersed in ideological fantasy today more than ever.

But perhaps Žižek's greatest achievement in *Sublime* is to show how both Hegel and Lacan identify a possibility for overcoming alienation and ideological operations through "subjective destitution." Subjective destitution, the last stage of Lacanian analysis, involves the insight that there is finally no big Other. What does this mean? Any totality is inconsistent with itself: symbolic reality is incomplete, unfinished, and internally contradictory. The belief in a symbolic universe that is Whole (the big Other) is based on fantasy. Or, as Hegel put it, the God of the beyond died on the cross. If the subject no longer presupposes himself as subject, he assumes the *nonexistence* of the big Other. This involves acknowledging and accepting the traumatic kernel of the utter meaninglessness of the Real; in short, I realize that my symbolic identity is based on a fantasy. Such acceptance acknowledges – rather than effaces – the gap between the Real and its (always inadequate) symbolization.

In several more recent works and in his public lectures, Žižek develops the above insight by apparently paradoxical claims like "Only an atheist can believe." It is thus not without significance that in the closing pages of *The Sublime Object of Ideology*, Žižek articulates a structural homology between his dialectical materialism and contemporary (a)theology (*Sublime*, pp. 229–30). In such ways, Žižek calls each of us to overcome alienation and the operations of ideology through what he has called (with reference to Kierkegaard) "a politics *between* fear and trembling."

In *The Sublime Object of Ideology*, Žižek supports democracy, but in an ambivalent way. The formally abstract democratic subject is a necessary fiction. What does this mean? In reality there is no "normal," there are only particular (de)formations of the empty and inconsistent, universal notion of democracy (*Sublime*, pp. 148–9). Insofar as democracy functions as the Master-Signifier, the task is to first *recognize its imposture*. De-fetishization is achieved by experiencing the big Other as barred: that is, recognizing that the Master-Signifier conceals not only a void, but also an obscene superego injunction to transgress and enjoy. The task is thus to annul oneself as subject, to accept subjective destitution, and to recognize that one's innermost treasure, one's unfathomable X (e.g., "Democracy!"), is worthless. In his next book, *For They Know Not What They Do*, Žižek will criticize his own position in *The Sublime Object* (including his previous support of democracy), and argue that the left today should not commit all its resources to the victory of democracy.[2]

This process of endless self-critique indicates the hysterical questioning that characterizes subjectivity as such (as *feminine*). Only through such confrontations with the Real as symbolic inconsistency can we hope to transform fantasy and desire, and to reinvent a new economy of enjoyment. Žižek argues in several works that it is precisely this subjective destitution ("my precious treasure is shit") that can prompt us to the act as a utopian leap through *darkness* that transforms symbolic subjectivity. In itself, the subject is the gap of being (cf. the Hegelian "night of the world" passage in the Jena writings); but in the decisive political act, subjectivity is constituted and utopia is realized.

---

[2] See, e.g., *For They Know Not What They Do: Enjoyment as a Political Factor* (London and New York: Verso, 1991), p. 270.

3

For They Know Not What They Do: Enjoyment as a Political Factor

Žižek traces – through the history of modern philosophy – the ideological manipulation of Real enjoyment (*jouissance*). Ideology manifests as a fantasy construction that blurs crucial distinctions; this phantasmatic ideological formation allows a subject to behave as though s/he belongs to a unified community that overcomes social antagonism. Social reality is made possible by ideological fantasy, which allows us to cope with the disturbing negativity of social antagonism. Žižek shows why the truth of any society is not encapsulated by any "positive" definition. Rather, the truth of a society involves the insurmountable antagonism of the Real; it is the primordial repression of the Real that spawns the multitude of competing definitions. Human infants respond to trauma/antagonism by symbolizing, and symbolic fictions serve as reactive attempts to cover over the inherent division or antagonism of society. Along the same lines, the symbolic subject is not a substantial entity, but an empty place that emerges as the inconsistency of socially constructed processes of subjectivization. And insofar as symbolic reality is always already structured by ideological fantasy, we must first "move the underground" of fantasy before transforming reality. Žižek analyzes a variety of examples that illustrate the self-defeating nature of ideological manipulations of enjoyment. Through these analyses, he demonstrates a new approach to the traditional philosophical problem of the relation between the universal and the particular. On the one hand, Žižek's dialectical development of Lacanian psychoanalysis illuminates the reasons why any formal system is inherently incomplete (e.g., implies at least one undecidable proposition). On the other hand, Žižek's psychoanalytic orientation enables an account of how irreducible social antagonism assumes

Žižek: A Reader's Guide, First Edition. Kelsey Wood.
© 2012 John Wiley & Sons, Inc. Published 2012 by John Wiley & Sons, Inc.

different forms as history progresses in unforeseeable directions. But in spite of historical contingency, in ideology the antithesis presupposes the same general form as the thesis, even though there is a change in the content of the thesis. The synthesis – as the negation of negation – is not a harmonious blending or full identity; rather it is the negation of the symbolic reality (the "positive" order) that had come to stand in for the originary void or incommensurability of the Real. Žižek's account of dialectical synthesis reveals our unconscious preoccupation with the trauma of the Real, and our complicity in the deployment of symbolic fictions which serve to mask this originary cut or asymmetry. The Real as the inconsistency of the symbolic register is thus a negative kind of universality: it is the encounter with (and the subsequent attempt to avoid) the Real that provokes the struggle for universality. Insofar as Hegelian synthesis marks the limits of the symbolic reality, Hegel's dialectic involves a "materialist" dimension, the same incommensurability that Lacan calls the Real. Žižek articulates a unique account of the relation between universal necessity and particular contingency. It is this dialectical materialist ontology that informs Žižek's critique of capitalist ideology.

> *In short, the problem with democracy is not that it is a democracy, but –*
> *to use the phrase introduced apropos of the NATO bombing of*
> *Yugoslavia – its "collateral damage": the fact that it is a form of State*
> *Power that involves certain relationships of production.*
> —Žižek, *For They Know Not What They Do:*
> *Enjoyment as a Political Factor*, p. lxxx

Žižek's *For They Know Not What They Do: Enjoyment as a Political Factor* (1991)[1] is the sequel to his first book in English, *The Sublime Object of Ideology. For They Know Not What They Do* (abbreviated *FTKN* below) is not easy reading; it is even more theoretically substantial than *Sublime*. For the reader already acquainted with Lacan and/or Žižek, *Sublime* is probably the best introduction to *FTKN*, since *Sublime* develops many of the same themes in a more accessible way. However, it is vital to keep in mind that in *FTKN*, Žižek revises his own earlier position in several ways. In *Sublime*, Žižek advocated democracy. But, as the opening quotation above indicates, in *FTKN*, he begins to formulate a bold, leftist critique of democracy. Also, in *FTKN*, Žižek revises his own earlier interpretation of Lacan:

---

[1]   Unless otherwise stated, page references for this work are to the following edition: *For They Know Not What They Do: Enjoyment as a Political Factor* (London and New York: Verso, 2002).

Although I still stand by the basic insights of *The Sublime Object*, it is clear to me, with hindsight, that it contains a series of intertwined weaknesses. First, there is the philosophical weakness: it basically endorses a quasi-transcendental reading of Lacan, focused on the notion of the Real as the impossible Thing-in-itself; in so doing, it opens the way to the celebration of failure: to the idea that every act ultimately misfires, and that the proper ethical stance is heroically to accept this failure. (*FTKN*, pp. xi–xii)

FTKN traces, through the history of modern philosophy, the ideological function of enjoyment. Put simply, in *FTKN* Žižek shows that because reality is structured by fantasy, "moving the underground" of fantasy is the first step in transforming reality.[2] This means that traversing the fantasy can enable us to reinvent our symbolic order through the act. Žižek offers a remarkable range of examples that indicate the self-defeating nature of various economies of enjoyment. In this context, "economy of enjoyment" refers to the way our symbolic desire helps us to "domesticate" Real *jouissance*. On the one hand, overproximity to the Real can lead to a psychotic disintegration of subjectivity and of symbolic reality. Psychosis is the massive presence of some intrusive Real (such as *jouissance*) that blocks the openness constitutive of symbolic reality (*Enjoy Your Symptom*, p. 119). On the other hand, without a minimum of enjoyment, life is not worth living. An economy of enjoyment is self-defeating if it leads either to the psychotic loss of reality *or* to the stifling of that minimum of *jouissance* without which life is not worth living. Simply put, symbolic desire can function more like a "firewall" to block the Real, or more like a mediator that leads to the traversal of the fantasy and to the Lacanian act. The act is linked to an ethics of the Real insofar as it can lead to a new mode of *jouissance*. Glyn Daly shows how an ethics of the Real involves a transformation of the imaginary, symbolic, and even modes of Real enjoyment:

> For Žižek, a confrontation with the obscenities of abundance capitalism also requires a transformation of the ethico-political imagination. It is no longer a question of developing ethical guidelines within the existing political framework (the various institutional and corporate "ethical committees") but of developing a politicization of ethics; an ethics of the

---

[2] Cf. the motto of Freud's *The Interpretation of Dreams* (which was taken from Virgil's *Aeneid*): "Flectere ni nequeo superos Acheronta movebo," meaning roughly, "If I cannot move the gods, I will stir up the underworld."

Real. The starting point here is an insistence on the unconditional autonomy of the subject; of accepting that as human beings we are ultimately responsible for our actions and being-in-the-world up to and including the construction of the capitalist system itself. Far from simple norm-making or refining/reinforcing existing social protocol, an ethics of the Real tends to emerge through norm-breaking and in finding new directions that, by definition, involve traumatic changes: i.e. the Real in genuine ethical challenge. An ethics of the Real does not simply defer to the impossible (or infinite Otherness) as an unsurpassable horizon that already marks every act as a failure, incomplete and so on. Rather, such an ethics is one that fully accepts contingency but which is nonetheless prepared to risk the impossible in the sense of breaking out of standardized positions. We might say that it is an ethics which is not only politically motivated but which also draws its strength from the political itself.[3]

The first step in transforming symbolic desire is moving the underground of fantasy, traversing the fantasy that supports our current symbolic order. Then interventions in the symbolic can produce changes in the Real.

In this regard, it is perhaps not without significance that the hegemonic ideology of late capitalism – liberal, multiculturalist democracy – proves to be self-undermining. For one thing, liberal global capitalism engenders its own obverse, namely militant nationalisms and other forms of intolerance. It is along these lines that Žižek analyzes the rise of racism and nationalism in Eastern Europe that followed the disintegration of the former Soviet Union. After the collapse of Soviet communism, what emerged was the brutal, exploitative rule by capital. Capitalist *disruption* – as described so well by Marx and Engels in *The Communist Manifesto*: "All that is solid melts into air" – did not lead to the recognition that it is capitalism itself that intensifies social divisions. Instead (in the vacuum left by the collapse of communism), as capitalism increasingly exacerbated social antagonism, this led to the formation of fantasy constructions of a stable nation that would (allegedly) be undivided by social antagonism. The ideological fantasy arose of a national enemy, an ethnic or religious Other who disrupts "natural" social stability. Žižek shows how this trend results from the late capitalist superego injunction to enjoy. For Žižek, the superego is manifested primarily an injunction

---

[3] Glyn Daly, "Slavoj Žižek: A Primer," available online at http://www.lacan.com/zizek-daly.htm.

to enjoy. It manifests as the obscene underside of the Law, since the public Law asks us to limit our selfishness for the good of society, but the superego injunction of late capitalism is to enjoy in ever more transgressive ways. In the economy of *jouissance* that is the postmodern, global capitalist (dis)order, surplus enjoyment is "imposed" or commanded. The apparent paradox here is that the absence of Law does not actualize "freedom." On the contrary, in the absence of symbolic authority, prohibition is universalized (e.g., self-imposed or unreflective). The explanation for this is that, although we experience enjoyment as transgressive, it is in fact something imposed. We never enjoy spontaneously, we always follow an obscene injunction: "The psychoanalytic name for this injunction, for this obscene call, 'Enjoy!', is superego" (*FTKN*, p. 10).

How is prohibition universalized today? Because *desire* is inherently transgressive, in a society where anything is permitted, enjoyment arises as a paradoxical hedonistic asceticism: in order to maximize pleasure, one must keep fit, moderate enjoyment, etc. Although prohibition incites the desire to transgress, prohibition also *relieves* the capitalist subject of the superego injunction to enjoy: "The external law regulates *pleasures* in order to deliver us from the superegotistical imposition of *enjoyment* which threatens to overflow our daily life" (*FTKN*, p. 241). Insofar as self-fulfillment must be combined with its own opposite (health food, no smoking, safe sex, etc.), access to enjoyment is perhaps even more blocked than it ever was:

> Therein consists the opposition between Law and superego: Law is the agency of prohibition which regulates the distribution of enjoyment on the basis of a common, shared renunciation (the "symbolic castration"), whereas superego marks a point at which *permitted* enjoyment, freedom-to-enjoy, is reversed into the *obligation* to enjoy – which, one must add, is the most effective way to block access to enjoyment. (*FTKN*, p. 237)

We all, to some extent, participate in (find enjoyment in) the reproduction of the symbolic fictions that structure social reality. What happens then, with the postmodern demise of symbolic order? With the undermining of the authority of the "virtual" – nonexistent but potentially efficacious – big Other, all that is solid melts into air, and all that is Holy is profaned (cf. *The Communist Manifesto*). This explains why many people today nostalgically long for discipline, or else attempt to cope with the disintegration of symbolic efficacy by the paranoid belief in some "Other of the Other" that sees all and controls political-economic events from behind the scenes. Even many liberal pseudo-leftists today willingly submit to ever-new forms of domination (academics in the USA are notorious for this), all the while fantasizing that somewhere there is an Other (or elite group) that has full knowledge, expertise, control, and *jouissance*. This paranoiac tendency is why the dominant theme of so many recent films and novels is the fantasy construction of some secret organization that covertly manipulates social institutions. The essential element in any ideology is the fantasy construction that supports the ideology. We fantasize that we might have full *jouissance*, if only it weren't for some Other who steals or threatens our enjoyment. This is an example of how an idiotic and excessive kernel of enjoyment ensures ideology's hold on the subject. Ideological fantasy both purports both to explain, and to offer a remedy for, all social antagonism.

The difficulty is to reinvent a more just symbolic order through the Lacanian act, without simply destroying Law as such. Human subjects *need* the big Other, because it functions as a kind of anonymous authority or social link (as when we say "One simply does not do that"). Even though the big Other does not literally exist, it nonetheless has virtual reality insofar as *we behave as though it exists*. This paradox of the reality of the virtual explains what Žižek means when he sometimes says that the big Other can "know" something. For example, if we all already know that the emperor has no clothes, then what changes when a child states this fact aloud in public? What causes embarrassment and *changes everything* is that now, the big Other "knows," and this dissolves the social link (*FTKN*, pp. 11–12). In this sense, appearances matter: the critique of ideology is never as simple as eliminating hypocrisy. But why should we, as Žižek puts it in the subtitle of this section of the book, "Let the Emperor have his clothes!" (*FTKN*, p. 11)? How do we reconcile this with Žižek's quotation, in the closing passages of the book, of Saint-Just's famous motto: "Nobody can reign innocently!"? Žižek argues that "the Jacobinical Terror was not a simple aberration or betrayal of the democratic project but, on the contrary, of a strictly democratic nature" (*FTKN*, p. 268). We will return to this question at the end of this chapter, but for now, it is important to realize that Žižek's aim is not to destroy all social links; his aim rather, is to clarify the duty of today's left. And the duty of the left today should *not* merely be to support democracy.

It is important to remember that according to Žižek's dialectical materialism, the big Other is nonexistent: symbolic authority is virtual; it is efficacious insofar as we behave as though the big Other exists. Moreover, subjectivity is not a positive, substantial entity but an incommensurability, a dialectical non-identity or "reflexive asymmetry" in symbolic reality. In his forward to the second edition of *FTKN* (2002), Žižek writes: "The basic insight elaborated in the first half of *For They Know Not What They Do* is that Hegelian dialectics and the Lacanian 'logic of the signifier' are two versions of the same matrix" (p. xviii). Žižek develops the link between Hegel and Lacan by arguing that the crucial achievement of German Idealism was the focus on subjectivity as the confrontation with negativity, madness, and "the night of the world." He argues that Hegelian dialectical inquiry is always disrupted from within by a moment of negativity that proves essential to the concept in question. And as already indicated, according to Žižek's reading of Hegel, any whole or totality is inherently inconsistent; any conceptual unification is incomplete and inconsistent.

Along the same lines, Žižek's subject as Real is an ontological difference that ruptures both individual and society, particular and universal. Žižek's aim is to evoke this gap, this irrepressible void, without lapsing into a fantasy of completeness. Žižek elegantly links the Lacanian insight that finally there is no big Other with developments in set theory and, by implication, with the incompleteness of quantum reality. He refers to set theory (in which any set includes the empty set as an element or subset), in order to articulate a logical space within which "the specific difference no longer functions as the difference between the elements against the background of the universal-neutral set" (*FTKN*, p. 43). Instead, the specific difference coincides with the difference between the universal set and its particular element. As Žižek puts it: "*the set is positioned at the same level as its elements*, it operates as one of its own elements, as the paradoxical element which 'is' the absence itself, the element-lack" (*FTKN*, p. 43).

Perhaps the primary achievement of *FTKN* is to elaborate such ontological insights in relation to major themes from Freudian and Lacanian psychoanalysis in order to reveal the unease (*Unbehagen*) of culture as such. For example, irreducible social antagonism (e.g., class struggle) takes different forms as history and technology develop in unpredictable ways. Although some commentators tend to underrate Žižek's *FTKN*, the book more fully develops certain theoretical points that were presented in a concise way in *The Sublime Object of Ideology*. For example, in *Sublime*, Žižek developed an account of the Hegelian logic of the "negation of negation," which is a kind of double, self-referential negating that does not involve a return to a positive identity through synthesis (cf. *Sublime*, p. 176). In *FTKN*, Žižek further develops his own earlier account of the negation of negation by showing how, in ideology, any antithesis – although presupposing the same understanding of what exists (the same form) as the thesis – nonetheless involves a transformation of the content of the thesis within the general limits of this formal dimension.

However, as the negation of the negation, the synthesis posits the difference as such, by marking the *inadequacy* of the determinate formal system that informs both the thesis and the antithesis. Žižek explains this difficult point by reference to Fredric Jameson's notion of the "vanishing mediator":

> This gap between the form and its notional content offers us also the key to the necessity of the "vanishing mediator": the passage from feudalism to Protestantism is not of the same nature as the passage from Protestantism to bourgeois everyday life with its privatized religion. The first passage concerns "content" (under the guise of preserving the religious form or even its strengthening, the crucial shift – the assertion of the ascetic-acquisitive stance in economic activity as the domain of the manifestation of Grace – takes place), whereas the second passage is a purely formal act, a change of form (as soon as Protestantism is realized as the ascetic-acquisitive stance, it can fall off as form). (*FTKN*, p. 185)

The transition from medieval corporatism to capitalist individualism became possible insofar as the Protestant work ethic was universalized. Once this ethic became central to intersubjective economic life as the ascetic-acquisitive stance, the transition from medieval feudalism to bourgeois capitalism was accomplished, and the religious ideals of Protestantism were then relegated to private life. Žižek illustrates throughout *FTKN* this ontological insight that the universal is not some determinate form or content; rather, the universal is precisely that point of possibility and impossibility that both allows and undermines any determinate, systematic account. His examples show how the Real of *jouissance* must be considered when evaluating the variety of ways of responding to late capitalism's superego injunction to enjoy.

Žižek's critique of global liberal capitalism – and its ideological supplement, pluralist "democracy" – hinges on the fact that the possibility of *true democracy* has long since been foreclosed by global capital. Thus, whereas today's right-wingers blatantly violate constitutional law in order to further the interests of an elite few, today's liberal pseudo-leftists reduce the space of politics proper to a question of cultural diversity, and simply promote "identity politics." The left today implicitly assumes that global capitalism is here to stay, in spite of the fact that the upheavals and crises of late capitalism are in the process of making religious fundamentalism and populist nationalism global phenomena. Today's leftists mistakenly equate class struggle with any other political struggle. But against democratic, populist, or nationalist accommodations with capitalism, Žižek's *For They Know Not What They Do: Enjoyment as a Political Factor* opens up the space for a radical political act which breaks free from vulgar, egotistic bourgeois life.

In what sense is enjoyment a political factor? Again, superego commands are all variations on one fundamental theme, the injunction to enjoy. Superego, as the injunction to enjoy, is thus opposed to the shared, public Law. The symbolic Law regulates the distribution of *jouissance* on the basis of shared and public renunciation; this is the Lacanian symbolic castration. However, in late capitalism, the freedom-to-enjoy has been turned into an obligation to enjoy (*FTKN*, p. 237). The cynic believes in nothing but the Real of enjoyment (p. 251).

But in light of the looming ecological catastrophe, the dismantling of the welfare state, and the fact that late capitalism has excluded, disempowered, and disenfranchised more and more workers around the world, Žižek's message is shifting the very terrain of contemporary political discourse. And his message, in a nutshell, is this: certain kinds of interventions in the symbolic dimension (e.g., in the realm of shared, public practices) can produce changes in the Real. Confrontation with the Real is the constitutive deadlock of symbolic desire. Žižek argues that, regarding the Lacanian motto "*le père ou pire*" ("the Father or worse"), the goal of psychoanalysis is *not* to bring about "successful" identification with the Father, but to induce the analysand to choose the *worst* (*FTKN*, p. 267). This means that we must dissolve the Father-as-symptom and fully assume the constitutive impossibility of desire: the duty of the left today is to "keep alive the memory of all lost causes, of all shattered and perverted dreams and hopes attached to leftist projects. The ethics which we have in mind here, apropos of this duty, is the ethics of the Cause *qua* Thing, the ethics of the Real which 'always returns to its place'" (*FTKN*, p. 271).

This leads to a question: What is the difference between psychotic "passage to act" (*passage à l'acte*) and an ethics of the Real, which reinvents a new symbolic order through the traversal of the fantasy and the Lacanian act? Glyn Daly argues that an ethics of the Real implies that we cannot look to any authoritative symbolic Other in order to find justification for our action (or inaction):

For Žižek an ethics of the Real (or Real ethics) means that we cannot rely on any form of symbolic Other that would endorse our (in)decisions and (in)actions: for example, the "neutral" financial data of the stockmarkets; the expert knowledge of Beck's "new modernity" scientists; the economic and military councils of the New World Order; the various (formal and informal) tribunals of political correctness; or any of the mysterious laws of God, nature or the market. What Žižek affirms is a radical culture of ethical identification for the left in which the alternative forms of militancy must first of all be militant with "themselves." That is to say, they must be militant in the fundamental ethical sense of not relying on any external/higher authority and in the development of a political imagination that, like Žižek's own thought, exhorts us to risk the impossible.[4]

In order to achieve an ethics of the Real, we must first of all be militant with *ourselves*. An ethics of the Real does not rely on any external, "higher" authority. Along these same lines, in his book *Violence* (2008), Žižek writes:

> It [Benjaminian "divine violence"] is just the sign of the injustice of the world, of the world being ethically "out of joint." This, however, does *not* imply that divine justice has a meaning: rather, it is a sign without meaning, and the temptation to be resisted is precisely the one which Job resisted successfully, the temptation to provide it with some "deeper meaning." What this entails is that, to put it in Badiou's terms, mythic violence belongs to the order of Being, while divine violence belongs to the order of Event: there are no "objective" criteria enabling us to identify an act of violence as divine; the same act that, to an external observer, is merely an outburst of violence can be divine for those engaged in it – there is no big Other guaranteeing its divine nature; the risk of reading and assuming it as divine is fully the subject's own.[5]

The topic of violence will be discussed thoroughly in chapter 23 of this book. But for now, the question is whether divine violence as "a sign without meaning" implies that we cannot distinguish between an act proper and the blind striking out of the *passage à l'acte*. How, if at all, can we distinguish an ethico-political act from the impotent violence of the psychotic "passage to act"? Is an ethics of the Real homologous to the neurotic return of the repressed?

In the closing paragraphs of *FTKN*, Žižek distinguishes between four different ethical attitudes known to Lacanian psychoanalytic theory: the hysteric's ethical imperative is to keep *desire* alive, the obsessional's ethical imperative is the Other's *demand*, and the pervert's ethical imperative

---

[4] Glyn Daly, "Slavoj Žižek: A Primer," available online at http://www.lacan.com/zizek-daly.htm.

[5] Slavoj Žižek, *Violence* (London: Verso, 2008), p. 200.

is to work for the Other's *enjoyment* (*FTKN*, p. 271). But in contrast to these three, Žižek associates an ethics of the Real with *drive*, and argues that the subject must not give way as to his drive. Žižek stresses that drive is not any kind of biological urge or instinct: "*the status of the drive itself is inherently ethical*. We are at the exact opposite of vitalist biologism: the image that most appropriately exemplifies drive is not 'blind animal thriving' but the ethical compulsion to mark repeatedly the memory of a lost Cause" (*FTKN*, p. 272).

Žižek emphasizes that this does not mean that we should simply *document* past trauma as accurately as possible: "such 'documentation' is a priori false, it transforms the trauma into a neutral, objective fact, whereas the essence of trauma is precisely that it is too horrible to be remembered, to be integrated into our symbolic universe" (*FTKN*, p. 272). The drive is the compulsion to mark again and again – by means of some symbolic gesture – the trauma as *trauma*, that is, in its very impossibility. This indicates the duty of the left today:

> This, then, is the point at which the Left must not "give way": it must preserve the traces of all historical traumas, dreams and catastrophes which the ruling ideology of the "End of History" would prefer to obliterate – it must become itself their living monument, so that as long as the Left is here, these traumas will remain marked. Such an attitude, far from confining the Left within a nostalgic infatuation with the past, is the only possibility for attaining a distance on the present, a distance which will enable us to discern signs of the New. (*FTKN*, p. 273)

4

Looking Awry: An Introduction to Jacques Lacan through Popular Culture

What we ordinarily consider to be "reality" is in fact a juxtaposition of the symbolic register and the imaginary register. The Lacanian Real, however, is *not* experienced as part of everyday reality. The Real permeates the imaginary and the symbolic registers. But it resists incorporation into shared, symbolic practices and intersubjective linguistic systems. In neurosis, the Real is the return of the repressed, and in psychosis, the Name/No! of the Father, which is foreclosed from the symbolic register, returns in the Real as overwhelming anxiety. Fantasy – like the symptom – supports the consistency of experience. This means that the register of the imaginary is not simply a realm of illusion, for it is primarily in dreams that we approach the Real as cause of desire. But to encounter the Real is to experience the dissolving of reality, and when this happens, some individuals are able to traverse ideological fantasy, undergo subjective destitution, and reinvent symbolic reality through the Lacanian act.

The basic presupposition of psychoanalytic interpretation, its methodologic a priori, is, however, that every final product of the dream work, every manifest dream content, contains at least one *ingredient that functions as a stopgap, as a filler holding the place of what is necessarily* lacking in *it. This is an element that at first sight fits perfectly into the organic whole of the manifest imaginary scene, but which effectively holds within it the place of what this imaginary scene must "repress," exclude, force out, in*

Žižek: A Reader's Guide, First Edition. Kelsey Wood.
© 2012 John Wiley & Sons, Inc. Published 2012 by John Wiley & Sons, Inc.

order to constitute itself. It is a kind of umbilical cord tying the imaginary
structure to the "repressed" process of its structuration.
—Žižek, *Looking Awry: An Introduction to Jacques*
Lacan through Popular Culture, p. 52

One of Žižek's most popular books is *Looking Awry: An Introduction to Jacques Lacan through Popular Culture* (1991).[1] In *Looking Awry*, Žižek refers to popular fiction and film in order to illustrate by way of example the meaning of such difficult Lacanian concepts as the split subject, the *sinthome*, the distinction between desire and drive, the gaze, *jouissance* (enjoyment) and, especially, the three registers of subjectivity: imaginary, symbolic, and Real. In his preface, Žižek describes the book as: "a reading of the most sublime theoretical motifs of Jacques Lacan together with and through exemplary cases of contemporary mass culture: not only Alfred Hitchcock, about whom there is now general agreement that he was, after all, a 'serious artist,' but also *film noir*, science fiction, detective novels, sentimental kitsch, and up – or down – to Stephen King" (*Looking*, p. vii). Žižek's clear writing style and numerous references to popular culture make *Looking Awry* more readable than most texts on Lacanian theory, but the analyses are occasionally rather concise, and the book will be more accessible to those who have already read Žižek's *The Sublime Object of Ideology* (1989).

Looking Awry is divided into three sections, and in the first – "How Real is Reality?" – Žižek deals with the most fundamental topic of the book, the Lacanian Real. Žižek first shows the extent to which our notion of reality is constituted by fantasy and the register of the imaginary. As Žižek puts it, reality as we experience it "rests on a certain 'repression,' on overlooking the real of our desire. This social reality is then nothing but a fragile, symbolic cobweb that can at any moment be torn aside by an intrusion of the real" (*Looking*, p. 17). Fantasy then, fills out the void or "black hole" of the Real. Although imaginary projections serve as efforts to escape the Real, such efforts are futile. Žižek shows why by articulating several different modalities of the Lacanian Real. One such modality is the return of the Real. That the repressed Real always returns may be seen once we consider how there are certain facts that we really already *know*, even though we still do not *believe* them. Our attitude toward global climate change illustrates this split:

---

[1] Unless otherwise stated, page references for this work are to the following edition: *Looking Awry: An Introduction to Jacques Lacan through Popular Culture* (Cambridge, MA, and London: MIT Press, 1992).

we are quite aware that it may already be too late, that we are already on the brink of catastrophe (of which the death throes of the European forests are just the harbinger), but nevertheless we do not believe it. We act as though it were only an exaggerated concern over a few trees, a few birds, and not literally a question of our survival. (*Looking*, pp. 27–8)

One of the ways that the Real returns then, is in the form of traumatic intrusions that disrupt the balance of everyday life. But the Real also *answers* insofar as it reinforces the balance of everyday existence (*Looking*, p. 29). Whereas the negativity of the Real resists symbolization, an answer of the Real is, on the contrary, a *support* of symbolization and interpretation. An answer of the Real is some event that, although in fact it is totally contingent, nonetheless serves for the subject as a confirmation or guarantee of symbolic efficacy and consistency. Because the imaginary and symbolic registers are informed from within by the register of the Real, any contingent coincidence may serve as an answer of the Real, if the event links together disparate moments of the subject's life into a texture that admits of interpretation. However, in order to be experienced as an answer of the Real, the contingent event must appear to be *found* by the subject, rather than *produced* by the subject: "we must, by structural necessity, fall prey to the illusion that the power of fascination belongs to the object as such" (*Looking*, p. 33).

Also, because the imaginary, the symbolic, and the Real are intertwined with one another, the Real may be directly *rendered* by, or contained in the symbolic form itself. Žižek refers to the abstract expressionist paintings Mark Rothko produced in the 1960s. These late Rothko paintings manifest Rothko's struggle to maintain the barrier that separates reality from the intrusive Real: "that is, to prevent the real (the central black square) from overflowing the entire field, if the difference between the figure and its background is lost, a psychotic autism is produced" (*Looking*, p. 19). A similar rendering of the Real in symbolic form occurs in cinema with the use of contemporary sound techniques that do not simply reproduce the expected sound of the film's depicted "reality" but rather heighten it or alter it in suggestive ways. The uncanny, surrealist effect of certain non-diegetic sound techniques can evoke the disturbing Real of the psychic reality *within* the very symbolic texture of the film itself.

After an evocative discussion of examples of symbolic renderings of the Real, Žižek gives a brief but penetrating analysis of the Lacanian notion of "knowledge in the Real." Lacan's investigations into the logic of the signifier reveal that there are irreducible paradoxes of universality and particularity implicit to the very symbolic formations that provide the texture of our social reality. One of the examples that Žižek discusses to illustrate knowledge in the Real itself is the developments in quantum physics that suggest the odd notion that nature knows its own laws and behaves accordingly. Subatomic particle physics is supposed to be an exact science (free of "subjectivity"). This makes it all the more striking that, in the last few decades, subatomic particle physics exhibits a homology with what Lacan referred to as knowledge in the Real.

Particle physics has repeatedly encountered phenomena that imply the suspension of the principle of local cause. That is, these phenomena seem to involve a transfer of information that would have to take place faster than is possible according to the theory of relativity: "This is the so-called Einstein-Podolsky-Rosen effect, where what we did in area *A* affects what happens in area *B*, without this being possible along the normal causal chain permitted by the speed of light" (*Looking*, p. 45). Žižek argues that to explain such phenomena, we must presuppose a kind of "knowledge in the Real":

> Let us take a two-particle system of zero-spin: if one of the particles in such a system has a spin UP, the other particle has a spin DOWN. Now suppose we separate the two particles in some way that does not affect their spin: one particle goes off in one direction and the other in the opposite direction. After we separate them, we send one of the particles through a magnetic field that gives it a spin UP: what happens is that the other particle acquires a spin DOWN (and vice versa, of course). Yet there is no possibility of communication or of a normal causal link between them, because the other particle had a spin DOWN immediately after we gave the first particle a spin UP, i.e., *before* the spin UP of the first particle could cause the spin DOWN of the other particle in the fastest way possible (by giving the signal with the speed of light). The question then arises: *How did the other particle "know" that we had given the first particle a spin UP?* We must presuppose a kind of "knowledge in the Real," as if a spin somehow "knows" what happens in another place and acts accordingly. (*Looking*, pp. 45–6)

In the concluding chapter of the book's first section, Žižek employs an analogy between the psychoanalytic procedure and the methods of fictional detectives (e.g., Sherlock Holmes or Philip Marlowe) in order to describe two typical ways in which we avoid the Real of our desire. The analyst, in the effort to lead the analysand to confront her desire, does not simply proceed after the manner of the detective in a classic "logic and deduction" story. The logical, deductive methods of the classical detective (e.g., Sherlock Holmes) help the reader avoid the Real of desire by dispelling the surreal quality of the intrusions of the Real into everyday reality: "the main function of the detective's 'rational explanation' is to break the spell they have upon us, i.e., to spare us the encounter with the real of our desire that these scenes stage" (*Looking*, p. 60).

By contrast, the hard-boiled detective (e.g., Philip Marlowe) does not dispel the dreamlike quality of the Real; instead, he becomes so enmeshed in the chaotic succession of events that he is often unable to effectively analyze and intervene in them. The hard-boiled detective approaches the Real of his desire (embodied in the *femme fatale*), and as a consequence undergoes a loss of everyday reality. But in rejecting the *femme fatale* and avoiding the Real of desire, the hard-boiled detective *breaks with* the radical ethics of the Real proposed by Lacan and Žižek. An ethics of the Real involves not giving way on one's desire – but persisting to the very end – even to the point of risking life itself.

In the second part of *Looking Awry*, "One Can Never Know Too Much about Hitchcock," Žižek approaches Hitchcock's films in three novel ways. First he articulates a dialectic of deception in the films of Hitchcock: "a dialectic in which those who really err are the non-duped" (*Looking*, p. ix). Then Žižek shows how Hitchcock's famous use of tracking shots involves a formal procedure, the aim of which is to "produce a 'blot,' a point from which the image looks at the spectator, the point of the 'gaze of the Other'" (*Looking*, p. ix). Finally, Žižek proposes that the main stages in Hitchcock's development proceed "from the Oedipal journey of the 1930s to the 'pathological narcissism,' dominated by the maternal superego, of the 1960s" (*Looking*, p. ix).

The third and final section of *Looking Awry* – "Fantasy, Bureaucracy, Democracy" – is devoted to Lacan's later developments of his theory. Žižek focuses on how this later version of Lacan's theory is relevant to the field of politics and ideology. It is important to remember that Žižek revises Marx's critique of ideology. According to Žižek, social reality is guided by a "fetishistic inversion." It is not reality that subjects fail to recognize, but the fantasy that is constitutive of their reality. Ideological fantasy is constitutive of social reality; ideology structures the symbolic reproduction of reality by providing a fantasy that masks the negativity of social antagonism.

Again, if a word is used as the Master-Signifier, then it functions in such a way so as to be indefinable. Some terms that function in certain discourses as the Master-Signifier are "God," "democracy," "liberty," "tolerance," and "nature." Because the Master-Signifier is utterly without intelligible significance, the mythic wholeness at the heart of any ideology proves to be nothing but a gap that is positivized in a phantasmic way in order to mask antagonism within the sociosymbolic order. Thus the sense of wholeness provided by ideology relies on some term that is essential to the system of interactions and yet always already indefinable within it. In the same way, the coherence of everyday experience is constituted when some "pathological" fantasy element functions as a stand-in for the repressed Real (e.g., the Real of social antagonism, or the Real of the Other's desire). Žižek explains this point in a clear and accessible way in his essay "Jacques Lacan's Four Discourses":

> Recall, again, Lacan's outrageous statements that, even if what a jealous husband claims about his wife (that she sleeps around with other men) is all true, his jealousy is still pathological. Along the same lines, one could say that, even if most of the Nazi claims about the Jews were true (they exploit Germans, they seduce German girls), their anti-Semitism would still be (and was) pathological – because it represses the true reason the Nazis needed anti-Semitism in order to sustain their ideological position. So, in the case of anti-Semitism, knowledge about what the Jews "really are" is a fake, irrelevant, while the only knowledge at the place of truth is the knowledge about why a Nazi needs a figure of the Jew to sustain his ideological edifice. In this precise sense, the analyst's discourse produces the master signifier, the swerve of the patient's knowledge, the surplus element that situates the patient's knowledge at the level of truth: after the master signifier is produced, even if nothing changes at the level of knowledge, the same knowledge as before starts to function in a different mode. The master signifier is the unconscious *sinthome*, the cipher of enjoyment, to which the subject was unknowingly subjected.[2]

In *Looking Awry*, Žižek indicates how the symbolic reality fixed in place by the Master-Signifier is sustained by a superego imperative that enjoins us to a performative: "to sustain itself, reality always requires a certain superego command, a certain 'So be it!' The status of the voice uttering this command is neither imaginary nor symbolic, it is *real*" (p. 130). This performative dimension indicates the limit of the "classical" version of Lacanian theory. The limit of the standard or classical interpretation of Lacan is determined by the field of discourse, of communication as meaning.

---

[2] Slavoj Žižek, "Jacques Lacan's Four Discourses," available online at http://www.lacan.com/zizfour.htm.

However, in his last years, Lacan found a way to break through the field of communication as meaning:

> After establishing the definitive, logically purified structure of communication, of the social bond, via the matrix of the four discourses, Lacan undertook to delineate the outlines of a certain "free-floating" space in which signifiers find themselves prior to their discursive binding, to their *articulation*. This is the space of a certain "prehistory" preceding the "story" of the social bond, i.e., of a certain psychotic kernel evading the discursive network. (*Looking*, p. 132)

What does this mean? Lacan's concept of the *sinthome* indicates the One of *jouis*-sense. In other words, the *sinthome* functions as a One in the sense of a freely floating signifier that is permeated by enjoyment. This *jouissance* is what makes the *sinthome* freely floating: enjoyment prevents it from being incorporated into chains of signifiers. Thus the *sinthome* functions as a One which is neither a symptom nor a fantasy; it is a kernel of enjoyment that fascinates but repels us. And yet, as such, the *sinthome* can bind together the three registers of subjectivity – the Real, the imaginary, and the symbolic – and thus serve to sustain our sense of reality (in Lacan's usage, *sinthome* involves wordplays on "symptom," "Saint," and "Saint Thomas").

But the *sinthome* is not a signifier in any ordinary sense, because it is directly enjoyed: as a cipher of enjoyment, its only "meaning" is the *jouissance* it provides. Insofar as it functions as a portal for enjoyment, the *sinthome* is so permeated with *jouissance* that it is not bound (like an ordinary signifier) into the chains of signifiers that constitute reality. The *sinthome* is not the symptom; it is not "the coded message to be deciphered by interpretation" (*Looking*, pp. 128–129). Instead, the *sinthome* is a freely floating core of "*jouis*-sense" or "enjoy-meant" that constitutes everyday reality by serving as the core of some ideology.

Žižek argues that the role of the *sinthome* in the "construction of the ideological edifice" forces us to rethink the criticism of ideology. Ideology is usually approached as if it were simply a mode of discourse: "as an enchainment of elements the meaning of which is overdetermined by their specific articulation, i.e., by the way some 'nodal point' (the Lacanian master-signifier) totalizes them into a homogeneous field" (*Looking*, p. 129). But the role of the *sinthome* compels us to acknowledge that it is not enough to "denounce the 'artificial' character of the ideological experience" (p. 129). In short, ideology is not just a discursive construction; rather, ideological fantasy is constitutive of symbolic reality.

Because of the "stupid materiality" of the *sinthome*, the sheer nullity of its immediate reality, it eludes discursive interpretation and escapes historical mediation. All we can do is to expose it so as to change "the precious gift into a gift of shit" (p. 129). In sum, instead of confronting the ideology with its repressed truth, we can only dissolve the social bond by "isolating the heinous kernel of its idiotic enjoyment" (p. 129).

All of this enables us to understand why Žižek concludes *Looking Awry* with an analysis of some of the deadlocks that limit democracy. The danger Žižek discerns in formal democracy is its *impotence*. After subtracting all positive contents (e.g., my status as an "intellectual") we are left with an ideal, leveled citizen of the planet that arouses no political enthusiasm. What then, could possibly motivate the process of abstraction that produces such an ideal, leveled citizen? In a startling move, Žižek argues that what motivates and enables the formal, democratic abstraction (the subtracting of all positive contents) is not simply global capitalism, *but also nationalism.*

But how could the ideal leveling of social differences – implicit to the process of abstraction through which the subject of democracy is produced – be motivated and enabled by nationalism? Žižek's answer is – to the dismay of proponents of "radical democracy" – all too plausible. In the first place, insofar as this democratic abstraction (the subtracting of all positive content) is realized, it must take the form of allegiance to a national cause. In the second place, this allegiance to a national cause functions as materialized enjoyment, that is, as the Freudian Thing (*das Ding*). In other words, it is in and through the national cause that subjects organize – in the form of a myth – their collective enjoyment. But insofar as the coherence of everyday experience is constituted when some pathological fantasy element functions as a stand-in for the repressed Real (e.g., the Real of social antagonism), nationalism is *the privileged domain* of the eruption of enjoyment into the social field (*Looking*, p. 165). For example, ethnic tensions always implicitly refer to the national Thing as materialized enjoyment: some Other is trying to steal our *jouissance*, or else has access to some secret and perverse enjoyment of "Their" own (*Looking*, p. 165).

In sum – and to repeat – there is no "neutral" and purely formal universality. That which is the true universal proves to be the repressed trauma, antagonism, or *jouissance* around which any symbolic order revolves. Moreover, this primordially repressed Real (e.g., enjoyment) always returns in one way or another, to disrupt symbolic order. Žižek argues that this irreducible dimension of repressed *jouissance* indicates the inherent deadlock of democracy.

Again, populist nationalism is the privileged domain of the eruption of the Freudian Thing as materialized enjoyment (cf. the *sinthome*) into the sociosymbolic order. But given the fact that "fantasies cannot coexist peacefully" (*Looking*, p. 168), what can we do, once we recognize the inherent deadlock of democracy? In the concluding section of *Looking Awry*, Žižek shows how the hegemonic ideology of late capitalism – liberal multiculturalist democracy – sustains itself through a fetishistic split. On page 168, he writes: "*I know very well* (that the democratic form is just a form spoiled by stains of 'pathological' imbalance), *but just the same* (I act as if democracy were possible)." Thus once we recognize the deadlock of democracy, it is clear what we do *not* do. Since ideology is more than a discursive construction, we do not simply presuppose some "neutral" universality as the space for compromise.

Why not? Because of the traumatic kernel of enjoyment that is constitutive of symbolic reality, the subject cannot simply be reduced to a place – not even an empty place – in the symbolic order. There is always an excessive something "more than itself," some phantasmic Thing – the *objet petit a* – that symbolic subjectivity circles around. Given certain disruptions that arose in the aftermath of the collapse of the Soviet Union, it is clear that liberal global capitalism spawns its own obverse, in the form of intolerant, militant nationalisms. As Žižek points out, the capitalist's appropriation of surplus value from the workers does not indicate "unfairness"; rather, the formal democracy of the market – the equivalence of market exchange – is, as Marx already recognized, *the very form of exploitation*: "surplus value is the 'material' remainder, the surplus contents, appropriated by the capitalist through the very form of the equivalent exchange between capital and the labor force" (*Looking*, pp. 166–7). The strategy for the left then, must involve bypassing the impotence of democracy by directly working to dissolve the capitalist social order through revealing that its "precious gift" is an idiotic kernel of masturbatory *jouissance*.

5

Enjoy Your Symptom! Jacques Lacan in Hollywood and Out

Žižek develops the Lacanian concepts of letter, woman, repetition, phallus, and father in order to analyze the ideological function of postmodern cynicism. He also elaborates the philosophical implications of Lacan's psychoanalytic theory in order to defend Lacan against the charge of "logocentrism" leveled by Derrida. To refute this charge, Žižek deploys illustrative examples from popular culture that clarify his Hegelian-Lacanian account of subjectivity as the *asymmetry* between (and within) three dimensions of experience: the imaginary, the symbolic, and the Real. The subject as such is feminine; the subject as such involves the hysterical question "Why am I what you say I am?" The subject *as the question* exposes the imposture of the phallic Master-Signifier. Thus the phallic, symbolic law proves to be itself a symptom. But the process of ideological subjectivization involves the covering-over of the constitutive (feminine) lack or inconsistency that is the subject as such. The Master-Signifier seems to ground reality, but because of insurmountable antagonism and inconsistency, the phallic signifier actually incarnates the lack or gap that is the Real of subjectivity. Simply put, the subject as such is feminine, and is bound up with the originary void of the Real; but symbolic fictions constitute reality by functioning as stand-ins to cover over the originary (feminine) subject position: this is why any symbolic system proves to be irreducibly inconsistent.

And what is this act *if not the moment when the subject who is its bearer* suspends *the network of symbolic fictions which serve as a support to his*

Žižek: A Reader's Guide, First Edition. Kelsey Wood.
© 2012 John Wiley & Sons, Inc. Published 2012 by John Wiley & Sons, Inc.

daily life and confronts again the radical negativity upon which they are founded?

—Žižek, *Enjoy Your Symptom!*
Jacques Lacan in Hollywood and Out, p. 53

One of Žižek's most intriguing books is *Enjoy Your Symptom! Jacques Lacan in Hollywood and Out* (1992).[1] In *Enjoy Your Symptom!* (abbreviated *Enjoy* below) Žižek uses examples from popular culture in order to improvise on five fundamental Lacanian motifs: letter, woman, repetition, phallus, and father.[2] *Enjoy* is not easy reading: it is not an introduction to Lacanian theory. The book is a substantial work in a new kind of theory, Žižek's revolutionary fusion of dialectical materialist philosophy and Lacanian psychoanalysis. But in order to grasp the significance of *Enjoy*, it is crucial to remember that Žižek is *not* simply offering psychoanalytic analyses of the films and books that he discusses. On the contrary, Žižek discusses familiar examples from literature and cinema only in order to clarify psychoanalytic/philosophical theory. Thus the same scene from a film might be used to help clarify different theoretical points. In addition, in this book Žižek does not simply *define* fundamental Lacanian concepts, but *applies* them: he uses letter, woman, repetition, phallus, and father as starting points for his own philosophical extrapolations on ontology, contemporary Western culture, and the ideological function of postmodern cynicism.

One of Žižek's aims is to defend Lacanian theory against charges of "logocentrism" leveled by the philosopher Jacques Derrida and his deconstructionist followers. "Logocentrism" is Derrida's term for the presumption that rational accounts are adequate to the task of explaining the nature of what exists. Žižek nullifies this critique by showing that the theme of Lacan's work is the incommensurability between the three modes of manifestation which together demarcate human existence: the symbolic, the Real, and the imaginary registers.

The imaginary register involves fantasies of unity, such as the ego. Again, the subject (unlike the ego) does not exist prior to the acquisition of language. The presymbolic, or better, *nonsymbolic* life substance is

---

[1]   Unless otherwise stated, page references for this work are to the following edition: *Enjoy Your Symptom! Jacques Lacan in Hollywood and Out*, rev. edn. (New York and London: Routledge, 2001).

[2]   The best introduction to *Enjoy Your Symptom!* is Žižek's first book in English, *The Sublime Object of Ideology*, which treats the same themes in a more expansive way.

enjoyment or *jouissance* (pleasure-in-pain), and enjoyment is Real. The symbolic subject, as a being of language, emerges through the renunciation of *jouissance* that is the toll which must be paid upon entry into the symbolic order. The symbolic register involves shared, rule-governed structures and practices such as language. After the acquisition of language the speaking subject remains divided between the imaginary (e.g., the ego and fantasies of unity) and the symbolic (e.g., linguistic concepts defined by difference or otherness). Formed by entry into language, subjectivity emerges at the price of "alienation." Lacan viewed *speech* as an act, or more precisely, an interaction between subject and other. *Language* however, is a pre-existing structure beyond the control of individual subjects. Language both constitutes and alienates subjectivity; the subject that is constituted through entry into the symbolic register is a divided subject. Alienation arises as the infant submits to the pre-existing, intersubjective, network of the symbolic order and becomes a subject of language. Insofar as the child submits to the Other and develops the linguistic dimension of subjectivity, the child *becomes* a circulating signifier in the symbolic network. It is by way of signifiers that any subject is represented both to itself and to other subjects, or, as Lacan expresses this, "The signifier represents the subject for another signifier."

However this does not mean that subjects use language to represent themselves; on the contrary, *language uses us* insofar as pre-existing linguistic structures are constitutive of the subject. The subject's alienation in and through language implies that a dimension of subjectivity is outside of the body: this externalized aspect of the subject is the pre-existing, intersubjective network, or the big Other. The alienated, speaking subject is characterized by the discord between private, imaginary experience and the intersubjective symbolic register.

The register of the Real is fundamental surd or gap; the Real is that which is left out of our imaginary-symbolic notion of reality. The Real of subjectivity permeates the imaginary and symbolic registers as a negativity that cannot be imagined or symbolized. The Real is this asymmetry or incommensurability between – and *within* – the imaginary and symbolic registers. Žižek focuses on this asymmetry, and analyzes the ways that imaginary identifications (such as the ego) prevent confrontation with the Real that disrupts symbolic order. The imaginary masks the very inconsistency of the symbolic that manifests the Real. Žižek's aim is to induce interventions in the symbolic so as to produce changes in the Real (e.g., to change our mode of *jouissance*).

Why Does a *Letter* Always Arrive at Its Destination?

The title of every chapter of *Enjoy* poses a question regarding a controversial thesis of Lacanian psychoanalysis. One of the difficulties of an initial approach to *Enjoy* is the fact that Žižek poses questions in one section of the book which are only answered in later sections; meanwhile, these later sections pose further questions even while they develop answers to earlier ones. Žižek's first chapter is called "Why Does a *Letter* Always Arrive at Its Destination?" What is a "letter" and why does it always arrive?

The agency of the letter involves the insight that the workings of the unconscious are disclosed through linguistic functions: a symptom is linguistic; it sends a message, like a letter addressed to the analyst. If Lacan's account of subjectivity is *not* logocentric, then why his claim, "The unconscious is structured like a language"? The answer, as Žižek shows, is that the symbolic constitutes but alienates the subject. In this regard, the reader should keep in mind that Lacan's approach is also a departure from structuralist linguistics insofar as Lacan highlights the gap and lack of movement between the *signifier* (the sound of a word or its written form) and the *signified* (the conceptual meaning). From early on Lacan recognized that a signifier such as an acoustic or graphic image does not have meaning in reference to some fixed, signified concept: signifiers do not merely call to mind a corresponding signified. For Lacan, the notion of a signifier is inseparable from the notion of structure: signifiers are differential elements in a structure; they are combined in signifying chains, primarily through metonymy.[3] Moreover, any instance of signification involves the alienation or split that is constitutive of subjectivity. Consequently, unlike an idealist or Jungian assertion of positive meanings, Lacan's "materialist," negative approach does not imply that the whole signifier (much less the whole process of signification) is present in the consciousness of any subject.

---

[3] Tony Myers explains the difference between metaphor and metonymy in the following way: "If you have an instance in a movie of a couple making love, but want to suggest the act rather than show it, the metaphorical way would be to show two rain drops conjoining on the window pane, and the metonymical way would be to show abandoned clothes strewn on the floor. In other words, a metaphor designates a resemblance in qualities, whereas a metonymy identifies a part of something in place of the whole thing." See Tony Myers' excellent book *Slavoj Žižek* (London: Routledge, 2003), p. 5. For Lacan, metonymy is the condition for metaphor, and *desire is a metonymy*.

The first chapter of *Enjoy* is an extrapolation from Lacan's concept of the letter. The letter designates the embodied, localized nature of any signifier, what Lacan describes as the "materiality" of the signifier. Materiality here does not mean "content," but refers to the priority of the fully contextualized signifier over the derivative signified. One way to evoke the meaning of Lacan's concept of the letter is to consider that figures of speech in the analysand's discourse are not accidental, but serve as mechanisms for both revealing and concealing unconscious connections. Here is how Bruce Fink puts this in his book *Lacan to the Letter*:

> The unconscious at work in dreams employs metonymy and metaphor, and the analysand in talking about his dreams employs virtually all of rhetoric's figures and tropes. *To the analyst, nothing is ever "just a figure of speech."* The analyst's mode of reading attends to both what is presented and what is not presented, to both speech and writing, to both what is enunciated and what is avoided. In essence, it reads all speech as a compromise formation, as produced by competing forces.[4]

Žižek elaborates on Lacan's concept of the letter by first distinguishing imaginary, symbolic, and Real dimensions *within* the letter. He then shows how these three registers are inextricably bound together in the letter. In the first place, to evoke the imaginary dimension of the letter, Žižek shows how a subject's self-recognition involves a process of imaginary identification. Because desire is of/for the Other's desire, a subject simultaneously recognizes and *misrecognizes* himself in the speech of the Other:

> a letter which "always arrives at its destination" points to the logic of recognition/misrecognition (*reconnaissance/méconnaissance*) elaborated in detail by Louis Althusser and his followers (Michel Pêcheux): the logic by means of which one (mis)recognizes oneself as the addressee of ideological interpellation. This illusion constitutive of the ideological order could be succinctly rendered by paraphrasing a formula of Barbara Johnson: "A letter always arrives at its destination *since its destination is wherever it arrives.*" (*Enjoy*, p. 10)

Secondly, the symbolic dimension of the letter involves the insistent role of the letter in the unconscious: the unconscious belongs to the symbolic register. To understand this, we must remember that desire is unconscious

[4] See Bruce Fink's *Lacan to the Letter* (Minneapolis: University of Minnesota Press, 2004), p. 75.

(unlike a want or a wish). Desire exists in the big Other; this means that the intersubjective symbolic network is the locus in which desire is manifested. In this sense, the unconscious is externalized in the big Other: it is the discourse of the Other. The Real of desire is manifested only through the symbolic, as the inconsistency or incompleteness of signification: desire shows up within the symbolic register, as a characteristic of signifiers (e.g., in alibis, evasions, distortions, or slips of the tongue).[5] Why then does the letter always return to the subject, inscribing itself in his life and organizing the intersubjective network around him? The answer – in its most concise form – is that the letter is not meant for one particular, individual recipient. The letter (like desire) has always already been inscribed in the intersubjective, symbolic network, and so cannot fail to arrive there:

> its true addressee is namely not the empirical other which may receive it or not, but the big Other, the symbolic order itself, which receives it *the moment the letter is put into circulation*, i.e., the moment the sender "externalizes" his message, delivers it to the Other, the moment the Other takes cognizance of the letter and thus disburdens the sender of responsibility for it. (*Enjoy*, p. 10)

Finally, to approach the Real dimension of the letter, Žižek focuses on that which resists symbolization, or rather, that which indicates the irreducible paradoxes that are inherent to any symbolic system: the inconsistency, incompleteness, undecidability, or redundancy of symbolization. In this regard, it is helpful to consider why Lacan locates desire not in consciousness, but in distortions of speech and other symbolic practices (e.g., slips of the tongue, bungled actions). Desire (insofar as it is Real) "speaks" through the distortions and redundancies of speech and symbolic practices. When we consider the Real dimension of the letter, we recognize that we always say *more* than we intend to say: we are unable to apprehend (much less control) the effects of our utterances on the intersubjective network of the symbolic register. The inevitable return of the Real – as the incompleteness and inconsistency of the imaginary and the symbolic – reveals finally that there is no big

---

[5] Žižek says of desire that as such, desire is always the desire to desire; it is never simply desire. Desire is always excessive because of this *reflexivity*: desire is the desire to desire. Thus the desiring subjectivity par excellence is that of a hysterical feminine subject. See Slavoj Žižek, *Interrogating the Real*, ed. Rex Butler and Scott Stephens (London: Continuum, 2005), p. 247, note 10.

Other; there can never be an all-encompassing metalanguage: "The crucial point here is that the imaginary, the symbolic, and the real dimension of 'a letter always arrives at its destination' are not external to each other: at the end of the imaginary as well as the symbolic itinerary, we encounter the Real" (*Enjoy*, p. 21).

Why is *Woman* a Symptom of Man?

In what sense is *woman* a symptom of man? The first thing to remember is that "woman" in this context refers to the feminine structure of the subject as such, and *not* to biological sex. The second thing to note is that Žižek's approach in this section presupposes a reader who is familiar with Lacanian theory, particularly Lacan's famous "logic of sexuation." Subjectivity, masculine or feminine, is a positioning in relation to language and the symbolic register. Any subject is subjected in one way or another to the "phallic function." The phallic function is associated with the alienating character of language and symbolic practices: it is the phallic function that institutes lack. Lacan's term "phallus" in this context evokes the *jouissance* that is renounced when the subject accepts the rules and prohibitions of the symbolic father. No one actually possesses the phallus, because phallus is the signifier of something that was always already lost. The phallus signifies desire, a lack in being; the phallus is how the unconscious nostalgically represents loss.

The child tries to be the object which it imagines the mother desires (the phallus). But as an imaginary object, the phallus can never be directly present in any subject's experience. For this reason, renouncing the attempt to be the imaginary phallus for the mother is crucial for children of *both* sexes. Lacan's term "symbolic castration" refers to this renunciation. Again, insofar as s/he has not accepted symbolic castration, a neurotic still tries to be the imagined object of desire for the mother.

The symbolic phallus is a signifier of desire and lack; just as a veil suggests the presence of something behind it, so the symbolic phallus suggests the presence of the object of desire. The symbolic phallus substitutes for the realization that desire can never be satisfied. Lacan's logic of sexuation revolves around the phallic function as symbolic castration. The feminine logic is the non-All, while the masculine logic is the universal and its constitutive exception. In the feminine logic of non-All, the set is incomplete, but there is no exception to it: a feminine subject is immersed in the symbolic register *without exception*. Finally the

Real of sexual difference is nothing in itself; it is simply the irreconcilable difference between the two logics. Let us consider some simple examples for the beginner in philosophy that may help give a sense of how this works.

The first example involves Descartes' *Meditations*. In *Meditations* 1 and 2, the project of methodic doubt is homologous to the feminine logic. The subject as such is feminine, and the subject as such – the feminine subject – is *the question*. Insofar as Descartes initially engages in his project of universal doubt, the subjectivity evoked by this radical questioning is not "thinking substance," but merely the empty place of the subject as the question, the subject as such: in other words, the subject as *feminine*. However, once Descartes isolates his first principle, the *cogito*, "I think therefore I am," he starts with this (allegedly) intuitive knowledge, and begins his attempt to deduce all other kinds of knowledge from it. This project fails: for one thing, it involves a couple of fallacious efforts to prove God's existence. But the main point for our purposes is that the process of beginning with the *cogito* and then attempting to deduce all knowledge from this "indubitable" first principle is homologous to the masculine logic. "Thinking substance" serves in this project of intuition/ deduction as the constitutive exception that grounds the sought-after universal knowledge.

Here is a second example. John Locke's philosophy involves an empiricist theory of knowledge (epistemology), and a dualist theory of reality (metaphysics). He argues that we receive simple ideas from the two kinds of substance, material substance (matter) and spiritual substance (soul). Out of these simple ideas our minds form complex ideas. Simple ideas of sensation are received into consciousness (through the sense organs) from material substance, and simple ideas of reflection are received into consciousness from spiritual substance. However, Locke acknowledges that we have no knowledge of substance as such, even though all knowledge implies substance (material and spiritual) as the origin of the two kinds of simple ideas from which all complex ideas are formed. Locke's philosophy is homologous to the masculine logic: substance as the source of simple ideas serves as the constitutive exception.

For the purposes of illustrating the difference between the masculine logic and the feminine logic, we can take Hume's version of empiricism to be something like Locke's: what Locke calls "simple ideas," Hume calls "impressions," and what Locke calls "complex ideas," Hume calls "ideas." However, in contrast to Locke's thinking, Hume's stricter version of empiricism implies that the word "substance" is a word with no meaning, since we have no impression of substance as such. There is no exception made in Hume's version of empiricism for the non-empirical postulate of substance as such. All our knowledge, then, is composed of impressions and the ideas which are faint, weak copies of impressions. In this sense, the set of impressions and ideas is "non-All": the set is incomplete, but there is no exception to it. In this regard, Hume's thinking is homologous to Lacan's feminine logic.

Here is a third example. Kant distinguishes between phenomena (things-for-us, appearances) and noumena (things-in-themselves). Knowledge achieves universality in being limited to phenomena (appearances) only; we can have no knowledge of the thing-in-itself. Nonetheless, we must presuppose the thing-in-itself as existing behind or beneath phenomena, especially in regard to moral choices, since the phenomenal self is determined, while the noumenal self is free. The exceptional status Kant grants to noumenal freedom is homologous to the masculine logic: the thing-in-itself serves as the constitutive exception to the universality of knowledge of phenomena (this is discussed in chapter 6 below, on *Tarrying with the Negative*).

For our present purpose of illustrating the masculine and the feminine logics, we can take Hegel's thinking to be something like Kant's but without the constitutive exception of the thing-in-itself. On this interpretation of Hegelian dialectic, appearances are all there is, but these appearances are incomplete and/or inconsistent with one another. According to Žižek's interpretation of Hegel, Absolute Knowledge is not a totality or a position of "omniscience." On the contrary, Žižek takes Absolute Knowledge to be the recognition that any totality is irreducibly inconsistent. Žižek interprets Hegelian Absolute Knowledge as the realization that there is no neutral position beyond the subject's position of enunciation. According to this reading, Hegelian dialectic is homologous to the feminine logic.

As a fourth and final example, consider the relativity of motion. Imagine that you are standing on a train, and you drop a coin. From your frame of reference, the coin drops approximately 27 inches in a straight line-segment from your hand towards the center of the earth. Now imagine a viewer on the station platform watching through the windows of the train as it speeds past the station at 90 miles per hour. The observer sees the coin leave your hand, and travel forward at 90 miles per hour in the time between when it leaves your hand and hits the floor of the train. So the coin actually moved significantly farther than 27 inches, and its path was a forward, downward-sloping curve. Now imagine an observer situated in space, who perceives the surface of the earth move beneath him as the planet rotates. From this frame of reference, the coin not only travels toward the center of the earth as well as forward with the movement of the train. In addition, the coin also travels through space at approximately 1000 miles per hour with the rotation of the earth. The coin then, moves significantly further than in the previous two frames of reference, and the path of the coin's motion is twisted by the earth's rotation. There are other frames of reference: the earth also revolves at enormous speed around the sun; the sun revolves at an even greater speed around the center of the Milky Way galaxy; the galaxy revolves around the center of the cluster of galaxies; the cluster revolves around the center of the super-cluster, and the supercluster itself moves.

In relation to this example, the masculine logic is exemplified if we imagine that there must be some definite, "objective" distance, path, or velocity of the coin's motion. For the masculine logic, this (incalculable) absolute motion is the exception that is constitutive of all the relative descriptions of the coin's motion from various frames of reference. The unknowable absolute motion serves (in the masculine logic) as that which allows the transition to all possible frames of reference. Žižek occasionally points out the ironic consequences of the masculine logic's notion of a neutral and disengaged perspective of all perspectives. It is certainly ironic if the notion of pure "objectivity" turns out to be nothing but a postulate of the subject.

In this example, the supposition of the absolute motion beyond all frames of reference is the exception that is constitutive for the masculine logic. The feminine logic in relation to this same example involves *accepting* each of the descriptions of the motion from the various frames of reference, while *denying* the meaning of any absolute distance and path that somehow exists behind or beyond the various perspectives. In sum, the feminine logic involves the insight that any one, whole, or totality is non-All.

Thus the Lacanian Real is not the absolute "perspective of all perspectives." Žižek emphasizes repeatedly that the Real is constituted retroactively as a result of recognizing the inconsistency of symbolic systems: once we encounter the Real, it is as if it always already was. Furthermore, regarding the above four examples, it might initially seem that simply removing the exception allows the transition from the masculine to the feminine logic. But the important point is that while the exception is *constitutive* for the masculine logic, the feminine logic of non-All needs no constitutive exception. Succinctly put, the feminine subject recognizes that the postulate of neutral, disengaged "objectivity" involves a fantasy. Symbolic reality is always fictional insofar as it depends on fantasy projections that cover over inconsistency. The feminine logic is open to the realization that the Master-Signifier is always meaningless within the very field of symbolic significance that it pins down or "quilts."[6] In other words, sovereignty relies on the logic of the universal and its constitutive (but meaningless) exception. To realize that the subject as such is distinct from the process of ideological subjectivization is to recognize that the Master is an impostor. Insofar as fantasy fills in the gaps of the symbolic system, meaning is imaginary, and the task for the feminine subject (the subject as such) is to traverse the fantasy. This we can do, because the subject as such is the *question*. As Žižek explains in various texts, Lacanian psychoanalysis implies a radical-emancipatory moment and the analyst functions as a revolutionary agent, insofar as the goal of analysis is to isolate and then to get rid of the Master-Signifier that structures "the subject's (ideologico-political) unconscious."[7]

All of this indicates why there can be no universal definition of "the" woman. At this point, we are now in a position to understand what Žižek means in *Enjoy* when he claims that woman is a symptom of man. In what way is a feminine subject a *symptom*? A symptom, like a letter, may be an address to the Other. In such cases, the symptom functions as a signifier, serving a linguistic function, sending a message to the analyst. In the early Lacan, the symptom is a formation of the unconscious that functions as a symbolic compromise between two conflicting desires. But in his later theory, Lacan articulated the symptom as Real, as pure *jouissance* that does not admit of interpretation. Žižek follows the later Lacan in his development of the concept of the symptom: it is in this sense that he intends the "enjoyment" of the symptom. When considered in relation to the symbolic, a symptom may function as a particle of Real *jouissance* that undermines universal definitions. Along these lines, because of her relation to the symbolic order, there can be no comprehensive and consistent definition of feminine subjectivity as such (*the* woman does not exist).

From early on, Lacan located the essence of human existence in *desire*. The subject of desire is the subject of the unconscious, and this subjectivity is constituted through signification: desire "exists" only in the inconsistencies and distortions of signification. Insofar as it is phallic, desire is related to the symbolic; but insofar as it manifests the nonsymbolic Real, the essential life substance (*jouissance*) is usually something of which the subject is unaware. This is why Žižek asserts the Real, as that

---

[6] See Žižek's *The Parallax View* (Cambridge, MA: MIT Press, 2006), pp. 253–4 on the non-All, and pp. 372–3 on the Master-Signifier.

[7] See Slavoj Žižek, "Jacques Lacan's Four Discourses," available online at http://www.lacan.com/zizfour.htm.

which eludes symbolization, to be the cause of desire. And as already indicated, he argues that the feminine subject position is subjectivity as such. But as a symptom, a feminine subject evokes the pleasure-in-pain of *jouissance*; her association with the essential life substance gives subjectivity whatever consistency it has. As Tony Myers expresses this:

> For if the symptom is what maintains the consistency of the subject, equally its dissolution will betray that consistency and the subject will disappear. Therefore, the thesis that "woman is the symptom of man" registers the fact that man only exists in so far as woman confers consistency upon him. Man, in other words, depends for his existence on woman.[8]

For a masculine subject, a feminine subject evokes the object of his fundamental fantasy, the fantasy that was formed in childhood in response to the enigma of the (m)Other's desire. This fundamental fantasy cannot ever be subjectivized; in order to function, it must remain repressed (*How to Read Lacan*, p. 59). In the fantasy of a masculine subject, feminine subjectivity functions as something Real which he believes will provide him anchorage for his existence outside the symbolic register. Like a masculine subject, a feminine subject is capable of phallic desire. But unlike a masculine subject, there is a feminine *jouissance* that is nonphallic, Other *jouissance*. "Nonphallic" here means that this supplementary, Other *jouissance* does not exist within the phallic symbolic order. Compared to the masculine subject, the feminine subject has access to another form of *jouissance* that is "more" (*encore*).[9] With reference to Lacan's late work, Žižek explains the sense in which woman is a symptom of man. In Lacan's last seminars and writings, the symptom is conceived as:

---

[8]   See Tony Myers, *Slavoj Žižek* (London: Routledge, 2003), p. 86.

[9]   In "The Liberal Utopia," Žižek criticizes Yannis Stavrakakis' interpretation of nonphallic other jouissance as "a *jouissance* beyond accumulation, domination and fantasy, an enjoyment of the not-all or not-whole." Stavrakakis argues that we achieve this *jouissance* by accomplishing "the sacrifice of the fantasmatic *objet petit a*" which can only "make this other *jouissance* attainable." Žižek argues that Stavrakakis fails to grasp the implications of the distinction between desire and drive, and the distinction between the *aim* and the *goal* of drive. Because of this, Stavrakakis reduces *objet petit a* to its role in fantasy, whereas for Lacan, *objet a* is another name for the Freudian "partial object." This means that *objet a* cannot be reduced to its role in fantasy which sustains desire. In short, Stavrakakis envisions a liberal utopia in which desire is not transgressive, but is able to function without the destabilizing excess of *objet petit a*. See Slavoj Žižek, "The Liberal Utopia," online at http://www.lacan.com/zizliberal.htm.

a particular signifying formation which confers on the subject its very ontological consistency, enabling it to structure its basic, constitutive relationship to *enjoyment* (*jouissance*) [...]: if the symptom is dissolved, the subject loses the ground under his feet, disintegrates. In this sense, "woman is a symptom of man" means that *man himself exists only through woman as his symptom*: all his ontological consistency hangs on, is suspended from his symptom, is "externalized" in his symptom. In other words, man literally *ex-sists*: his entire being lies "out there," in woman. Woman, on the other hand, does *not* exist, she *insists*, which is why she does not come to be through man only – there is something in her that escapes the relation to man, the reference to the phallic signifier; and, as is well known, Lacan attempted to capture this excess by the notion of a *"not-all" feminine jouissance*. (*Enjoy*, pp. 155–6)

Like feminine subjectivity, the *act* is akin to the symbolic undecidability of the Real. The act is not founded in the symbolic register, in ideology, or in any psychological content. The act is founded only in itself; the act is excluded from the intersubjective network of the big Other insofar as it suspends the performative power of the phallic Master-Signifier, and therefore of the other signifiers that are fixed in place by the Master-Signifier. In an act, symbolic imperatives no longer oblige. Žižek describes the act as a withdrawal from symbolic reality that allows us to begin again from the "zero point" of freedom that Hegel called "abstract negativity" (*Enjoy*, p. 43). Žižek links the act as symbolic suicide to the death drive as radical autonomy: "woman, taken 'in herself,' outside the relation to man, embodies the death drive, apprehended as a radical, most elementary ethical attitude of uncompromising insistence, of 'not giving way as to ...' Woman is therefore no longer conceived as fundamentally 'passive' in contrast to male activity: the act as such, in its most fundamental dimension, is 'feminine'" (*Enjoy*, p. 156).

The act communicates nothing and expects nothing; in the act, the feminine subject renounces support in the symbolic big Other. This renunciation involves a withdrawal so complete that the subject has nothing whatsoever left to lose, not even renunciation itself.

Why is Every Act a *Repetition*?

Over the course of psychoanalytic treatment, the analyst discerns that in the speech of the analysand, certain meaningless signifiers persist and are repeated. Lacan's concept of the letter refers to the repetition of signifiers of *jouissance* that continuously return and cause the subject suffering.

Repetition is a feature of signification, and is linked to the way the subject receives back from the Other his own (repressed) message in inverted (unrepressed) form. Žižek's account of repetition focuses on the act of a feminine subject. Supplementary, "Other *jouissance*" is manifested in the ethical act of the feminine subject, who does not choose the symbolic Father, but instead chooses the worst, the exception, that which is left out of the symbolic order (*Enjoy*, p. 78). Žižek develops this psychoanalytic concept of the act as repetition in relation to Kierkegaard's philosophical account of repetition: "Repetition as act is to be distinguished from its other modalities; that is to say, the status of the repetition with Kierkegaard is triple, according to his triad of the *esthetical, ethical,* and *religious* stages (or, to name their Lacanian equivalents, Imaginary, Symbolic, and Real)" (*Enjoy*, p. 78).

Though only possible against the background of the symbolic, an act is an encounter with the abyss of the Real. The act as the repetition of an experience of *impossibility* belongs to the Real:

> This is how Lacan conceives the difference between repetition of a signifier and repetition *qua* traumatic encounter with the Real: the repetition of a signifier repeats the symbolic *trait unaire*, the mark to which the subject is reduced, and thus constitutes the ideal order of the Law, whereas "traumatism" designates precisely the reemergent failure to integrate some "impossible" kernel of the Real. (*Enjoy*, p. 79)

What the act repeats is the encounter with the ethical-symbolic undecidability of the Real. Put simply, the act of a feminine subject involves an identification with those who are excluded, those who function as the excremental remainder, and as such, stick out of the symbolic order. In this way, Žižek links Lacan's notion of the Real as an "unhistorical" traumatic kernel to the moment of negativity, madness, or unreason inherent to (his reading of) Hegelian dialectic. According to Žižek, when Hegel compares a proposition with itself, he exposes the discord between the speaker's intended meaning and what the speaker effectively said (*Enjoy*, p. 26, note 28). Hegel articulates this nonrational moment of discord as the constitutive exception *within* universality: Hegelian dialectic requires this point at which universality is suspended.

By showing how, beginning with Kierkegaard, critics of Hegelian dialectic overlooked this non-synthesized negativity, Žižek both reinscribes Hegel and shows why Lacanian theory is not a logocentric power discourse: "Lacan's fundamental thesis is that the Master is by definition an *imposter*: the Master is somebody who, upon finding himself at the place of the constitutive lack in the structure, acts as if he holds the reins of that surplus, of the mysterious X which eludes the grasp of the structure" (*Enjoy*, p. 103).

Why Does the *Phallus* Appear?

Initially the phallus functions as an imaginary object that the infant assumes satisfies the mother's desire, until the paternal function dispels the imaginary unity between mother and child. When the child realizes that rules limit the satisfaction of desire, phallus then functions symbolically. The symbolic phallus is a signifier of lack, and recognizing that he can never be the phallus is how the masculine subject accepts symbolic castration. But accepting symbolic castration is accompanied by the fantasy of an obscene father *not* subjected to prohibitions; this imaginary primordial father functions as the constitutive exception to "universal" law.

The feminine psychic structure is another way of relating to the phallic function and the symbolic register. Feminine subjects are capable of phallic *jouissance* like masculine subjects, but feminine sexuation is not entirely phallic. Insofar as *jouissance* is sexual, it is phallic and does not relate to the Other as such. But, as discussed above, feminine subjects are also capable of supplementary, Other *jouissance* which is nonphallic, not confined by the prohibitions of the symbolic father. Put succinctly, instead of pretending or hoping to *have* the symbolic phallus, a feminine subject – through masquerade – can *be* the phallic signifier of desire for a masculine subject.

As the signifier of lost *jouissance*, phallus fuses desire with symbolic signification. In this sense, the phallic signifier is an index of its own impossibility: as the signifier of symbolic castration, phallus signifies its own absence. In sum, phallus appears because it signifies the fundamental division of subjectivity; it is the privileged signifier of desire and lost *jouissance*.

Why Are There Always Two *Fathers*?

The symbolic Father refers to the agency of the public Law, as opposed to the mythical and obscene, primordial father of unrestrained enjoyment. The Name/No of the Father (*le nom du père*) involves the name and the symbolic identity in and through which we are inscribed into the sociosymbolic community. Symbolic castration implies that speaking beings are socialized animals, and this means that direct access to the Real of enjoyment is barred. Symbolic castration frees the child from the burden of trying to be the phallus for the mother. Instead of imaginary identification centering on the desire of the mother, it can identify with the symbolic Father. The intervention of the symbolic Father corresponds with the acquisition of language, and the child's identification with the paternal function unifies its desire with the law. Although the authoritative "father figure" in the West has traditionally been male, even in a matriarchal society individuals are subjected to something homologous to what Lacan referred to as the Name/No! of the Father (the agency of public Law). This implies that for all symbolic subjects, sexual relationships must proceed under the sign of the Name/No of the Father. In short, sexual enjoyment is possible only if *jouissance* has been renounced as the primary goal of existence.

Again, superego is formed insofar as the child internalizes the Name/ No of the Father. However, Žižek emphasizes the dual nature of the superego. Superego has a symbolic side – the public law – but also a hidden side, an obscene injunction to transgress. The symbolic Law serves to regulate the subject's *jouissance*. But the dark underside of this Law is a superego injunction to the unrestrained *jouissance* of the imaginary, primal father. This is the obscene superego injunction of late capitalism: "Enjoy!"

Conclusion: Why is *Reality* Always Multiple?

Žižek shows how the recognition of Real antagonism enables us to distance ourselves from the ideology of late capitalism. According to Žižek's dialectical materialism, the negativity of Hegelian dialectic is homologous to the ineffaceable trauma or antagonism of the Lacanian Real. This version of materialism does not presuppose any "neutral" reality which is distorted by various representations of it; nor does it imply any disengaged standpoint from which reality is observed and described. One of Žižek's primary aims is to dispel imaginary neutrality and consistency in order to disclose the Real *jouissance* that both forms and disrupts any symbolic order.

Some deconstructionist critics argue that Žižek emphasizes symbolic structures while neglecting contingent factors, claiming that he elevates historically relative phenomena to the level of transcendental universality.

Žižek demonstrates that this presupposes the Real to be temporally prior to the symbolic. To summarize, Žižek argues that this view presupposes the naive and ordinary, linear or "historical" notion of time (X must exist before Y, which exists before Z). Against this, Žižek argues throughout his works that a free act can reconfigure the entire field of symbolic reality, in a way that retroactively creates its own possibility. Again, the kind of universality opened up by the feminine logic of "not-all" involves the act, which is a confrontation with the Real as a *negative* a priori: if we encounter the Real through the Lacanian act, it is as if the Real always already was. That which is always "repeated" in the act of a feminine subject is not any positive content, but rather the engagement with the inconsistency of the masculine logic (universality and its constitutive exception).

The ethical act of a feminine subject involves choosing the "worse" instead of choosing the symbolic Father, insofar as she identifies with *what is left out* of the symbolic order. How are we to understand this? In the psychoanalytic account of "socialization," the subject emerges from the encounter between the presymbolic life substance of *jouissance* with the symbolic order. This encounter is constitutive of any subject; this means that to be included in the intersubjective symbolic network is to have been constituted by a forced choice. The subject (as capable of a *free* choice) does not exist prior to the "choice" of the symbolic order over the presymbolic enjoyment. The choice of symbolic subjectivity is forced insofar as the subject is only free after she has been constituted by choosing the symbolic community:

> The choice of community, the "social contract," is a paradoxical choice where I maintain the freedom of choice only if I "make the right choice": if I choose the "other" of the community, I stand to lose the very freedom, the very possibility of choice (in clinical terms: I choose psychosis). What is sacrificed in the act of choice is of course the Thing, the incestuous Object that embodies impossible enjoyment – the paradox consisting in the fact that the incestuous Object *comes to be through being lost*, i.e., that it is not given prior to its loss. For *that* reason, the choice is forced: its terms are incomparable, what I cede in order to gain inclusion in the community of symbolic exchange and distribution of goods is in one sense "all" (the Object of desire) and in another sense "nothing at all" (since it is in itself impossible, i.e., since, in the case of its choice, I lose all). (*Enjoy*, p. 75)

In the choice between the symbolic Father or the worse ("*le père ou pire*"), any split subject – anyone who is not psychotic – has always already accepted the forced "choice" of the Name of the Father, and thus entered the symbolic community. This constitutive choice is between bad and worse: if the worse is anxiety, nonetheless, the alternative is the forced choice of symbolic community, which is bad in the sense that it involves giving ground relative to one's desire, and thus contracting an indelible guilt (*Enjoy*, p. 75). This explains the sense in which the psychotic is "free" (pp. 75–6). The psychotic took the choice seriously (not as forced), and rejected the symbolic community, choosing instead the "impossible" opposite of the Name of the Father. This impossible opposite of symbolic community is the "nonsymbolizable object," *objet petit a* (p. 75).

But again, is there any distinguishing mark of the ethical *act* of the feminine subject? In other words, when – if ever – is it possible to distinguish, on the one hand, the ethico-political act (of a *neurotic*) from, on the other hand, the (*psychotic*) suspension of symbolic order? We are now in a position to look at this question more closely. In *Looking Awry*, Žižek introduced a distinction between "acting out" and the "*passage à l'acte*":

> Broadly speaking, acting out is still a symbolic act, an act addressed to the big Other, whereas a "passage to act" suspends the dimension of the big Other as the act is transposed into the dimension of the real. In other words, acting out is an attempt to break through a symbolic deadlock (an impossibility of symbolization, of putting into words) by means of an act, even though this act still functions as the bearer of some ciphered message. Through this act we attempt (in a "crazy" way, true) to honor a certain debt, to wipe out a certain guilt, to embody a certain reproach to the Other, etc. [...] The "passage to act" entails in contrast an exit from the symbolic network, a dissolution of the social bond. We could say by *acting out*, we identify ourselves with the symptom as Lacan conceived it in the '50s (the ciphered message addressed to the Other), whereas by *passage à l'acte*, we identify with the *sinthome* as the pathological "tic" structuring the real kernel of our enjoyment [...]. (*Looking Awry*, p. 139)

Acting out as the culmination of hysterical questioning is thoroughly coordinated with the parameters of truth; but, in contrast to this, the *passage à l'acte* suspends the dimension of truth. Truth has the structure of a (symbolic) fiction, and because of this, truth and Real enjoyment (*jouissance*) are not compatible (*Looking*, p. 140). Unlike the passage to act, acting out involves identification with the symptom as a ciphered message to the symbolic big Other, and this implies that acting out may be correlated with traversing the fantasy in and through the ethico-political act. When we identify with a *social* symptom: "we traverse and subvert the fantasy frame that determines the field of social meaning, the ideological self-understanding of a given society, i.e., the frame within which, precisely, the 'symptom' appears as some alien, disturbing intrusion, and not as the point of eruption of the otherwise hidden truth of the existing social order" (*Looking Awry*, p. 140).

In *Enjoy Your Symptom!*, Žižek argues that after the (originary, constitutive) forced choice of symbolic order, a subject can repeat the choice and rid herself of the guilt she brought upon herself originally, insofar as choosing the Name of the Father (in the forced choice) implied giving way on her desire. This first time of the choice was bad, but this second time of the choice – its repetition – is worse, since it involves "excommunication" from the intersubjective, symbolic network: "Therein consists the Lacanian definition of the authentic ethical act: an act which reaches the utter limit of the primordial forced choice and repeats it in the reverse sense. Such an act presents the only moment when we are effectively 'free.' Antigone is 'free' after she has been excommunicated from the community" (*Enjoy Your Symptom!*, p. 77). In her ethico-political act, Antigone refuses to give way on her desire. In this sense her act "remains throughout determined by the coordinates of truth" (*Looking Awry*, p. 140). In short, even though her act separates her from the symbolic community – it is a kind of symbolic suicide – Antigone identifies with the "symptom," she does not identify with the *sinthome* that structures the Real kernel of enjoyment.

How does Žižek counter the postmodern claims that individuals are too cynical to believe in ideologies anymore, therefore we now inhabit a post-ideological world? Žižek undermines this claim by delineating the ways in which we postmodern, cynical subjects nonetheless rely on fantasmatic supports (such as the belief in some Other who still believes) that enable us to avoid confronting the Real.

6

Tarrying with the Negative: Kant, Hegel, and the Critique of Ideology

In this book, Žižek argues that Lacanian theory reaffirms a conception of universal truth and is therefore opposed to cognitive and ethical relativism. He amends Lacan's occasional disparaging remarks about philosophy by developing the philosophical dimension of Lacanian psychoanalytic theory, and, in the process, argues that Lacan is one of the preeminent philosophers of our time. Philosophy involves a distancing from the artificial character of the Master-Signifier, and Žižek argues that Lacan (like Plato, Kant, Hegel, and Marx) accomplishes this critical distantiation. By articulating the Hegelian theme of "tarrying with the negative" in light of Lacanian theory, Žižek reveals the connection between the self-reflexive negativity of German Idealism, the Freudian concept of the death drive, and the Lacanian Real. Because the void of the Real underlies the symbolic construction of reality, Hegel's *Aufhebung* (sublation) is a "re-marking," an incomplete re-inscription which leaves an indivisible remainder. Thus the notorious Hegelian "Absolute Knowledge" involves recognizing the inconsistency of symbolic reality, and is therefore homologous to the Lacanian *passe*, the moment when the analysand comes to occupy the place of the analyst through experiencing the lack in the symbolic register. Ideology, in contrast to this, depends on a fantasy that masks this hole or lack in the symbolic order.

The two crucial breaks in the history of philosophy, Plato's and Kant's, occurred as a reaction to new relativistic attitudes which threatened to demolish the traditional corpus of knowledge: in Plato's case, the logical argumentation of the sophists undermined the mythical foundations of

Žižek: A Reader's Guide, First Edition. Kelsey Wood.
© 2012 John Wiley & Sons, Inc. Published 2012 by John Wiley & Sons, Inc.

the traditional mores; in Kant's case, empiricists (such as Hume) under-mined the foundations of the Leibnizean-Wolfian rationalist metaphysics. In both cases, the solution offered is not a return to the traditional attitude but a new founding gesture which "beats the sophists at their own game," i.e., which surmounts the relativism of the sophists by way of its own radicalization (Plato accepts the argumentative procedure of the soph-ists; Kant accepts Hume's burial of the traditional metaphysics). And it is our hypothesis that Lacan opens up the possibility of another repetition of the same gesture

—Žižek, Tarrying with the Negative:
Kant, Hegel, and the Critique of Ideology, p. 4

One of Žižek's most theoretically substantial books is *Tarrying with the Negative: Kant, Hegel, and the Critique of Ideology* (1993).[1] In *Tarrying with the Negative* (abbreviated *Tarrying* below), Žižek argues, against decon-structionists (e.g., Jacques Derrida, Judith Butler) and postmodernists (e.g., Richard Rorty and Jean-François Lyotard), that Hegel makes the-matic a fundamental negativity that prevents any complete dialectical synthesis. He develops in some detail his reading of Hegel through Lacan and, in the process, indicates how nationalistic identity is based on a fantasy of consistency and harmonious synthesis. The mythical point of origin around which nationalisms revolve is actually a hole or rupture in the symbolic order; this gap is "positivized" through the actions of believ-ers in a way that camouflages Real social antagonism within the regime. In sum, nationalisms are based on a fantasy of originary social harmony and unity.

Žižek begins by claiming that philosophy enables us to distance our-selves from such fantasies of unity, and from the artificial and contin-gent Master-Signifier (*Tarrying*, p. 2). Philosophy reinvents theory by revealing current presuppositions about the conditions of possibility for truth. He argues that Lacan (like Kant, Hegel, and Marx) accom-plishes this abstraction from starting points. Moreover, Lacanian theory (like the philosophies of Plato and Kant) opposes cognitive and ethical relativism and reaffirms a conception of universal truth. In this sense, Lacan is a transcendental philosopher: Lacan's work was an endeavor to uncover the transcendental conditions of possibility for *desire*. With

[1] Unless otherwise stated, page references for this work are to the following edition: *Tarrying with the Negative: Kant, Hegel, and the Critique of Ideology* (Durham, NC: Duke University Press, 1993).

95

reference to Kant's *Critique of Pure Reason*, Žižek argues that Lacan offers a critique of pure desire:

> Are not all his fundamental concepts so many keys to the enigma of desire? Desire is constituted by "symbolic castration," the original loss of the *Thing*; the void of this loss is filled out by *objet petit a*, the fantasy-object; this loss occurs on account of our being "embedded" in the symbolic universe which derails the "natural" circuit of our needs; etc., etc. (*Tarrying*, p. 3)

Žižek demonstrates how Lacanian analysis reveals the produced and artificial character of the Master-Signifier. When a subject identifies with an ideology, the Master-Signifier's lack of content is "filled in" by its performative dimension. That is, my very identification with an ideology retroactively creates an illusion that the content with which I identify was always already there: "when the subject recognizes himself in an ideological call, he automatically overlooks the fact that this very formal act of recognition creates the content one recognizes oneself in" (*Tarrying*, p. 73). But – against the misconception that Lacanian theory is just another form of postmodern relativism – Žižek clarifies the sense in which Lacan's approach reinvigorates the concept of universality. For Lacan, the universal truth of any situation is revealed *through* contingency: "The perception of Lacan as 'anti-essentialist' or 'deconstructionist' falls prey to the same illusion as that of perceiving Plato as just one among the sophists. [...] Lacan accepts the 'deconstructionist' motif of radical contingency, but turns this motif against itself, using it to assert his commitment to Truth *as contingent*" (p. 4).

In *Tarrying*, Žižek indicates that postmodern relativism – the ideology of late capitalism – is self-referentially inconsistent insofar as it implicitly offers a synoptic view of the Whole even while it explicitly denies the possibility of any synoptic view of the Whole. By making thematic the moment of negativity inherent to both German Idealism and Lacanian psychoanalytic theory, Žižek articulates an account of universal truth that avoids this absurdity. His dialectical materialism enables a new approach to truth that hinges on the insight that any totality (or Whole) is always internally inconsistent. Lacan demonstrated that subjectivity cannot be conceived in any positive way; instead, the subject is split, decentered, and out of place with regard to symbolic "reality." Along these lines, Kant bequeathed to his German Idealist followers (Fichte, Schelling, Hegel) a notion of subjectivity as a dialectical split or void. For Kant, the negativity of the thinking subject implies that the "I think" is always empty on the phenomenal level (*Tarrying*, p. 16). The subject as Real is dislocated from, and cannot be found in the symbolic universe. And, as intimated by Kant, the symbolic reality is inherently ruptured by Real antinomy: "there is no way for us to imagine in a consistent way the universe as a Whole; that is, as soon as we do it, we obtain two antinomical, mutually exclusive versions of the universe as a Whole" (p. 83).

Žižek links this "negative" ontology to current events, and by way of examples, reveals the limitations of a broad range of philosophical and political positions. Because of a widespread failure to recognize the negativity implicit to Hegelian dialectics and the Lacanian Real, deconstructionists, pragmatists, and neoliberals all miss the dialectical paradox that is implicit to any symbolic order. But dialectical materialism both exposes and embraces this paradox, and shows how those approaches that fail to recognize dialectical paradox undermine themselves. For example, what appears as a problem to an abstract approach proves to be a necessary constituent of the unproblematic state of things that we imagine ourselves to be progressing toward. However, because no "unproblematic" state of things exists prior to "problems," it can happen that the more we get rid of the alleged problem, the more we lose what we were trying to preserve. Žižek argues that what appears to be a problem for neoliberalism actually proves to be part of the solution. Neoliberalism overlooks "the degree to which, in today's complex economies, the very 'normal' functioning of the market can be secured only by way of the state actively intervening in social security, ecology, law enforcement, etc.; left to itself, the market mechanism is bound to destroy itself" (*Tarrying*, p. 93). This dialectical paradox implies that the proposed solution can actually exacerbate the problem, metastasizing the root cause of the problem. And the reverse also holds: that which appears, from an abstract perspective, to be a problem may actually turn out to be its own solution (p. 93).

But in light of this dialectical paradox, precisely how do we ascertain the truth of a sociosymbolic system? Adherents of any ideology are generally not cognizant of the hidden underside (the repressed truth) of the social reality. Žižek argues throughout his works that any symbolic system implies some primordially repressed Other, and in societies founded on the exclusion of some particular group – that functions as the religious, racial, or ethnic Other – this exclusion may encapsulate the truth of what is wrong with the sociosymbolic order. According to Žižek's dialectical materialist understanding of truth, universal truth is revealed in and through historical contingency (for example, this century's *oppressors* include descendants of the last century's *oppressed*). The universal truth

of a situation is disclosed through a historically relative locus in the constellation of social positions: those who are disenfranchised experience
the truth which is repressed from the hegemonic ideology.

"I or He or It (the Thing) Which Thinks"

To illustrate how the constitution of symbolic order involves the primordial repression of some Other, Žižek analyzes the thought of several
modern philosophers, beginning with Descartes. Against the usual
scholarly interpretation, Žižek argues that Descartes' methodic doubt
does not merely establish the autonomous subject as a thinking substance. In a startling reversal, Žižek demonstrates that the standard
interpretation of Descartes' *cogito ergo sum* ("I think therefore I exist") as
implying the existence of *res cogitans* (a "thinking thing") – ignores the
negativity implicit to Descartes' project of radical doubt. What does
"negativity" mean in this context? For one thing, Descartes' methodic
doubt involves a withdrawal inward, away from the socially constituted,
symbolic dimension of personal identity. Žižek argues that – in this
withdrawal inward, away from sociosymbolic identity – Descartes'
method of isolating the *cogito* anticipates both the negativity of the subject in German Idealism, and the split subject of Lacanian theory. The
process of symbolic subjectivization involves the in-corporation of the
hegemonic ideology of society. However, the subject as Real is the void
inherent to any symbolic order.

This is why Žižek argues that when Lacan speaks of *cogito*, he means
the exact opposite of subjectivization: "the 'subject' qua $ emerges not
via subjectivization-narrativization, i.e., via the 'individual myth' constructed from the decentered pieces of tradition; instead, the subject
emerges *at the very moment when the individual loses its support in the network of tradition*; it coincides with the void that remains after the framework of symbolic memory is suspended" (*Tarrying*, p. 42).

By reinterpreting Cartesian subjectivity in terms of radical doubt, the
withdrawal inward, and the confrontation with madness, Žižek evokes a
subject that is not a positively existing thinking thing, but is instead a
kind of splitting or lack of symmetry. The subject as such is "unified"
with the sociosymbolic order only insofar as both the subject and symbolic reality are split by the Real: "Lacan resolves the worn-out problem
of the relationship between the individual and society via an elegant reference to precisely this moment of Hegel's philosophy: psychoanalytic
theory enables us to recognize their "reconciliation" – the "mediation" of

the Individual and the Universal – in the very splitting that runs through both of them" (*Tarrying*, p. 30).

Because Žižek's approach to the subject emphasizes this irreducible "splitting" or void inherent to symbolic identity, it avoids the extremes of, on the one hand, rampant subjectivism (e.g. the completely autonomous subject of the Enlightenment Project) and, on the other hand, the postmodern disappearance of the subject (that is, the subject as a mere function of language).

Cogito and the Sexual Difference

Descartes himself retreated from the abyss opened up by methodic doubt, the confrontation with madness, and the hypothesis of the Evil Deceiver. Immanuel Kant was the first to articulate the implicit paradoxes of Cartesian subjectivity as *res cogitans* ("thinking thing"). By distinguishing between phenomena ("things for us") and noumena ("things in themselves"), Kant shows, on the one hand, that I can never perceive my understanding as a phenomenon; but, on the other hand, neither can I ever step outside of myself to understand myself as the noumenal Thing which is doing the understanding. Kant showed that it is not possible to locate the subject in any (allegedly) organic hierarchy. The subject is not an element of some (alleged) Whole in which everything has its "natural" place. On the contrary, Kant anticipates Lacan insofar as the subject is "in the most radical sense 'out of joint'; it constitutively lacks its own place, which is why Lacan designates it by the mathem $, the 'barred' *S*" (*Tarrying*, p. 12).

The distinction between the "I" as Cartesian "thinking substance" and as Kantian transcendental apperception is encapsulated in the insight that: "it is not legitimate to use 'I think' as a complete phrase, since it calls for a continuation – 'I think that … (it will rain, you are right, we shall win …)'" (*Tarrying*, p. 13). This distinction – between the "I" as thinking substance and as an empty "I think that …" – exposes Descartes' *reification* of consciousness: "he wrongly concludes that, in the empty 'I think' which accompanies every representation of an object, we get hold of a positive entity, *res cogitans* (a 'small piece of the world,' as Husserl puts it), which thinks and is transparent to itself in its capacity to think" (*Tarrying*, p. 13).

Unlike Descartes, Kant reveals an asymmetry or topological discord *within subjectivity*, between the unknowable substance which thinks and the empty form "I think." For Kant the existence of thoughts in consciousness

99

in no way implies that I have access to myself as thinking substance. However, in spite of his own achievement of this insight, Kant's philosophical anthropology, in fact his entire metaphysics, lapses into inconsistency: "Kant himself commits an error when, in his *Critique of Practical Reason*, he conceives of freedom (the postulate of practical reason) as a noumenal Thing; what gets obfuscated thereby is his fundamental insight according to which I retain my capacity of a spontaneous-autonomous agent precisely and only insofar as I am not accessible to myself as Thing" (*Tarrying*, p. 15). In sum, Kant, like Descartes, departed from his own insight into subjectivity and freedom.

However, regarding sexual difference, Žižek argues that Kant formulated the inconsistency inherent to universality by means of his distinction between two types of logical antinomy (mathematical and dynamical). Moreover – as Joan Copjec shows – the Kantian antinomies prefigure Lacan's logic of sexuation.[2] Kant describes two asymmetrical antinomies of symbolization, the dynamic and the mathematical. Put succinctly, the dynamic antinomies of universality and its constitutive exception parallel the masculine structure of subjectivity, while the mathematical antinomies of "not-all" are homologous to the feminine structure. As Žižek puts it:

> Paradoxical as it may sound, *the Kantian antinomies designate the moment at which sexual difference is for the first time inscribed in the philosophical discourse*, not in the guise of the opposition between the two contradictory poles of every antinomy (the universe is finite / the universe is infinite, etc.), but in the guise of the difference in the two types of antinomies. (*Tarrying*, pp. 56–7)

In sum, Kant's transcendental turn is the beginning of a *dialectical* account of the subject; the subject is a form of split or asymmetrical universality.

Along these lines, according to Lacanian theory, self-consciousness is *not* self-transparency. On the contrary, self-consciousness is decentered in a way that makes it the very opposite of self-transparency: "Lacan's point is not that full self-consciousness is impossible since something always eludes the grasp of my conscious ego. Instead, it is the far more paradoxical thesis that *this decentered hard kernel which eludes my grasp is ultimately self-consciousness itself*; as to its status, self-consciousness is an external object out of my reach" (*Tarrying*, pp. 66–7). Insofar as subjectivity is inherently divided from itself, the Other is inscribed into who

---

[2] See Joan Copjec's excellent book, *Supposing the Subject* (London and New York: Verso, 1994).

I am. Nonetheless, the intersubjective symbolic network (the big Other) cannot provide some common "substance" that overcomes the split or decentering of the subject: "Precisely insofar as I am $, I cannot conceive of myself as participating at [sic] some common substance, i.e., this substance necessarily opposes itself to me in the guise of the Other Subject" (p. 69).

On Radical Evil and Related Matters

Žižek acknowledges that Kant's account of subjectivity as a dialectical gap or asymmetry anticipates, in some ways, the Lacanian Real. But he also argues that both Kant and Schelling fail to adequately formulate the problematic of freedom and radical Evil. According to Žižek, it is not until Hegel that we get a more adequate formulation: "When Hegel, in his *Lectures on the Philosophy of Religion,* conceives of the very act of becoming human, of passage of animal into man, as the Fall into sin, he is more penetrating: the possible space for Good is opened up by the original choice of radical Evil which disrupts the pattern of the organic substantial Whole" (*Tarrying,* p. 96).

In such ways, Žižek argues that the socially defined Good functions so as to mask a more originary choice of Evil. The ultimate paradigm in the sociosymbolic register of how Good masks the egotism of radical Evil is the (right-wing) effort to: "(re)construct society as a harmonious, organic, nonantagonistic edifice" (*Tarrying,* p. 97). Thus the very gaze of nostalgia can be the locus of Evil. The socially defined Good masks the more originary (and distinctively *human*) choice of radical Evil.

The subject as the void in the symbolic order serves as the mediator that enables historical reinventions of symbolic order. How does this occur? A "vanishing mediator" serves as the missing link between two symbolic orders, which facilitates the transition between the two and then disappears. Žižek illustrates the concept of the vanishing mediator with the following example:

> from the standpoint of the precapitalist corporate society, capitalism is Evil, disruptive, it unsettles the delicate balance of the closed precapitalist economy – why, precisely? Because it presents a case of a "predicate" – a secondary, subordinated moment of the social totality (money) – which, in a kind of *hubris,* "runs amok" and elevates itself into an End-in-itself. However, once capitalism achieves a new balance of its self-reproductive circuit and becomes its own mediating totality, i.e., once it establishes itself as a system

101

which "posits its own presuppositions," the site of "Evil" is radically displaced: what now counts as "evil" are precisely the left-overs of the previous "Good" – islands of resistance of precapitalism which disturb the untroubled circulation of Capital, the new form of Good. (*Tarrying*, pp. 97–8)

Žižek uses such reversals to illustrate the link between Hegelian dialectic and the later Lacan's dialectic of desire. According to Hegel, the "negation of negation" results in an affirmation that is different from the affirmation that was originally negated.

As Žižek repeatedly demonstrates, the Hegelian dialectical process never culminates in any full synthesis that encompasses and neutralizes all difference.[3] Along these lines, for Lacan the passage from the physiological *need* of the newborn to the *demand* of the child: "produces a new object which replaces the lost-sublated object of need – *objet petit a*, the object-cause of desire" (*Tarrying*, pp. 111–12). Put simply, *objet petit a* is a fantasy object that fills out or "positivizes" an ineffaceable lack: namely, the lack we encounter whenever we obtain any positive object of symbolic desire.[4] Insofar as desire is inherently transgressive, no positive object can ever satisfy it. The Real of desire is a lack that cannot be filled; in this sense, desire is the desire to desire. Consequently, any notion of social relations that implies harmonious filling of this lack that is constitutive of subjectivity rests on a fantasy. Any harmonious Whole is imaginary; because of the Real, all totality is internally inconsistent.

---

[3] Commentators aligned with the Essex School of discourse theory (e.g. Yannis Stavrakakis) try to link Žižek with the "postmarxism" of Ernesto Laclau and Chantal Mouffe. However, in numerous works, Žižek has successfully refuted the interpretations of Lacan implicit to postmarxist theory and to the related project of "radical democracy." In sum, Žižek argues that, though these interpretations are right to emphasize the Real of social antagonism, they do not recognize the Real of Capital. Democracy is not radical enough, insofar as it is inherently corrupted by its accommodation to capitalism. See Judith Butler, Ernesto Laclau, and Slavoj Žižek, *Contingency, Hegemony, Universality: Contemporary Dialogues on the Left* (London and New York: Verso, 2000).

[4] Žižek criticizes Yannis Stavrakakis for failing to understand the role of the Lacanian *objet petit a*: "in total contradiction to Lacan, Stavrakakis reduces *objet petit a* to its role in fantasy – *objet a* is that excessive X which magically transforms the partial objects which occupy the place of the lack in the Other into the utopian promise of the impossible fullness of *jouissance*. What Stavrakakis proposes is thus the vision of a society in which desire functions without *objet a*, without the destabilizing excess which transforms it into a 'cataclysmic desire of fantasy' – as Stavrakakis puts it in a symptomatically tautological way, we should learn to 'really enjoy our partial enjoyment.' For Lacan, on the contrary, *objet a* is a(nother) name for the Freudian 'partial object,' which is why it cannot be reduced to its role in fantasy which sustains desire." See Žižek, "The Liberal Utopia," online at http://www.lacan.com/zizliberal.htm.

Hegel's "Logic of Essence" as a Theory of Ideology

In the pivotal section of *Tarrying* (chapter 4), Žižek articulates his dialectical materialist interpretation of Hegel. This section of *Tarrying* is Žižek at his best. In it, he shows that interpretation is a direct intervention of the symbolic in the Real; in other words, the notion or concept of a thing affects that thing's existence. This efficacy of the symbolic implies that there are entities whose very existence depends on non-knowledge; for example, in psychoanalysis, the word can affect the Real of the symptom: when interpretation leads to knowledge, the symptom may cease to exist. Thus the very existence of a symptom may depend on its *not* being understood through symbolic interpretation. In such ways, Žižek argues that the meaning of "existence" in Hegelian dialectic is much more sophisticated than the way Kant conceived of existence.

Žižek undermines the usual notion of "Hegel's idealism" by considering, in detail, Hegel's actual arguments in light of Lacanian theory. Žižek first shows that for Hegel, an excessive moment of conflictuality is inherent to reason itself. Then Žižek develops the link between this constitutive "madness of reason" and the Freudian death drive as the excessive moment of "unreason" that is constitutive of subjectivity as such. According to the standard, naive interpretation of Hegel, Hegelian dialectic culminates in a rationalistic moment: all dialectical oppositions are ultimately resolved in a harmonious synthesis free from contradiction. There is a variant reading of Hegel, slightly less naive than the typical interpretation described above, according to which Hegelian dialectic involves a tension between a rationalist logic and a different kind of "logic," one that involves contradictions that undermine rationalism. According to this interpretation, Hegelian dialectic is the effort to bring together rational structure with the conflictuality of life. Žižek argues against both the first, naive interpretation as well as the second, variant reading.

On Žižek's reading of Hegelian dialectic, reason or rationality is itself the locus of contradiction and conflict; rationality is the ultimate excess or site of conflict and fundamental antagonism. Žižek does not simply deny that there is, in Hegel, a tension between rationalism as opposed to conflict and contradiction. But the crucial distinction of Žižek's interpretation of Hegel is that he locates this very tension *within* reason itself. So when reason struggles to overcome contradiction and antagonism, it is fighting against itself, against a deep and ineradicable split that is inherent

103

to rationality. There is a moment of unreason that is constitutive of reason, and this is why when reason fights its "opposite" it is struggling against itself. Reason for Hegel essentially involves the excess of madness (cf. the famous "night of the world" passage from the *Jenaer Realphilosophie* manuscripts). Žižek links the Real, as the inherent inconsistency and incompleteness of the symbolic register, to Hegelian dialectic and explains how the latter implies this "unhistorical" traumatic kernel as the constitutive exception within universality: Hegelian dialectic *requires* this moment of negativity in which universality (symbolic efficacy) is suspended.

As an illustration of this, whereas Kant's approach to freedom implied that subjectivity involves immediate access to the noumenal, Hegel's approach to subjectivity never implies this movement from the phenomenal to the noumenal. Instead, Hegelian dialectic grapples with the problem of how – within being – phenomena, or appearances, ever arise as such. In other words, Kant emphasizes the split between phenomena and noumena; but Hegel re-introduces this split throughout existence itself. If we only have access to appearances, how could the term "appearance" as such have meaning, since there is nothing that is not an appearance? Žižek argues that this is Hegel's problematic, and his interpretation of Hegel highlights the moment of fundamental negativity that prevents any fully realized dialectical synthesis.

Žižek views the Lacanian theory of the late 1940s and early 1950s as Hegelian, and evokes Lacan's Hegelianism by way of considering the passive role of the analyst in the psychoanalytic cure. The passivity of the analyst facilitates the patient's overcoming of external obstacles by provoking the patient to recognize his own inauthentic self-deception (*Tarrying*, p. 143). If the analyst removes external hindrances, the patient's "inner" narrative (i.e., his web of excuses) will collapse due to its inherent inconsistency. Viewed in this light, everything hinges on how the subject recognizes and responds to the (internal and external) constellation or configuration of possibility. External obstacles serve precisely to configure the subject's options in any given set of circumstances. The task for the subject is to accept the burden of responsibility by letting go of excuses and then to exploit the circumstances by deploying the only potentials he has: namely, the ones that are configured by the external set of obstacles.

The fundamental antagonism of the second part of Hegel's *Science of Logic* – Hegel's logic of essence – is the antagonism between *ground* and *conditions*. "Ground" means the inner essence or true nature of a thing, and "conditions" refers to the external circumstances or conditions of possibility that allow this same inner essence or nature to be realized. In the second part of his *Logic*, Hegel shows that it is impossible to achieve a synthesis between ground and conditions, because there is no common measure between the two. In the third part of *Logic*, Hegel will surpass this incommensurability by way of the "subjective logic" of Notion (*Tarrying*, p. 141). One of Žižek's main points is that this surpassing does not efface the opposition, but preserves it; in fact, preserving opposition is precisely what is meant by "tarrying with the negative." The elements that are "combined" are juxtaposed in such a way that the antagonism and opposition between them is preserved undiminished; in other words, the difference is posited as such. Žižek argues that in reason itself, antagonism is not merely *preserved*; if anything, contradiction is *enhanced* within rationality. The upshot of this is that – although ground and conditions are incommensurable – it is also impossible to completely separate them from one another. To tarry with the negative involves the recognition that certain antagonisms are irreducible (e.g., the opposition between ground and conditions). Thus any synthesis or identity between the two elements essentially involves (irresolvable) antagonism or contradiction: according to this dialectic, *even a logical tautology implies contradiction*. In such ways, Žižek argues against the usual interpretations of Hegel by highlighting the impossibility of any fully realized harmonious synthesis.

Insofar as Hegel's "Logic of Essence" implies that contradiction and antagonism are the essence of reason, Hegelian dialectic can provide the basis for the critique of ideology. In *Tarrying*, Žižek's aim is to disclose irreducible antagonism by dispelling imaginary unity. By showing the link between the Real and the non-synthesized negativity inherent to Hegelian dialectic, Žižek refutes the postmodernist claim that Lacanian theory is a logocentric power discourse.

Enjoy Your Nation as Yourself!

In *Tarrying*, Žižek argues that the more the logic of global capitalism becomes universal, the more nationalism and "irrational fundamentalism" will develop to oppose the logic of Capital (pp. 219–20). Nationalistic identity involves a fantasy that masks irreducible social antagonism and enables the belief in organic social harmony and unity. In such ways, fantasy works as the element in ideology that masks the inconsistency of the symbolic, big Other. However, ideology cannot keep repressed all awareness of class antagonism within the regime, because it revolves around the Master-Signifier, a word with no meaning that is positivized through the unreflective (and inconsistent) actions of believers.

Žižek discusses the liberal-democratic notion of universality as a neutral medium or framework for compromise, and demonstrates how this vacuous notion of universality serves the ideology of capitalism. Is liberal democracy – and its implicit compromise with capitalism – the only option for the left today? How do leftists oppose nationalism without relying on the liberal-democratic fantasy of a "neutral space" for dialogue and compromise? Žižek answers by reviving the Hegelian, concrete universality, which is realized only through the engaged and properly political act of taking sides. Because the universal truth of a sociosymbolic order is revealed only through the position of that society's excluded, abject Other, it is only through a politics of identification with this disenfranchised Other that we traverse the fantasies implicit to nationalism and racism. In this way, we can achieve the solidarity of a common struggle, and pass to the act proper. Through the act we traverse the fantasy, encounter the Real, and renounce all symbolic ties. Insofar as the act is a repetition of unrealized potential within the current symbolic actuality, a revolutionary collective may change the entire coordinates of reality. It is always possible to reactualize emancipatory possibilities that are repressed by the current, hegemonic ideology.

As the foregoing indicates, *Tarrying* is not only Žižek's fusion of Lacanian theory with dialectical materialist ontology. Beyond this aspect of the book, there is also a timely ethico-political message. After the ontological preparation, Žižek articulates the theme of "tarrying with the negative" in terms of social antagonism, and argues for an openly partisan and committed (though unorthodox) Marxist stance. But at this critical juncture in the history of human existence, is there really any possibility of gaining critical distance from postmodern relativism, the ideology of multinational, corporate capitalism? In short, just because we know that there is no big Other, how can we make the collapse of the big Other part of our experience?

Žižek highlights the urgency of such questions: "One is tempted to risk a hyperbole and to affirm that *everything*, from the fate of so-called 'Western civilization' up to the survival of humanity in the ecological crisis, hangs on the answer" (*Tarrying*, p. 5). In the book's final chapter, Žižek urges that at this critical juncture in world history, we must be realists, and demand the impossible. The concluding sentences reiterate Žižek's claim that the fate of humanity may hinge on whether or not we recognize that our symbolic order is internally inconsistent: "The crucial, hitherto underestimated ideological impact of the coming ecological crisis will be precisely to make the 'collapse of the big Other' part of our everyday experience [...] Perhaps, however, our very physical survival hinges on our ability to consummate the act of assuming fully the 'nonexistence of the Other,' of *tarrying with the negative*" (*Tarrying*, p. 237).

7

The Metastases of Enjoyment: On Women and Causality

In Part I of this book, Žižek develops his critique of late capitalist ideology by arguing against typical accounts of the origins of the Bosnian conflict, which focus on ethnic and religious tensions. Žižek's analysis shows that the cause of ethnic and religious conflicts is not "the clash of cultures" or the lack of tolerance; these are pseudo-explanations that mask the power struggle implicit to world-market globalization. In the power relations of global capital, violence plays a structural role insofar as the economy functions as a "transcendental" (structural) principle. In Part I Žižek also develops the Hegelian-Lacanian theme of the master/slave dialectic, arguing that there is a hidden link between the inherent violence of capitalist ideology and feminine enjoyment. In Part II, Žižek delineates contours of this link by analyzing the status of women in late capitalism. Žižek argues that it is not the external Other who threatens our enjoyment and our identity. On the contrary, access to enjoyment is always limited (because *jouissance* is Real), and every symbolic identity is inherently inconsistent. The Other is some locus in/of symbolic reality upon which subjects who are indoctrinated into the hegemonic ideology project the intrinsic antagonism of their own symbolic identity.

> *Here one can specify Lacan's thesis that an analyst is authorized only by himself: an analysand becomes an analyst upon assuming that his desire has no support in the Other, that the authorization of his desire can come only from himself.*
>
> —Žižek, *The Metastases of Enjoyment: On Women and Causality*, pp. 72–3

Žižek: A Reader's Guide, First Edition. Kelsey Wood.
© 2012 John Wiley & Sons, Inc. Published 2012 by John Wiley & Sons, Inc.

One of Žižek's most provocative books is *The Metastases of Enjoyment: On Women and Causality* (1994).[1] *The Metastases of Enjoyment* (abbreviated *Metastases* below), builds on Žižek's previous analyses of enjoyment as a political factor. As already mentioned, enjoyment is never simply pleasure; it is usually experienced as discomfort or even suffering. Enjoyment is the aim of the drives and as such, it is something of which the subject is usually not aware. Enjoyment manifests as an odd fascination accompanied by pain, disgust, or horror. In his introduction to *Metastases*, Žižek describes enjoyment as "the primordial generative element" – the underlying cause of otherwise inexplicable behavior – and indicates the dangers that arise when enjoyment is the motivator of human behavior.

What makes *Metastases* such a provocative book? Žižek first leads us to recognize that our behavior is inconsistent and apparently inexplicable, then he forces us to confront an unflattering, but plausible, explanation for this behavior. Žižek claims that a prime example of behavior motivated by unconscious enjoyment was the West's quavering indecision during the Bosnian war. Why were subjects in Western liberal democracies strangely compelled to look at horrible images of murdered children, raped women, and starving prisoners? Why did the West, on the one hand, loudly proclaim its compassion for victims of the conflict, and yet, on the other hand, merely offer (inadequate) humanitarian aid, when a decisive military intervention could have ended the horrifying violence? Wouldn't a true ethico-political act involve not only saving the victims, but also destroying those who made them victims? Žižek argues in *Metastases* that our liberal indecision – and our ineffectual expressions of "compassion" – are symptomatic of the false guilt feelings that accompany narcissistic satisfaction ("we are all right while things are going badly for them"). But once we accept this psychologically penetrating insight, then something much more difficult to acknowledge follows: namely that the unconscious motivator (the hidden cause) of the West's failure to break the siege of Sarajevo was *enjoyment*: that is, our horrified fascination with the fantasy image of the helpless "Balkan victim."

Along these same lines, Žižek claims that what proved to be unbearable to Western observers was not the horrific suffering of the residents of Sarajevo – but the notion that these people were just ordinary citizens like ourselves. This is why Western liberal-democratic subjects were completely unable to recognize the deeper political-economic causes of

---

[1] Unless otherwise stated, page references for this work are to the following edition: *The Metastases of Enjoyment: On Women and Causality* (London and New York: Verso, 2005).

the Bosnian conflict, preferring superficial, "de-politicized" accounts that focused on ethnic and cultural differences.

In Part I of *Metastases*, Žižek refutes standard accounts of the cause of the Bosnian conflict which focus on the clash of cultures, especially ethnic and religious intolerance. Žižek argues that these pseudo-explanations not only mask the true cause, but in the long run, actually serve the interests of capitalist globalism. Put succinctly, the root of the problem is not cultural differences or the lack of tolerance; the true cause lies beneath the ethnic and religious tensions, in the implicit power struggles of world-market globalization. In sum, violence has a structural role in the power relations of global capitalism.

How is the excess and imbalance of global capital linked to the psychotic "loss of reality"? The psychotic *passage à l'acte* does not occur when something is lacking in reality, but on the contrary, when there is too much of a Thing in reality. The subject disappears in the full presence of the object of his fantasy, the symbolic texture of his reality disintegrates, and the kernel of enjoyment within him is laid open to attack (*Metastases*, p. 77). When this occurs, every ethnic otherness is seen as a threat to his enjoyment:

> In other words, the skinhead who gets into a fury and starts to beat "them" up without any "deeper" rational or ideological foundation, simply because "it makes him feel good," is none other than the narcissistic individual of the so-called "society of consumption" in a different modality: the line that separates them is extremely thin; it consists of a purely formal conversion, since we are dealing with one and the same fundamental attitude inscribed either inside or outside the ideological framework of what is "socially permissible." (*Metastases*, p. 81)

Also in Part I, Žižek articulates some of the implications of the Lacanian distinction between the four discourses or social links (the master's, the university's, the hysteric's, and the analyst's). The four discourses demarcate four different subject positions as structural possibilities for ways of relating to the symbolic register. These analyses do not only clarify the meaning of the ethical act of a feminine subject (or hero); in addition, Žižek points out a hidden link between feminine enjoyment on the one hand, and, on the other, the relations of domination inherent to capitalism:

> At the top and on the bottom we have two flat positions: the saint is ethical (he does not compromise his desire) and moral (he considers the Good of others), whereas the scoundrel is immoral (he violates moral norms) and unethical (what he is after is not desire but pleasures and profits, so he

110

lacks any firm principles). Far more interesting are the two horizontal positions expressing an inherent antagonism: the hero is immoral yet ethical – that is to say, he violates (or rather, suspends the validity of) existing explicit moral norms in the name of a higher ethics of life, historical Necessity, and so on, whereas superego designates the very opposite of the hero, an unethical moral Law, a Law in which an obscene enjoyment sticks to obedience to the moral norms (say, a severe teacher who torments his pupils for the sake of their own good, and is not ready to acknowledge his own sadistic involvement in this torment). (*Metastases*, p. 67)

In Part II, Žižek analyzes the status of the feminine subject in the discourses and symbolic practices of late capitalism. These analyses outline the contours of the link between feminine enjoyment and the structural role of violence in capitalist ideology. Žižek shows how the same power relations and inherent violence that configure global capitalism also determine the discursive position (and social status) of feminine subjects. In order to understand this, we should review Lacan's "logic of sexuation" (in *Seminar XX: Encore*).

Žižek's account of the universal as correlative with its exception corresponds with Lacan's definition of the masculine subject position in the logic of sexuation. The constitutive exception which establishes the universality of masculinity is the mythical father of Freud's *Totem and Taboo*, the primordial father who (allegedly) enjoyed completely and possessed all women before he was murdered by his sons. Out of guilt for this (imaginary) patricide, masculine subjects become subject to symbolic castration (inhibition and repression). The transition from the general set of all men to the universal man is thus enabled by the constitutive exception: the universal in this sense is not empirical generality, but is founded in and through the exception.

But in contrast to this, Žižek's Hegelian elaboration of Lacan emphasizes the ethico-political implications of the feminine subject position. The feminine subject position implies a different relation to the big Other (the signifying order) than that implied by the masculine subject position. The feminine logic of non-all exposes the fictional nature of symbolic universality; the feminine logic reveals the lack in the symbolic order. Feminine subjects disclose the imposture of the Master by showing that the phallic signifier is ultimately subordinated to the feminine logic of non-all. The feminine subject is the subject as such, because the feminine universality (as non-all) makes possible the masculine logic of symbolic universality, which is founded on a constitutive exception. Masculine subjectivity is a reaction to – or an *exception* to – feminine subjectivity, in the sense that a masculine subject experiences a feminine subject as if she

111

were the object cause of desire, the *objet petit a*. It is the *objet petit a* that serves as the subject's defense against symbolic castration. In the big Other – the intersubjective, symbolic register – *objet petit a* functions as the remainder of Real enjoyment, the *jouissance* that is the repressed, traumatic underside of the Master-Signifier.

Once we recognize the lack in symbolic "reality," we realize that it is the *objet petit a*, and not the phallic signifier, that functions as the condition of both possibility and impossibility for symbolic universality. The inconsistency in the symbolic order that *objet petit a* (is imagined to) remedy is the parallax gap on which masculine universality is wrecked: in the masculine logic, symbolic concepts are not really universal; they are supplemented by fantasies of completeness. We can never say the whole truth, not because there aren't enough words, but because words are not enough. This can help us see why Žižek argues in *Metastases* (as in his other works) that the universal is not conceptual; instead, we must conceive of universality as a struggle for conceptualization. As the remainder of repressed enjoyment, *objet petit a* is the underside of the symbolic register. It is because of this originary repression that Žižek emphasizes the distinction between, on the one hand, the exclusion of the Real that opens up the empty place of masculine universality and, on the other hand, the subsequent struggles for hegemony of different particular contents to occupy this place of the Master-Signifier.

In the last chapter of *Metastases*, and in the book's appendix, Žižek argues that nationalistic mobilizations involve the element of fantasy at work in ideology. He reiterates his claim that the cause of the West's failure to end the suffering in Sarajevo during the Bosnian conflict was our fixation on the fantasy image of "the Balkan victim." Our intervention was inadequate because of our unconscious desire to *maintain* the ideologically charged image of the helpless victim, reduced to the level of animal suffering. This explains why

> the West provided just enough humanitarian aid for the city to survive, exerted just enough pressure on the Serbs to prevent them from occupying the city; yet this pressure was not strong enough to break the siege and allow the city to breathe freely – as if the unavowed desire was to preserve Sarajevo in a kind of atemporal freeze, between the two deaths, in the guise of a living dead, a victim eternalized in its suffering. (*Metastases*, p. 213)

Right-wing power (and the masculine logic which underlies it) is held in place by an obscene, phantasmatic underside. Žižek shows that beneath the public law, the superego functions as the injunction to enjoy, to adopt the mantle of the (mythical) primordial father of unbridled *jouissance*. This injunction to transgress, this obscene underside of the public law, sustains the "triumph" of liberal, global capitalism. Nationalistic mobilizations involve a relationship toward a phantasmatic Thing, which represents the incarnation of enjoyment. How is the illusion of community sustained today in a world disrupted by the power struggles inherent to global capitalism? In short, the sense of community is *sustained by racist fantasy*. Racial tensions result from imagining that some other group threatens our enjoyment, or has a privileged relationship to enjoyment. Why do white racists in the USA say that "All 'blacks' look alike"? White racists do not really look at African Americans; they do not want to see the Other.[2] Many white racist workers in the USA imagine that they are part of the same "community" with the wealthy elite that exploits workers and despises "white trash."

But in spite of our alleged freedoms today, we cynical, postmodern subjects – finding ourselves overwhelmed by the injunction to transgress and the burden of choosing every aspect of our very existence – compensate for the decline in symbolic efficacy by voluntarily subjecting ourselves to ever new forms of constraint: in short, we demand that the Other act on our behalf. Instead of recognizing that Capital itself is the ultimate power of deterritorialization, we blame the disintegration of symbolic order on some (religious, racial, ethnic) Other. This "postmodern racism" is inherent to the multiculturalist and (allegedly) tolerant reduction of the sphere of politics proper to the clash of cultures. When all conflicts are presupposed to arise from cultural or ethnic differences, we not only miss the true causes of the conflict. More seriously, the presupposition functions so as to depoliticize all problems: the result is a cynical subject. This is why the resigned, postmodern subject of late capitalism views anyone with political principles as a dangerous fanatic. Moreover, as Žižek has argued in more recent writings, "the opposition between rightist populism and liberal tolerance is a false one."[3] In other words, democratic openness is based on exclusion, and right-wing populism and liberal tolerance are two sides of the same coin. This explains why there are forms of racism that involve a rejection of Muslims, for example, *with the false claim that all Muslims are racist.*

[2] See Ralph Ellison, *Invisible Man* (New York: Vintage Books, 1995).
[3] See Slavoj Žižek, "A Vile Logic to Anders Breivik's Choice of Target," online at http://www.guardian.co.uk/commentisfree/2011/aug/08/anders-behring-breivik-pim-fortuyn. Žižek argues that Breivik's "vile logic" exemplifies the widening intersection of right-wing populism with liberal tolerance and political correctness.

This implicit moment of racism in liberal "tolerance" is also manifested in the way that the worldwide triumph of liberal democracy has led to the development of a new ideological formation, the universalization of the fantasy image of the helpless victim:

> So the much-advertised liberal-democratic "right to difference" and anti-Eurocentrism appear in their true light: the Third World other is recognized as a victim – that is to say, *in so far as he is a victim.* The true object of anxiety is the other no longer prepared to play the role of victim – such an other is promptly denounced as a "terrorist," a "fundamentalist," and so on. The Somalis, for example, undergo a true Kleinian splitting into a "good" and a "bad" object – on the one hand the good object: passive victims, suffering starving children and women; on the other the bad object: fanatical warlords who care more for their power or their ideological goals than for the welfare of their own people. The good other dwells in the anonymous passive universality of a victim – the moment we encounter an actual/active other, there is always something with which to reproach him: being patriarchal, fanatical, intolerant … (*Metastases*, p. 215)

All of this supports Žižek's initial, provocative claim, which at first seemed so outrageous, that unconscious enjoyment was the cause of the West's indecision during the Bosnian war. It is the enjoyment provided by ideological formations – such as the fantasy image of the victim – that explains the failure of Western intervention in the Bosnian conflict.

8

The Indivisible Remainder: On Schelling and Related Matters

The primary aim of this book is to expose the repressed Real as the "symptomal kernel" of relations of domination. Žižek shows how the power of capitalist ideology is consolidated through our unreflective complicity in it. How does Žižek follow through on this insight? He emphatically does not resort to the typical leftist strategy of simply undermining or subverting order. Instead, Žižek investigates the question of how order first emerges from disorder. What split or alienation within subjectivity allows the hegemonic ideological order to maintain itself? Žižek develops the psychoanalytic insight that the unconscious figure of the father is a *falsification*: the version of the father figure (e.g., God, or the capitalist Master) that informs our unconscious behaviors is a *père-version*, an imposter. It is this imaginary father figure which allows us to find enjoyment through our symptom. In developing his account of the split subject, Žižek articulates the hidden, materialist dimension in Schelling's *Weltalter* drafts as well as in Hegelian dialectic. He then argues that a reinvigorated dialectical materialism – informed by Lacanian psychoanalytic theory – enables us to discern the way beyond ideology. Dialectical materialism informs emancipatory politics by showing that the subject as such is the "part of no part" of the body politic. In sum, the subject as such is *proletarian*: the crises of late capitalism make all of us substanceless subjectivity, "proletarians" who are alienated from our own symbolic reality.

Every Organization of Sense, every universal conceptual scheme by means of which we endeavor to comprehend reality, is in itself – at its most fundamental, for structural reasons and not merely due to contingent circumstances – biased, out of balance, "crazy," minimally "paranoiac"

Žižek: A Reader's Guide, First Edition. Kelsey Wood.
© 2012 John Wiley & Sons, Inc. Published 2012 by John Wiley & Sons, Inc.

(as the early Lacan would have put it): its imposition disturbs the "natural order of things" and throws the universe off balance. In other words, there is no neutral Universality: every Universality, every attempt at All, at a global comprehension, bears the indelible mark of a "pathological" exclusiveness of One – that is, hinges on the "partiality" of its position of enunciation. So, again, it is not sufficient to say that no conceptual structure is perfectly neutral, that it fails to comprehend reality in a truly impartial way; the point is, rather, that the status of this "bias" is a priori, structural."

—Žižek, *The Indivisible Remainder:*
On Schelling and Related Matters, p. 76

One of Žižek's most theoretically speculative books is *The Indivisible Remainder: On Schelling and Related Matters* (1996).[1] In *Indivisible*, Žižek clarifies his version of dialectical materialism by investigating F. W. J. von Schelling's struggle in *Die Weltalter* (*The Ages of the World*) to mediate the contradiction in metaphysics between idealism and materialism.

Kant left to his German idealist followers (Fichte, Schelling, Hegel) a notion of things-in-themselves (noumena) as the negativity intrinsic to any attempted dialectical synthesis. In other words, because we have no access to things-in-themselves, our knowledge of both material objects and of human subjects is limited to phenomena as appearances or things-for-us. Schelling further develops this dialectical negativity or incompleteness by clarifying the way the identity of *anything* is split, alienated, and "outside" of itself. To summarize, for Schelling and Lacan, any synthesis (identity) involves an indivisible remainder that undermines it. Identity is always divided or split; any identity implies a contradiction. In *Indivisible*, Žižek develops this account of alienated identity and articulates the materialist aspect of German Idealism, primarily focusing on the second of Schelling's three *Weltalter* drafts but with reference also to Hegelian dialectics.

Underlying Žižek's analysis of alienation in this book is Lacan's distinction between imaginary, symbolic, and Real. Again, the imaginary register is manifested primarily in fantasies of wholeness and unity which mask Real disunity (e.g., the "fragmentary" character of the infant's experience). At the origin of such fantasies of completeness is the narcissistic identification with the visual image of one's body which occurs in

---

[1] Unless otherwise stated, page references for this work are to the following edition: *The Indivisible Remainder: On Schelling and Related Matters* (London and New York: Verso, 2007).

the mirror phase of early childhood development. But any self-identity based on images is alienated insofar as imaginary identification is externalized and egotistic; in fact, the ego remains throughout life a fantasy of completeness and consistency. However, unlike the imaginary ego, the symbolic identity of the subject is a way of relating to the social networks constituted through language and the social prohibitions which regulate desire. The symbolic register involves intersubjective, rule-governed practices such as linguistic chains of signifiers (e.g. words) which are defined by relations of difference. But what we experience as reality is an imaginary-symbolic fiction: any symbolic universe involves fantasies of wholeness which facilitate the comforting illusion of unified reality. The development of the symbolic register of subjectivity does *not* remedy the alienation of imaginary identification: with the acquisition of language, the subject is further alienated in the signifier. If the imaginary ego is alienation in an image, then the symbolic subject is alienation in the signifier, the word.

Upon entering the symbolic register, the Real of subjectivity is externalized in the word. Of course, for Schelling, this "transubstantiation" in the word has Christian-mystical connotations (the Fall from paradise into knowledge; the Word which, in the beginning, was with God and was God, etc.). But Žižek's interpretation is not focused on theology or mysticism; he remains orientated toward the implications for metapsychology, philosophy, and the critique of ideology. But – regarding the subject's alienation in the signifier – it is important to note that if the process of subjectivization reduces the subject to a circulating signifier in the symbolic order, nonetheless the subject as such (as feminine) involves the hysterical questioning of symbolic identity, authority, and ideological interpellation.

Žižek argues that Schelling, like Lacan, offers an account of how the *Ideal* – thought – arises from the *Real* (from the clash of presymbolic drives). Although the Lacanian-Schellingian Real designates the limit of the symbolic register, in addition it indicates the beyond of reality. One way to see that the Real is not a purely negative category involves desire. Although desire is manifested as the inconsistency of the symbolic order, it is the Real as drive that serves as the "driving force" of desiring (*Indivisible*, p. 97). If we assert that symbolic reality conceals the traumatic Real (e.g., the presymbolic vortex of drives) then this implies that the symbolic arises from the Real, as a reaction to the Real. This primordial repression of the Real means that the Real of drive permeates but eludes symbolic reality. But it is important to remember that the Real does not "exist," it insists. This implies that although the Real – as the libidinal dynamics of drive – accounts for the incompleteness of the symbolic, nonetheless, the Real is constituted retroactively, as the "indivisible remainder" of symbolization. Put simply, insofar as the Real cannot be symbolized or imagined (cannot be incorporated into reality), it is "impossible," and this impossibility of the Real imparts to it a horrifying quality:

> The Ground is [...] the traumatic Thing, the point of simultaneous attraction and repulsion, which stands for the vortex of Life itself threatening to draw us into its depressive abyss. And does not this pre-predicative vortex of the Real point directly towards the Lacanian *jouissance*? Does not Schelling himself determine the Real [*das Reale*] as the circular movement of "irrational" (i.e. pre-logical, pre-symbolic) drives which find satisfaction in the very "meaningless" repetition of their circular path? For Schelling (as well as for Lacan) this Real is the Limit, the ultimate obstacle on account of which every "semantic idealism," every attempt to deploy the Absolute as a self-enclosed matrix generating all possible significations of Being, is destined to fail. (*Indivisible*, p. 75)

Beneath what we experience as reality there is an occluded, horrifying vortex of Real drive. Žižek argues that Schelling was the first philosopher to recognize that the incompleteness of imaginary-symbolic reality is linked to the Real. But significantly, even more primordial than the pre-symbolic ground of Real drive, there is an irrational abyss of free will that is the potential for radical evil. Symbolic reality is a defense formation against both the Real of primordial drive and the madness of ungrounded, free decision.

What are the implications of the Real for philosophy? Simply put, the problem that haunts idealism is that there is no reality outside the mind. By contrast, dialectical materialism refines this problematic and shows why there can be *no mind outside reality*: that is, there is no metalanguage, no God's-eye view, no perspective of all perspectives. For dialectical materialism, any totality is always contradictory/inconsistent (this holds for the subject, the object, and any "relation" between them). Because the Real of drive undermines any attempt to achieve dialectical synthesis, there can be no overarching synthesis which unifies various symbolic practices. Furthermore, any particular symbolic "system" (e.g. theoretical physics) is, in fact, divided *against itself* by the Real. Even further, any individual human subject's symbolic identity is irremediably divided against itself. There is no mind outside of symbolic reality, but if we analyze the metonymical sliding of signifiers into one another, we uncover fantasy as well as the primordially repressed Real, because the registers of the imaginary and of the Real permeate the symbolic reality.

Žižek locates the origin of dialectical materialism in a particular moment or problematic in the philosophy of Schelling (cf. *Weltalter*, second draft, 1813). In his introduction, Žižek writes: "This book was written in the hope that it will contribute to our perception of Schelling's *Weltalter* drafts as one of the seminal works of materialism" (*Indivisible*, p. 7). Žižek interprets the second of Schelling's three accounts of the genesis of God as prefiguring the Lacanian account of the origins and structure of subjectivity: "In short, Schelling's *Weltalter* is to be read as a *metapsychological* work in the strict Freudian sense of the term" (p. 9). Žižek – who, in other texts, describes himself as "a fighting atheist" – reads Schelling's account of the origin of God as an allegory for the origin of the subject; therefore it is unsurprising that he calls Schelling's notion of God "a fantasy-formation at its purest" (p. 22), and claims it is "a 'psychotic,' mad God" (p. 24). This indicates that one of the "blind spots" in Schelling involves ideology: "it may well be that the 'official' ideology of our society is Christian spirituality, but its actual foundation is none the less the idolatry of the Golden Calf: money" (*Indivisible*, p. 4). Readers approaching *Indivisible* for the first time might find it helpful to think of Schelling's "God" as Žižek's Real (the fundamental split of subjectivity).

Žižek views Schelling in terms of Fredric Jameson's notion of "vanishing mediator," the missing link between two situations or symbolizations: a vanishing mediator facilitates the transition between two terms and then disappears. Žižek's subject (as Real) is, like Schelling's God, the vanishing mediator between two situations. Before the beginning, in unbearable anxiety and *jouissance*, the subject as Real is the psychotic antagonism between the will to contraction and the will to expansion. And although this subject of drive is already a "one," the true beginning of subjectivity is the ascent from drive to desire – from the Real to the symbolic – or, in Schelling's terms, from God to the Word. But significantly, even after the ascent from the Real to the symbolic, at the limit of existence we encounter the horrible Real. For this reason, the subject can never consciously experience the fundamental fantasy which constitutes and guarantees the kernel of her being (cf. Žižek, *The Plague of Fantasies*, p. 121, *The Parallax View*, p. 171). In the encounter with the Real, symbolic identity and reality can disintegrate; i.e., any "normal" neurotic is potentially psychotic.

Žižek delineates the contours of the Lacanian Real through analysis of Schelling's investigation of the problem of free will versus determinism. The investigation into freedom provides insight into the incommensurability that is the Real: "For Schelling, then, the primordial, radically contingent fact, a fact which can in no way be accounted for, is freedom itself, a freedom bound by nothing, a freedom which, in a sense, *is* Nothing; and the problem is, rather, how this Nothing of the abyss of primordial freedom becomes entangled in the causal chains of reason" (*Indivisible*, p. 16). Significantly, Schelling asserts a radical split between consciousness and freedom: the free act, as the essence of the human, is situated in the Real kernel of subjectivity which precedes consciousness (p. 18). In an unconscious, primordial act of decision, potential subjectivity "contracts" its being.

In the formation of self, this originary contraction must occur before the expansion that signifies the effective freedom of the subject; this originary contraction is a condition of possibility for any symbolic differentiation. The transition from the Real of drive to the intersubjective network of the symbolic is a contraction in the guise of an expansion: "In the (verbal) sign, I – as it were – *find myself outside myself*, I posit my unity outside myself, in a signifier which represents me" (*Indivisible*, p. 43). This contraction/expansion into symbolic rules is a defensive masking of the disquieting abyss of primordial freedom. Thus guidelines make possible the subject's effective (limited) freedom: "Finally, when all is said and done, this is what *self-identity* is about: a self-identity is never fully transparent – the more it is 'self-,' the more it implies a minimum of opaque contraction which holds it together and thus prevents it from dispersing" (p. 26).

There is no "mind" outside reality, but a subject cannot be reduced to its actual presence (in symbolic subjectivization). Throughout her existence, a subject's "project," the possibility of what she might become, is her very existence. This means that freedom is "outside of" the mind. Žižek argues that it is the act of freedom as *unconscious* decision that opens up the lived temporality of the subject:

> the "unconscious" is not primarily the Real in its opposition to the Ideal; in its most radical dimension, the "unconscious" is, rather, the very act of decision/differentiation by means of which the Ideal establishes itself in its opposition to the Real and imposes its Order on to the Real, the act by means of which the rotary motion of drives is "repressed" into the eternal past. (*Indivisible*, pp. 76–7)

The transition from the Real to the symbolic is the act of decision or differentiation through which the subject resolves the agonizing, psychotic clash of drives, and breaks out of this vicious cycle into temporal succession. The chaotic pulsation of drives, as Real, is always already past: not once present and now past, but *past from the beginning of time*; that is, temporality begins with the ascent from the Real of antagonistic drives into symbolic differentiation. The split of subjectivity is the present: the present is the repression of antagonistic drives through symbolic differentiation: "The undifferentiated pulsation of drives is thus supplanted by the stable network of differences which sustains the self-identity of the differentiated entities: in its most elementary dimension, the Word is the medium of differentiation" (*Indivisible*, p. 33).

To recapitulate: the beginning proper is a free act of decision that differentiates between past and present and thereby represses the unbearable anxiety of the preceding closed circuit of drives. Schelling's ground (*Grund*) of existence is the clash of primordial drives; but "beneath" this ground, however, is a more primal ground (*Urgrund*), which is the indifference and nothingness of the abyssal freedom. The ascent to subjectivity begins in a primordial contraction, as an anonymous abyss of freedom gets caught up in a rotary antagonism of contraction and expansion, a whirlpool of opposed drives. This Real vortex of drives is irrational, but it is constitutive of rationality. Reason – and the symbolic in general – arises through the disavowal of drive and the alienation in the word: the beginning occurs when one finds the word which breaks the vicious cycle of conflicting drives. Thus the subject that results from symbolic subjectivization remains irremediably alienated from itself:

> The crucial point not to be missed here is that in so far as we are dealing with *Subject*, [it is] the contraction of the subject outside himself, in an external sign, which resolves the tension, the "inner dispute," of contraction and expansion. The paradox of the Word is therefore that its emergence resolves the tension of the pre-symbolic antagonism, but at a price: the Word, the contraction of the Self outside the Self, involves an irretrievable externalization-alienation [...]. (*Indivisible*, p. 46)

Although in *Indivisible*, Žižek employs Schelling's Christian-mystical terminology, it is important to recognize that he discerns – behind this terminology – Schelling's philosophical insight into nature and the limits of scientific discourse. Schelling anticipates dialectical materialism by apprehending that the incompleteness of formal systems implies the incompleteness of reality. This is why Žižek argues in Part II of *Indivisible* that developments in quantum physics support dialectical materialism by showing that *the universe itself, not just our knowledge of it*, is incomplete. For Žižek there is a homology between the subject (especially its abyssal free will) and the incompleteness of the quantum universe. Because reality is symbolic, in nature itself we encounter the constitutive deadlock of symbolization.

But what are the implications of this constitutive "deadlock of symbolization" for Žižek's critique of ideology? How does ideology relate to the alienated self and irreducible symbolic inconsistency? The answer is surprisingly simple: he utilizes this very inconsistency as the basis for his critique of ideology. That is, instead of resorting to the typical leftist strategy of subverting order, Žižek goes to the root of the problem by investigating the question as to how order first emerges from disorder. What split or alienation within subjectivity allows an ideological order to maintain itself? In *Indivisible*, Žižek's answer is that the "symptomal kernel" of ideology allows us to find *jouissance* through our symptom. If *jouissance* is the painful satisfaction the subject obtains from his symptom, then we participate in sustaining the very system of domination that oppresses us. We rely on the figure of the dominating Master so that we can avoid the impasse of desire:

> the "ideological" is not only the false, mystifying presentation of raw coercion as "genuine" domination and authentic respect for the Master, but also – perhaps even more so – the illusory misrecognition of the inner "hold" a figure of authority exerts upon us, that is, the notion that we are merely yielding to external coercion when effectively, at the level of the unconscious libidinal economy, we need the Master in order to avoid the deadlock of our desire. (*Indivisible*, p. 207)

In such ways Žižek shows how our unreflective complicity in the very power relations that oppress us consolidates the power of capitalist ideology. He does not offer any neutral and disengaged, "objective" resolution of social antagonism; however, Žižek's dialectical materialism *does* establish the existence of ideology and *does* subject it to critique.

The successful functioning of ideology depends on the stupidity of its subjects. But more and more today – in an era of postmodern cynicism – ideology can openly display "the secret of its functioning (its constitutive idiocy, which traditional, pre-cynical ideology had to keep secret) *without in the least affecting its efficiency*" (*Indivisible*, p. 201). Because the recognition of Real antagonism is not ideology, dialectical materialism is capable of exposing ideology to critique; dialectical materialism can expose the workings of ideology *without* espousing ideology. It does this by showing how the imaginary register produces fantasies of wholeness which mask the (irreducible, Real) antagonism inherent to the symbolic big Other.

Fantasy conceals the inconsistency in the symbolic order and occludes the constitutive void in the Other. Ideological fantasy masks the lack, the (allegedly) "lost" *jouissance*, which results upon language acquisition and entry into the symbolic register. One such fantasy of wholeness in ideology today is related to "nature" in its function as the Master-Signifier:

> in ideology, opposites coincide: both the New Age "holistic" notion of man as a part of the natural-spiritual global process, and the notion of man as derailed nature, as an entity "out of joint," are ideological – what both notions "repress" is the fact that *there is no (balanced, self-enclosed) Nature* to be thrown out of joint by man's *hubris* (or to whose harmonious Way man has to adapt). (*Indivisible*, p. 235, note 31)

Ideological fantasy occludes the incompleteness of reality, and thereby lures subjects to imagine and to behave as though it is possible (for some Other) to access the *jouissance* we lost when we became subjects. Racist fantasy, for example, leads subjects to behave as though "they" are threatening "our" *jouissance*. But the symbolic big Other is inherently antagonistic; therefore there is no unambiguous answer to the question of desire: "What does the Other want from me?" Ideology is any set of symbolic practices that (explicitly or implicitly) offers answers to this unanswerable question.

And finally, the possibility of traversing the fantasy (for example, in the act of a revolutionary collective of subjects) lies in the irremediable split of the symbolic register of subjectivity. In order to apprehend this Real that is the indivisible remainder of symbolization, the subject as self-relating negativity must be distinguished from the process of subjectivization and ideological interpellation:

> That is to say: the very aim of the psychoanalytic process is, of course, to induce the subject to renounce the "secret treasure" which forms the kernel of his phantasmic identity; this renunciation of *agalma*, the "going-through the fantasy [*traversée du fantasme*]," is strictly equivalent to the act of "subjective destitution." However, the subject prior to interpellation–subjectivization is not this imaginary depth which allegedly precedes the process of interpellation, but the very void which remains once the phantasmic space is emptied of its content – when, that is, to paraphrase Mallarmé's *Un coup de dés*, nothing takes place but the place itself. The process of interpellation fills out an empty place which must already be here if this process is to take place. (*Indivisible*, pp. 166–7)

In other words, the freedom to overcome ideology arises from the very gap which ideological fantasy attempts to cover over. Ideology is overcome through the recognition of, and engagement with, the very antagonism and lack that ideology tries to conceal. In sum, no process of symbolic subjectivization can ever really resolve the anxiety provoked by the hysterical question regarding the desire of the Other: since the subject as such is the hysterical question, and since any symbolic reality is inherently inconsistent, the repressed Real will always return to disrupt symbolic order.

9

The Plague of Fantasies

The "plague of fantasies" refers primarily to the flood of audiovisual representations to which subjects are exposed today. These images blur the subject's reasoning and facilitate ideological manipulation. Žižek suggests that of all the antagonisms that characterize our epoch, the central antagonism is the one between abstraction on the one hand, and, on the other, pseudo-concrete images that are charged with phantasmatic significance. Žižek demonstrates that the (allegedly) "post-ideological" experience of subjects today remains structured by abstraction: his examples of abstraction here include digitalization as well as speculative market relations. Žižek relates these developments in symbolic practices to the Real of enjoyment and to the Real of capital. In addition to the inherent ideological element at work in symbolic practices, the fantasies that deluge today's subject also serve an ideological function, namely the manipulation of the subject's relation to Real *jouissance*. Žižek develops the Lacanian notion of fantasy and illustrates through examples how fantasy supports our sense of reality. There is no reality without fantasy; symbolic order is dependent on the fantasy that supplements it. Fantasy supplements symbolic reality by providing a sense of closure or completeness. Ideology not only permeates everyday life, but more importantly, the phantasmatic images that sustain an ideological edifice are externalized as intersubjective, symbolic practices. However, because the locus of psychoanalytic knowledge is the intersection of the symbolic law and its obverse – the obscene superego injunction to transgress – Lacanian theory provides a way to break out of the vicious cycle of desire supported by law and its transgression. The critique of ideology shows that the Other does not threaten our enjoyment; the Other does not possess what we lack. This recognition allows the possibility

Žižek: A Reader's Guide, First Edition. Kelsey Wood.
© 2012 John Wiley & Sons, Inc. Published 2012 by John Wiley & Sons, Inc.

of traversing the fantasy, encountering the unrepresentable Real, and, through the Lacanian act, overcoming the manipulations of ideology. In sum, Lacanian theory is not simply a pessimistic assertion of the eternal status of ideology: against this reading, Žižek affirms that it is possible to twist out of the masculine logic of ideological subjectivization and actualize the feminine Real of subjectivity through identification with the excluded, abject, and lacking Other.

> *If we subtract fantasy from reality, then reality itself loses its consistency and disintegrates. To choose between "either accepting reality or choosing fantasy" is wrong: if we really want to change or escape our social reality, the first thing to do is change our fantasies that make us fit this reality."*
> —Žižek, "Return of the Natives," in *New Statesman*,
> 4 March 2010

One of Žižek's most sustained engagements with Lacanian psychoanalytic theory is *The Plague of Fantasies* (1997).[1] In *Plague*, Žižek analyzes the flood of pseudo-concrete images that bombard contemporary subjects. By analyzing postmodern culture in light of Lacanian concepts like fantasy, the unconscious, the Name of the Father, symbolic castration, *objet petit a*, desire, gaze, fetishism, and the Real of *jouissance*, Žižek formulates an incisive critique of liberal capitalist ideology.

The fundamental insight of Žižek's dialectical materialism is that any identity is displaced from itself. Žižek articulates this alienation in terms of the three fundamental registers of the Lacanian theoretical space: the Real, the symbolic, and the imaginary. The imaginary register is the locus of the emergence of the ego in the mirror phase. The imaginary involves fantasies of consistency (such as the ego) with which we identify. By contrast, the symbolic register is the network of language and communication. But any symbolic order proves to be incomplete and inconsistent, and the Real is manifested as the inherent limit of the symbolic. Thus belief is symbolic and inconsistent, whereas knowledge is Real and involves the recognition of irreducible inconsistency: "the status of the (Lacanian) big Other *qua* symbolic institution is that of belief (trust), not that of knowledge, since belief is symbolic and knowledge is real" (*Plague*, p. 107). Again, the Real is ultimately the focus of all Žižek's analyses. We experience reality insofar as some traumatic Real is primordially repressed:

---

[1] Unless otherwise stated, page references for this work are to the following edition: *The Plague of Fantasies* (London and New York: Verso, 1997).

126

What distinguishes man from animals is thus again the excessive fixation on the trauma (of the lost object, of the scene of some shattering *jouissance*, etc.); what sets the dynamism that pertains to the human condition in motion is the very fact that some traumatic X eludes every symbolization. "Trauma" is that kernel of the Same which returns again and again, disrupting any symbolic identity. (*Plague*, p. 95)

Fantasies of wholeness mask Real trauma or antagonism by filling the gaps of the symbolic universe. However, with the inevitable return of the repressed Real, one's symbolic identity is disrupted: to encounter the Real is to experience the disintegration of reality.

But *jouissance* is Real, and without *jouissance*, life loses its meaning. As surplus enjoyment, *jouissance* is not pleasure: it is enjoyment beyond the pleasure principle; enjoyment is an odd fascination or pleasure-in-pain, of which the subject is usually unaware. Fantasy structures and animates *jouissance*, while simultaneously serving as a protective shield against its lethal excess. Every ideology relies upon and manipulates an economy of *jouissance*, and psychoanalysis enhances the critique of ideology by revealing how surplus enjoyment operates on various levels. As with all of Žižek's books and lectures, *Plague* functions like the intervention of the psychoanalyst in the clinic: Žižek's aim is not simply to change the beliefs of his analysand (his reader). He also provokes us into confronting the Real of enjoyment and traversing the ideological fantasy that binds us to liberal global capitalism.

Fantasy is an "unwritten framework which tells us how we are to understand the letter of the Law" (*Plague*, p. 29). In chapter 1, Žižek discusses seven features of fantasy: (1) fantasy's transcendental schematism, (2) the intersubjective character of fantasy, (3) fantasy as concealment of antagonism through narrative, (4) the "fall" into symbolic castration and Law, (5) fantasy as staged for the gaze of the Other, (6) the inherent transgression and violence of symbolic Law, and (7) the empty gesture.

(1) Fantasy's transcendental schematism   Fantasy is not belief: fantasy is imaginary while belief is symbolic. But neither is fantasy a private, hallucinatory escape; instead, fantasy is constitutive of symbolic reality. The imaginary ego is a fantasy of completeness and consistency, but the symbolic subject is irremediably divided in its very formation. Becoming a subject involves accepting "symbolic castration"; to accept symbolic castration is to accept that one can never be the phallus – the missing object of desire – for the mother. After the acquisition of language, access to *jouissance* is mediated by the symbolic order. For the symbolic subject, it seems (in retrospect) that the presymbolic self was the bodily incarnation of enjoyment, as if the opening of the symbolic dimension evacuated *jouissance* from the body; it seems that the word is somehow the murder of the thing, that symbolic concepts cannot adequately represent "the stuff of life."

The symbolic big Other, the intersubjective, social network of signifiers, is structured around a void (the repressed Real). Fantasy provides the coordinates of reality by filling the gap of symbolic inconsistency: "One of the most elementary definitions of ideology, therefore, is: a symbolic field which contains such a filler holding the place of some structural impossibility" (*Plague*, p. 76). Žižek interprets the Lacanian thesis that "truth has the structure of a fiction" to mean that symbolic reality is constituted through the primordial exclusion of some Real trauma or antagonism. This is why symbolic reality, like truth, is never "whole." Along these lines, the locus of ideological fantasy is not some private, inner belief. On the contrary, ideological fantasy is externalized, in the sincerity of (unconscious) intersubjective practices: "not in what people think that they are doing, but in their actual social activity itself" (p. 105). In this sense, "the truth is out there." To encounter the truth, we do not plumb the deeps of the mind; instead we analyze that which is *externalized* in the inconsistency of sociosymbolic practices. Even the analysis of architectural designs may reveal the Real social antagonism that is masked by the hegemonic ideology, such as:

> the Soviet Union of the 1930s, which put on top of a flat multistorey office building a gigantic statue of the idealized New Man, or a couple: in the span of a couple of years, the tendency to flatten the office building (the actual workplace for living people) more and more became clearly discernible, so that it changed increasingly into a mere pedestal for the larger-than-life statue – does not this external, material feature of architectural design reveal the "truth" of the Stalinist ideology in which actual, living people are reduced to instruments, sacrificed as the pedestal for the spectre of the future New Man, an ideological monster which crushes actual living men under his feet? (*Plague*, pp. 3–4)

In our age of postmodern cynicism, subjects are aware that the symbolic order is inconsistent, and yet, perversely, behave in ways that ignore this incoherence; Žižek's term for this is "fetishist disavowal." By occluding the lack that underlies desire, the fantasy framework allows the simultaneous denial and recognition of symbolic castration. Fantasy is a kind of fixation that masks the displacement that *is* the symbolic subject.

(2) Fantasy is intersubjective   Fantasy does not simply stage unrealized desires, but teaches us how to desire. Fantasy tells me what I am for the Other: fantasy is our attempt to form an identity that would make us an object of the Other's desire. The object of fantasy (*objet petit a*) is that imagined treasure within me, on account of which I perceive myself as worthy of the Other's desire (*Plague*, p. 8). Intersubjective, ideological fantasy constitutes reality by offering an imaginary meaning in response to the Real of trauma or antagonism; it structures enjoyment so as to make us accept social relations of domination, to keep us attached to the Master (pp. 48–9). This can help us to grasp why Žižek argues that racist fantasy (e.g., the anti-Semitic figure of the Jew) is never the positive cause of social antagonism; social antagonism is Real and irreducible. In sum, racist fantasy is an attempt to answer the question of what society expects from me: for example, "We" must prevent "Them" from stealing "Our" enjoyment. Alternatively, racist fantasy can manifest as: "They enjoy in strange and alien ways."

(3) Fantasy conceals antagonism through narrative   Žižek's analyses of the psychology of racism do not contrast racism as such with color prejudice as a manifestation of racism. Thus Žižek argues that "it has been the Jews who have been chosen as the object of racism *par excellence*".[2] In *Plague*, Žižek develops an account of how racist fantasy conceals Real antagonism through narrative. The racist figure of the Jew, for example – as the alleged cause of social imbalance – is a phantasmatic attempt to cover over the disturbing Real of social antagonism. Because any symbolic network, any big Other, is inherently antagonistic, there is no consistent answer to the hysterical question: "What does the Other desire of me?" In response to this unanswerable question, intersubjective fantasy provides a mythical narrative: "fantasy is the primordial form of *narrative*, which serves to occult some original deadlock" (*Plague*, p. 10). The original deadlock (of the Other's desire) is Real; thus the subject's inability to discover a consistent answer to the question of desire exposes the lack in the symbolic register left by the repressed Real. The object of fantasy – *objet petit a* – is an attempt to fill this lack. Hence symbolic desire and Real *jouissance* are inherently antagonistic:

> So how is it possible to couple desire and *jouissance*, to guarantee a minimum of *jouissance* within the space of desire? It is the famous Lacanian *objet petit a* that mediates between the incompatible domains of desire and

2   See Slavoj Žižek, *The Sublime Object of Ideology* (London: Verso, 1989), p. 115. Also see *Jacques Lacan: Critical Evaluations in Cultural Theory*, ed. Slavoj Žižek (London and New York: Routledge, 2003), p. 362.

jouissance. In what precise sense is *objet petit a* the object-cause of desire? The *objet petit a* is not what we desire, what we are after, but, rather, that which sets our desire in motion, in the sense of the formal frame which confers consistency on our desire: [...] *objet petit a* as the cause of desire is nothing other than this formal frame of consistency. (*Plague*, p. 39)

But if we renounce *jouissance* in order to enter into the symbolic register, then doesn't Real enjoyment exist in a substantial way prior to the "fall" into symbolic subjectivity? On the contrary, the paradox which must be accepted here is that in the formation of the subject, we renounce something *we never had*. In other words, the emergence of the object of fantasy strictly coincides with its loss (*Plague*, p. 13). The symbolic (divided) subject has never had full access to *jouissance* and never will, since in the encounter with the Real, symbolic identity disintegrates.

In several of his works, Žižek clarifies a fundamental ambiguity in Lacanian theory by distinguishing between different senses of the Real. Different modes of the Real are the result of different ways of distancing ourselves from "ordinary" reality. This distantiation may involve primarily the imaginary register (the Real as a distorted image), or it may involve primarily the symbolic register (the Real as an empty structure constituted retroactively). Or, in some contexts – Žižek refers here to contemporary art – this distantiation may manifest the Real as Real: the Real "itself." Žižek explains this in an essay called "The Matrix, or Two Sides of Perversion," where he writes:

> The emergence of excremental objects which are out of place is thus strictly correlative to the emergence of the place without any object in it, of the empty frame as such. Consequently, the Real in contemporary art has three dimensions, which somehow repeat within the Real the triad of Imaginary-Symbolic-Real. The Real is first here as the anamorphotic stain, the anamorphotic distortion of the direct image of reality – as a distorted image, as a pure semblance that "subjectivizes" objective reality. Then, the Real is here as the empty place, as a structure, a construction which is never here, experienced as such, but can only be retroactively constructed and has to be presupposed as such – the Real as symbolic construction. Finally, the Real is the obscene excremental Object out of place, the Real "itself." This last Real, if isolated, is a mere fetish whose fascinating/captivating presence masks the structural Real, in the same way that, in the Nazi anti-Semitism, Jew as the excremental Object is the Real that masks the unbearable "structural" Real of the social antagonism. – These three dimensions of the Real result from the three modes to acquire a distance towards "ordinary" reality: one submits this reality to anamorphic distortion; one introduces an

object that has no place in it; one subtracts/erases all content (objects) of reality, so that all that remains is the very empty place these objects were filling in.[3]

This indicates the sense in which the Real is constituted retroactively: renunciation itself creates the spectre of the loss of full enjoyment. This is why, regarding the Real of class antagonism, Žižek writes:

> The repressed past is never known "as such," it can become known only in the very process of its transformation, since the interpretation itself intervenes in its object and changes it: for Marx, the truth about the past (class struggle, the antagonism which permeates the entire past history) can become visible only to a subject caught up in the process of its revolutionary transformation." (*Plague*, pp. 90–91)

Repetition is never the reoccurrence of the identical constellation of all contingent particulars. Pure identity is a fantasy, but the symbolic register is a system of differences. No two symbolic realities are ever identical (because no "one" is identical to itself). But insofar as any symbolic order is constituted through primordial repression, the "sameness" that reoccurs involves the encounter with the repressed Real in ever new, historical conditions.

(4) The "fall" into symbolic castration and Law This account of repetition as the primordial repression constitutive to any symbolic order enables us to understand why symbolic castration – as the prohibition of incestuous enjoyment – is the "loss" of a phantasmatic mother–child union (*Plague*, p. 15). With the development beyond the imaginary ego to the symbolic (castrated) subject, the child is not actually deprived of any of its previous experiences. Instead, a spectral, "purely potential, nonexistent X" is added. In comparison to this phantasmatic, "lost" *jouissance*, actual experiences seem hopelessly inadequate. Thus psychoanalysis transforms misery into the *common unhappiness which results from accepting symbolic castration:* psychopathology results from the refusal of castration. But it is not possible to fully accept symbolic castration; therefore, the position of the neurotic (who accepts castration in an incomplete and inconsistent way) is the closest anyone comes to being "normal." The neurotic merely *represses* castration; this is why it returns in the signifying

---

[3] Slavoj Žižek, "The Matrix, or Two Sides of Perversion," in *Philosophy Today*, Celina, 1999, vol. 43. This essay is available online at http://www.egs.edu/faculty/slavoj-zizek/articles/the-matrix-or-two-sides-of-perversion/.

chain, in his speech and symbolic practices. More seriously, the pervert *disavows* castration, but re-enacts it in fantasy. Most seriously of all, the psychotic behaves as though the (virtual) threat of castration does not exist. This is because the Name or No of the Father is *foreclosed* entirely from the mental universe of the psychotic.

Žižek reveals the link between fantasy and (allegedly transgressive) perversion, by showing how fantasy re-enacts the installation of the symbolic Law, of the Name/No! of the Father:

> the phantasmic narrative does not stage the suspension-transgression of the Law, but *the very act of its installation*, of the intervention of the cut of symbolic castration – what the fantasy endeavors to stage is ultimately the "impossible" scene of castration. For this reason, fantasy as such is, in its very notion, close to perversion: the perverse ritual stages the act of castration, of the primordial loss which allows the subject to enter the symbolic order." (*Plague*, p. 14)

As Žižek points out, it is ironic that the pervert is widely believed to be one who transgresses the public Law, violating the rules of decent, "normal" behavior. But in contrast to this, Žižek's account shows that, in making himself the instrument of the Other's desire – and in assuming that he knows *what it is* that the Other desires – the pervert re-enacts symbolic castration again and again. This shows that, far from being the transgressor *par excellence*, the pervert is, on the contrary, he who "effectively longs for the very rule of Law" (*Plague*, p. 14).

(5) Fantasy is staged for the gaze of the Other As constitutive of desire, fantasy must remain implicit, since fantasy functions as *both* the support of the symbolic order *and* its inherent transgression. The obscene superego injunction to enjoy is bound up with the fantasy that direct access to full *jouissance* is possible and desirable. But Žižek argues that ideological fantasy – like perversion – both acknowledges and disavows symbolic castration. The ultimate perverse fantasy is the fantasy that I am nothing but an instrument of the Other's *jouissance*; I am deprived of my own enjoyment (by symbolic castration), and my role is to ensure the enjoyment of the Other. And insofar as nothing fascinates me more than the Other's gaze, gaze can function as the fetish-object *par excellence* (*Plague*, pp. 103–4). The mother's gaze signifies desire; gaze is how we first encounter the desire of the Other. For subjects, gaze is not seeing with the eye; gaze is the ultimate object of fantasy: "Apropos of a phantasmic scene, the question to be asked is thus always for which gaze is it staged? Which narrative is it destined to support?" (p. 16). But since truth arises through engagement in struggle, the neutral gaze of the innocent observer is nonexistent (*Plague*, p. 18). In sum, the notion of "objectivity" as a kind of disengaged, neutral gaze is a fantasy construction.

(6) Law is transgressive and violent Violence and transgression are inherent to the installation of symbolic order, and since the power edifice is split from within, it is vulnerable. Any discourse of power relies on a mechanism of self-censorship, and power discourse remains operative only if the censorship is *unspoken*. Žižek's example here is the effectiveness of conservative populist political discourse. Today's conservative populism views government itself as an enemy, and serves the interests of the wealthy and powerful elite by keeping the working class divided. The libidinal economy of today's conservative populism thrives by manipulating the racist fantasy (e.g., "They" are stealing "Our" *jouissance*). But for conservative populist discourse to be effective, its racism must remain unspoken. Populist conservatism censors itself and thereby *increases* the effectiveness of its discourse; its implicit racism is more symbolically efficient than overt racism would be.

However, since the symbolic register has more "reality" than the void beneath it, "an appearance is never 'merely an appearance,' it profoundly affects the *actual* sociosymbolic position of those concerned" (*Plague*, p. 26). Therefore, it makes all the difference in the world whether or not some things *remain unspeakable* or whether they become viewed as acceptable: once the big Other knows it, the entire libidinal economy changes. This is why leftists today must ensure that racist, sexist, and similar (right-wing) discourses remain unspeakable:

> Today, in the face of the emergence of new racism and sexism, the strategy should be to *make such enunciations unutterable*, so that anyone relying on them automatically disqualifies himself (like, in our universe, those who refer approvingly to fascism). [...] the position here should be quite unashamedly "dogmatic" and "terrorist": this is *not* a matter for "open, rational, democratic discussion." (*Plague*, p. 26)

In sum, open "democratic" discussion and compromise is *not* an option in the face of the emerging racism and sexism of today's right-wing populists.

(7) The Empty Gesture To prevent the dissolution of the social link, fantasy sustains freedom of choice by *confining* freedom of choice, "by preventing the choice which, although formally allowed, would, if in fact made, ruin the system" (*Plague*, p. 29). One structuring element which reinforces any sociosymbolic order then, is the empty gesture. When a gesture is made that is meant to be rejected, its rejection results in a pact of solidarity: the social link is solidified through what remains unspoken, e.g. the mutual acceptance of unwritten rules. But what happens if the other to whom the offer to be rejected is made actually accepts the offer? Taking the empty gesture seriously reveals that the choice was a forced choice. If the *semblance* of freedom is treated as *actual* freedom, the social link – as the system of domination based on unwritten rules – dissolves. Unwritten rules prevent such choices:

> In other words, the act of taking the empty gesture (the offer to be rejected) literally – to treat the forced choice as a true choice – is, perhaps, one of the ways to put into practice what Lacan calls "traversing the fantasy": in accomplishing this act, the subject suspends the phantasmic frame of unwritten rules which tell him how to choose freely – no wonder the consequences of this act are so catastrophic. (*Plague*, p. 29)

Any social order is vulnerable because the system must formally allow choices which cannot actually be made without dissolving the social link (*Plague*, p. 28). And although fantasy shields us from the Real of surplus enjoyment, fantasy is also a conduit to the Real, for fantasy is permeated by enjoyment. Fantasy *cannot* adequately shield us from the Real, since fantasy also transmits the Real. With the return of the repressed Real and subsequent disintegration of my symbolic identity, I recognize that the only support of my identity as a subject is imaginary, and I undergo subjective destitution (pp. 9–10). Subjective destitution involves acknowledging that *nothing* in me merits the Other's desire. This shattering realization opens the space for the act, in which one risks everything by traversing the fantasy. The hero traverses the fantasy and recognizes that the (imaginary) treasure within her is worthless. She abandons the fake position and identifies with the empty place in the symbolic order, fully assuming the position of the excluded one – even at the risk of life itself (p. 148). Traversing the fantasy through the ethical or political act is only possible against the background of symbolic reality.

However, the act proper is not symbolic; rather, it involves an encounter with the Real. This is one of the reasons why Žižek argues against the postmodernist claim that science is "just another local narrative grounded in its specific pragmatic conditions" (*Plague*, pp. 159–60). Science is open to a kind of negative universality insofar as it relates to the mathematical Real "beneath" the symbolic universe (p. 160). The experience of reality depends on this openness to the *beyond* of the symbolic universe: "Or, to put it in ontological terms: the moment the function of the dark spot which keeps open the space for something for which there is no place in our reality is suspended, we lose our very 'sense of reality'" (*Plague*, p. 163).

10

The Ticklish Subject: The Absent Centre of Political Ontology

Žižek reveals the inadequacy of a presumption shared by the three predominant contemporary philosophical orientations: Heidegger's ontology, French post-political theory, and Anglo-American cultural studies. Because the mainstreams of contemporary Western thinking all conceive Cartesian subjectivity as self-transparent thinking substance, these modes of "overcoming Cartesianism" all miss the hidden truth of subjectivity. The standard interpretation of Descartes' *cogito* – as implying the existence of *res cogitans*, a "thinking thing" – ignores the *negative* dimension of Descartes' project of radical doubt. More generally, Žižek shows that because today's three predominant philosophical orientations do not recognize the philosophical import of Lacanian psychoanalysis, they cannot provide grounds for an effective critique of ideology. Žižek's account of the *cogito* highlights the subject as the question, and opens up the possibility of a way of thinking that is outside of, and more originary than, subjectivization as (mis) recognition. In sum, Žižek shows that subjectivity as such implies the subversion of ideological subjectivization.

The division it mobilizes is not the division between two well-defined social groups, but the division, which runs "diagonally" to the social division in the order of Being, between those who recognize themselves in the call of the Truth-Event, becoming its followers, and those who deny or ignore it."

—Žižek, *The Ticklish Subject*, p. 227

Žižek: A Reader's Guide, First Edition. Kelsey Wood.
© 2012 John Wiley & Sons, Inc. Published 2012 by John Wiley & Sons, Inc.

"A spectre is haunting Western academia … the spectre of the Cartesian subject." So begins Žižek's *The Ticklish Subject: The Absent Centre of Political Ontology* (1999).[1] *The Ticklish Subject* is a nuanced elaboration of Žižek's Hegelian-Lacanian understanding of subjectivity. The book traces through the history of modern philosophy the disavowed truth of subjectivity, or, to put it simply: the hidden functioning of the unconscious. But what, or rather who, is the ticklish subject? His answer is that *you* are: the human subject is the focus of inquiry in this text. One of the primary achievements of *The Ticklish Subject* is to show that even the most intimate personal experience involves a potentially emancipatory universal dimension. The introduction describes the threefold aim of the book:

> The three parts of the book focus on today's three main fields in which subjectivity is at stake: the tradition of German Idealism; post-Althusserian political philosophy; the "deconstructionist" shift from Subject to the problematic of multiple subject-positions and subjectivizations. Each part starts with a chapter on a crucial author whose work represents an exemplary critique of Cartesian subjectivity; a second chapter then deals with the vicissitudes of the fundamental notion that underlies the preceding chapter (subjectivity in German Idealism; political subjectivization; the "Oedipus complex" as the psychoanalytic account of the emergence of the subject). (*Ticklish*, p. 2)

The Ticklish Subject shows the inadequacy of the presumption shared by all three of these contemporary philosophical orientations: Heidegger's ontology, French "post-political" theory, and Anglo-American cultural studies. These interpretations of Descartes' *cogito ergo sum* ignore the functional role of "I think therefore I exist" within the broader project of methodic doubt; consequently, they overlook the radical implications of Descartes' withdrawal inward, away from the socially constituted dimension of personal identity. The three mainstreams of contemporary Western philosophy all conceive Cartesian subjectivity as a self-transparent thinking substance. Because of this – Žižek argues – proponents of these three modes of opposition to (what they refer to as) "Cartesianism" miss the hidden truth of subjectivity: the confrontation with madness, and the subsequent effort to start with a clean slate. Insofar as they overlook the traumatic kernel – the disavowed radical potentiality – that is the

---

[1] Unless otherwise stated, page references for this work, abbreviated *Ticklish*, are to the following edition: *The Ticklish Subject: The Absent Centre of Political Ontology* (London and New York: Verso, 2000).

obverse of "I think, therefore I am," the predominant philosophical notions of subjectivity do not provide adequate grounds for an effective critique of global capitalism's liberal-democratic ideology.

In order to provide these potentially emancipatory grounds, Žižek advances a genealogy of the *divided* subject. He shows how this split or alienated subject was implicit in the philosophies of Descartes, Kant, and Hegel, and explicit in Freudian and Lacanian psychoanalytic theory. He discloses both the disturbing core of subjectivity as well as the hidden, obscene rules that sustain even supposedly civilized cultures: "The point, of course, is not to return to the *cogito* in the guise in which this notion has dominated modern thought (the self-transparent thinking subject), but to bring to light its forgotten obverse, the excessive, unacknowledged kernel of the *cogito*, which is far from the pacifying image of the transparent Self" (*Ticklish*, p. 2). Žižek's approach to consciousness reveals the functioning of an excessive limit-moment of inhuman non-consciousness. It shows in what sense this opaque moment of failure or madness is constitutive of *all* human subjectivity.

In *The Ticklish Subject*, Žižek develops his insight into the materialist dimension of negativity implicit to Hegelian dialectic. The negativity of the Real permeates formal-symbolic systems as a moment of undecidability or paradox; by making thematic the Real as an "irreducibly external element" that is inherent to symbolic subjectivity, Žižek shows the sense in which Hegelian dialectic already prefigured both the materialism of Marx as well as the Freudian notion of the death drives. The Hegelian negativity that indicates human autonomy is manifested in our preoccupation with questions about the meaning of life, and in our capacity to act *against* our own spontaneous inclinations. Along these lines, Freud recognized that an evolutionary or a biological account of human existence seems inadequate to explain why neurotics repeat patterns of behavior that cause them suffering. Such observations led Freud to map the uncanny workings of what he referred to as *Todestriebe* ("death drives"), a self-sabotaging aspect of human existence that seems to elude any biological or physiological account of the human organism, instincts, etc.

Žižek makes manifest the philosophical dignity of Freud's psycho-analytic insight. Against the misguided notion that human beings are always determined by unconscious forces, Žižek asserts the subversive potential of human spontaneity and the possibility of radical autonomy implicit to Freud's notion of death drive. Žižek's account of death drive links this Freudian acknowledgment of human autonomy with the negativity implicit to Hegelian dialectic. Dialectic for Žižek is always ruptured by some nonrational element that prevents the complete, consistent understanding of any whole or totality. He argues that developments in twentieth-century mathematics and science – particularly in quantum mechanics – are in accord with the negativity implicit to Hegelian dialectic: in short, any determinate system is always ruptured from within by inconsistency. The universe itself is incomplete, or "non-all."

Žižek argues that consciousness is always integrally linked to such lack or disruption, to an experience that something has gone wrong. The Lacanian subject does not manifest the "object character" of the imaginary ego. Instead of manifesting the wholeness of an image, the subject is the gap of being: the subject is not a substantial entity but rather a lack of symmetry in the world picture. *The Ticklish Subject* focuses precisely on this fundamental incommensurability, and in the process reveals how imaginary ego identifications may occlude the confrontation with the Real: as a fantasy of consistency or wholeness, the ego can mask the formally undecidable moment that disrupts symbolic practices. Žižek's critique of the capitalist injunction to enjoy hinges on this void at the heart of subjectivity, this non-economic failure of self-interest that lies "beyond the pleasure principle." In regard to traditional problems of metaphysics and epistemology, we might say that Žižek's point is not that we need to resolve the separation between knowing and being; the point is *to think this gap itself* without introducing any imaginary sense of completeness. Žižek shows that the only thing that "unifies" knowing and being is the same lack or inconsistency inherent to both of them.

The first part of *The Ticklish Subject* locates the accomplishment of German Idealism in its affirmation of subjectivity as the confrontation with negativity and madness (cf. Hegel on the "night of the world"). Žižek shows that Heidegger failed to recognize the implications of Hegel's understanding of subjectivity as self-relating negativity, and this explains Heidegger's failure to account for the transition from individual authenticity to the authentic political act of a collective of individuals. Heidegger's Nazism then, was not simply a brief, stupid error, but was systemic throughout his entire corpus, waiting to erupt like a psychotic *passage à l'acte*.

The second part of the book reveals the inadequacy of the notion of subjectivity in recent French political philosophy, especially the work of Alain Badiou. Although Žižek's thinking in many ways accords with Badiou's logic of being and event, nonetheless, Žižek argues that Badiou remains too idealistic. Badiou distinguishes between, on the one hand, being as order or structure and, on the other hand, the *event* as a spontaneous act of creation *ex nihilo*. An event, for example, would be the French Revolution, which cannot simply be explained as emerging causally from pre-existing social conditions. Badiou's distinction between being as the given order and event as the utterly magical moment of truth is homologous to Kant's problematic distinction between *phenomena* (things-for-us) and *noumena* (things-in-themselves). Žižek shows that Badiou provokes questions he leaves unanswered: for example, *how* does being erupt as event? How does the order of being as structure make possible the event in the first place? That is, how can we think the *unity* of being and event?

Žižek's central effort in *The Ticklish Subject* is to show how his dialectical materialist approach to subjectivity casts new light on questions with which Badiou fails to engage. For Žižek, truth arises through struggle, and is revealed only through the position of the abject other (thus the truth of Nazism was disclosed not to Heidegger, but to the Jews). Žižek urges that only if we put ourselves into the position of the abject other – by getting rid of the injunction to enjoy and undergoing "subjective destitution" – will the truth happen through us. Žižek shows how subjectivity as such "is this domain 'beyond the good,' in which a human being encounters the death-drive as the utmost limit of human experience, and pays the price by undergoing a radical 'subjective destitution,' by being reduced to an excremental remainder" (*Ticklish*, p. 161). Žižek's point is that this limit-experience is the irreducible and constitutive condition of subjectivity *in its truth*.

In chapter 5 of *The Ticklish Subject*, Žižek pursues his account of divided subjectivity first by responding to criticism from Judith Butler. Why does Žižek devote an entire chapter to Butler's work? His painstaking treatment of Butler's work reveals the moment of failure in, not only "identity politics," but also contemporary Anglo-American cultural studies in general. Butler's criticism of Lacan is typical of postmodernist objections to Lacanian theory, namely that Lacan's emphasis on symbolic structure makes him insensitive to the contingencies of historical development. Butler claims that Lacan takes historically relative and accidental phenomena to be *a priori*, transcendental structures. Žižek's careful and thorough response shows that Butler implicitly presupposes that the Real is *temporally* prior to the symbolic. In other words, Butler overlooks the possibility that the Real is produced retroactively, as the remainder of symbolization:

> In other words, it is not that we have homosexuals, fetishists, and other perverts *in spite of* the normative fact of sexual difference – that is, as proofs

of the failure of sexual difference to impose its norm; it is not that sexual difference is the ultimate point of reference which anchors the contingent drifting of sexuality; it is, on the contrary, on account of the gap which forever persists between the real of sexual difference and the determinate forms of heterosexual symbolic norms that we have the multitude of "perverse" forms of sexuality. (*Ticklish*, p. 273)

For Lacan sexual difference is Real precisely insofar as it can never be translated into a norm which fixes the subject's identity. Butler elevates a contingent symbolic reality (a norm) beyond the ontic to the ontological level and thereby falls into the very error she tries to locate in Lacan's thinking.

To put the problem concisely, a paradox of self-reference undermines any effort to show that it is *universally* true that every historical period is determined by *non-universal* constructs. But Žižek's dialectical materialist approach avoids the inconsistency of this positive formulation by evoking the Real as a negative kind of universality, a negative *a priori*. What is universal is not any concept, or norm, or anything positive; instead, the universal is the lack or inconsistency that spawns the struggle for hegemony between various concepts, norms, definitions, or positive contents. The Real is not a kind of Kantian thing-in-itself, which because of our finitude we can only comprehend inadequately. The Real is manifested, rather, in the irreducible inconsistency of symbolic reality. In sum, Butler seems not to consider the Real as constituted *retroactively*, as the failure of symbolic systems.

In such ways, Žižek's Hegelian-Lacanian analysis indicates that any "positive" ontology implies conceptual deadlock. Language itself is ultimately self-referential.[2] Regarding nominalism and realism, he writes:

> Both standard philosophical versions, "realist" and "nominalist," fail to account for this struggle for the Universal. According to the realist account, there is a "true" content of the notion of the political to be unearthed by a true theory, so that once we gain access to this content, we can measure how close to it different theories of the political have come. The nominalist account, on the contrary, reduces the whole problem to the different nominal definitions of the term: there is no real conflict; the two parties are simply using the word "political" in a different sense, conferring on it a different scope.
>
> What both accounts miss, what disappears in both of them, is the antagonism, the struggle inscribed into the very heart of the "thing itself."

[2] Slavoj Žižek, *In Defense of Lost Causes* (London and New York: Verso, 2008), p. 3.

In the realist account, there is a true content of the universal notion to be discovered, and the struggle is simply the conflict between different erroneous readings of it – that is, it arises out of our misperception of the true content. In the nominalist account, struggle again arises out of an epistemological confusion, and is thus neutralized into a peaceful coexistence of the plurality of meanings. What gets lost in both cases is the fact that the struggle for hegemony (for the particular content which will function as the stand-in for the universality of the political) is groundless: the ultimate Real which cannot be further grounded in some ontological structure. (*Ticklish*, pp. 181–2)

However, as we will see, Žižek's version of dialectical materialism *does* show a way to surpass conceptual deadlocks relating to universality and specific difference.[3] Žižek does not simply resolve paradoxes of universality and singularity. Instead, in a kind of Hegelian *Aufhebung*, he shows how his dialectical materialist approach incorporates the paradoxical tension or antagonism: paradox is overcome insofar as it is embraced in its very insolubility. The moment of paradox indicates proximity to the repressed Real, the universal incommensurability against which any particular symbolic constellation is a reactive formation.

The Ticklish Subject articulates the universal as a void or impossibility that is not simply determinate or systematic, but is rather that which marks the intrinsic limit of any determinate symbolic "system." Žižek illustrates this point by way of reference to the Frankfurt School of Western Marxism. Whereas Habermas did not recognize the significance of the negative dimension of dialectic, Horkheimer and Adorno understood that the truth of the Enlightenment emerges only in its moments of troubling excess: "the only way to reach the truth of some notion or project is to focus on where this project went wrong" (*Ticklish*, p. 347).

One implication of Žižek's approach is that Marx's analysis of political economy may be seen to anticipate Lacan's distinction between fundamental types of social links as *discourses*: Marx's critique of capitalism elucidates the disavowed truth of capitalist discourse. Marx showed how the capitalist, insofar as he is concerned with maximizing profits, is unconcerned with knowledge as such. However, in order to more effectively appropriate surplus value from the workers, the capitalist master co-opts the discourses of religion, philosophy, and even science.

---

[3] For an overview of Žižek's philosophy, see Adrian Johnston, *Žižek's Ontology: A Transcendental Materialist Theory of Subjectivity* (Evanston: Northwestern University Press, 2008).

In this respect, Marx's problematic distinction between the fundamental relations of production – as opposed to the ideology of the superstructure – paves the way for Lacan's analysis of how the discourse of the university is always already in the service of the discourse of the master. The functional role of the university is to provide any sort of rationalizations that serve the master.

In political-economic life, imaginary projections of unity serve to mask irreducible social antagonisms. Žižek shows how the success of global capitalist ideology is based on the ego as an object, as an imaginary identification with a fixed, specular image. Imaginary ego identifications and the subject's alienation in language facilitate the development of capitalist globalism. However, Žižek urges that emancipation may be achieved if we recognize that the indefinable central term, the Master-Signifier (e.g., Democracy, Freedom, Nature), is necessary to ideology but is never encountered in any subject's experience. The ideological function of the Master-Signifier is to conceal – by means of imposture – not only the vacuous surd at the heart of the Law, but also some obscene superego injunction. In contrast to the hegemonic functioning of the superego in Freud's Victorian era, the predominant superego injunction of late capitalism is to forget about corruption, inequity of opportunity, and the looming ecological catastrophe and simply "Enjoy!"

The Ticklish Subject shows how today, in spite of the decline of the paternal metaphor and the inefficacy of ethical-political principles, global capitalist relations of production actually structure an ever more prohibitive and homogenized social reality:

> The true horror lies not in the particular content hidden beneath the universality of global Capital but, rather, in the fact that Capital is effectively an anonymous global machine blindly running its course; that there is in fact no particular Secret Agent animating it. The horror is not the (particular living) ghost in the (dead universal) machine, but the (dead universal) machine in the very heart of each (particular living) ghost. The conclusion to be drawn is thus that the problematic of multiculturalism (the hybrid coexistence of diverse cultural life-worlds) which imposes itself today is the form of appearance of its opposite, of the massive presence of capitalism as *global* world system: it bears witness to the unprecedented homogenization of today's world. (*Ticklish*, p. 218)

Multiculturalism – as well as postmodern efforts to reduce truth to "narratives" or "solidarity of belief" – simply further the interests of global capital. Žižek notes wryly that liberal pseudo-leftists really know all of this, but the problem is that they want to maintain their relatively comfortable lifestyles (bought at the expense of suffering in the Third World), and meanwhile to maintain the pose of revolutionary "beautiful souls." Postmodern "post-politics" replaces the recognition of global ideological divisions with an emphasis on the collaboration of enlightened experts, technocrats, and specialists who negotiate to reach compromises. Such pragmatic "administration of social matters" accepts in advance the very global capitalist framework that determines the profitability of the compromise (*Ticklish*, p. 199). This suspension of the space for authentic politics leads to what Žižek calls "postmodern racism," which ignores the universal rights of the political subject, proliferates divisions along cultural lines, and prevents the working class from politicizing its predicament.

Even more seriously, according to Žižek, post-politics no longer merely represses the political, but forecloses it. Thus instead of violence as the neurotic "return of the repressed," we see signs of a new kind of irrational and excessive violence. This new manifestation of violence results from the (psychotic) foreclosure of the Name of the Father that leads to a "return in the Real." This violence is thus akin to the psychotic *passage a l'acte*: "a cruelty whose manifestations range from 'fundamentalist' racist and/or religious slaughter to the 'senseless' outbursts of violence by adolescents and the homeless in our megalopolises, a violence one is tempted to call *Id*-Evil, a violence grounded in no utilitarian or ideological reason" (*Ticklish*, p. 198).

Where then, is the power to combat such foreclosure? *The Ticklish Subject* shows that the subversive power of subjectivity arises only when the subject annuls himself as subject: the acknowledgment of the integral division or gap in subjectivity allows the move from subjection to subjective destitution. Insofar as the subject concedes to the inherent failure of symbolic practices, he no longer presupposes himself as a unified subject. He acknowledges the nonexistence of the symbolic big Other and the monstrosity of the Real. Such acceptance involves the full assertion – rather than the effacement – of the gap between the Real and its symbolization.

In contrast to the artificial object character of the imaginary capitalist ego, *The Ticklish Subject* discloses the "empty place" of the subject as a purely structural function, and shows that this functioning emerges only as the withdrawal from one's substantial identity, as the disintegration of the "self" that is situated and defined within a communal universe of meaning. Put simply, Žižek calls us to be ever more critical of our struggle to maintain our self-deceptions, and of the ideological props that sustain our relatively comfortable numbness. All it takes to break free from the manipulations of ideology is the courage to remain true to our symbolic desire. Žižek's analysis of the symbolic subject as radical negativity opens up the space for a true *act* which ignores the false dilemma of a forced choice and redefines the very parameters of meaning.

11

The Art of the Ridiculous Sublime: On David Lynch's Lost Highway

Cinema, like fantasy, teaches us how to desire. Fantasy not only supports our sense of everyday reality; it also serves as a defense against the Real. The films of David Lynch make thematic the discord between imaginary-symbolic reality and the "impossible" Real. The characteristically postmodern effect created by Lynch's films arises from the juxtaposition of fantasy over against the intrusive Real. The enigma of postmodernity is evoked by the "art of the ridiculous sublime" insofar as we are forced to confront our own fundamental fantasy. This confrontation opens the possibility of traversing the fantasy by way of the act. The act as symbolic suicide reinvents the symbolic, and founds a new reality.

Žižek's Lacan is not the Lacan of post-structuralism, the theorist of the floating signifier, but the Lacan of the Real, the first category in the famous Lacanian triad of the Real, the Imaginary, and the Symbolic. The most under-represented of the Lacanian categories, the Real is also the most unfathomable because it is fundamentally impenetrable and cannot be assimilated to the symbolic order of language and communication (the fabric of daily life); nor does it belong to the Imaginary, the domain of images with which we identify and which capture our attention
　　　　　　—Marek Wieczorek, "Introduction," in Žižek, *The Art of the Ridiculous Sublime: On David Lynch's Lost Highway*

Žižek: A Reader's Guide, First Edition. Kelsey Wood.
© 2012 John Wiley & Sons, Inc. Published 2012 by John Wiley & Sons, Inc.

One of Žižek's more sustained engagements with film theory is *The Art of the Ridiculous Sublime* (2000; abbreviated *Ridiculous Sublime* below).[1] But like many of Žižek's works, *Ridiculous Sublime* is extraordinarily broad in scope: it ranges beyond film theory and psychoanalysis into political philosophy, ethics, and even the role of fantasy in cyberspace. However, the metaphysical motif of the book involves the ambiguity of fantasy as a conduit to the Real.

According to Žižek's dialectical materialism, any totality is an inconsistent totality; identity is displaced from itself. For example, my identity as a symbolic subject is based on a fundamental fantasy which I cannot consciously experience. The symbolic order is internally inconsistent because of some repressed Real; what we experience as reality is constituted through the primordial repression of the Real. Fantasy constitutes our lived sense of the coherence of reality by masking the Real, and by occluding the inconsistency that results from the repression of the Real (e.g., the repression of trauma or antagonism). In order to evoke the Real, Žižek approaches the films of David Lynch in light of complementary antagonisms such as ridiculous/sublime, Law/transgression, and reality/fantasy: "This essay is an attempt to unravel the enigma of this coincidence of opposites, which is, in a way, the enigma of 'postmodernity' itself" (*Ridiculous Sublime*, p. 3).

Žižek illustrates the inconsistency of the symbolic order by showing how even the strictest moral code is ruptured by an inherent injunction to transgression. The coincidence of the opposites Law/transgression shows up in the film *Casablanca*, about three quarters into the film, as the ambiguity of the famous fade-out during the encounter between Rick and Ilsa. The ambiguity of this scene, and especially the fade-out, is engendered by the odd juxtaposition of contrary signals. There are clear indications in the film that Ilsa and Rick *did* have sex during the interlude, but there are also, at the same time, clear indications that they did *not* have sex:

> To put it in Lacanian terms: during the infamous 3½ seconds, Ilsa and Rick did not do it for the big Other, the order of public appearance, but they did do it for our dirty fantasmatic imagination. This is the structure of inherent transgression at its purest, and Hollywood needs BOTH levels in order to function. [...] And, to link this to psychoanalytic terms, this opposition is, of course, the opposition between symbolic Law (Ego-Ideal) and

---

[1] Unless otherwise stated, page references for this work are to the following edition: *The Art of the Ridiculous Sublime* (Seattle: The Walter Chapin Simpson Center for the Humanities, University of Washington, 2000).

obscene superego: at the level of the public symbolic Law, nothing happens, the text is clean, while, at another level, it bombards the spectator with the superego injunction, "Enjoy!" (*Ridiculous Sublime*, p. 5)

Žižek considers the role of the unconscious in all of this. He segues from the "structure of inherent transgression" in the above-mentioned scene from *Casablanca* into an account of why psychoanalysis is needed for the critique of ideology:

> We can locate the need for psychoanalysis at a very precise point: what we are not aware of is not some deeply repressed secret content but *the essential character of the appearance itself*. Appearances DO matter: you can have your multiple dirty fantasies, but it matters which of them will be integrated into the public domain of the symbolic Law, of the big Other. (*Ridiculous Sublime*, p. 6)

The unconscious is not a truth buried deep in the mind. On the contrary, Žižek argues that the truth is outside, externalized in the shared and public realm of appearances. In other words, what we typical postmodern cynics remain unaware of is that any symbolic order (or discourse of power) must "keep up appearances," especially since, behind the public face of symbolic law, there is an obscene injunction to transgress. In several of his works, Žižek shows how the Law is actually *reinforced* insofar as the symbolic order allows and even implicitly encourages certain kinds of transgression. But because appearances are efficacious in human behavior, certain things must remain implicit and unspoken (e.g., rightist populism is more effective insofar as its racism remains unspoken). To explicitly state things that "we know but do not know that we know" would weaken the symbolic order. This is what Žižek means by disavowal, or "the fetishistic split" (*Ridiculous Sublime*, p. 5). The public, symbolic Law is sustained by obscene, transgressive fantasies; the Law itself *generates* its own obscene supplement (p. 6). This is why it matters very much that certain things remain unspoken: "keeping up appearances" means that the obscene superego injunction to transgress must not be explicitly inscribed into the intersubjective, symbolic register of language, communication, and Law. The attentive reader should already recognize how Žižek's remarks here in chapter 1 of *Ridiculous Sublime* resonate with his justifiably famous critiques of liberal democracy as the ideology of global capitalism. Žižek's dialectical materialist critique of ideology shows that the task for the left involves not only opposing right-wingers, but also exposing the complicity between liberal democracy (the ideology of global capitalism) and rightist populism. As Žižek has argued in more recent writings, the opposition between right-wing populism and liberal tolerance is a false opposition.[2] How can rightist populism and liberal tolerance be two sides of the same coin? For one thing, democratic "openness" itself is based on *exclusion*: we are only "tolerant" of the Other who fits into our fantasy framework (e.g., the depoliticized, passive victim).

But if any symbolic order has a public Law which is supplemented by an obscene nightly law, in the form of a superego injunction to transgress, how can we break out of this vicious cycle? How can we free ourselves from ideology? Again, Žižek argues that the way out is through the act of the feminine subject. In this book, as in virtually all of his other works, Žižek emphasizes the radical emancipatory potential of feminine subjectivity, and highlights the subversive aspect of the feminine subject in her relation to masculine authority. This is why Section 2 of *Ridiculous Sublime* focuses on the feminine act.

Section 2, "The Feminine Act," presupposes some familiarity with Lacan's "logic of sexuation" (cf. Lacan's *Seminar XX: Encore*). The masculine logic implies a rule which is (allegedly) universal. However, masculine universality is constituted by an exception: the universality of the rule is produced through an exception to the rule. Put simply, the masculine logic is like saying: "in principle yes, *but* ..." The logic of feminine subjectivity is different; the feminine logic acknowledges that the rule is inconsistent. However, there are no exceptions to the rule, even though the rule is non-all. For example, according to the feminine logic, the set is all there is, but the set itself is incomplete. In Žižek's works, the masculine logic is shown to be a reaction to the more fundamental feminine logic. This means that the masculine logic (of the exception) *itself* functions as the exception to the feminine logic. Put succinctly, the subject as such is feminine, and this is the reason that in *film noir*, the subversive impact of the *femme fatale* points toward the radical emancipatory potential of subjectivity as Real.

Now we are in a position to understand why Žižek analyzes the role of the doomed *femme fatale* of the older *noir* films as well as the predatory, aggressive *femme fatale* of new *noir*, and shows how both these versions are ensnared in the fantasy formations of the masculine subject position:

---

[2] See Slavoj Žižek, "A Vile Logic to Anders Breivik's Choice of Target," online at http://www.guardian.co.uk/commentisfree/2011/aug/08/anders-behring-breivik-pim-fortuyn.

Both versions of the *femme fatale* – the classic *noir* version as well as the postmodern version – are thus flawed, caught in an ideological trap, and it is our contention that the way out of this trap is provided by David Lynch's *Lost Highway*, a film which effectively functions as a kind of meta-commentary on the opposition between the classic and postmodern *noir femme fatale*." (*Ridiculous Sublime*, p. 13)

Žižek argues that the theme of *Lost Highway* is the desire of the Other, specifically, the enigma of feminine desire. But we desire through the Other; this means that desire is externalized in the symbolic register, as the distortion of chains of signifiers. *Lost Highway* evokes the redemptive potential of the feminine act insofar as the film decomposes the masculine fantasy: Lynch reveals the inconsistency of fantasy. In fact, as Žižek demonstrates, neither the fantasy that sustains symbolic reality, nor the symbolic reality, nor some combination of both, offers a way for the protagonist to acquire distance from the traumatic Real of surplus enjoyment or pleasure-in-pain (*jouissance*). As symbolic, desire is opposed to Real *jouissance*. In *Lost Highway* the Real – as impossible to symbolize – is manifested by the curvature of the symbolic space of desire. Žižek argues that this accounts for the impossible, surrealistic circularity of the film's narrative structure:

> Much more productive is to insist on how the very circular form of narrative in *Lost Highway* directly renders the circularity of the psychoanalytic process. That is to say, a crucial ingredient of Lynch's universe is a phrase, a signifying chain, which resonates as a Real that insists and always returns – a kind of basic formula that suspends and cuts across time: in *Dune*, it is "the sleeper must awake"; in "Twin Peaks," "the owls are not what they seem"; in *Blue Velvet*, "Daddy wants to fuck"; and, of course, in *Lost Highway*, the phrase which is the first and the last spoken words in the film, "Dick Laurant is dead," announcing the death of the obscene paternal figure (Mr. Eddy). The entire narrative of the film takes place in the suspension of time between these two moments. (*Ridiculous Sublime*, p. 17)

The Real shows up as the circularity, inconsistency, or displacement inherent to the symbolic register and to symbolic identity. The symbolic identity of the subject is split insofar as there can be no full and transparent self-consciousness. Another way that the Real is manifested in the film is the impossibility of the masculine protagonist (Fred/Pete) encountering *himself*.

Žižek analyzes three crucial scenes which define the three characters to whom the protagonist attempts to relate: "Dick Laurant as the excessive/ obscene superego father, Mystery-Man as timeless/spaceless synchronous

Knowledge, Alice as the fantasy screen of excessive enjoyment" (*Ridiculous Sublime*, p. 18). These three scenes show how the repressed Real inevitably returns as the antagonism or trauma underlying our symbolic identity and shared public practices.

The first key scene shows that Dick Laurant/Mr. Eddy is a paradoxical figure insofar as he represents *both* the respect for the symbolic law *and* the excessive enjoyment of the mythical, primordial father; he is: "physically hyperactive, hectic, exaggerated, and as such already inherently *ridiculous*" (*Ridiculous Sublime*, p. 19). Žižek discusses other similar examples of obscene paternal figures in Lynch's films in order to show the association between symbolic law and the fantasy of the primordial father, who is the imaginary exception which constitutes masculine universality.

In the second crucial scene of *Lost Highway*, the obscene and excessive phallic enjoyment of the violent paternal figure is complemented by the pure asexual Knowledge of the Mystery-Man. If the evil but ridiculous Dick Laurant represents the surplus enjoyment of the imaginary primal father, Laurant's friend, the Mystery-Man, is anything but ridiculous; he is a spooky, even nightmarish figure, who can be in two places at once. Like the director of a film, he can manipulate emotions. The Mystery-Man represents pure, asexual Knowledge; he knows the protagonist better than the protagonist knows himself: "Against this background, one should conceive of the Mystery-Man as the ultimate horror of the Other who has a direct access to our (the subject's) fundamental fantasy" (*Ridiculous Sublime*, p. 20).

Again, the fundamental fantasy is the very core of my subjectivity; it functions as a transcendental schema which constitutes my unique symbolic reality. But the paradox of the fundamental fantasy is that if I approach it directly, the coherence of my subjectivity dissolves. The horror of the Mystery-Man involves the realization that my identity is displaced from itself: I myself have no access to the innermost, unique kernel of my own subjectivity, even though some Other might have this knowledge. Again, in Lynch's films, the Real is manifested in and through the displacement of apparent unities into a coincidence of opposites, such as this complementarity between two contrasting figures of evil: evil as violent, excessive enjoyment as opposed to evil as the cold, disinterested gaze of omnipotence.

The third revelatory scene involves Alice as the object of the male protagonist's fundamental fantasy. Alice is in a dark house, where she stands opposite a movie screen on which is projected a pornographic scene of Alice engaged in coitus *a tergo* with a large and powerful man:

Is this house of pornography the last in a series of hellish places in Lynch's films, places in which one encounters the final (not truth but) fantasmatic lie (the other two best known are the Red Lodge in "Twin Peaks" and Frank's apartment in *Blue Velvet*)? This site is that of the fundamental fantasy staging the primordial scene of *jouissance*, and the whole problem is how to "traverse" it, to acquire a distance from it. And, again, this side by side confrontation of the real person with her fantasmatic image seems to condense the overall structure of the film that posits aseptic, drab, everyday reality alongside the fantasmatic Real of a nightmarish *jouissance*.

Significantly, Žižek argues against New Age interpretations of Lynch's films, which enjoin us to break through the rules and boundaries of social life to the subconscious flow of life energy. This is why Žižek emphasizes that this fundamental fantasy of the primordial scene of *jouissance* (cf. the Freudian "primal scene") is *not the truth but a lie*, and the problem is how to traverse this fantasmatic lie, to acquire a distance from it (*Ridiculous Sublime*, p. 20).

Žižek argues that it is possible to change our fantasy, and hence to reinvent our symbolic reality. Moreover, interventions in the symbolic may produce changes in the Real. Lynch's films indicate this redemptive possibility by a unique effect of extraneation: "Lynch DECOMPOSES the ordinary 'sense of reality' sustained by fantasy into, on the one side, pure, aseptic reality and, on the other side, fantasy: reality and fantasy no longer relate vertically (fantasy beneath reality, sustaining it), but horizontally (side by side)" (*Ridiculous Sublime*, p. 21). Along these lines, Lacanian theory decomposes the ordinary sense of "self." The subject is split; it is not a psychological unity. And insofar as we have no direct access to our own fundamental fantasy, it is as if our innermost feelings are produced by an uncanny mechanism not under our control.

Even our hatred is produced through the Other, or "canned," like the imbecilic, pre-recorded laughter that accompanies a TV sitcom. Moreover, the Lacanian tradition holds that the only affect which does not lie is anxiety. From this psychoanalytic perspective, we should be suspicious of any persuasive *narrative*. Consistency is a sign of the influence of fantasy, while certain kinds of inconsistency indicate the proximity of the Real. The subject as Real is the split or displacement inherent to the symbolic order:

> The subject himself emerges through such a displacement of his innermost self-experience onto the "reified" symbolic order. This is one way to read the Lacanian mathem of the subject, the "barred subject," $: what empties the subject is the fact of being deprived of his innermost fantasmatic kernel

which is transposed onto the "reified" big Other. Because of this, there is no subject without the minimally "reified" symbolic institution. (*Ridiculous Sublime*, p. 27)

In Section 6 of *Ridiculous Sublime* ("Fathers, Fathers Everywhere"), Žižek distinguishes between imaginary, Real, and symbolic functions of father figures in film. Žižek is arguing against both New Age, obscurantist approaches to film as well as postmodern, relativistic interpretations. What surprises many postmodern liberals is that Žižek's work is not simply directed toward undermining symbolic authority as such. On the contrary, just as symbolic desire is opposed to Real *jouissance*, so the Father as bearer of authority can prevent the breakdown of symbolic Law into the senseless violence of Id-Evil. Neither the ineffectual and benign – imaginary – maternal father (of postmodernism) nor the father of unrestrained – Real – enjoyment (implicit to New Age jargon about discovering our "life energy") can prevent the disintegration of symbolic authority.

What both the New Age and the postmodern approaches miss is "the father as the bearer of symbolic authority, the Name of the Father, the prohibitory 'castrating' agency that enables the subject's entry into the symbolic order, and thus into the domain of *desire*" (*Ridiculous Sublime*, p. 31). If the Name of the Father is *foreclosed*, the individual becomes psychotic and has no gender: only neurotics, who *repress* the Name of the Father, have gender. But, on the other hand, after the Father has enabled the subject to enter the symbolic order, the point is not to (try to) unambiguously identify with the Father as bearer of symbolic authority.

On the contrary, in the choice between "the Father or worse" (*le père ou pire*), the feminine subject – the hero – chooses the worse. Because the subject as such is the hysterical question, the role of the analyst is not to facilitate identification with symbolic authority. On the contrary, the analyst is subversive insofar as s/he enables the insight that *the symbolic order cannot guarantee the subject's identity*. Žižek describes this aspect of the role of the analyst in an essay on Lacan's four discourses:

> The crucial point not to be missed here is how the late Lacan's identification of the subjective position of the analyst as that of *objet petit a* presents an act of radical self-criticism. Earlier, in the 1950's, Lacan conceived the analyst not as the small other (*a*), but, on the contrary, as a kind of stand-in for the big Other (A, the anonymous symbolic order). At this level, the function of the analyst was to frustrate the subject's imaginary misrecognitions and to make them accept their proper symbolic place within the circuit of symbolic exchange, the place that effectively (and unbeknownst to them) determines

their symbolic identity. Later, however, the analyst stands precisely for the ultimate inconsistency and failure of the big Other, that is, for the symbolic order's inability to guarantee the subject's symbolic identity.[3]

Through her identification with the inconsistency and failure of the symbolic order (the locus of the excluded or disenfranchised Other), the feminine subject remains true to her desire, and thereby breaks the vicious cycle of the Law and its obscene superego injunction to transgressive enjoyment. This indicates a way to distinguish the ethico-political act from the blind striking out of the psychotic *passage à l'acte*.

To conclude, in *The Art of the Ridiculous Sublime*, Žižek shows how David Lynch's films exploit the discord between imaginary-symbolic reality and the seemingly impossible Real. In their juxtaposition of idyllic fantasy over against the unbearable, intrusive Real, Lynch's films evoke the enigma of postmodernity. Lynch's "art of the ridiculous sublime" forces us to confront the comic horror of our own fundamental fantasy. This confrontation renders visible the inconsistency of the fantasmatic support of the symbolic order, and thereby opens the possibility of traversing the fantasy through the act.

The feminine act reinvents the symbolic register in a way which actualizes radical-emancipatory potential. The inconsistency of the fantasy support of ideology and symbolic authority thus provides the basis for the founding of a new reality, and a new symbolic identity. And because interventions in the symbolic may effect changes in Real *jouissance*, the act of a feminine subject may even inaugurate a new economy of enjoyment.

---

[3] Cf. Slavoj Žižek, "Jacques Lacan's Four Discourses," available online at http://www.lacan.com/zizfour.htm.

12

The Fragile Absolute: or, Why is the Christian Legacy Worth Fighting For?

Žižek addresses the postmodern return of the religious, and urges that Marxists should appropriate the subversive core of Christianity. Žižek argues that the best way to encapsulate the gist of an epoch is to focus on the disavowed "ghosts" that haunt it, and our epoch, he argues, is haunted by the spectral power of Capital. Capital functions today as the disavowed Real, insofar as our imaginary-symbolic reality is an answer to the repressed and monstrous excesses of capital. In this sense, symbolic "reality" and the spectral apparition of the Real are co-dependent. But how does all of this relate to religion? In contrast to pagan religions (such as mystery cults) that revolved around a secret domain of orgiastic enjoyment, Judaism subordinated enjoyment to the Father's Law. Christianity, however, involves the passage from Law to Love. Žižek shows that in Christian theology, eternity is the inconceivable "event" or "cut" that opens up and sustains temporality. The Christian event of conversion is analogous to the Lacanian *act*. As a form of symbolic suicide, the act is linked with the Real: it first *disrupts* and then *reforms* the symbolic register in unpredictable ways. Conversion, like the Lacanian act, is an intervention in the symbolic texture of temporal reality that can change the effects of the nontemporal Real.

One of the most deplorable aspects of the postmodern era and its so-called "thought" is the return of the religious dimension in all its different guises: from Christian and other fundamentalisms, through the multitude of New Age spiritualisms, up to the emerging religious sensitivity within deconstructionism itself (so-called "post-secular" thought). How is a

Žižek: A Reader's Guide, First Edition. Kelsey Wood.
© 2012 John Wiley & Sons, Inc. Published 2012 by John Wiley & Sons, Inc.

Marxist, by definition a "fighting materialist" (Lenin), to counter this massive onslaught of obscurantism?
—Žižek, *The Fragile Absolute: or, Why is the Christian Legacy Worth Fighting For?* p. 1

One of Žižek's most thorough analyses of religion is *The Fragile Absolute: or, Why is the Christian Legacy Worth Fighting For?* (2000).[1] In this book, Žižek uses the psychoanalytic theory of Jacques Lacan in order to reactualize – for leftists today – the subversive, radical-emancipatory kernel of Christianity. And as usual, Žižek's approach is anything but "as usual." This becomes clear after the first paragraph, which is addressed to Marxist materialists. In the second paragraph, in an apparent reversal, Žižek asserts that there is a direct lineage from Christianity to Marxism, and further, "the authentic Christian legacy is much too precious to be left to the fundamentalist freaks" (*Fragile*, p. 2). Moreover, Christians and Marxists should now be fighting on the same side against New Age spiritualisms. And for those not yet perplexed (and/or annoyed), Žižek next indicates that this book will also deal with the philosophical problem of *repetition* (in the anti-essentialist Hegelian sense). Thus as Marxists/ Christians, we must not fetishize the "authentic" disciples of Jesus as opposed to the later reinvention of Christianity by Saint Paul, because: "*there is no Christ outside Saint Paul*; in exactly the same way, there is no 'authentic Marx' that can be approached directly, bypassing Lenin" (*Fragile*, p. 2). In a nutshell, like all of Žižek's works, *The Fragile Absolute* cannot be put in a nutshell.

In the first chapter of *Fragile*, "Giving Up the Balkan Ghost," Žižek (obliquely) addresses his Slovenian origins, and defuses the charge (leveled by Ian Parker et al.) that he is too much identified with these origins and associations. He also shows how the liberal rhetoric of tolerance for the Other masks various forms of racism, such as "reflexive racism." Even *respect for the other's culture can be used as an excuse* for strengthening walls and borders. As Žižek puts it on page 6: "was not the official argument for apartheid in the old South Africa that black culture should be preserved in its uniqueness, not dissipated in the Western melting-pot?" This example indicates the sense in which rightist populism and liberal tolerance – a tolerance based on the exclusion of the intrusive Other – are two sides of the same coin. Again, even racism

---

[1] Unless otherwise stated, page references for this work, abbreviated *Fragile*, are to the following edition: *The Fragile Absolute: or, Why is the Christian Legacy Worth Fighting For?* (London and New York: Verso, 2001).

itself can be used an excuse for a racist agenda, as when white, right-wing populists in the USA complain that African Americans are racists. Žižek develops ideas along these lines in several texts. For example, "One of Jacques Lacan's more outrageous statements is that, even if what a jealous husband claims about his unfaithful wife is all true, his jealousy is still pathological."[2] In the same way, even if it *were* true that African Americans are all racists, the right-wing populist complaint is still pathological.

These examples indicate how the global reflexivization of today's societies has led to the loss of a sense of shame and the proliferation of excuses for injustice and evil, as in the case of the neo-Nazi skinhead, "who, when he is really pressed for the reasons for his violence, suddenly starts to talk like social workers, sociologists and social psychologists, quoting diminished social mobility, rising insecurity, the disintegration of paternal authority, lack of maternal love in his early childhood" (*Fragile*, p. 9). Meanwhile, contemporary critical and political discourse is permeated by the fantasy that we have finally achieved a "post-ideological," purely pragmatic era. No one seems to notice that legitimate political struggles are misrepresented as depoliticized ethnic/cultural conflicts, or that the term "worker" has virtually disappeared, replaced by the term "immigrants." Political-economic critique has been reduced to liberal jargon, as the brutal exploitation of workers and the poor is buried under an avalanche of misguided and ineffectual multiculturalist proclamations against the lack of "tolerance for Otherness" (p. 10). Žižek decisively rejects such blather, and indicates the strategy for true leftists: "the way to fight ethnic *hatred* effectively is not through its immediate counterpart, ethnic *tolerance*; on the contrary, what we need is *even more hatred*, but proper *political* hatred: hatred directed at the common political enemy" (p. 11).

Who is this common political enemy? Today it is the imposition of the world market which undermines local ethnic traditions, and even undermines the nation-state itself. The sociosymbolic reality of people involved in production processes is determined by the more fundamental, "abstract" logic of Capital, such as financial speculation on futures. Guided by the goal of maximizing profits, abstract financial speculation is indifferent to the suffering of people. In this sense, Capital functions as the disavowed Real which informs socio-ideological, symbolic reality (p. 15).

[2] See Slavoj Žižek, "Today Iraq, Tomorrow … Democracy," from *In These Times*, March 26, 2003, online at http://www.lacan.com/zizek-today.htm.

Marx was thus correct in asserting that capitalism's incessant drive to maximize profits implies an inherent contradiction or obstacle insofar as this self-enhancing dynamics of productivity undermines its own material conditions. One way that capitalism's inherent obstacle is manifested is that the full development of productive forces is inevitably (and repeatedly) thwarted by socially disastrous economic crises. But orthodox Marxists may be in for a disappointment, for the Žižek giveth, and the Žižek taketh away: Marx's mistake, he points out, was to conclude that Communism would be able to remove the inherent obstacle of capitalism while maintaining productivity. Against this, Žižek argues that:

> the "condition of impossibility" of the full deployment of productive forces is simultaneously its "condition of possibility": if we abolish the obstacle, the inherent contradiction of capitalism, we do not get the fully unleashed drive to productivity finally delivered of its impediment, we lose precisely this productivity that seemed to be generated and simultaneously thwarted by capitalism [...]. (*Fragile*, pp. 17–18)

From Žižek's Lacanian psychoanalytic perspective, the *obstacle* to fully realized desire is itself the crucial inter-mediator which makes the object desirable. Marx's mistake was thus to presuppose that it is possible to have expanding productivity – the object of desire – in the absence of the inherent obstacle, namely the capitalist's appropriation of surplus value (p. 21). Crucial here is the link between the libidinal economy sustained by surplus enjoyment (*jouissance*) and the capitalist economy sustained by surplus value. The paradox is that the more profit we make, the more we want; the more we acquire some partial object of desire, the more desire as such remains unsatisfied, "the more you possess it, the greater the lack" (p. 24). Žižek's dialectical materialism incorporates this paradox by showing how symbolic reality acquires definition only insofar as "presence" is disclosed over against nonpresence, or lack (p. 32). In other words, we maintain our sense of reality only insofar as the traumatic Real of *surplus enjoyment* is kept at a minimal distance. The full presence of "the very Thing" would provoke a psychotic collapse (p. 39). This does not imply the simplistic conclusion that capitalism's injunction to enjoy makes us crazy; Žižek argues in several works that the antagonisms which limit capitalism are *internal* to capitalism.[3] The key point here is that the

---

[3] Slavoj Žižek and Glyn Daly, *Conversations with Žižek* (Cambridge: Polity Press, 2004), p. 152.

libidinal economy of capitalism revolves around the lethal enjoyment which *must* be kept at a distance by symbolic Law.

To paraphrase Marx, the Real of drive is manifested in capitalism insofar as the circulation of money as capital becomes an end in itself, when the expansion of value occurs only in and through this constantly renewed movement. This is why Žižek argues in several of his works that, in the libidinal dynamics of capitalism, the *goal* of drive must be distinguished from the *aim* of drive: if the goal of capitalism is to maximize profits, nonetheless its true aim is simply the endless circulation of capital. It is the endless circulation of capital in world-market globalization that has now led to the postmodern dissolution of social links, of discourses, and of Law. This is why Marx was correct in his arguments that capitalism dissolves "all that is solid." We can see this disintegration in the late capitalist decline in symbolic efficacy (e.g. the postmodernist claim that truth is solidarity of belief and science is just another narrative).

Žižek analyzes this process of dissolution in chapter 4 of *Fragile*. In Lacanian psychoanalytic theory, modes of discourse function as social links. In this connection, Žižek shows how traditionally, the "discourse of the Master" sustained the symbolic identity of the subject through the Master-Signifier, his title or mandate (*Fragile*, p. 43). Fidelity to this gives the subject his ethical dignity. Such identification with the Master-Signifier is conducive to the tragic mode of existence. Tragedy arises insofar as the subject tries to sustain his fidelity to the mission which gives coherence to existence. This inevitably fails because of some (Real) remainder which resists the Master-Signifier. Today, by contrast, there is the slippery, postmodern, capitalist subject, who lacks any ethical dignity because he lacks support in the Master-Signifier. The postmodern subject's only "consistency" lies in his comical inconsistency, in the dissolving of all that is solid, in the melting into air of all social links and traditions, and in the undermining of all symbolic mandate and authority (pp. 42–3). Although postmodernists reject references to the Real of the logic of Capital as being too "essentialist," Žižek shrewdly notes that "today's postmodern politics *does* have a limit: it encounters the Real when it touches the point of actually disturbing the free functioning of Capital" (pp. 54–5).

One way the Real of Capital informs symbolic narratives/reality today is the ideological fantasy of the helpless victim. Real enjoyment (*jouissance*) as pleasure-in-pain is manifested by our Western fascination with the fantasy formation of the passive, suffering victim. Instead of decisive military action to definitively resolve political conflicts, NATO strategy (e.g., in Kosovo) ensures that certain populations *remain passive victims* who are dependent on aid, instead of becoming active military-political forces on their own: "The crucial point is thus to recognize clearly in this ideology of global victimization, in this identification of the (human) subject as 'something that can be hurt,' the mode of ideology that fits today's global capitalism" (*Fragile*, p. 60). Instead of recognizing that the true cause of such conflicts is the power struggles inherent to the world-market, we accept depoliticized accounts (e.g., the clash of cultures). But such depoliticized explanations – accounts that reduce political struggles to cultural clashes – overlook the systemic violence of capitalism, and the very economy of surplus enjoyment that undermines symbolic order.

Žižek's analysis in *The Fragile Absolute* indicates how, in the opposition between imaginary fantasy and symbolic reality, it is our fantasy which discloses the Real of *jouissance*. Better than our explicit rationalizations, our films implicitly reveal the monstrous truth of surplus enjoyment as Real. In *Fragile*, as in many of his other works, Žižek uses film to segue into discussion of how the inconsistency of both fantasy and reality points toward the primordially repressed Real. Even images of cata-strophic violence in film can serve as a protective shield against the Real, and against the abyssal "madness" of the ungrounded, Lacanian act.

But again, the radical alienation or decentrement of the symbolic subject means that I, as a subject, have no access to my own fundamental fantasy, to the way things "really seem to me" (*Fragile*, p. 84). All of this indicates how Žižek's psychoanalytically informed dialectical material-ism shows that the emergence of any imaginary-symbolic reality is always a response to "some monstrous excess in the Real" (p. 92). Any symbolic order functions only insofar as it relies on fantasy to mask the inherent violence of its own founding Event (the primordial repression of Real *jouissance*). Moreover, any possible narrative of this very Event finally proves to be a fantasy which serves to distance us from the Real of surplus enjoyment.

Žižek argues that in Christian theology, the notion of Eternity is homologous to the Lacanian Real. Eternity is the inconceivable "Event" or "cut" that opens up and sustains temporality. Like the Real, Eternity is excluded so that temporal reality maintains consistency: "If then, we claim that each concrete historical constellation generates its own eternity, this does *not* simply mean that Eternity is the ideological myth generated by historical reality: Eternity is, rather, that which is *excluded* so that historical reality can maintain its consistency" (*Fragile*, p. 96).

The radical decentrement of the subject (the inaccessibility of the fantasy framework of our reality) seems to imply that we are caught in a closed loop. But the Lacanian act is an encounter with the Real as the deadlock or inconsistency of the symbolic. Thus the only way to break out of imaginary-symbolic reality is the ungrounded act, which literally emerges *ex nihilo*, from nothing and nobody. The "good news" of Christianity is that a conversion experience is an act which breaks through the symbolic texture of reality in a way which can even alter the effects of the nontemporal Real: a genuine conversion experience is a temporal event that can change the eternal. In terms of Lacanian psychoanalysis, the act disrupts and then reforms the symbolic order in unpredictable ways. Such an intervention in the symbolic can even transform our mode of Real *jouissance*.

Žižek illustrates such transformation with reference to religion. Ancient pagan religions involved a domain of sacred enjoyment, and New Age neo-paganism enjoins us to realize our "true self" by discovering our creative "life energy." However, in contrast to paganism, the Judaic tradition subordinates *jouissance* to the Law of the Father. But Žižek argues that the historical passage from Judaism to Christianity is homologous to the passage, in Lacanian theory, from the "masculine" logic of sexuation to the "feminine" logic. Again, in order to comprehend the significance of the masculine and the feminine subject positions, it is important to bear in mind that these are two different ways of relating to the symbolic register, two different modalities of symbolic identification. The masculine subject position involves the logic of universality constituted by an exception. For example, according to the masculine logic, the coherence of any series is constituted through reference to the Master-Signifier which grounds the series. Žižek argues that in the masculine logic, the series itself is exceptional; it is a series of exceptions (*Fragile*, p. 115). But again, in *Seminar XX: Encore* (1972–3), Lacan developed the feminine logic of "non-all" (not-whole). For the feminine logic, the series is not universal, but incomplete; however, there is no exception to the series. The feminine logic of non-all implies that the Master-Signifier is just the most efficient or most established member of the series (*Fragile*, p. 116).

According to Lacan, psychoanalysis should enable the subject to free herself from reliance on the Master-Signifier, which guarantees the consistency of the symbolic order. This is why Lacan argued that the Master-Signifier is ultimately an imposture, an empty signifier, a word with no consistent meaning; in this sense, what binds a society together is shared ignorance. But Žižek contrasts the masculine logic of Judaism with the feminine logic of Christianity, which involves love as the paradoxes of the feminine non-all. The libidinal economy of Judaism is fundamentally that of Law and its transgression. But through forgiveness and salvation, Christianity offers the possibility of twisting out of the masculine logic of Law and its transgression. Love as non-all involves identification with the lack in the symbolic law. Thus the passage from Judaism to Christianity is the passage from Law to Love:

> As every true Christian knows, love is the *work* of love – the hard and arduous work of repeated "uncoupling" in which, again and again, we have to disengage ourselves from the inertia that constrains us to identify with the particular order we were born into. Through the Christian work of compassionate love, we discern in what was hitherto a disturbing foreign body, tolerated and even modestly supported by us so that we were not too bothered by it, a subject, with its crushed dreams and desires – it is *this* Christian heritage of "uncoupling" that is threatened by today's "fundamentalisms," especially when they proclaim themselves Christian. Does not fascism ultimately involve the return to the pagan mores which, rejecting the love of one's enemy, cultivate full identification with one's own ethnic community? (*Fragile*, pp. 128–9)

Žižek argues that such love involves the paradoxes of the feminine logic of non-All. Love is not an exception to the All of knowledge, but a "nothing" which reveals the incompleteness of the field of knowledge (pp. 146–7).

The true subversion of the Law does not consist in doing the necessary but dirty thing (which actually sustains the ruling ideology). The subversive core of Christianity involves doing what is explicitly allowed according to the public face of the Law, but prohibited at the level of unwritten rules: "when Christ claims that he is here merely to *fulfil* the [Jewish] Law, he thereby bears witness to how his act effectively *cancels* the Law" (*Fragile*, p. 148). In this sense, the feminine act suspends the ethical (as defined by Law) through what is, in effect, a properly *political* decision (p. 155). If a community of believers identifies with those who are the outcasts of the social order, and then engages in such a political act, the subversive core of Christianity might be actualized.

13

On Belief

In this book, Žižek builds on his insights in *The Fragile Absolute*, and argues for a dialectical materialist version of "living in Christ," a Christian-materialism that is both informed by Lacanian theory and grounded in the Gospel. Žižek uses examples from popular culture to illustrate how Western versions of Asiatic spirituality are the perfect ideological supplements to global capitalism. Therefore Marxists and Christians should work together to oppose New Age, pagan spiritualism. Unlike the futile, pagan quest for self-fulfillment, both Marxism and Christianity involve the acceptance of imperfection as well as unconditional ethical engagement. What St Paul's institutionalized version of Christianity accomplished against the Roman Empire, Marxists today must accomplish against the Empire of liberal-global capitalism. To facilitate this transformation, Žižek re-inscribes insights and commitments from Christianity into his own unorthodox version of Marxist dialectical materialism.

> *What if sexual difference is not simply a biological fact, but the Real of an antagonism that* defines humanity, *so that once sexual difference is abolished, a human being effectively becomes indistinguishable from a machine?*
> —Žižek, *On Belief*, p. 43

In Žižek's *On Belief* (2001),[1] he further develops ideas which he introduced in his previous book on religion, *The Fragile Absolute*. Žižek begins, in his

[1] Unless otherwise stated, page references for this work are to the following edition: *On Belief* (London and New York: Routledge, 2004).

Žižek: A Reader's Guide, First Edition. Kelsey Wood.
© 2012 John Wiley & Sons, Inc. Published 2012 by John Wiley & Sons, Inc.

introduction, by indicating that *On Belief* will show why leftists today should endorse a materialist version of Christianity. This re-inscription of Christianity will displace the "original" and put it to work, fulfilling its unrealized, radical-emancipatory potential. Žižek shows how St Paul already performed such a displacement and re-inscription, just as Lenin did with Marxism, and Jacques Lacan did with Freudian psychoanalysis (*On Belief* pp. 2–3). Thus the first, most basic idea to grasp in order to understand this book is that Žižek is not talking about Christianity as it is, but as it might be. He evokes the subversive potential of Christianity in order to prepare the way for a radical leftist reinvention of Christianity, a materialist version of "living in Christ," inspired by the Gospel, but also grounded in the psychoanalytic theory of Jacques Lacan and the dialectical philosophy of Hegel and Marx. In *On Belief*, Žižek displaces Christianity and "puts it to work," re-inscribing it into contemporary political discourse. The surprising result is a return to Lenin.

Žižek states bluntly at the outset that this return to Lenin must not involve adjusting the theory through pragmatic compromises, so that nothing really changes. Nor should it be confused with liberal, pseudo-leftist nostalgia for the good old revolutionary times:

> In contrast to this false radical Leftist's position (who wants true democracy for the people, but without the secret police to fight counter-revolution, without their academic privileges being threatened), a Leninist, like a Conservative, is *authentic* in the sense of fully *assuming the consequences of his choice,* i.e. of being fully aware of what it actually means to take power and to exert it. (*On Belief*, p. 4)

Žižek calls us to reactualize "Lenin's unconditional will to intervene," in such a way that our intervention will change the coordinates of the entire situation (*On Belief*, p. 3). Today, more than ever, leftists must not be afraid to pass to the radical-emancipatory act, and fully assume the dirty work of realizing political change. What St Paul's re-inscription of early Christianity did to the Roman Empire, leftists today must do to the Empire of global liberal-capitalism (p. 5).

Žižek urges that, at this critical juncture in human history, Marxists and Christians must fight together against Gnosticism, New Age spiritualism, and Western Buddhism. Arguing that all three of these function today as ideological supplements to global capitalism, Žižek contrasts them with Marxism and Christianity, both of which involve the acceptance of imperfection, and both of which involve unconditional ethical engagement. But Žižek's Marxism is unorthodox; this becomes apparent in chapter 1, when he affirms the dialectical coincidence of the two "opposites," rational discourse and myth:

> Myth is thus the Real of *logos*: the foreign intruder, impossible to get rid of, impossible to remain fully within it. Therein resides the lesson of Adorno's and Horkheimer's *Dialectic of Enlightenment*: enlightenment always already "contaminates" the mythical naive immediacy; enlightenment itself is mythical, i.e. its own grounding gesture *repeats* the mythical operation. And what is "postmodernism" if not the ultimate *defeat* of the Enlightenment in its very triumph: when the dialectic of enlightenment reaches its apogee, the dynamic, rootless postindustrial society *directly generates its own myth*. The technological reductionism of the cognitivist partisans of Artificial Intelligence and the pagan mythic imaginary of sorcery, of mysterious magic powers, etc., are strictly the two sides of the same phenomenon: the defeat of modernity in its very triumph. (*On Belief*, pp. 11–12)

Žižek draws the connection here with psychoanalysis in the following way. The subject's symbolic universe is sustained through *fetish*. Fetish functions as a fiction which enables the subject to keep Real trauma repressed. *Symptom*, however, is the eruption of the repressed trauma into the symbolic universe (*On Belief*, p. 13). In this sense, Western Buddhism functions as a fetish which allows adherents to participate fully in the ruthless capitalist system while sustaining the lie that they are somehow detached from it. The Western Buddhist dismisses the truth of his capitalist existence as a mere game (p. 15). But as opposed to such a *comic* evasion of the truth of capitalism, psychoanalysis is inherently anti-capitalistic and inherently *tragic*. It is not Buddhism, but psychoanalysis which reveals the irresolvable antagonism of the symbolic order and the uncanny, disjointed, and displaced character of symbolic identity.

Along these lines, it is not orthodox Marxism but a psychoanalytically informed dialectical materialism that exposes the connection between the capitalist economy of surplus value and the libidinal economy of surplus enjoyment (*jouissance*). The perversion of late capitalism is manifest in the obscene superego injunction to ever more consumption, self-fulfillment, and enjoyment (*On Belief*, pp. 20–21). Production creates the fantasmatic "need" for the objects it produces, turning subjects into consumers. However, no excess of capitalist consumption can efface the originary lack which is constitutive of the subject. Moreover, this capitalist injunction to enjoy, this incitement to ever further transgression, is linked to the postmodern disintegration of symbolic order and the loss of the social link. This is why, in his *Seminar XX: Encore*, Lacan emphasized the lack of rapport implied by enjoyment, pointing out the idiotic and solitary character of *jouissance* (*On Belief*, p. 23). Žižek discerns this idiotic, solitary enjoyment in our immersion in cyberspace. The immersion in cyberspace reduces the subject to a windowless, Leibnizean monad, with no way to know whether we are in touch with a "real other" beyond our PC screen (pp. 26–7).

Regarding the postmodern decline of symbolic efficacy, Žižek cautions against the hasty abandonment of the old conceptual coordinates of thinking:

> Today, in a time of continuous rapid changes, from the "digital revolution" to the retreat of old social forms, thought is more than ever exposed to the temptation of "losing its nerve," of precociously abandoning the old conceptual coordinates. The media constantly bombard us with the need to abandon the "old paradigms": if we are to survive, we have to change our most fundamental notions of what constitutes personal identity, society, environment, etc. New Age wisdom claims that we are entering a new "post-human" era; postmodern political thought tells us that we are entering post-industrial societies, in which the old categories of labor, collectivity, class, etc., are theoretical zombies, no longer applicable to the dynamics of modernization. The Third Way ideology and political practice is effectively THE model of this defeat, of this inability to recognize how the New is here to enable the Old to survive. Against this temptation, one should rather follow the unsurpassed model of Pascal and ask the difficult question: how are we to remain faithful to the Old in the new conditions? ONLY in this way can we generate something effectively New. (*On Belief*, pp. 32–3)

The temptation to be avoided today is that we abandon theory and lapse into hasty, *pre-theoretical generalizations*, such as the liberal tendency to reduce fascism and communism to two equal and opposite forms of "totalitarianism."

Against this, Žižek argues that Stalinist Socialism with its ruthless technological mobilization, manipulation of human beings, and Gulags, was a tragic perversion of a noble *emancipatory* project. By contrast, Nazism was an *anti-emancipatory* project which went all too well. Against Heidegger, Žižek points out that it was *not* Nazism, but Communism which had an inner greatness, namely its liberating potential. Nazism, by contrast, was totally perverse through and through from the very beginning. The Holocaust was not a tragic perversion of some (alleged) "inner greatness" of the Nazi project: on the contrary, the Holocaust *was* the Nazi project (*On Belief*, p. 39).

Žižek also argues against pre-theoretical generalizations which would reduce the human subject to either a machine or an animal: "This is the lesson of both psychoanalysis and the Judeo-Christian tradition: the specific human vocation does not rely on the development of man's inherent potentials (on the awakening of the dormant spiritual forces OR of some genetic program); it is triggered by an external traumatic encounter, by the encounter of the Other's desire in its impenetrability" (*On Belief*, p. 47).

According to Žižek's interpretation of the Judeo-Christian tradition, the passage from God to the Word is homologous to the beginning of subjectivity in the ascent from drive to desire, from the Real to the symbolic. The subject as Real is the antagonism between the will to contraction and the will to expansion. In order to cope with trauma, human subjects *symbolize*; the human infant enters the symbolic register only as a reaction to trauma, and the mode of this reacting is not genetically determined in advance (*On Belief*, pp. 47–8). Thus the proper object of psychoanalysis is not the animalistic, biological body, but the speaking, symbolic subject as the *gap* or split between *jouissance* and language. And against the Buddhist claim that animals, just as much as humans, are equal in not wanting suffering, Žižek points out that the psychoanalytic concept of drive designates the human subject's paradoxical ability to want unhappiness, to find excessive pleasure in suffering itself (*On Belief*, p. 63). Animals do not desire; desire is not biological need, nor is it the childish demand for proof of love.

On the contrary, desire is a defense against "the painful turmoil of excessive *jouissance*" (*On Belief*, p. 77). Thus symbolic law is not simply the result of rational deliberation or compromise; the true Law/ Prohibition is imposed by desire itself. In this sense, Law *is* desire. Real *jouissance* is excessive, and as a reaction to this anxiety-provoking excess, the pacifying symbolic network structures and distorts enjoyment into what we call "reality" (p. 80). Along these lines, religion – like Law – is not simply an institution contrived through human ingenuity to serve a social function, for "Gods are of the Real" (p. 82).

However, in this connection, it is crucial to keep in mind that for Lacan and Žižek the Real does not "exist" – after the manner of a thing or property – either within or "beyond" reality. Again, the Real does not exist, it insists. Even the Real of drive does not "exist" temporally prior to desire and symbolization. It is because the repressed Real is immanent to symbolic reality that it is impossible to symbolize the Real. In other words, if drive is prior to desire, it is ontologically prior rather than temporally prior. Lacan defines drive as the split subject in relation to the demands of the parents, and there is no temporality prior to subjectivity. The Real, like the religious notion of eternity, is excluded so that historical reality can maintain its consistency. The Real of drive is that against which the symbolic has always already arisen.

But if the Real as such is, in a sense, "impossible," does this mean that it is inaccessible? Is it the case, as deconstructionists claim, that Otherness and the Event of the Lacanian act are never encountered but always "to come," always deferred? Against this deconstructionist mantra, Žižek emphasizes that the Real as impossible *does* happen: "the 'Real as impossible' means that THE IMPOSSIBLE DOES HAPPEN, that 'miracles' like Love (or political revolution: 'in some respects, a revolution is a miracle,' Lenin said in 1921) DO occur" (*On Belief*, p. 84).

In *On Belief*, Žižek distinguishes the Lacanian act proper from hysterical acting out, from the psychotic *passage à l'acte*, and from the symbolic act:

> In the hysterical acting out, the subject stages, in a kind of theatrical performance, the compromise solution of the trauma she is unable to cope with. In the *psychotic passage à l'acte*, the deadlock is so debilitating that the subject cannot even imagine a way out – the only thing he can do is to strike blindly in the real, to release his frustration in the meaningless outburst of destructive energy. The symbolic act is best conceived of as the purely formal, self-referential, gesture of the self-assertion of one's subjective position. (pp. 84–5)

Unlike acting out, the passage to act, and the symbolic act, *the act proper* reconfigures the symbolic coordinates of the subject's situation. Though it is possible only against the background of symbolic reality, the Lacanian act as an encounter with the Real radically reinvents the subject's symbolic reality and her symbolic identity. Thus the act proper has an affinity with the impossible Real, as does Lacan's concept of the split subject, who "exists only through his own impossibility" (*On Belief*, p. 89).

This can help us to understand why Žižek contrasts symbolic desire with Christian love. Desire is caught up in the inconsistency of the symbolic register; desire thrives on the difference between the limited satisfaction we actually obtain, as opposed to the more full satisfaction we were seeking. For desire, *this* (whatever I have just attained) is not *that* (which I desire). By contrast, love – like the act proper – is an "impossible" miracle, in which this *is* that:

> love FULLY ACCEPTS that "this IS that" – that the woman with all her weakness and common features IS the Thing I unconditionally love; that Christ, this wretched man, IS the living God. Again, to avoid a fatal misunderstanding: the point is not that we should "renounce transcendence" and fully accept the limited human person as our love object, since "this is

all there is": transcendence is not abolished, but rendered ACCESSIBLE –
it shines through in this very clumsy and miserable being that I love. (*On
Belief*, p. 90)

The perfection of Christian love is thus "the loving attachment to the
Other's imperfection" (*On Belief*, p. 147). But how does this dialectical
materialist version of Christianity differ from the standard versions?

In the first place, according to Žižek's Christian-materialism, there is
no Hell and no Paradise: "there is simply NO PLACE in the Christian
edifice for an afterlife" (*On Belief*, p. 91). However, the main difference is
that Žižek asserts that the "spark of divinity" in human beings is that
which *prevents* us from being fully human, from achieving self-identity:
"the purely spiritual dimension towards which all humans strive, the
'divinity' is rather a kind of obstacle, of a 'bone in the throat' – it is
something, that unfathomable X, on account of which man cannot ever
become MAN, self-identical" (p. 90). If Christ, as the only Son of the
Father, was the unique case of "man = God," then after Christ's death,
"there is no place for any God of Beyond" (p. 91). Žižek, like Hegel,
interprets the crucifixion to mean that God really did die on the Cross.
Afterward, all that remains is the community of believers, joined in the
Holy Spirit. This reading explains why Žižek argues that Christianity as
such involves a moment of atheism, so that "only an atheist can believe."

This explains why, in the closing paragraphs of *On Belief*, Žižek asserts
that God's abandonment of his Son on the Cross signals God's
fundamental *imperfection* (p. 146). At both Matthew 27:46 and Mark
15:34, Christ is said to have cried out: "My God, my God, why have you
forsaken me?" In the New Testament, there are only seven quotations
attributed to Christ on the Cross. Significantly, this questioning cry
(which appears in both Matthew and Mark), is the only saying that
appears in more than one, parallel account of the crucifixion. Because
this question also occurs in the opening line of Psalm 21, some Christians
(especially those who consider themselves to be "fundamentalists") try
to evade the implications of Christ's question by claiming that Christ was
only quoting a psalm, etc. By contrast, some contemporary Christian
theologians point out that at this most decisive moment in the Gospels,
the Father seems to have deserted the Son. Like these latter theologians
(and unlike the so-called Christian "fundamentalists"), Žižek argues that
by uttering this questioning cry, Christ was announcing his mortality and
separation, as a human subject, from God: this gulf of separation, this
moment – not only of death, *but of atheism* – distinguishes the Christian
notion of God.

The Christian notion of rebirth is, in Lacanian psychoanalytic terms, the symbolic suicide implicit to the act. The act is "the possibility of new possibilities" (*On Belief*, p. 101). It is rebirth through the act which enables us to change our fundamental fantasy, to re-vision the secret treasure within us, and reinvent our very identity: "God is thus ultimately the name for the purely negative gesture of meaningless sacrifice, of giving up what matters most to us" (p. 150).

In conclusion, Žižek's dialectical materialism shows the way for subjects to break out of the ideological manipulations of global capitalism. The inconsistency in the symbolic texture of reality is irreducible (Real). Moreover, this inherent antagonism is also necessary for symbolic law to function. But it is this very gap that enables subjects to encounter the Real as the "outside" which is somehow *immanent* to the symbolic order. The Real is the "extimate" kernel of the symbolic order: the Real is intimately a part of the symbolic, and yet the Real may not be symbolized. Žižek argues that *faith without belief* – "faith" as the unconditional engagement with the Real – is the only true utopia.

Thus Žižek's call for a return to Lenin does *not* mean adopting Lenin's positive political procedures today. But if Lenin himself (his writings and actions, etc.) has been inscribed into the symbolic register, then is it not the case that the "authentic" Lenin has been misrepresented? So what is it about Lenin that we should return to or displace/re-inscribe? Again, "repetition" is not the recontextualization of some positive content; it is the repetition of a Real antagonism or negativity that is left out of the symbolic order. *On Belief* shows that Žižek's concept of repetition implies that the task for a revolutionary collective today is to return to what Lenin tried, and failed, to accomplish. If our revolutionary attempt to realize the impossible fails again, nonetheless we will *fail better* this time.

14

The Fright of Real Tears: Krzysztof Kieślowski between Theory and Post-Theory

Žižek engages with recent film theory in order to intervene in the debate between, on the one hand, what is usually referred to in this context as "Theory" and, on the other hand, the cognitivist "Post-Theory" of David Bordwell, Noel Carroll, and others. Žižek argues that, despite superficial appearances, what is called Theory in film studies has virtually nothing in common with Lacanian psycho-analytic theory. Consequently, when Bordwell (or other advocates of Post-Theory) attack such authors as Laura Mulvey or Kaja Silverman, they are in no way engaging with Lacan. In *The Fright of Real Tears*, Žižek shows how both Theory and Post-Theory fail to comprehend the relevance of Lacan for film theory. Žižek demonstrates a Lacanian approach to film theory by deploying psychoanalytic categories as well as insights from continental philosophy, and develops a nuanced and multifaceted interpretation of Krzysztof Kieślowski's films. The overarching theme of the book is Žižek's elaboration of the Real as that which makes impossible any rapport between the masculine and the feminine subject.

Lacan provided the ultimate formulation of this impossibility in his "formulae of sexuation": the masculine side combines universality with its constitutive exception, while the feminine side asserts the non-all as the paradoxical obverse of this lack of exception. One should read the two levels that define each position as "appearance versus truth": the upper level provides the "appearance," while the lower level discloses its "truth." The "appearance" of the masculine position is that of Universality, while

Žižek: A Reader's Guide, First Edition. Kelsey Wood.
© 2012 John Wiley & Sons, Inc. Published 2012 by John Wiley & Sons, Inc.

its "truth" is the constitutive Exception/transgression (say, the Hero-Master who violates the Law in order to constitute it); the "appearance" of the feminine position is the mysterious Exception, the Feminine which resists the universal symbolic order, while its "truth" is that there is nothing outside *the symbolic order, no exception.*

—Žižek, *The Fright of Real Tears: Krzysztof Kieślowski between Theory and Post-Theory,* p. 91

Perhaps Žižek's most penetrating intervention into film theory is *The Fright of Real Tears: Krzysztof Kieślowski between Theory and Post-Theory* (2001).[1] As always with Žižek's works, the reader of *Fright* gets much more than he bargained for. In the first part of the book, Žižek redefines the coordinates of the controversy in today's cinema studies between "Theory" and "Post-Theory" by demonstrating decisively that *both sides are wrong,* both sides misrepresent the psychoanalytic theory of Jacques Lacan.[2] Against the reductivist readings of Lacan presupposed by both Theorists and Post-Theorists, Žižek indicates a way beyond the controversy by deploying properly Lacanian concepts in order to reveal ideological tensions in the films of Kieślowski. Krzysztof Kieślowski (1941–1996) began his career as a brilliant documentary film maker in Poland during the 1970s. But once Kieślowski abandoned documentaries and turned to fiction, he became one of the greatest film makers of the twentieth century. In the second part of *Fright,* Žižek analyses the fundamental motifs of Kieślowski's entire oeuvre. The third part of *Fright* consists of a detailed interpretation of Kieślowski's three greatest works: *Decalogue* (1988), *The Double Life of Veronique* (1991), and *Colours* (1993–4).

Fright is an impressive and complex book, and not Žižek's most accessible. One hurdle for the general reader is to grasp the significance of theoretical concepts derived from Lacanian psychoanalysis (e.g. suture, gaze, impossible subjectivity, interface). But the more subtle dimension of the work involves the way Žižek utilizes Lacanian categories in order to develop his own anti-essentialist version of Hegelian dialectics. Žižek puts Lacanian categories to work by re-inscribing them within his own dialectical materialist philosophy:

[1] Unless otherwise stated, page references for this work are to the following edition: *The Fright of Real Tears: Krzysztof Kieślowski between Theory and Post-Theory* (London: British Film Institute, 2001).
[2] See Gopalan Ravindran's excellent essay "Žižek's *The Fright of Real Tears*: Theory, Post-Theory and Kieślowski," in *International Journal of Žižek Studies,* vol. 1/3 (2007): *Žižek and Cinema,* available online at http://zizekstudies.org/index.php/ijzs/issue/view/5.

the fundamental lesson of dialectics is that universality as such emerges, is articulated "for itself," only within a set of particular conditions. (All great historical assertions of *universal* values, from Ancient Roman Stoicism to modern human rights, are firmly embedded in a *concrete* social constellation.) However, one should avoid here the historicist trap: this unique circumstance does not account for the "truth" and universal scope of the analysed phenomenon. It is precisely against such hasty historicisers that one should refer to Marx's famous observation apropos of Homer: it is easy to explain how Homer's poetry emerged from early Greek society; what is much more difficult to explain is its universal appeal, i.e. why it continues to exert its charm even today. (*Fright*, p. 8)

In *Fright*, Žižek shows that what holds for Homer also holds for Kieślowski: it is easy to show how Kieślowski's work emerged from its social and political context; what is much more difficult to explain is its universal appeal.

Žižek illuminates the individual character of Kieślowski's work in a Hegelian way, by approaching this individuality via the dialectical tension between universality and particularity. That Hegel is a constant reference for Žižek in this work is apparent even in his organization of *Fright* into three parts (Universal, Particular, and Individual) which refer to Hegel's *Science of Logic*. On the face of things, it initially seems clear that the concept of *universality* involves sameness, and the concept of *particularity* involves difference. But according to Žižek's dialectical materialism, the *individual* identity of anything (e.g. the films of Kieślowski) does not arise through harmonious synthesis. Symbolic identity and reality imply a fundamental displacement. For example, symbolic identity functions as a kind of "mask" insofar as it involves the repression of impulses or antagonisms which are held to be inadmissible (*Fright*, p. 74). Thus there is no pure self-identity: symbolic identity implies contradiction which results from the repression of some Real trauma or antagonism.

All of this indicates that *Fright* is much more than a book about movies. Žižek acknowledges as much in his introduction, when he states that his aim is "not to talk *about* his [Kieślowski's] work, but to refer to his work in order to accomplish the *work* of Theory" (*Fright*, p. 9). Žižek views the conflict in film studies between deconstructionist Theory and cognitivist Post-Theory as emblematic of a wider crisis in cultural studies:

What looms in the background is a whole set of dilemmas, from the purely epistemological to politico-ideological ones: do cultural studies provide an adequate instrument to counteract global capitalism, or are they simply the ultimate expression of its cultural logic? Will cognitive scientists and other representatives of the so-called "Third Culture" succeed in replacing cultural critics as the new model of "public intellectuals"? (*Fright*, p. 2)

In *Fright* Žižek combines sophisticated philosophical and metapsychological insights with his unique brand of ironic humor. An example of his irony is found on page 130 of *Fright*, when Žižek analyses the role of "framing" in the interpretation of a painting. The irony is that this analysis repeats an account in the Introduction of his (alleged) "total bluff" about framing at a round table discussion. Žižek is (in)famous for employing irony and occasionally crude humor to intentionally distance non-philosophers: he literally *dares* the careless reader to dismiss him as a comedian or provocateur. But hasty critics should be wary of falling into one of Žižek's traps. It is difficult to discredit Žižek by quoting him out of context, because he always comes back to where he started (the Real). Informing his apparently disorganized writings is an extremely sophisticated dialectical logic which proves to be profoundly resilient and difficult to refute.

In Part 1 of *Fright*, Žižek reveals the inadequacy of the Post-Theory of David Bordwell and Noel Carroll (cf. Bordwell and Carroll, *Post-Theory: Reconstructing Film Studies*, 1985). Against the reductionistic scientism of the Post-Theorists, Žižek does not merely *claim* that theory is alive and well, he demonstrates this, first by revealing the fatal limitations of Post-Theory, and then by employing Lacanian categories to analyze not only Kieślowski's films but also the works of a wide range of film makers and authors. One limitation of the quasi-scientific approach of the Post-Theorists arises from their emphasis on physical, material reality and the private consciousness of the perceiver. This approach amounts to a dismissal of the history of ideas, and what Lacan called the symbolic register: that is, the intersubjective realm of language, signifying representations, and systems of rules (as well as the exceptions which delimit any rule's functioning). The narrow focus of the Post-Theorists leads them to "behave as if there were no Marx, Freud, semiotic theory of ideology, i.e. as if we can magically return to some kind of naiveté before things like the unconscious, the overdetermination of our lives by the decentred symbolic processes, and so forth became part of our theoretical awareness" (*Fright*, p. 14). But the Post-Theorist's exclusion of psychoanalytic and philosophical theory comes back – like the repressed Real – to haunt him, showing that, in some ways, "Post-Theory" is effectively "Pre-Theory." As Žižek points out, the alleged "professionalism" of Post-Theory is finally just another name for profound political resignation (p. 13). Moreover, their "fright of real theory" leads Post-Theorists to mistakenly direct their anti-Lacanian diatribes against deconstructionists and other postmodernists: Post-Theorists fail even to correctly identify the very Lacanians they are trying to refute. Žižek responds to this with wry humor: "in the global field designated by Post-Theorists as that of Theory, we are dealing with a [...] 'case of the missing Lacanians': except for Joan Copjec, myself and some of my Slovene colleagues, I know of no cinema theorist who effectively accepts Lacan as his or her ultimate background" (pp. 1–2).

More seriously, in their attacks on Theory as such, Post-Theorists employ two *mutually exclusive* arguments. On the one hand, Post-Theorists argue that Theory purports to be a grand theory of everything against which one should oppose modest, empirically verifiable programs for research. But, on the other hand, Post-Theorists also argue that Theorists reduce meaningful, basic questions to relativistic discussions of the historical conditions of the emergence of cinematic perceptions (*Fright*, p. 14). Furthermore, cognitivist Post-Theorists claim that their approach is "dialectical" but, as Žižek points out: "What Post-Theorists mean by a 'dialectical approach' is simply the notion of cognition as the gradual process of our always limited knowledge through the testing of specific hypotheses. [...] the cognitivist speaks from the safe position of the excluded observer" (pp. 14–15). Although they claim that their approach is dialectical, Post-Theorists in fact remain within parameters outlined long ago by Karl Popper, the most dismissive critic of Hegelian dialectics of all (p. 15). Thus when Bordwell claims to have identified a "trans-cultural universal," his unfamiliarity with Hegelian dialectics prevents him from realizing that "the very relationship between trans-cultural universals and culture-specific features is not an ahistorical constant, but historically overdetermined: *the very notion of a trans-cultural universal means different things in different cultures*" (*Fright*, p. 17).

Against the Post-Theorist's implicitly inconsistent notion of universality, Žižek deploys the Hegelian concept of concrete universality. Concrete universality is not simply a texture of particular situations in which some specific content hegemonizes the universal notion. In contrast to this, Žižek insists that Hegelian concrete universality implies that *the exception is the rule*. In other words, none of the particular instantiations of the universal notion fully actualizes its meaning. In this sense, the Hegelian concept of concrete universality anticipates the Lacanian Real, insofar as any possible constellation of particular exemplifications revolves around some central impossibility of symbolization. Žižek thus interprets concrete universality in light of the *failure* of totalization: any totality is inherently incomplete/inconsistent. And, along the same lines, because the subject's "position of enunciation" is irreducibly part of the process of disclosure, this position is indelibly inscribed into that which is disclosed (*Fright*, p. 15). As a result, there can be no neutral, objective definition of reality, because any allegedly "trans-cultural universal" ultimately turns out to be just another perspective:

> does the fact a non-Western (or even a medieval Western) painting can appear to us extremely confusing not indicate that there are no simple trans-cultural functions of guiding attention? In short, while the problem-solution model of historical research can undoubtedly lead to a lot of precise and enlightening insights, one should nonetheless insist that the procedures of posing problems and finding solutions to them always and by definition occur within a certain ideological context that determines which problems are crucial and which solutions acceptable. (*Fright*, p. 17)

In such ways, Žižek quite effectively shows that Post-Theory implies a philosophically untenable notion of universality. In contrast to the approach of the Post-Theorists, Žižek's dialectical materialism may be viewed as a "universal perspectivism," insofar as the universal functions as a negative *a priori*:

> at every stage of the dialectical process, the concrete figure "colours" the totality of the process, i.e. the universal frame of the process becomes part of (or, rather, drawn into) the particular content. To put it in Ernesto Laclau's terms, at every stage its particular content is not only a subspecies of the universality of the total process: it "hegemonises" this very universality, the "dialectical process" is nothing but the name for this permanent shift of the particular content which "hegemonises" the universality. (*Fright*, pp. 23–4)

Again, this means that universality is the struggle for universality, insofar as the sameness of anything does not consist in any of the various perspectives on it, or in the combination of all these perspectives. Any perspective finally proves to be inconsistent, just as any totality of perspectives is incomplete and inconsistent with itself. The only universal sameness is this irreducible difference or inconsistency, which permeates any symbolic system, reality, or identity (cf. Heidegger on "ontological difference," Derrida on *différance*, and Lacan on the Real).

Žižek's explicit arguments against Post-Theory in the first part of *Fright* are implicitly furthered by his analyses in the remainder of the book. The upshot is that only the application of theory allows the viewer to gain insight into the sociopolitical, psychological, and philosophical dimensions of film.

Post-Theorists argue that Lacanian terms such as suture, gaze, impossible subjectivity, and interface have no empirically verifiable meaning. Žižek responds by devoting two chapters to the concept of *suture*, and his analyses reveal the links between Lacanian psychoanalysis, cinema theory, and the critique of ideology. On page 56 of *Fright*, he defines suture as "the structurally necessary *short-circuit* between different levels (style, narrative, the economic conditions of the studio system of production, etc.). In Lacanian theory, suture is a conjunction of the imaginary and the symbolic, a conjunction which stands for "the paradoxical element which, within a given field, holds the place of its constitutive Outside." Suture does not provide closure, but introduces an element that *prevents* closure: "a 'symptomal torsion' embodied in the 'supernumerary' element which, while it is part of the situation, has no place within it."[3] Simply put, it is suture as a process (as a verb) that prevents the consistent, complete existence of suture (as a noun). Thus the key insight underlying the concept of suture is that, although Real trauma/antagonism permeates any symbolic representation (or diegetic reality in film), the Real can only be pointed to as that which distorts reality.[4] Because the Real is manifested as the inconsistency or lack of symbolic reality, the "wholeness" of the narrative content is signified only by reaching *beyond* the explicit narrative, and including some formal features to stand in for the repressed Real. In this sense, suture means that the *external* limit of symbolic reality is reflected back *within* symbolic reality, as the impossibility of totalization: "suture is the exact opposite of the illusory, self-enclosed totality that successfully erases the decentred traces of the production process: suture means that, precisely, such self-enclosure is *a priori* impossible, that the excluded externality always leaves its traces" (*Fright*, p. 58). Or, as Žižek puts it on page 32: "the limit between the social and its exteriority, the non-social, can only articulate

---

[3] Slavoj Žižek, *Iraq: The Borrowed Kettle* (London: Verso, 2004), p. 102.

[4] On the notion of suture, Žižek writes: "The most coherent effort to explain the relations among the various terms we have been discussing, the impossible real, the master-signifier, the non-denumerable subject and its repetition, is found in Miller's article on the theory of 'suture.'" See *Jacques Lacan: Critical Evaluations in Cultural Theory* (London: Routledge, 2003), p. 119. Miller's article on suture and the elements of the logic of the signifier was published in French in *Cahiers pour l'analyse*, vol. 1, Winter 1966. Subsequently an English version translated by Jacqueline Rose appeared in *Screen*, vol. 18, Winter 1978. A version of Miller's article is available online at http://www.lacan.com/symptom8_articles/miller8.html.

itself in the guise of a difference (by mapping itself onto a difference) between the elements of social space. In other words, although radical antagonism can only be represented in a distorted way, through the particular differences internal to the system, it *has* to be represented."

To clarify the concept of *gaze*, Žižek quotes Lacan, who in his *Seminar I* (1954) spoke of gaze in the following way: "I can feel myself under the gaze of someone whose eyes I do not see, not even discern. All that is necessary is for something to signify to me that there may be others there. This window, if it gets a bit dark, and if I have reasons for thinking that there is someone behind it, is straight-away a gaze" (*Fright*, p. 34). Gaze belongs to the imaginary register; it is purely fantasmatic. But it is experienced as though it is in the object, not in the perceiving subject: gaze is the point from which the object seems to regard the spectator. Along these lines, the concept of *impossible subjectivity* involves the free-floating gaze which belongs to no determinate subject, as for example:

> when, in the middle of a shot unambiguously marked as subjective, the spectator is all of a sudden compelled to acknowledge that *there is no possible subject within the space of diegetic reality who can occupy the point of view of this shot*. So we are not dealing here with the simple reversal of a subjective into an objective shot, but in constructing a place of *impossible* subjectivity, a subjectivity which taints the very objectivity with a flavour of unspeakable, monstrous evil." (*Fright*, p. 36)

What if the exchange of subjective and objective shots fails to produce the effect of suture? Such a situation calls for the effect of *interface* (*Fright*, p. 39). Interface is the uncanny redoubling of a character with a spectral image, reflection, or shadow. Insofar as the spectral image evokes the repressed Real, interface operates at a more primordial level than does suture (p. 52). Žižek succinctly describes the effect of interface as follows: "when the gap can no longer be filled by an additional signifier, it is filled by a spectral *object*, in a shot which, in the guise of the spectral screen, includes its own counter-shot" (p. 54).

In Parts 2 and 3 of *Fright*, Žižek reveals the technical complexities, the psychological subtlety, and the ethical profundity of Kieślowski's films. As a documentary film maker, Kieślowski's talent was to reveal the drabness as well as the heroism of day to day existence in the socialist bloc near the end of the Cold War era. Fairly early on, however, Kieślowski abandoned the documentary approach and turned to fiction. In Part 2 of *Fright*, Žižek argues that this choice was a profoundly *ethical* decision, and to support this, he quotes Kieślowski himself:

Not everything can be described. That's the documentary's great problem. It catches itself in its own trap. ... If I'm making a film about love, I can't go into a bedroom if real people are making love there. ... I noticed, when making documentaries, that the closer I wanted to get to an individual, the more objects which interested me shut themselves off. That's probably why I changed to features. There's no problem there. I need a couple to make love in bed, that's fine. Of course, it might be difficult to find an actress who's willing to take off her bra, but then you just find one who is. ... I can even buy some glycerine, put some drops in her eyes and the actress will cry. I managed to photograph some real tears several times. It's something completely different. But now I've got glycerine. I'm frightened of real tears. In fact, I don't even know whether I've got the right to photograph them. At such times I feel like somebody who's found himself in a realm which is, in fact, out of bounds. That's the main reason why I escaped from documentaries.[5]

Žižek agrees with Kieślowski that there is something unwarranted, even obscene, about probing into another's intimacy. And significantly, as Žižek shows, this motif of the dialectical tension between documentary reality and fiction – as the problem of trespass on the Other's real intimacy – runs through several of Kieślowski's later films. Thus an important thematic element in Kieślowski's films is the transgressive attraction of the Real, as well as the ethical function of *shame* (*Fright*, p. 73).

Žižek argues that all of Kieślowski's work involves this ethical dimension; thus several of his protagonists are faced with fundamental (even potentially fatal) decisions, such as the choice of whether to commit themselves to a vocation, or to remain in the relative safety of their everyday existence: "From Kieślowski's early documentaries to *Veronique* runs the straight line of reflection upon the fundamental ethical choice between mission and life: the spontaneous flow of life tending towards calm is interrupted by the violent intrusion of interpellation" (*Fright*, pp. 160–61).

[5] *Kieślowski on Kieślowski*, ed. Danusia Stok (London: Faber and Faber, 1993), p. 86; cited in Žižek, *The Fright of Real Tears*, p. 72.

15

Did Somebody Say Totalitarianism? Five Interventions in the (Mis)use of a Notion

Žižek argues that the term "totalitarianism" functions as a stopgap; instead of enabling thought, it prevents us from thinking. Academia today is infected with a kind of pseudo-leftist irrationalism, because for postmodernists the concept of universality is unreflectively conflated with mechanisms of domination. Against the global capitalist ideology of liberal democracy, Žižek articulates a type of universality that does not function as the presupposition of a neutral space for pragmatic compromise, but rather as a fundamentally antagonistic or negative *a priori*. As Žižek had already put it in *For They Know Not What They Do*, because of a minimal logical temporality, even A = A produces the effect of pure contradiction. The identity of an entity with itself is the coincidence of this entity with the empty place of its inscription. Identity-with-itself is another name for self-referential negativity, for the negative relationship that defines one's identity.[1] This concept of identity as contradiction facilitates Žižek's articulation of a universality that precedes and makes possible all subsequent *struggles* for universality. Based on this conception of universality as fundamental negativity, Žižek clarifies the essential difference between fascism and communism, and identifies a redemptive dimension that was implicit in even the darkest time of Stalinism.

On the "Celestial Seasonings" green tea packet there is a short explanation of its benefits: "Green tea is a natural source of antioxidants, which neutralize harmful molecules in the body known as free radicals. By

---

[1] Žižek, *For They Know Not What They Do* (London and New York: Verso, 2002), pp. 35–6.

Žižek: A Reader's Guide, First Edition. Kelsey Wood.
© 2012 John Wiley & Sons, Inc. Published 2012 by John Wiley & Sons, Inc.

taming free radicals, antioxidants help the body maintain its natural health." Mutatis mutandis, is not the notion of totalitarianism one of the main ideological antioxidants, whose function throughout its career was to tame free radicals, and thus to help the social body to maintain its politico-ideological good health?
—Slavoj Žižek, *Did Somebody Say Totalitarianism: Five Interventions in the (Mis)use of a Notion*, p. 1

One of Žižek's most controversial and contentious works is *Did Somebody Say Totalitarianism? Five Interventions in the (Mis)use of a Notion* (2001).[2] This book (abbreviated *Totalitarianism* below) is a pointed attack on contemporary political attitudes, especially among today's liberal but "self-professed 'radical' academia" (p. 1). Žižek's introduction introduces the thesis of the book, namely that the notion of totalitarianism today functions as a kind of "ideological antioxidant," the purpose of which is to tame free radicals, prevent thinking, and thereby sustain the illusion of concord in late capitalist society. In *Totalitarianism*, Žižek shows that the liberal-democratic consensus on totalitarianism defines it with a reference to the Holocaust as the ultimate evil, to the Gulag as the (alleged) truth of communism, to the rise of ethnic/religious fundamentalisms, and to the deconstructionist mantra that the root of totalitarianism is the concept of universality. Žižek analyzes all four of these references, and boldly attacks the liberal-democratic consensus itself.

The sting of *Totalitarianism* is that Žižek directs his fire, not so much against right-wing conservatives, as against the left – more specifically, against pseudo-leftist liberals – especially postmodernist academics. Žižek indicates how our alleged academic freedom is, in fact, constrained by numerous unwritten prohibitions. These unwritten rules operate at a pre-conscious level to ensure that the ideology of liberal global capitalism is never seriously questioned: "One of these unwritten rules concerns the unquestioned ubiquity of the need to 'contextualize' or 'situate' one's position: the easiest way to score points automatically in a debate is to claim that the opponent's position is not properly 'situated' in a historical context" (*Totalitarianism*, p. 1). Many postmodernists interpret historicism as epistemic and ethical relativism; but historicist advocates of epistemic relativism implicitly appeal to the very universality they explicitly deny. However, postmodernists remain blithely untroubled by

---

[2] Unless otherwise stated, page references for this work are to the following edition: *Did Somebody Say Totalitarianism? Five Interventions in the (Mis)use of a Notion* (London and New York: Verso, 2002).

the paradox of self-reference implicit to relativism; as Žižek wryly observes: "Rationality as such gets a bad press today" (p. 7).

Žižek argues that historicism is not only false but, moreover, functions today as the ideology of world-market globalization. Epistemic and ethical relativism involve refusals of awareness, and Žižek shows that the relativist's emphasis on historical contingency is *not radical enough*. Because symbolic fictions shape people's behavior, the symbolic order has "reality"; it has a kind of virtual reality. The symbolic big Other is "the virtual order that regulates intersubjective space" (*Totalitarianism*, p. 254). The limit of historicism involves its failure to acknowledge the power of abstraction: "the circulation of Capital is the force of radical 'deterritorialization' (to use Deleuze's term) which, in its very functioning, actively ignores specific conditions and cannot be 'rooted' in them" (p. 2). But most academics today conform to the unwritten prohibition against questioning the global capitalist ideology of relativism; the postmodern left, for example, automatically conflates any form of universality with "totalitarianism." Žižek argues that the left today (ca. 2001) has simply accepted the notion that capitalism is here to stay, and one sign of this is the common but misguided phantasmatic image of communism and fascism as equal and opposite extremes of totalitarianism which exist on the same spectrum.

One of Žižek's primary aims in *Totalitarianism* is to show that this image is deceptive: the splitting of our political space into the Left and the Right cannot be translated into any "metalanguage." There is no common language between left and right; there is no neutral standard, no "objective" common ground of universality by which to compare them according to the same criteria of evaluation. Simply put, these are not two extremes on the same "neutral" scale or spectrum; this is nothing but an inherently illusory image. In contrast to this imagined "neutral space" for compromise, the political field is homologous to the difference between feminine and masculine subjects, in which "there is no sexual rapport."

Just as the logic of feminine sexuation gives rise to *a completely different concept of universality* than does the masculine logic, so also does the left differ from the right: there are simply no common denominators to link the two incommensurable symbolic universes. Thus a true leftist, Žižek argues, is one who behaves in such a way so as to acknowledge that this lack of rapport – this sociosymbolic inconsistency – is Real and irreducible. By contrast, pseudo-leftist liberals believe that there *is* a common measure by which to compare the two symbolic universes. Self-professed "leftist" liberals succumb to the fantasy of a neutral and "objective" universal standard of evaluation. Against this, Žižek argues that universality *is an engagement in the struggle for universality* that involves fully identifying with the excluded "excremental remainder" of today's capitalist sociosymbolic order (e.g. slum-dwellers, the homeless, and the stateless). Žižek argues that the postmodern left (particularly academics who prize their privileges) has unthinkingly adopted the basic coordinates of liberal capitalism. It is thus no accident that any serious political inquiry which throws into question the existing order is immediately perceived as totalitarian. The postmodern left's unreflective references to totalitarianism reinforce the unwritten rule against questioning the liberal-democratic hegemony which sustains global capitalism. Moreover this vague notion of totalitarianism does not function as a theoretical concept which facilitates further insight, but as a *stopgap* which prevents us from acquiring any insight at all (*Totalitarianism*, p. 3).

To combat such "pseudo-leftist irrationalism," Žižek articulates a kind of universality that functions neither as the foundation for eternally unchanging knowledge, nor as an allegedly neutral space for pragmatic compromise. Against both of these forms of sophistry, Žižek deploys the Hegelian concept of concrete universality as a fundamentally antagonistic, negative *a priori*. He interprets concrete universality as the inherent negativity that ruptures from within any symbolic order, any constellation of situated particulars. Viewed in this way, concrete universality involves the Real antagonism that makes any totalization inherently inconsistent. And because the concept of concrete universality is articulated in terms of situated particularity, Žižek cannot be accused of overlooking the moment of truth implicit to the emphasis on historical contingency.

The truly infuriating thing for many pseudo-leftist liberals is that Žižek actually does reveal the triviality of postmodern so-called "thought" – not to mention the inherently *reactionary* character of such academic fashions as identity politics and "deep ecology."[3] Žižek accomplishes this

---

[3] Žižek explains this with reference to Deleuze: "I think that what is fundamentally wrong with [identity politics] is that ultimate authenticity is based on the idea that only the person who is immediately affected by circumstances can tell the true story about his or her suffering – let's say only a gay black woman can really know and say what it means to be a gay black woman, and so on. But, as Deleuze puts it somewhere, the reference to your unique experience as the basis of ethical argument always ends up in a reactionary position. For example, the main excuse of many Nazis after the Second World War was always along the lines of: yes, you can condemn us in general terms, but can you imagine what it meant to be a German in the 1930s?" See Slavoj Žižek and Glyn Daly, *Conversations with Žižek* (Cambridge: Polity Press, 2004), p. 142. In other texts, Žižek uses the word "reactionary" to characterize the ultraconservative opposition to progressive social change and

by using categories from the psychoanalytic theory of Jacques Lacan to reactualize Hegelian dialectics. One example which indicates the potency of Žižek's dialectical materialism involves the Lacanian concept of desire, which is always transgressive. Lacan found the desire of the Miser to be of especial interest, because the Miser's desire is *excessive in its very moderation*. In *Totalitarianism*, Žižek refers to this example in order to concisely link Lacanian psychoanalysis, Hegelian dialectics, and a Marxist-style critique of capitalist ideology:

> Marx claimed that, in the series production-distribution-exchange-consumption, the term "production" is doubly inscribed, it is simultaneously one of the terms in the series and the structuring principle of the entire series: in production as one of the terms of the series, production (as the structuring principle) "encounters itself in its oppositional determination," as Marx put it, using the precise Hegelian term. And the same goes for desire: there are different species of desire (i.e., of the excessive attachment that undermines the pleasure principle); among these species, desire "as such" encounters itself in its "oppositional determination" in the guise of the miser and its thrift, the very opposite of the transgressive move of desire.[4]

Thrift (moderation) as an expression of the Miser's (immoderate) desire shows how the transgressive exception *is directly inscribed into the series of desired objects*. The series of objects involves an inconsistency (e.g. the negativity implied by oppositional determination) which is constitutive of the series even as it is inscribed within the series. The symbolic big Other is thus structured around the void of a central antagonism. This subtle but forceful example indicates why professional philosophers find it so difficult to refute Žižek's anti-essentialist (i.e. materialist) development of Hegelian dialectics. In such ways, Žižek's dialectical materialism evokes the homology between capitalism's economy of surplus value (i.e. profit) and the libidinal economy of excessive enjoyment (*jouissance* as pleasure-in-pain).

Yet another aspect of Žižek's work which professional philosophers find troublesome is his "Christian-materialism." One philosopher in the

---

emancipatory politics; he associates reactionary ideas with mysticism, sentimentality, racism, misogyny, Buddhist resignation, and paganism.

[4] Slavoj Žižek "From the Myth to Agape," in *Journal of European Psychoanalysis*, number 8–9, Winter–Fall 1999, available online at http://www.psychomedia.it/jep/number8-9/zizek. htm. Also see Žižek's *Did Somebody Say Totalitarianism: Five Interventions in the (Mis)use of a Notion* (London: Verso, 2001), p. 40.

USA even makes the (rather paranoid) suggestion that Žižek is just playing an elaborate joke on posterity by purporting to combine inherently irreconcilable elements of Marxism and Christianity.[5] Oddly, in the same review, the author refers to Žižek as a "Stalinist," even though Žižek discusses at length – in *Totalitarianism* and in various other works – the perversity of Stalinism. But, regarding religion in general, Žižek emphasizes that myth is inseparable from logos (cf. *On Belief*, p. 11). We unreflectively give in to the temptation to believe in God because "God is unconscious" (p. 88). Žižek also makes it clear that for dialectical materialism, it is the radical-emancipatory potential of the ethical act (e.g. love of imperfect humanity) which links Christianity and Marxism. Thus Žižek states unequivocally that there is no place in Christianity for the notion of an afterlife (cf. *On Belief*, p. 91). Moreover, the God of "beyond" died on the cross with his Son, impotent to save either himself or his Son (*Totalitarianism*, pp. 50–51).

According to Žižek, Christ's sacrifice is a radically meaningless, excessive act: in other words, it is an act of *love* for imperfect humanity. Furthermore, Žižek argues that the theological notion of sacrifice as "payment for sin" *is itself the sin* (*Totalitarianism*, p. 52). To put it in terms of Lacanian psychoanalysis, Žižek interprets Christ's death as showing humanity that we can twist free of the vicious cycle of symbolic Law and its obscene supplement, the superego injunction to transgress. The Good News of Christianity is that Christ erases sins through love of fallen humanity; an ethical act retroactively erases sins without trace. Here again Žižek flaunts academic fashion, clearly demonstrating that he is no political cynic: an act committed out of love for humanity can bring "a New Beginning" (p. 53). Žižek argues that Christian love emerges insofar as the Other is loved not in spite of but *because of* his lack and imperfection. Therefore, if God can be loved, he must be imperfect and lacking (p. 57). That is, we do not love the Other by overcoming some "intolerance" toward him (intolerance allegedly grounded in our reluctance to admit some repressed similarity to him). The problem is not that this superficial view is wrong in every case, but that it *presupposes that love is always fundamentally narcissistic*, as in Aristotle's claim that "a friend is another self." Against this, Lacanians argue that "self" (i.e. ego) is a fantasy image of wholeness or consistency. Thus for Žižek, Christian love implies that the true Otherness is not the repressed heterogeneity *within us*, but

---

[5] See Adrian Johnston's "Review – The Fright of Real Tears," available online at http://metapsychology.mentalhelp.net/poc/view_doc.php?type=book&id=720.

(as Hegel might have said) the "Otherness of the Other itself to itself" (p. 57). In short, Christian love points toward the Lacanian ethics of the Real. As opposed to the fantasmatic register of the imaginary, and to the intersubjective network of the symbolic big Other, the Real designates an enigmatic, even traumatic encounter which cannot be imagined or symbolized adequately. Žižek argues that the Real in this sense – the Otherness of the Other itself to itself – is the very condition of human freedom: "Freedom is ultimately *nothing but* the space opened up by the traumatic encounter, the space to be filled in by its contingent/inadequate symbolizations/translations" (p. 58).

The "normal" neurotic responds to the traumatic encounter with the Real – e.g. the desire of the Other – by symbolizing; thus, unlike (some of) the postmodern leftists he opposes, Žižek does not attempt to undermine symbolic authority as such. Instead, he investigates the way order arises, and carefully analyses the structural differences between symbolic orders, for example, between Nazism and Stalinism. He takes this approach because the symbolic order (including the prohibitions of the symbolic Father) alleviates the stifling anxiety produced by the overproximity of the Real. Žižek explains this concisely by asserting that "father" is the solution to the deadlock, the symbolization which functions as a compromise formation and/or a symptom that "alleviates the unbearable anxiety of directly confronting the Void of the Other's desire" (*Totalitarianism*, p. 60). The task for all of us (neurotics) who have repressed the traumatic encounter with the Real, is thus to reform our symbolic universe *by encountering the Real again, for example, through love.* To put this in terms of Lacanian psychoanalysis, the task for the subject is to achieve an ethics of the Real by assuming the position of the analyst. This means embracing the insight that any symbolic order is irreducibly inconsistent, that is, fully accepting that the intersubjective symbolic network – the big Other – ultimately does not exist. This explains Žižek's assertion that "only the psychoanalyst who endorses the nonexistence of the big Other is a true atheist" (p. 89).

Because the symbolic big Other finally does not exist, communication occurs only in and through miscommunication: a successful communication in Lacan's sense of the term involves responding not to what the Other intended to say, but to the Other's *repressed* message (*Totalitarianism*, p. 95). If I am not aware of the repressed dimension of what I say to you, how can we communicate? Put succinctly, we communicate successfully insofar as I receive back from you my message in its inverted, "true" form. This indicates the truly radical dimension of Lacan's linguistic reinvention of psychoanalysis, insofar as I will no doubt vehemently deny ever having implied any such thing. The nonexistence of the big Other means that a successful (i.e. "true") communication usually occurs without either participant being consciously aware of it. The truth is *externalized*, alienated from consciousness in the inconsistency of the symbolic register. This Lacanian insight not only casts new light on several traditional problems of philosophy, it also indicates why Žižek argues in *Totalitarianism* (and elsewhere) that those who claim our era is "post-ideological" are dangerously wrong.

The critique of ideology is not only requisite due to the disconnect between what we say and what we do. More to the point, the critique of ideology is imperative today insofar as there are things we know to be true, even though we do not *believe* them. One example of this fetishist disavowal involves global climate change: even if I know perfectly well that the practices of multinational corporations today are putting at risk the very survival of Homo sapiens, I behave as if I do not know this.

Again, Žižek's dialectical materialist conception of universality essentially involves fundamental antagonism or incommensurability (cf. the Hegelian notion of oppositional determination). This negative form of universality is linked to the Real and, as such, it both precedes and informs all subsequent struggles for symbolic hegemony. Based on this, Žižek articulates an ethics of the Real, which enables him to clarify essential differences between fascism and communism. In chapter 3 of *Totalitarianism*, Žižek discusses at some length the perversity of Stalinist Communism and its numerous evils, such as mass murder, the show trials, and the Gulags. In spite of his detailed discussion of such evils, Žižek argues nonetheless that there was always "a redemptive dimension" of communism, even during the darkest time of Stalinism (*Totalitarianism*, p. 88). The problem with the Stalinist Communists, he argues, was not that they were ruthlessly dedicated to the cause of communism, but that *they forgot this cause*: "they were not pure enough, and got caught up in the *perverse* economy of duty: 'I know this is heavy and can be painful, but what can I do? This is my duty ...'" (p. 111). Moreover, the ideology of Stalinism involved a regression to a (pre-Leninist) belief in an "objectivist logic" of necessary stages of development (p. 112). Žižek shows, by contrast, how Lenin was always ready to intervene, transforming the coordinates of a situation, even when everyone around him (including his wife) was convinced that because the time was not yet ripe, Lenin must be mad: "Lenin's point is [...]: ultimately *there is no objective logic of the 'necessary stages of development,'* since 'complications' arising from the intricate texture of concrete situations and/or from the unanticipated results of 'subjective' interventions always disrupt the smooth course of things" (p. 115). In other words, Lenin effectively recognized – to put it in Lacanian terms – that the big Other does not exist. By contrast, Stalinists did not recognize this.

What about the common image of fascism and communism as two equal and opposite extremes of totalitarian evil, to the right and to the left of "moderate" liberal capitalism? The first thing to note is that Žižek thoroughly analyzes the horrors and miserable failures of "actually existing Socialism," especially Stalinism. Thus he cannot be accused of defending communism out of ignorance (e.g. because he only experienced the rather "soft" Yugoslav variety). Žižek even argues that in order to realize the possibility of a communist alternative to capitalism today, leftists must fully confront the horrors of Stalinism. In order for true leftists today to re-inscribe the communist hypothesis and reinvent today's global-capitalist symbolic order, we cannot close our eyes to the failures of Communist regimes. The failure to encounter the Real trauma of Stalinism explains Žižek's criticisms of the Frankfurt School of Western Marxism:

> "Stalinism" (really existing socialism) was thus for the Frankfurt School a traumatic topic apropos of which it HAD to remain silent – this silence was the only way for them to retain their inconsistent position of the underlying solidarity with the Western liberal democracy, without losing their official mask of its "radical" Leftist critique. Openly acknowledging this solidarity would deprive them of their "radical" aura, changing them into another version of the Cold War anti-Communist Leftist liberals, while showing too much sympathy for the "really existing Socialism" would force them to betray their unacknowledged basic commitment.[6]

Even though he scrutinizes the perversity of Stalinism, nonetheless Žižek (like Alain Badiou) also reminds us that "actually existing Socialism" was for several decades an effective force against the rule of global capital (*Totalitarianism*, p. 130). And at the time of this writing (ca. 2010) – more than two decades after what both Žižek and Badiou call "the obscure disaster" of the collapse of European Communism – when many economists concur that we are entering another great depression, even the miserable failures of actual Communist regimes cannot efface the oppositional role these regimes play as what both Žižek and

---

[6] Slavoj Žižek "Heiner Mueller out of Joint," available online at http://www.lacan.com/mueller.htm. Also see Žižek's *Did Somebody Say Totalitarianism: Five Interventions in the (Mis)use of a Notion* (London: Verso, 2001), p. 93.

Fredric Jameson call "liberated territories" (p. 131). Since capitalism today "defines and structures the *totality* of human civilization," in spite of their miserable failures, Communist regimes at least hold open the possibility of an escape from the logic of world-market capitalism, with its inevitably recurring crises (pp. 130–31). It is thus no accident that so many anti-Communist dissidents finally ended up bitterly criticizing capitalism. As Žižek points out: "What anti-Communist dissidents such as Havel overlook, then, is that the very space from which they criticised and denounced terror and misery was opened and sustained by Communism's attempt to escape the logic of capitalism" (p. 131).

In several works Žižek argues that in right-wing authoritarian regimes, everyone is fully aware that behind the conservative populist rhetoric there is really nothing but greed and the lust for power. By contrast, even in left-wing "totalitarian" regimes, the leaders really act out of (what is perceived as) virtue.[7] But to concisely summarize the main thrust of Žižek's argument here, the essential difference between Nazism and Stalinism is indicated by the difference between the extermination camps of the Nazis and the forced labor camps (Gulags) of the Stalinists. The Nazi extermination camps produced the *passive* "Muslim," who was "reduced to the apathetic vegetative existence of a living death through physical terror" (*Totalitarianism*, pp. 87–8). By contrast, Stalinism produced victims of show trials, who were themselves forced to *actively* forsake their dignity. Žižek argues that Stalinist ideology "even at its most 'totalitarian,' still exudes an emancipatory potential" (p. 131). And even in the Gulag, the collective participation in material production sustained a sense of communist solidarity (p. 135). In his brief essay, "The Two Totalitarianisms," Žižek clarifies the differences between Nazism and Stalinism in an accessible and convincing way:

> Till now, to put it straightforwardly, Stalinism hasn't been rejected in the same way as Nazism. We are fully aware of its monstrous aspects, but still find *Ostalgie* acceptable: you can make *Goodbye Lenin!*, but *Goodbye Hitler!* is unthinkable. Why? To take another example: in Germany, many CDs featuring old East German Revolutionary and Party songs, from "Stalin, Freund, Genosse" to "Die Partei hat immer Recht," are easy to find. You would have to look rather harder for a collection of Nazi songs. Even at this anecdotal level, the difference between the Nazi and Stalinist universes is clear, just as it is when we recall that in the Stalinist show trials, the accused

---

[7] For example, see Slavoj Žižek, *Tarrying with the Negative: Kant, Hegel, and the Critique of Ideology* (Durham, NC: Duke University Press, 1993), pp. 100–101.

had publicly to confess his crimes and give an account of how he came to commit them, whereas the Nazis would never have required a Jew to confess that he was involved in a Jewish plot against the German nation. The reason is clear. Stalinism conceived itself as part of the Enlightenment tradition, according to which, truth being accessible to any rational man, no matter how depraved, everyone must be regarded as responsible for his crimes. But for the Nazis the guilt of the Jews was a fact of their biological constitution: there was no need to prove they were guilty, since they were guilty by virtue of being Jews. In the Stalinist ideological imaginary, universal reason is objectivised in the guise of the inexorable laws of historical progress, and we are all its servants, the leader included. A Nazi leader, having delivered a speech, stood and silently accepted the applause, but under Stalinism, when the obligatory applause exploded at the end of the leader's speech, he stood up and joined in. [...] Consider the fact that, on Stalin's birthday, prisoners would send him congratulatory telegrams from the darkest gulags: it isn't possible to imagine a Jew in Auschwitz sending Hitler such a telegram. It is a tasteless distinction, but it supports the contention that under Stalin, the ruling ideology presupposed a space in which the leader and his subjects could meet as servants of Historical Reason. Under Stalin, all people were, theoretically, equal. We do not find in Nazism any equivalent to the dissident Communists who risked their lives fighting what they perceived as the "bureaucratic deformation" of socialism in the USSR and its empire: there was no one in Nazi Germany who advocated "Nazism with a human face."[8]

But many politically cynical and opportunistic academics in Western societies today have effaced these distinctions. We have no sense of community or solidarity; on the contrary, we are paranoid and/or pathologically narcissistic, and we willingly submit to authority and increasing encroachments on academic freedom. This is because we are complicit in the excesses of global capital: we treat human beings in the Third World as if they are mere virtual entities in cyberspace, to be exploited and even killed (*Totalitarianism*, p. 136). Meanwhile, in sweat shops worldwide, from Mexico to Guatemala to Brazil to China, workers toil to produce products for our consumption and enjoyment, products which they could never afford to purchase (p. 137). We Western academics all too willingly submit to administrative authority and unwritten prohibitions against critical thinking, all the while preoccupying ourselves with vicious

---

[8] See Slavoj Žižek, "The Two Totalitarianisms," in *London Review of Books*, vol. 27, number 6, March 17, 2005, p. 8; the essay is available online at http://www.lrb.co.uk/v27/n06/slavoj-zizek/the-two-totalitarianisms.

maneuverings in order to secure our petty little privileges. Our political cynicism, rationalizations, and lethargy make it easy for our leaders to invade other countries in order to exploit the natural resources there. We are blind to our own participation in the excesses of global capitalism; we remain willfully ignorant of the fact that our "freedom" to consume cheap products is bought at the price of unimaginable suffering in the Third World. In other writings, Žižek has argued that Stalinism was the *symptom* of capitalism:

> We should not succumb to the temptation of reducing capitalism to a mere form of appearance of the more fundamental ontological attitude of technological domination; we should rather insist, in the Marxian mode, that the capitalist logic of integrating the surplus into the functioning of the system is the fundamental fact. Stalinist "totalitarianism" was the capitalist logic of self-propelling productivity liberated from its capitalist form, which is why it failed: Stalinism was the symptom of capitalism.[9]

Liberal, pseudo-leftist academics find it easy to scoff at such claims. But we have no conception of what would really be involved in creating a society in which material production and creative fulfillment through labor were *not* subordinated to the capitalist logic of exploitation for profit: "against the standard liberal demonizing vision of Stalin as a perverse Master systematically pursuing a diabolical plan of mass murder, is that this extremely brutal violent exercise of power as power over life and death coincided with – or, rather, was the expression of, its exact opposite, a total incapacity to govern the country through 'normal' authority and executive measures" (*Totalitarianism*, p. 119).

The implicit reference here to Hegelian oppositional determination in no way justifies Stalin's crimes. However, it does support Žižek's arguments that Nazism was a racist and genocidal project through and through, from its very inception (as even a cursory reading of Hitler's *Mein Kampf* indicates). Communism, however – not just in spite of, but even *because of* its perversion under Stalin – retained the character of *a radical-emancipatory movement* which went wrong. This idea that a principled, emancipatory movement nonetheless sometimes goes wrong can help us to understand why, in *The Fright of Real Tears*, Žižek associates Stalinist propaganda with what he calls "proto-Fascism."[10]

---

[9] See Slavoj Žižek, "Jacques Lacan's Four Discourses," available online at http://www. lacan.com/zizfour.htm.

[10] See Žižek, *The Fright of Real Tears: Krzysztof Kieślowski Between Theory and Post-Theory* (London: British Film Institute), p. 189, note 59: "Therein resides Capra's proto-Fascism:

Žižek concludes *Totalitarianism* with a Marxist argument. Cyberspace affects everyone in the world today in one way or another, and it enables the digital control of our everyday existence on a scale never before possible: "The digitalisation of our daily lives, in effect, makes possible a Big brother control in comparison with which the old Communist secret police supervision cannot but look like primitive child's play" (p. 256). How do we ensure that this control is not exercised by and for the wealthy, powerful elite few? How do we change the sociosymbolic order from capitalist exploitation to an order which allows symbolic identification with those who are outcast and disenfranchised today (e.g. the millions of stateless slum-dwellers)? Instead of retreating ever further into our pathological narcissism, we should engage in the collective labor of building a communist world. And a good way to start would be by making cyberspace the property of the people, for example (as Žižek suggests in more recent writings), by socializing Microsoft.[11]

---

in his rendering of 'ordinary people' as *already* naive and good, not as struggling toward this goal, in the same way the Stalinist films presented the Soviet citizens as *already* good – in a kind of Kantian paralogism, 'goodness' becomes a direct, positive quality, not an elusive feature that only appears in magic moments."

[11] Slavoj Žižek and Glyn Daly, *Conversations with Žižek* (Cambridge: Polity Press, 2004), p. 154.

16

Welcome to the Desert of the Real

In the months following the tragic events of September 11, 2001, the United States of America missed an opportunity to recognize and to confront the inconsistency of liberal-global capitalism. But despite widely broadcast claims that nothing would ever be the same again, the USA reasserted the same old ideological commitments. Instead of encountering the Real as the inherent limit moment of our imaginary-symbolic reality – and thereby opening the possibility for the Lacanian act – the USA reaffirmed and reinforced its capitalist ideology. Žižek analyzes this failure and develops a spirited critique of global capitalist ideology.

> *That is the ultimate paradox of democracy: within the existing political order, every campaign against corruption ends up being co-opted by the populist extreme Right.*
> —Žižek, *Welcome to the Desert of the Real: Five Essays on September 11 and Related Dates*, p. 79

One of Žižek's more lively and remarkable interventions is *Welcome to the Desert of the Real: Five Essays on September 11 and Related Dates* (2002).[1]

---

[1] Unless otherwise stated, page references for this work are to the following edition: *Welcome to the Desert of the Real: Five Essays on September 11 and Related Dates* (London and New York: Verso, 2002).

Žižek: A Reader's Guide, First Edition. Kelsey Wood.
© 2012 John Wiley & Sons, Inc. Published 2012 by John Wiley & Sons, Inc.

This book (abbreviated *Welcome* below) is a pointed attack on the ideology of global liberal capitalism.

Žižek argues that the choice we are offered today between either "democracy" or fundamentalism involves the fallacy of false dilemma. Moreover, it is a *forced* choice: within the coordinates of our sociosymbolic order, no one is really free to choose fundamentalism, unless he also wants to be treated as a dangerous fanatic and to be hounded by the authorities. Žižek's introduction presents the thesis of the book, namely that this forced choice – which is imposed on us by the hegemonic ideology of liberal democracy – obscures the fact that what passes for democracy today is *not* the only possible alternative to fundamentalism (*Welcome*, p. 3).

Žižek argues that the defining feature of the twentieth century was its emphasis on the encounter with Real antagonism or trauma, as opposed to the imaginary-symbolic reality of everyday experience. However, this "passion for the Real" ultimately devolved into pure spectacle, as in both the Stalinist show trials as well as the publicity-oriented terrorist acts which we still face today. Thus the primary reason that terrorists destroyed the World Trade Center (WTC) towers on September 11, 2001, was not simply to kill people, or even to inflict damage on the financial system, "but *for the spectacular effect of it*," to horrify us and to publicize their cause (p. 11).

Žižek contrasts the way the twentieth century passion for the Real devolved into pure semblance, with the way today, the postmodern passion for semblance is inclining more and more toward the traumatic and intrusive Real (*Welcome*, pp. 9–10). This dialectical dynamic culminates in a paradoxical coincidence of opposites, as in today's market, where "we find a whole series of products deprived of their malignant properties: coffee without caffeine, cream without fat, beer without alcohol ..." (p. 10). Cyberspace offers virtual sex, which is sex without sex, and the digital technology of warfare lends a semblance of plausibility to promises of war without casualties (on our side), which is effectively "warfare without warfare" (p. 11).

Along the same lines, today's liberal, politically correct, and (allegedly) tolerant multiculturalism presupposes a bland and homogenized Other, one who "dances fascinating dances and has an ecologically sound holistic approach," but who is somehow lacking any of the intrusive, traumatic characteristics of a Real neighbor (alcoholism, wife-beating, patriarchy, homophobia). Multiculturalist tolerance is based on a narcissistic notion of love, completely different from Žižek's Christian-materialist love, which enjoins us to love the kind of Other it would actually be very difficult (and meaningful) to love. The problem is not only that the Hollywood ideological apparatus leads us to view the world as deprived of its traumatic Real. The uncanny effect of late capitalism – an effect produced through, among other things, corporate media, advertisements to turn children into nagging little consumers, as well as the addiction to electronic games and virtual reality – is that *our actual social existence has taken on the character of virtual reality*, or a fake performance (*Welcome*, pp. 13–14). More and more we treat persons as virtual entities. We behave in an artificial, cunning, and even paranoid way, like agents in a spy story. We *create* the very enemy who inhabits our dark fantasies.

Žižek argues that on the one hand, fantasy can provide a pacifying scenario that helps us domesticate the anxiety-provoking Real. But on the other hand, fantasy itself can evoke the shattering and inassimilable Real (*Welcome*, p. 18). The horror of the WTC attacks was intensified because we were in fact already (unconsciously) prepared for them, due to ideological fantasy. The attacks were "libidinally invested" with horrifying power insofar as we had been repeatedly warned by the media of the terrorist threat, as well as being conditioned for decades by Hollywood disaster movies. The shock of the events was intensified because "America got what it fantasized about" (pp. 15–16). Not only do terrorists develop strategies based on Hollywood films and information widely available on the internet, but, as Žižek points out, the Pentagon even sought the advice – in October 2001 – of Hollywood directors who specialize in disaster films, in order to more effectively prepare against future threats. Furthermore, beginning in November 2001, White House advisors met with Hollywood executives to coordinate the so-called "war against terror" (i.e. the invasion of Iraq) by spreading ideological fantasies in the USA and to viewers of Hollywood films around the world (*Welcome*, p. 16). All of this supports Žižek's argument that Hollywood functions as an "ideological state apparatus" which to some extent even engenders the very threat it indoctrinates us against. Again, what was most horrifying about the tragedy of September 11 was that what we had fantasized about entered our reality: the libidinally charged fantasy image entered into what we experience as "reality" and shattered it (p. 16).

What can we possibly do to counteract the effects of ideology and effectively prevent such tragedies? One way psychoanalysis can be of help here is by enabling us to recognize – in what we experience as *mere fiction* (e.g. disaster movies) – the kernel of the Real which "we are able to sustain only if we fictionalize it" (*Welcome*, p. 19). Put succinctly, we must recognize the dimension of fiction which permeates the symbolic order which we experience as reality. The true opposite of the intrusive/ traumatic Real is our experience of reality. For this reason, Real trauma which we are not yet ready to face (except in its fictional guise) can haunt us even more than the "normal" shocks we experience in our reality (p. 22). This indicates the meaning of the Lacanian dictum that the Real does not "exist," it *insists*. Here Žižek draws the connection to his own (unorthodox) communist politics:

> When I miss a crucial opportunity, and fail to make a move that would "change everything," the very nonexistence of what I *should have done* will haunt me forever: although what I did not do does not exist, its spectre continues to insist. In an outstanding reading of Walter Benjamin's "Theses on the Philosophy of History," Eric Santner elaborates Benjamin's notion that a present revolutionary intervention repeats/redeems past failed attempts: the "symptoms" – past traces which are retroactively redeemed through the "miracle" of the revolutionary intervention – are "not so much forgotten deeds, but rather forgotten *failures* to act, failures to *suspend* the force of social bond inhibiting acts of solidarity with society's 'others'" [...]. (*Welcome*, pp. 22–3)

We must not simply abandon the passion for the Real, and reduce our lives to keeping up appearances. Instead, we must ensure that our orientation toward the Real is not fake, so that it does *not* devolve into – or remain – the (postmodern) passion for mere semblance.

Another way that Žižek's psychoanalytically informed dialectical materialism can help us sustain an orientation toward the Real is by making us aware that underneath the public face of symbolic Law there is an obscene superego injunction to transgress this Law. Thus the ethical-political hero can sometimes transform the coordinates of symbolic reality simply by sticking to the letter of the Law, and ignoring the superego injunction to transgress. Since it is the shared *transgression* of the symbolic Law which characterizes capitalist society, one step toward transformation of the global capitalist symbolic order involves recognition of the Real dimension of class antagonism which ideology attempts to efface. Recognizing the extent to which (the repressed Real of) class antagonism shapes our behavior is one of the prerequisites for any collective political act which would effectively reinvent the sociosymbolic order.

In such ways, Žižek argues that revolutionary violence can sometimes free us from the vicious cycle of Law and the unconscious superego injunction to transgress the Law. The liberating, revolutionary "Leninist" violence is characterized by fidelity to a symbolic order which enables identification with those who are currently disenfranchised and outcast. But any revolution involves the dirty work of seizing control, as well as the "heroic gesture of fully assuming" the obscene underside of Power (*Welcome*, p. 30). Nonetheless, Žižek distinguishes between the "reactionary" and the "progressive" passion for the Real. The *progressive* passion for the Real involves recognizing the Real of class antagonism (p. 31). By contrast, the *reactionary* passion for the Real is motivated by the passion for purification, as in the Nazi project of racist genocide: "Take Nazi ideology: the Jew as its Real is a spectre evoked in order to conceal social antagonism – that is, the figure of the Jew enables us to perceive social totality as an organic whole" (p. 32).[2]

There is an invisible border separating the digitalized First World from "the desert of the Real" which is the Third World (*Welcome*, p. 33). In the First World, our awareness that "we live in an insulated artificial universe" induces the paranoiac notion that we are under the constant threat of destruction (p. 33). Misrepresenting the cause of terrorism as the clash of cultural traditions is our typical recourse, since this depoliticized approach leaves our ideological commitments unexamined. Against such ideological mystification, Žižek argues that terrorism is related to the functioning of the Real of capital. This Real is manifested in and through abstract "structural" decisions (e.g. of the International Monetary Fund and the World Trade Organization) which not only ignore – but contribute to – the suffering of millions in the Third World. Žižek describes what happens after IMF specialists and corporate boards make decisions about "restructuring." These abstract decisions, made by financial specialists in plush offices in the First World, "affect thousands, sometimes causing terrifying havoc and destruction, but the link between these 'structural' decisions and the painful reality of millions is broken; the 'specialists' taking the decisions are unable to imagine the consequences, since they measure the effects of these decisions in abstract terms (a country can be 'financially sane' even if millions in it are starving)" (*Welcome*, p. 36). The root cause of (highly visible) acts of terrorism is the (invisible) systemic violence of capitalism (p. 49).

Like the functioning of capital, war is also becoming less visible and more *abstract*. It is becoming more and more difficult to determine whether or not we are in a war, and whether or not we have an enemy:

[2] In various works, Žižek describes reactionary politics as the extremely conservative opposition to progressive social change. Reactionary ideologies such as Nazism involve the fantasy that "natural" and "organic" social harmony could be restored if only the Other (Jews, Blacks, gays, immigrants, leftists) could be disenfranchised and excluded.

With the spread of the anthrax panic in October 2001, the West got the first taste of this new "invisible" warfare in which – an aspect we should always bear in mind – we, ordinary citizens, are totally dependent on the authorities for information about what is going on: we see and hear nothing; all we know comes from the official media. A superpower bombing a desolate desert country and, at the same time, hostage to invisible bacteria – this, not the WTC explosions, is the first image of twenty-first-century warfare. (*Welcome*, p. 37)

Such a scenario is homologous to the way, in Lacanian theory, the public face of symbolic Law is doubled by the obscene superego injunction to transgress. Žižek highlights this dialectical coincidence of opposites: "are not 'international terrorist organizations' the obscene double of the big multinational corporations – the ultimate rhizomatic machine, omnipresent, albeit with no clear territorial base? Are they not the form in which nationalist and/or religious 'fundamentalism' accommodated itself to global capitalism?" (p. 38). But rhizomatic cells of resistance are not enough. Žižek doubts that resistance to the global capitalist order will ever be effective without a unified political agenda, the recognition of a common political enemy, and a shared commitment to a cause that we value more than life itself.

However, unlike many individuals in the Third World, we in First World countries are so decadent in our love of material comforts and luxuries that we cannot even imagine anymore a cause for which we would sacrifice our life (*Welcome*, p. 40). Žižek argues that the absurdity of our typical depoliticized misrepresentations of each and every conflict as merely another clash of civilizations ignores the fact that *all* such conflicts are related to global capitalism. In addition, the most horrific slaughters (Rwanda, Congo, Sierra Leone) occurred *within* a civilization, and were clearly related to world-market globalization (p. 41). We ask ourselves "Why do they hate us?" conveniently overlooking our close ties to Israel, as well as our manipulations which ensure that oil-rich nations (e.g. Saudi Arabia and Kuwait) *remain undemocratic* so that we can exploit their oil, since "any democratic awakening could give rise to anti-American attitudes" (p. 42). The only effective way to prevent such tragedies as what happened on September 11 from occurring not only here but *anywhere*, is to recognize that the root cause of terrorist/militarist violence is global capitalism (p. 49).

Hegelian categories always underlie Žižek's reasoning. Žižek argues that global capitalism functions as a Hegelian inconsistent totality; it is a dialectical unity of itself and its other (*Welcome*, p. 51). Thus in the case of the forced choice between Bin Laden or Bush, *both* alternatives are wrong, and the choice proposed to us is not a true choice. The only ethical stance is solidarity with all victims, the victims of global capitalist exploitation *and* the victims of terrorism. Such an ethics of the Real involves a negative form of universality, a universality of the Real as irreducible symbolic inconsistency: "The actual universality is not the never-won neutral space of translation from one particular culture to another, but, rather, the violent experience of how, across the cultural divide, we share the same antagonism" (p. 66). Thus a true leftist is one who recognizes that antagonism is irreducible and Real, while a reactionary is anyone who believes in the fantasy of an organically unified social body. What prevented people of all nations who opposed both Bush *and* Bin Laden from joining forces? What leftists worldwide need is not just "the readiness to save victims, but also – even more, perhaps – the ruthless dedication to annihilating those who made them victims" (p. 68). In sum, what we lack is *ethical courage.*

One way to concisely summarize *Welcome* is to say that this book shows why it is impossible in today's capitalist societies for the same individual to combine these three features: conviction of belief, intelligence, and honesty. If he believes and is intelligent, then he is not honest. If he is intelligent and honest, then he cannot believe. If he is honest and believes, then he cannot be intelligent (*Welcome*, p. 71). How can we, in capitalist societies today, intelligently and sincerely believe? We cannot go back to a pre-capitalist world; we must change capitalism from within. Our new collectivity needs to avoid the evils of both world-market globalization and state bureaucracy. Before such a reinvention of the symbolic order is possible, we need to recognize that liberal democracy is not the answer. This can only be achieved through ethical courage. The true ethical courage involves the ability to *thoroughly question one's own position* (p. 75). Not only this, but we must refuse the forced choice:

> The democratic political order is of its very nature susceptible to corruption. The ultimate choice is: do we accept and endorse this corruption in a spirit of realistic resigned wisdom, or can we summon up the courage to formulate a Leftist alternative to democracy in order to break the vicious cycle of democratic corruption and the Rightist campaigns to get rid of it? (*Welcome*, p. 79)

If we do summon up ethical courage, what will our ethics of the Real look like? For one thing, there is always something *simple* in an ethical act (*Welcome*, p. 113). Moreover, the act involves the Other. As already indicated, Žižek urges that the left today must invent a new collectivity: to look not *at* one another, but to look *with* one another, together, toward a third point, namely the cause for which we are both fighting (p. 85). A consistent ethical stance will reject pragmatic-utilitarian reasoning (p. 104). If, in some "ticking clock" terrorist scenario, we must resort to doing the impermissible (e.g. torture), we must simply do it without elevating what we had to do into a universal principle. Only in this way can we retain a sense of the *wrongness* of what we had to do (p. 103). Pragmatic-utilitarianism effaces this sense of wrongness, by offering a pseudo-justification for the impermissible.

But if we are faced with a forced choice, an ethical act can be as simple as refusing to participate (*Welcome*, p. 116). Insofar as it ignores the forced choice and transforms the entire coordinates of the situation, we can recognize the ethical act by its "impossible" or "miraculous" character (p. 117). However, an ethics of the Real is not a form of irrationalism, but a dialectical *radicalization* of rationality: "Today's rise of 'irrational' violence should therefore be conceived as strictly correlative to the depoliticization of our societies, that is, to the disappearance of the proper political dimension, its translation into different levels of 'administration' of social affairs" (*Welcome*, pp. 132–3).

As opposed to being another example of irrational violence, an ethical or political act is a transfiguration of rationality itself, a reinvention of the symbolic coordinates of reality. In sum, an ethics of the Real hinges on an act which provides radically new, unforeseen standards of rational evaluation. The political act accomplishes this by retroactively changing the very reality of the situation into which it intervenes, and thereby creating its own conditions of possibility. Unrealized emancipatory possibilities are retroactively redeemed through the miracle of revolutionary intervention (*Welcome*, pp. 22–3).

17

The Puppet and the Dwarf:
The Perverse Core of Christianity

In this book Žižek urges that the left must reclaim the untapped, subversive kernel
of Christianity. He develops the revolutionary potential of Christianity as an
alternative to Christianity's *perverse* core. The subversive kernel of Christianity,
Žižek argues, is accessible only to a dialectical materialist approach. Furthermore,
the egalitarian ideals of dialectical materialism are accessible especially to those
who have gone through the (non-perverse) Christian experience. The emancipatory potential of Christianity involves the insight that Christ's death on the cross
reveals God's impotence, i.e., the nonexistence of the big Other. Žižek's Christian-
materialism highlights something which was already emphasized by Hegel,
namely that the "God of Beyond" really did die on the cross, and after his death,
God returns only as the spirit of the community of believers, not in person. Along
these lines, in the Hegelian "night of the world," the subject does not survive.
Subjective destitution involves the experience of losing one's "self." In this experience, the symbolic texture of reality (the big Other) disintegrates, as does one's
symbolic identity. Symbolic subjectivity must then be completely reinvented
from nothing, or "born again" (in Lacanian terms, through the *act* one becomes
a different subject). The ethico-political act involves identification with the gap in
the symbolic order, the place occupied by the excluded, disenfranchised Other.
The act as reinventing one's symbolic identity is homologous to the Christian
notions of spiritual rebirth and salvation. Žižek argues that the achievement of
Christianity is to elevate a loving and imperfect, divided subject to the place of
God. But moreover, St Paul's institutionalization of Christianity was a revolutionary act against the Roman Empire. Where is the possibility for such a
revolutionary act today? Žižek urges that dialectical materialism must reinvigorate Christian theology – and vice versa – if leftists are to realize their primary aim:

Žižek: A Reader's Guide, First Edition. Kelsey Wood.

namely, forming a revolutionary collective capable of combating the violence of global socioeconomic inequality.

> *The point of this book is that, at the very core of Christianity, there is another dimension. When Christ dies, what dies with him is the secret hope discernible in "Father, why hast thou forsaken me?": the hope that there is a father who has abandoned me. The "Holy Spirit" is the community deprived of its support in the big Other. The point of Christianity as the religion of atheism is not the vulgar humanist one that the becoming-man-of-God reveals that man is the secret of God (Feuerbach et al.); rather, it attacks the religious hard core that survives even humanism, even up to Stalinism, with its belief in History as the "big Other" that decides on the "objective meaning" of our deeds.*
>
> —Žižek, *The Puppet and the Dwarf: The Perverse Core of Christianity,* p. 171

One of Slavoj Žižek's more passionate interventions is *The Puppet and the Dwarf: The Perverse Core of Christianity* (2003).[1] This book (abbreviated *Puppet* below) involves a reversal of Walter Benjamin's first thesis on the philosophy of history. Referring to the story of an automaton constructed to win every chess game (thanks to a dwarf hiding inside the base and pulling the strings), Benjamin wrote: "The puppet called 'historical materialism' is to win all the time. It can easily be a match for anyone if it enlists the services of theology, which today, as we know, is wizened and has to keep out of sight."[2]

In his introduction, Žižek agrees with Robert Pfaller's thesis that traditional, pre-modern societies did not believe directly, but through a distance; pre-modern belief was essentially a form of politeness or ritual (*Puppet,* p. 6). In contrast with this, directly and fully assuming belief is a modern phenomenon: "this explains, for instance, why Enlightenment critics misread 'primitive' myths – they first took the notion that a tribe originated from a fish or a bird as a literal direct belief, then rejected it as stupid, 'fetishist,' naive. They thereby imposed their own notion of belief on the 'primitivized' Other" (p. 6). But with reference to today's *postmodern* and (allegedly) skeptical sociosymbolic order, Žižek argues

---

[1] Unless otherwise stated, page references for this work are to the following edition: *The Puppet and the Dwarf: The Perverse Core of Christianity* (Cambridge, MA: MIT Press, 2003).
[2] Cf. Walter Benjamin, *Essays and Reflections,* ed. Hannah Arendt (New York: Schocken Books, 1969), p. 253.

that "today, we believe more than ever" (p. 6). However, our fear of directly assuming our belief entails that we distance ourselves ironically from belief, all the while relying on the figure of some Other who believes directly and immediately. One manifestation of this postmodern disavowal of belief is what Žižek calls "the 'postsecular' Messianic turn of deconstruction" (p. 3). Thanks to this ironic distantiation from (or externalization of) belief, today – in spite of ongoing scientific developments – theology has been given a new lease on life. But today (in contrast to the situation in Walter Benjamin's time) historical materialism is now "practiced as it were under cover, rarely called by its proper name" (p. 3).

All of this helps to explain why Žižek articulates the theme of this book by *reversing* Benjamin's thesis to read: "The puppet called 'theology' is to win all the time. It can easily be a match for anyone if it enlists the service of historical materialism, which today, as we know, is wizened and has to keep out of sight" (*Puppet*, p. 3). Against the prevailing cynicism of today's postmodern, global capitalist societies, Žižek argues that *the question of belief matters more than ever*. In his introduction, Žižek explains that his intent in *Puppet* is to show how today it is possible for honest and intelligent subjects to believe directly and immediately in a cause, provided it is the right cause. And the right cause for our postmodern cynical time, Žižek argues, is Christian-materialism: "My claim here is not merely that I am a materialist through and through, and that the subversive kernel of Christianity is accessible also to a materialist approach; my thesis is much stronger: this kernel is accessible *only* to a materialist approach – and vice versa: to become a true dialectical materialist, one should go through the Christian experience" (p. 6).

In *Puppet*, Žižek aligns himself strongly against postmodernism, and the "Messianic" turn of deconstruction. He asserts his Christian-materialism to be an antidote to the endless postmodern deferrals of belief. Today, it is possible to *directly and immediately* assume Christian-materialist belief because Christian-materialism maintains an orientation toward the Real – as opposed to the imaginary and symbolic registers – by way of dialectical materialism's affinity with contemporary science (e.g. the radical Copenhagen interpretation of quantum mechanics).

This indicates why Žižek argues that the left today must appropriate what he calls the subversive kernel of Christianity: this subversive kernel is the revolutionary potential of Christianity – its radical-emancipatory moment – that runs counter to Christianity's *perverse* core. To highlight the contrast between Christianity's (good) subversive potential and its (bad) perverse core, Žižek emphasizes something which Hegel also recognized, namely that the "God of Beyond" died on the cross, and now God exists *only* as the Holy Spirit of the community of believers. As Lacan put this: "The Holy Spirit is the entry of the signifier into the world" (*Puppet*, p. 9).

The death of God on the cross is homologous to the Hegelian "night of the world" – the loss of personal identity brought about through tarrying with the negativity of the Real – insofar as the subject's symbolic identity does *not* survive. Undergoing subjective destitution means losing one's essence and passing over into the Other. In this experience, the symbolic texture of reality and of personal identity dissolves, and must be completely reinvented *from nothing*. In other words, after the Lacanian *act*, one is not the same subject one was before. Put simply, this means that we avoid the perverse core of Christianity and realize its subversive (materialist) potential only by acknowledging the death of God and the impossibility of any afterlife; only in this way can the honest and intelligent subject truly be "born again."

Žižek associates Christianity's radical-emancipatory, subversive kernel with the Kierkegaardian concept of *becoming*: "not yet the established positive dogma, but the violent gesture of positing it" (*Puppet*, p. 10). This concept of Christianity-in-becoming allows us to see why Žižek associates St Paul with Lenin; the connection is not so much the positive results of either St Paul's or Lenin's procedures, but the utopian moment of "law-constituting violence" (cf. Walter Benjamin) which precedes and informs the reinvention of the symbolic order. Violence as Žižek uses the term here does not mean senseless destruction, but rather indicates the positing of a new symbolic order, a new orthodoxy or institutionalization that would repeat for today's time the unrealized emancipatory potential of previous revolutionary moments in history. Žižek's references to Kierkegaard indicate the significance of the return to Lenin. Leftists today need to return to Lenin in his *becoming*, not to Lenin as an artifact of the USSR, but to Lenin the strategist of revolution, exploiting the openness of a contingent situation, and to Lenin on the morning after, imposing a new symbolic order.

And although many readers of *Puppet* may not notice, it is significant that Žižek both begins and ends this book with references to Hegelian sublation (*Aufhebung*, literally "out/up-lifting"). In Žižek's dialectical materialism – even in its "Christian" formulation – Hegel is the alpha and the omega (cf. *Puppet*, pp. 3, 171). Žižek's focus on the moment of negativity implicit to Hegelian dialectic explains why, in his own Christian-materialism, the ethical act involves giving up the promise of Eternity for the sake of the common and imperfect love of mortal human beings (p. 13).

Žižek contrasts Christian-materialism with Buddhism, which "fully assumes the Void as the only true Good" (*Puppet*, p. 23), and also assumes the reactionary image of society as an organic unity. In contrast to this reactionary moment inherent to Buddhism, Žižek argues that Christian-materialism is able to "pass 'beyond nothing,' into what Hegel called 'tarrying with the negative': to return to a phenomenal reality which is 'beyond nothing,' to a Something which gives body to the Nothing" (p. 23). To put this difficult Hegelian insight into simpler theological terms, Žižek is arguing that we should recognize that the gap which separates God from Himself – Father from Son from Holy Spirit – this very gap *is* God (p. 25). To express this same insight in terms of Lacanian psychoanalytic theory, this means that Žižek associates the Christian notion of God with the Lacanian Real. If the Real has no substantial existence, nonetheless, any possible symbolic order is a historically contingent reaction formation that revolves around some primordially repressed Real. Žižek argues that the Hegelian Absolute, like the Lacanian Real, is inherently antagonistic, "at war with itself," and hence cannot function as an ontological ground for the (reactionary) notion of society as a harmonious, organic unity (p. 28).

This recognition of irreducible antagonism contrasts with the Buddhist notion of the Void, which as a "transcendent world of formlessness" is unified with the world of temporal form (*Puppet*, p. 27). Buddhism adapts itself both to global capitalism (consider the example of "corporate Zen") as well as to fascism. Thus it is no accident that D. T. Suzuki – credited with introducing Zen Buddhism to the West – supported Japanese militarism in the 1930s. This shows that, unlike Christianity, Buddhist meditation as a spiritual technique is "an ethically neutral instrument, which can be put to different sociopolitical uses, from the most peaceful to the most destructive" (p. 31). Žižek shows that the Buddhist all-encompassing Compassion is opposed to the "intolerance" of Christian love, which "is a violent passion to introduce a Difference, a gap in the order of being, to privilege and elevate some object at the expense of others" (pp. 32–3).

In *Puppet*, Žižek refers several times to the Christian theologian (and writer of detective fiction) G. K. Chesterton. Chesterton is especially important to Žižek because he consistently affirmed an apparently paradoxical assertion. In various writings, Chesterton: "deploys the same conceptual matrix – that of asserting the truly subversive, even revolutionary, character of orthodoxy" (*Puppet*, p. 35). Žižek refers to Chesterton in order to substantiate his own dialectical materialist argument that Christianity in its *becoming* involves the search for orthodoxy, "exactly like Lenin's search for the authentic Marxist orthodoxy" (p. 35). Thus

Žižek's Christian-materialism is staunchly opposed to today's postmodern cynicism with regard to great Causes and the desire to change the world (p. 38).

To illustrate this opposition, Žižek alludes to Nietzsche, by indicating how our political cynicism and apathy has led to "the deadlock of today's Last Men, 'postmodern' individuals who reject all 'higher' goals as terrorist, and dedicate their life to survival replete with more and more refined and artificially excited/aroused small pleasures" (*Puppet*, p. 39). Žižek points out that Lacan already revealed the futility, hypocrisy, and inconsistency of such a life devoted to happiness as artificially aroused desire: "In our daily lives, we (pretend to) desire things that we do not really desire, so that, ultimately, the worst thing that can happen is for us to get what we 'officially' desire" (p. 43). Along the same lines, today's liberal, pseudo-leftist academics constantly bombard the capitalist system with demands which they do *not* really desire to be met:

> When, for example, "radical" academics demand full rights for immigrants and the opening of borders to them, are they aware that the direct implementation of this demand would, for obvious reasons, inundate the developed Western countries with millions of newcomers, thus provoking a violent racist working-class backlash that would then endanger the privileged position of these very academics? Of course they are, but they count on the fact that their demand will not be met – in this way, they can hypocritically retain their clear radical conscience while continuing to enjoy their privileged position. (*Puppet*, pp. 43–4)

Today's privileged, liberal academics *pretend* to desire things that they do not *really* desire. But this is hypocritical because they secretly realize that the worst thing that could happen for them would be to get what they "officially" desire. Such hypocrisy indicates the betrayal of desire. Posing as revolutionary "beautiful souls" allows so-called radical academics to find enjoyment in making impossible demands while maintaining their privileged position. They pretend to desire revolution without really desiring revolution.

In contrast to this false desire mobilized by egotistical fantasy and fetishist disavowal, Žižek enjoins us to the passion for the Real. The authentic act for Žižek is not a brief revolutionary dream or fantasy of utopia. Instead, he calls for what Badiou calls "fidelity to the event." Such fidelity involves the resolved commitment to invent a new and lasting symbolic order. Žižek's concept of the act thus involves the encounter with the Real, and the identification with the Other that is excluded from our symbolic reality. The act requires that the ethical imperative to revolution be sustained after the revolution, in the arduous work of reinventing a new sociosymbolic order, an order that would include today's disenfranchised, the outcasts of global capitalism.

Žižek argues that for Lacan, the other side of desire – desire's truly subversive side – involves resisting the superego injunction to transgress, resisting the obscene injunction to enjoyment (*jouissance*). Such resistance is required because, in succumbing to this perverse injunction to enjoy, we *compromise* our desire: "That is to say: for Lacan, the status of desire is inherently ethical: 'not to compromise one's desire' ultimately equals 'do your duty'" (*Puppet*, p. 49). The crucial factor – to determine in what our duty consists – is that we avoid the perverse belief in the existence of some all-encompassing and consistent, symbolic big Other. The pervert is he who desperately tries to evade the nonexistence of the big Other (e.g. the death of God) by identifying with the symbolic Law to the point of imagining himself to be the instrument of this Law. In contrast to the standard view of perversion (as subversive of law), Žižek reveals perversion to be a deeply conservative, nostalgic strategy for evading the nonexistence of the big Other:

> Perversion is a double strategy to counteract this nonexistence: an (ultimately deeply conservative, nostalgic) attempt to install the law artificially, *in the desperate hope that we will then take this self-posited limitation "seriously,"* and, in a complementary way, a no less desperate attempt to codify the very transgression of the Law. In the perverse reading of Christianity, God first threw humanity into Sin in order to create the opportunity for saving it through Christ's sacrifice; in the perverse reading of Hegel, the Absolute plays a game with itself – it first separates itself from itself, introduces a gap of self-misrecognition, in order to reconcile itself with itself again. (*Puppet*, p. 53)

As the above quotation indicates, one way to summarize Žižek's achievement in *Puppet* is to say that he successfully articulates a non-perverse interpretation of Christianity (Christian-materialism) and a non-perverse, "anti-essentialist" reading of Hegel (dialectical materialism). Žižek's analyses in *Puppet* also expose the contrast between, on the one hand, Lenin-in-becoming and, on the other hand, the perversion that was Stalinism.

The passion for the Real can be destructive if it involves the endeavor to extract from the Other the kernel of her being, *objet petit a*, that which is in her more than herself (*Puppet*, p. 59). With regard to Žižek's argument at this point, it is important to remember that, in Lacanian theory, the Other refers both to the radical alterity of another subject as well as to the intersubjective symbolic network that mediates between subjects. The mother is the child's first Other, and the castration complex arises when the child realizes her incompleteness (she lacks the phallus). The Other is also woman: woman is "the Other sex" for *both* males and females. The tendency in popular psychology toward "mother-blaming" is reversed in Lacanian psychoanalysis: "the true problem is the mother who *enjoys* (her child), and the true stake of the game is to escape this closure. The true anxiety is this being-caught in the Other's *jouissance*" (p. 59). The overwhelming presence of the Other's Real *jouissance* (enjoyment as pleasure-in-pain) produces anxiety, and prevents me from sustaining an open space for my desire. The paradoxical feature of desire as such is that it involves maintaining a distance between myself and what I desire (p. 60). This indicates the opposition between symbolic desire and Real *jouissance*. My desire of the Other is intensified only insofar as I am able to sustain the distance between myself and the Other, who remains enigmatic precisely because of this distance. By contrast, the Other's *jouissance* is most overwhelming in its direct proximity to me (p. 61).

This opposition between desire and enjoyment is also manifested insofar as the paternal symbolic Law functions as a screen to shield us from the Real *jouissance* of the mother. By accepting symbolic castration and the prohibitions of the symbolic Father, the subject's *jouissance* becomes phallic *jouissance*, which allows the subject to sustain desire (*Puppet*, p. 63). The passion for the Real has two sides, "purification" and "subtraction." When deceptive symbolic reality is violently peeled away, we confront the traumatic and intrusive Real; this is *purification* (p. 64). But in contrast to purification, *subtraction* begins with the Void of negativity, with the reduction of determinate content, and then establishes a "difference between this Void and an element that functions as its stand-in" (p. 64). Thus subtraction discloses an element which belongs to a set but has no place within the set. In politics, this "part with no-part" is those who are disenfranchised by the symbolic order.

Žižek's Christian-materialism enjoins us to fully identify with these outcasts, and to engage in a collective project to reinvent a symbolic order which would recognize that the excluded ones are the representatives of the human subject as such. Žižek argues in *Puppet* that Christ's divinity was his symbolic mandate conferred on him for fully assuming the place (including the humiliation and suffering) of the outcast, excluded Other:

We are one with God only when God is no longer one with Himself, but abandons Himself, "internalizes" the radical distance which separates us from Him. Our radical experience of separation from God is the very feature which unites us with Him – not in the usual mystical sense that only through such an experience do we open ourselves to the radical Otherness of God, but in a sense similar to the one in which Kant claims that humiliation and pain are the only transcendental feelings: it is preposterous to think that I can identify myself with the divine bliss – only when I experience the infinite pain of separation from God do I share an experience with God Himself (Christ on the Cross). (*Puppet*, p. 91)

This indicates how we can live without compromising our desire: we move from symbolic Law to excessive love (which violently introduces a difference), and back to symbolic Law. But if we avoid this move – from Law to Love and back – for the sake of "safety" (opportunistically avoiding risk), then we lose the very life we were trying to preserve.

We are only really alive when we are ready to risk everything for the sake of the excess of life (*Puppet*, p. 95). Christianity's relation to Jewish Law is encapsulated in St Paul's notion of a struggling universality, a struggle for universality which is embodied in those who are excluded and outcast by the current system:

its logic is: "it is those who are excluded, with no proper place within the global order, who directly embody true universality, who represent the Whole in contrast to all others who stand only for their particular interests." Lacking any specific difference, such a paradoxical element stands for the absolute difference, for pure Difference as such. In this precise sense, Pauline universality is not mute universality as the empty neutral container of its particular content, but a "struggling universality," a universality the actual existence of which is a radical division which cuts through the entire particular content. (*Puppet*, p. 109)

In its incompleteness, Christian-materialist love is *higher* than completeness. Žižek elegantly discloses the homology between St Paul's remarks on love and the feminine logic of sexuation. Even when the field of knowledge leaves no exception, knowledge remains *incomplete*.

Love is the "nothing" which makes even the complete series or field of knowledge incomplete. When I love, I am a Nothing which is paradoxically made more by the very awareness of my lack (*Puppet*, p. 115). Žižek argues that the achievement of Christianity is to elevate a loving, imperfect being (a fragile, divided subject) to the place of God. Lacan's *masculine* logic of sexuation (universality and its constitutive exception) is at work

209

in the way "sin" is the exception which sustains the Law. But love evokes Lacan's *feminine* logic of sexuation (the paradoxes of the non-All). The feminine logic of non-All does not mean that there is some part of woman outside of the symbolic order, but indicates, rather, the *failure* of totalization. The masculine attempt to achieve universal totalization takes place through universality's constitutive exception. However, in the feminine logic of sexuation there is no exception to the phallic function. Thus a feminine subject is immersed in the symbolic order more fully than a masculine subject: she is immersed in the symbolic *without exception*. Along these lines, love is not outside of Law; love is manifested as a total immersion within symbolic Law, which breaks the vicious cycle of Law and the obscene superego injunction to transgress.

Žižek claims that the key to Christ is already prefigured by the meaningless suffering of Job: "Job's properly ethical dignity lies in the way he persistently rejects the notion that his suffering can have any meaning, either punishment for his past sins or the trial of his faith" (*Puppet*, p. 125). This lack of closure signals the nonexistence of the big Other, and this is why Žižek links the story of Job to a moment of atheism implicit to Christianity, a moment when God himself was an atheist: "Christ's 'Father, why hast thou forsaken me?' is not a complaint to the *omnipotent* but capricious God-Father whose ways are indecipherable to us, finite humans. In contrast to this, Christ's cry on the cross hints at an *impotent* God" (p. 126). Žižek argues that God is not just and God is not unjust: God is simply impotent. Again, in Lacanian terms this means that the big Other does not exist; in other words, any possible symbolic order is ultimately inconsistent and divided against itself. The obscene superego supplement to the symbolic Law functions to *mask* this impotence of the big Other. But, by contrast, Žižek's Christian-materialism highlights this impotence: "no obscene superego supplement accompanies its public message" (p. 127). Concisely put, the hidden secret of Christianity is that there is no hidden secret.

To conclude, in *The Puppet and the Dwarf*, Žižek argues that the Lacanian act – traversing the fantasy, encountering the Real, undergoing subjective destitution, and reinventing one's symbolic identity – is homologous to the process indicated by the Christian notions of forgiveness, salvation, and spiritual rebirth. The subversive, radical-emancipatory core of Christianity consists in its evocation of God's impotence, that is, the nonexistence of the big Other:

> In what is perhaps the highest example of Hegelian *Aufhebung*, it is possible today to redeem this core of Christianity only in the gesture of abandoning

the shell of its institutional organization (and, even more so, of its specific religious experience). The gap here is irreducible: either one drops the religious form, or one maintains the form, but loses the essence. That is the ultimate heroic gesture that awaits Christianity: in order to save its treasure, it has to sacrifice itself – like Christ, who had to die so that Christianity could emerge. (*Puppet*, p. 171)

18

Organs without Bodies: On Deleuze and Consequences

Since the 1990s, Deleuze has been a central reference in both continental philosophy and Anglo-American cultural studies. In this book Žižek reveals two logics – two conceptual oppositions – that structure the work of Deleuze. On the one hand, there is the well-known figure of Deleuze who (under the influence of Felix Guattari) articulated in *Anti-Oedipus* a critique of psychoanalysis. Žižek argues that this "Guattarized" Deleuze is exploited to justify identity politics, which is inherently reactionary and furthers the interests of global-liberal capitalism. This figure of Deleuze – although widely believed to be "radical" by academic pseudo-leftists – ultimately functions as an ideologist of today's digital capitalism. But on the other hand, there is the "absolute Deleuze," the author of two books that Žižek regards highly: namely *Difference and Repetition* and *The Logic of Sense*. Against the predominant but one-sided (mis)reading of Deleuze, Žižek develops a more comprehensive and thorough reading that argues for a previously unrecognized affinity between Deleuze, Hegel, and Lacanian psychoanalysis.

During the shooting of David Lean's Doctor Zhivago *in a Madrid suburb in 1964, a crowd of Spanish statists had to sing the "Internationale" in a scene involving a mass demonstration. The movie team was astonished to discover that they all knew the song and were singing it with such a passion that the Francoist police intervened, thinking that they were dealing with a real political manifestation. Even more, when, late in the evening (the scene was to take place in darkness), people living in the*

Žižek: A Reader's Guide, First Edition. Kelsey Wood.
© 2012 John Wiley & Sons, Inc. Published 2012 by John Wiley & Sons, Inc.

nearby houses heard the echoes of the song, they opened up bottles and started to dance in the street, wrongly presuming that Franco had died and the Socialists had taken power.

This book is dedicated to those magic moments of illusory freedom (which, in a way, were precisely not simply illusory) and to the hopes thwarted by the return to "normal" reality.

—Žižek, *Organs without Bodies: On Deleuze and Consequences*, p. xii

Several decades ago, Michel Foucault predicted that the twentieth century would someday be viewed as "Deleuzian," and this prediction has in large part come true. But from Slavoj Žižek's perspective, the hard kernel of Deleuze's thinking was diluted by the popular but one-sided appropriation of a few Deleuzian notions applied (generally without rigor) in cultural studies, film theory, and by the anti-globalists. One of Žižek's most underrated books – at least in the USA – is *Organs without Bodies: On Deleuze and Consequences* (2003).[1] This book (abbreviated *Organs* below) shows that, as opposed to the popular figure of a "Guattarized" Deleuze, which has been appropriated by the anti-globalist left, there is another, more philosophically profound Deleuze (*Organs*, p. xi). In *Organs*, Žižek uncovers an interpretation of Deleuze that is covered over by the focus on the "Guattarized" Deleuze.

We should note that Deleuze – unlike many of his admirers – was a careful and thorough student of philosophy; Deleuze studied Spinoza, Leibniz, Hume, Kant, Nietzsche, and Bergson, to name a few. And Deleuze once said about his own work that he was trying to "bugger" the philosopher he was interpreting – to create a monstrous offspring – but in such a way that this child proves to have been always already immanent to that philosopher's opus. However, the offspring is displaced and transformed, so that the philosopher would not want to take it as his own. In this Deleuzian sense, Žižek makes a baby with Deleuze, a child which, on the one hand, Deleuze *would not be able to deny*, but which is, on the other hand, a "monstrous" offspring Deleuze would not be happy to see.[2]

It should also be noted that Žižek's title *Organs without Bodies* involves a reversal of Deleuze's and Guattari's notion of the "body without organs" (cf. *Anti-Oedipus* and *Mille Plateaux*). In Deleuze/Guattari, a

---

[1]   Unless otherwise stated, page references for this work are to the following edition: *Organs without Bodies: On Deleuze and Consequences* (London and New York: Routledge, 2004).

[2]   Simon Gros originally developed this idea and shared it with me.

213

body without organs is something like the excess of the flux of change. A body without organs is a virtual dimension of unstable potentialities which has not been organ-ized; a body without organs is a collection of striving, multi-directional flows.

In the first part of *Organs*, Žižek outlines the opposition between the two Deleuzes – the early Deleuze as oppose to the later, "Guattarized" Deleuze – and then indicates how the tension between them runs through the Deleuzian corpus. In the second part of *Organs*, Žižek traces the consequences of the same opposition in relation to science, art, and politics.

Žižek analyzes the core of Deleuze's thought, and in the process shows the affinity of this thought with both Hegel and Lacan (both of whom Deleuze opposed). For some Deleuzian readers, *Organs without Bodies* can provide a therapeutic shock, insofar as Žižek actually takes Deleuze more seriously as a philosopher than do many Deleuze enthusiasts. In other words, this book can function for some Deleuzian disciples as the intrusive return of the repressed Real. But if the careful reader persists in analyzing the thought of Deleuze as thoroughly as Žižek does, then she must engage with Deleuze *the philosopher*. And before attempting to refute Žižek's arguments, she must also do the hard work of understanding Žižek's dialectical-materialist reinvention of Hegel and Lacan. This indicates one of the main achievements of *Organs without Bodies*, namely, to make it impossible for uninformed critics of Žižek to rely on their own non-philosophical appropriations of vaguely Deleuzian notions while remaining blissfully ignorant of Hegelian dialectics and of Lacanian psychoanalytic theory. Žižek accomplishes this by repeatedly demonstrating the extent to which Deleuze himself articulates (allegedly) original insights which, in fact, were already anticipated in Hegelian dialectics and Lacanian theory.

This is one of the things which makes *Organs* so provocative and controversial: Žižek effectively indicates how, in spite of Deleuze's *explicit* opposition to Hegel, nonetheless Deleuze's own thinking *implicitly* involves Hegelian categories, for example, the paradoxical coupling of opposites such as "transcendental" and "empirical." By forgetting Hegel, Deleuze inadvertently repeats him:

> Deleuze even enjoins us to forget Hegel. This absolute rejection, this urge to "stupidize" Hegel, to present a straw man image of him (as amply demonstrated by Malabou), conceals, of course, a disavowed affinity. Fredric Jameson already drew attention to the fact that the central reference of *Anti-Oedipus*, the underlying scheme of its larger historical framework, is "The Pre-Capitalist Modes of Production," the long fragment from the

Grundrisse manuscripts in which we encounter Marx at his most Hegelian
(its entire scheme of the global historical movement relying on the Hegelian
process from substance to subject). And, what about the other key
Deleuzian concept literally taken over from Hegel, that of the "concrete
universal"? (What Deleuze aims at with the "concrete universality" is the
formal generative model of a process of BECOMING as opposed to the
"abstract" universals [genuses and species] that serve to categorize modes
of being, of established reality.) Is Deleuze's critique of the Platonic logic
of ideal universal types designating the same quality (set of properties) in
the elements comprised by the type not strangely close to Hegel's critique
of abstract universality? (*Organs*, pp. 49–50)

Even though Žižek's reading (or reinvention) of Hegelian dialectics is
actually remarkably clear, nonetheless the reader who is new to Hegel
must *engage* in the struggle for truth, and do the hard work of learning.

But occasionally Žižek addresses readers who are unfamiliar with
Hegel, as when – on page 50 of *Organs* – he explains the Hegelian "self-
movement of the Notion." In order to understand the Hegelian
"Notion"(*Begriff*), the most difficult thing for those of us trained in the
Anglo-American approach to philosophy is to first forget about empirical
generalizations or the nominalist use of the term "notion." For Hegel, the
Notion is not strictly distinguished from objects, since the Notion is constitutive of objects. As an illustration of this, let us take Notion to mean
"concept." In what sense could a concept be said to be constitutive of an
object? Simply put, this means that the distinction between an object and
a concept (which qualifies that object) can neither be rigorously maintained nor entirely dispensed with. For example, the distinction between
a concept and an object is itself a *conceptual* distinction. Moreover, concepts are not defined in isolation, but only through relations of difference
with one another, and also in relation to objects. But in comparison to
this reference to concepts and objects, Žižek's own explanation of the
Notion and its "self movement" is both clearer and more profound in its
implications:

What is, effectively, the Hegelian "self-movement of the Notion" about?
Recall a boring academic textbook that, apropos of a philosophical problem
or discipline, enumerates the series of predominant opinions or claims:
"The philosopher A claimed that the soul is immortal, while the philosopher
B claimed that there is no soul, and the philosopher C that the soul is only
the form of the body…" There is something blatantly ridiculous and
inadequate in presenting such a panoply of "opinions of philosophers" –
why? We, the readers, somehow "feel" that this is not philosophy, that a

"true" philosophy must systematically account for this very multitude of "opinions" (positions), not just enumerate them. In short, what we expect is to get a report on how one "opinion" arises out of the inconsistencies or insufficiencies of another "opinion" so that the chain of these "opinions" forms an organic Whole – or, as Hegel would have put it, the history of philosophy itself is part of philosophy, not just a comparative report on whether and how different "opinions" are right or wrong. This organic interweaving of "opinions" (positions) is what Hegel calls the "self-movement of the Notion." (*Organs*, p. 50)

In discussing the Hegelian Notion, Žižek highlights the fact that Hegel anticipates Lacan's logic of feminine sexuation by showing why the universal cannot be understood as the neutral container of its species:

> And, what is the Hegelian *Begriff* ["Notion"] as opposed to the nominalist "notion," the result of abstracting shared features from a series of particular objects? Often, we stumble on a particular case that does not fully "fit" its universal species, that is "atypical"; the next step is to acknowledge that *every* particular is "atypical," that *the universal species exists only in exceptions*, that there is a structural tension between the Universal and the Particular. At this point, we become aware that the Universal is no longer just an empty neutral container of its subspecies but an entity in tension with each and every one of its species. The universal Notion thus acquires a dynamics of its own. More precisely, the true Universal *is* this very antagonistic dynamics between the Universal and the Particular. It is at this point that we pass from "abstract" to "concrete" Universal – at the point when we acknowledge that every Particular is an "exception," and, consequently, that the Universal, far from "containing" its particular content, *excludes* it (or is excluded *by* it). This exclusion renders the Universal itself particular (it is not truly universal, since it cannot grasp or contain its particular content), yet this very failure is its strength: the Universal is thus simultaneously posited as the Particular. (*Organs*, pp. 50–51)

As already indicated, Žižek demonstrates throughout his works that the universal is not an empty, neutral container of its subspecies, and he argues that this notion of neutral universality actually serves to reinforce the hegemonic liberal-capitalist ideology.

Žižek argues that in spite of Deleuze's opposition to Hegel, Deleuze is much more Hegelian than Deleuze himself realized. He asserts that the story of the "Hegelian Deleuze" goes on and on (*Organs*, p. 51), and throughout the book, he gives numerous detailed examples in support of this claim. But in order to grasp the significance of Žižek's examples, the reader must keep in mind that Žižek articulates the Hegelian *Aufhebung* ("sublation") as a re-marking that leaves an indivisible remainder. Thus the Hegelian "negation of the negation" does not involve any return to positive identity. Negativity is not reduced to a passing moment in the self-mediating process of dialectical synthesis (cf. *The Sublime Object of Ideology*, p. 176). Hegelian dialectic preserves the difference, and posits the difference as such, and this negativity *attests to the freedom of the subject*. Thus for Žižek, Deleuze's opposition to Hegel is part and parcel of his failure (along with many leftist philosophers and theorists of culture), to adequately think through the unrealized potential for liberation implicit to the concept of the subject as self-relating negativity. Again, Žižek relates this Hegelian negativity to the radical autonomy indicated by the death drive.

But what about Deleuze's famous "anti-Oedipal" critique of psychoanalysis? In response to this, Žižek demonstrates that in the psychoanalytical theory of Jacques Lacan, the Oedipus complex functions in such a way as to produce a multitude of ambiguous meanings not encompassed by the ideological process of "subjectivization." Put simply, the Oedipus complex leads beyond both the "natural" *and* the social dimensions of desire, to the Real of the Other's desire. But insofar as the trauma/antagonism of the Real eludes both fantasy and symbolization, Oedipus proves to be an agent of the very "deterritorialization" and heterogeneity made thematic by Deleuze:

> And, insofar as the passage from sexed animals to humans involves a qualitative leap marked by the emergence of the symbolic order, one is tempted to establish here the connection with Lacan's *il n'y a pas de rapport sexuel*: the passage to language, *the* medium of communication, far from bringing about the pacification of the antagonism, the reconciliation of the opposed sexes in the universal symbolic medium, raises antagonism itself to the level of the absolute. With humans, what was before (in the animal kingdom) a struggle of two opposed forces within the same field, is raised into the absolute antagonism that cuts from within the universal medium itself. The access to universality is paid for by a total impossibility of communication, of common measure, between the sexes: *the price paid for the universalization-symbolization of sexuality is the sexuation of symbolic universality itself.* Instead of the reconciliation of the sexual opposition in the universality of language, universality itself gets split, caught in the antagonism. (*Organs*, p. 146)

But what, precisely, is the antagonism which Žižek discloses between two aspects of Deleuze's thinking?

In the first place, there is Deleuze and Guattari's well-known critique of psychoanalysis in *Anti-Oedipus* and their celebration of the productive multitude of becoming against the reified order of being as representation. Again, in *Organs*, Žižek argues that notions borrowed from Deleuze/ Guattari have been easily incorporated into the liberal-democratic ideology that sustains global capitalism.

But in contrast to this familiar, "Guattarized" Deleuze, there is the earlier Deleuze. In order to comprehend why Žižek argues that the earlier Deleuze is more profound than the later Deleuze/Guattari, it is crucial to keep in mind that Žižek's anti-essentialist interpretation of Hegelian dialectics does not rely on the masculine logic of universality and its constitutive exception (cf. Lacan's famous "Logic of Sexuation," from *Seminar XX: Encore*). Žižek identifies in the earlier Deleuze – prior to the influence of Guattari – the recognition that reality does not need some exception standing outside of it. For this earlier Deleuze, the only meaningful sense of the Kantian Thing-in-itself is the immanent limitation of appearances as such, the way that any phenomenal entity or meaning is always already divided against itself, or irreducibly inconsistent. This is the "Schellingian" Deleuze, who in *The Logic of Sense* articulated a kind of transcendental empiricism, and recognized the sterility of the incorporeal flux of becoming that is implied by the notion of the Sense-Event. The cause is not *outside* of what it explains (this would be Kant's masculine logic); rather, as Schelling and Hegel both emphasized, the cause belongs to appearances as appearances, appearances that have no otherworldly, or "more substantial" support. As Žižek shows, this position is homologous to Lacan's feminine logic of sexuation and the negative universality of the non-all. And just as for Lacan the subject as such is feminine, so the feminine logic of sexuation (the non-all) is more fundamental than the masculine logic (universality and its constitutive exception).

Žižek is often accused by so-called "leftists" of criticizing political strategies and movements without offering any plan or blueprint for the future. This criticism ignores Žižek's developments of the implications of the big Other's nonexistence. And yet, in numerous works, Žižek has decisively sided with Alain Badiou's "communist hypothesis," and discussed at length the political consequences of this position. But what are the political implications of the Deleuzian notion of the multitude? What would a "multitude in power" look like? Žižek develops this question as follows:

> Calls for the defense of particular (cultural, ethnic) identities being threatened by global dynamics coexist with the demands for more global mobility (against the new barriers imposed by capitalism, which concern, above all, the free movement of individuals). Is it, then, true that these

218

tendencies (these *lignes de fruite*, as Deleuze would have put it) can coexist in a nonantagonistic way, as parts of the same global network of resistance? One is tempted to answer this claim by applying to it Laclau's notion of the chain of equivalences: of course, this logic of multitude functions, because we are still dealing with *resistance*. However, what about when – if this really is the desire and will of these movements – "we take it over"? What will the "multitude in power" look like? (*Organs*, p. 198)

Žižek argues that a multitudinous network of resistance existed in opposition to the Communist Party hegemony during the last years of the USSR. But this multitude only functioned so long as it was *united against a common enemy* (the Party hegemony). Once this multitude took power, "the game was over" (*Organs*, p. 198). In sum, the multitude only functions as "the ethicopoetic shadowy double of the existing positive state power structure" (*Organs*, p. 199).

To conclude, Deleuze's earlier "transcendental empiricism" is homologous to Žižek's dialectical-materialist re-inscription of Hegel and Lacan insofar as subjectivity emerges from material-libidinal interactions, but is not reducible to these pre-subjective interactions. However, in contrast to this, the later "Guattarized" version of Deleuze involves a retreat from the radical implications of Deleuze's earlier work. Although the later Deleuze is believed to be "radical" by many postmodernist academics, Žižek argues that, on the contrary, the shift from the early to the late Deleuze is marked by an *evasion*. Deleuze evades the truly radical implications of the concept of the Lacanian act. Thus the popular appropriation of Deleuze/Guattari – in spite of its alleged radicality – in fact serves to sustain the liberal-democratic ideology of global capitalism.

19

Iraq: The Borrowed Kettle

After *Welcome to the Desert of the Real* this is Žižek's second book on the so-called "war on terror." In Iraq: The Borrowed Kettle, Žižek focuses on the Real as the inherent inconsistency of the symbolic network. Arguing that the symbolic big Other believes for us, Žižek exposes inconsistency of the symbolic order, and indicates how these inconsistencies are covered over by the manipulations of ideological rhetoric. For example, the mutual inconsistency of our "justifications" for the invasion of Iraq mirrors the strange logic of dreams; and for Žižek, such inconsistency indicates our unconscious effort to repress some disturbing truth.

The whole plea – for this dream is nothing else – recalls vividly the defence offered by a man who was accused by his neighbour of having returned a kettle in a damaged condition. In the first place, he had returned the kettle undamaged; in the second place it already had holes in it when he borrowed it; and in the third place, he had never borrowed it at all.
—Sigmund Freud, *The Interpretation of Dreams*

One of Žižek's sharpest and most pertinent interventions is *Iraq: The Borrowed Kettle* (2004).[1] In this book (abbreviated *Iraq* below) Žižek further develops arguments from *Welcome to the Desert of the Real* (2002)

---

[1]   Unless otherwise stated, page references for this work are to the following edition: *Iraq: The Borrowed Kettle* (London and New York: Verso, 2005).

Žižek: A Reader's Guide, First Edition. Kelsey Wood.
© 2012 John Wiley & Sons, Inc. Published 2012 by John Wiley & Sons, Inc.

concerning the so-called "war on terror." Žižek begins the book by quoting Herman Goering, speaking at the Nuremburg trials in 1946: "Of course the people don't want war. ... But after all, it is the leaders of the country who determine the policy, and it's always a simple matter to drag the people along" (*Iraq*, p. 1).

Žižek goes on to show that the truth of the justifications for the war in Iraq is revealed in the very inconsistency between them; for Žižek (as for both Sigmund Freud and Jacques Lacan), such inconsistency indicates unconscious efforts to deny or repress some disturbing truth. To highlight the inconsistency between the justifications for the US attack, Žižek employs the famous distinction developed by Lacan between three dimensions of experience: imaginary, symbolic, and Real. But it is the *shift* from one justification for the war to another that is the starting point of Žižek's analysis. This "parallax" shift of perspective reveals the inconsistency between the *imaginary* of ideological rhetoric, the *symbolic* of political hegemony, and the *Real* of the economy.

The imaginary justification for the invasion of Iraq in 2003 was the ideological belief in Western democracy. But it soon became clear that the US attack on Iraq was not carried out in order to improve the human rights of 26 million Iraqis (*Iraq*, p. 8). With regard to the symbolic register, the reason for the invasion was so that the political elite in the USA could assert its global dominance and impose the new rules of international relations. According to this new symbolic order, the USA brutally asserts its unconditional hegemony (p. 4). Even the pretence of neutral international law is dropped, as the USA paternalistically defines its allies' interest for them (p. 14). The message conveyed by the USA is now: "we are going to do this whether you agree or disagree, and if you are not with us, then you are with the terrorists." But regarding the register of the Real, the (initially) disavowed reason for the invasion was economic. However, Žižek is careful to point out that in this Lacanian triad of imaginary-symbolic-Real, each of these three levels has some degree of autonomy, and none of them is simply a mere semblance (*Iraq*, p. 4). For example, ideological fantasy produces effects in people's behavior, and has an impact on people's lives. This indicates how fantasy is *constitutive of* symbolic reality. But again, with regard to the triad of imaginary-symbolic-Real, "it is not that one is the 'truth' of the others; the 'truth' is, rather, the very shift of perspective between them" (*Iraq*, p. 6).

Nonetheless it is clear that, in the justifications for the war, the economy initially functioned as the disavowed Real. This finally became evident in June 2003, with the public statement by Paul Wolfowitz that the issue of weapons of mass destruction was only a "bureaucratic excuse," and that the primary motivation was control of Iraq's oil reserves (*Iraq*, p. 5). As always, the focus of Žižek's analysis is the Real as that which disrupts and marks the limit of the intersubjective, symbolic network. By showing how the sociosymbolic big Other believes for us, Žižek reveals the manipulations of ideological rhetoric. This approach enables Žižek to offer an even more convincing account than did Paul Wolfowitz of the way the economy functions as the repressed Real that produces symbolic inconsistency. Wolfowitz asserted that other countries (e.g. North Korea) pose a greater threat to global security than does Iraq; however, Iraq is swimming in a sea of oil.

In contrast to this, Žižek's analysis is both broader and more incisive. Given that China today functions in large part to provide a state-controlled labor force – which is then exploited by capitalists in the USA – where, exactly, is the most effective opposition to authoritarian global capitalism to be found?

> Here, I would like to propose the hypothesis that the US-Iraq war was, in terms of its actual sociopolitical content, *the first war between the USA and Europe*. That is to say: what if, as some economists have already suggested, the true economic aim of the war was not primarily the control of oil reserves but the strengthening of the US dollar, the prevention of the dollar's defeat against the euro, the prevention of the collapse of a dollar which is less and less "covered" by "real" value (think of the immense US debt)? (*Iraq*, p. 36)

Only if such disturbing possibilities are explicitly acknowledged within the intersubjective symbolic network can they ever really be encountered; in other words, the "truth" of our actions will remain repressed so long as the big Other is merely *presumed* not to recognize it. In other words, we believe the way we desire: through the Other. This means that there are things that we know, but do not yet know that we know them. The danger is that such repressed "unknown knowns" (things we already know although we do not know that we know them) control us, we do not control them.

In this book, Žižek indicates how and why such repressed truths can continue to dominate us *even after* we become aware of how they function. His name for this is "fetishist disavowal." Fetishist disavowal involves the stance of "I *know* very well that XYZ; nonetheless, I do not behave as if and/or believe that XYZ." For example, even though we know this already, do most citizens in the USA today behave as if and/or believe that the original predictions used to justify the US invasion of Iraq have proven false? Žižek reminds us: "No weapons of mass destruction were used, or even discovered; there were no fanatical Arab suicide bombers (until very recently); almost no oil wells were ignited; there were no determined Republican Guard divisions defending Baghdad to the end and risking the destruction of the city – in short, Iraq proved to be a paper tiger which basically collapsed under US pressure" (*Iraq*, pp. 16–17). Žižek acknowledges that Saddam did have (at least at one time) weapons of mass destruction (pp. 51, 65). And we should add that the US political elite was in a position to know this, since Dow Chemical provided some of these weapons to Saddam (p. 65).

But if the aim of the US invasion was the suppression of Muslim fundamentalism, then the attack on the secular, socialist nation of Iraq "was not only a failure, but it even strengthened the very cause it tried to combat" (*Iraq*, p. 15). Why have recent US interventions abroad tended to produce exactly what they were (allegedly) intended to prevent? In the case of the Iraq war (and the war in Afghanistan), US intervention is producing an anti-American Muslim front (p. 18). It is inconceivable that the US political elite has not noticed this correlation. And it is significant that, before the invasion, the US government deliberately fostered a climate of fear among (many of) its citizens: fear of an ecological catastrophe caused by burning oil wells, fear of high US casualties, and fear of a terrorist attack (pp. 15–16). Saddam was painted as a fundamentalist madman, when in fact he was just another ruthlessly "pragmatic" leader trying to grab and maintain power (p. 17).

All of this raises the possibility that the true goal of the US invasion involved not only strengthening the dollar against the euro, but also *repressing* whatever remains of the radical-emancipatory potential of "democracy" in the USA. Given this possibility:

> We should therefore be very careful not to fight false battles: the debates about how evil Saddam was, even about the cost of the war, and so forth, are red herrings. The focus should be on what actually transpires in our societies, on what kind of society is emerging *here and now* as the result of the "war on terror." The ultimate result of the war will be a change in *our* political order. (*Iraq*, p. 19)

The problem today is not that the USA is a new Roman Empire, policing the globe in the vacuum left after the end of the Cold War. On the contrary, the problem is that the USA is *not* such a global Empire. The USA merely *pretends* to be the global policeman, while actually behaving like just another nation-state, pursuing its own particular interests against other polities (*Iraq*, p. 19). The USA's political elite maintains its power by ensuring that its citizens are "more equal" (economically) than any other citizens in the world (p. 20). If we ordinary citizens are addicted to petroleum, are our corporate and political elite nothing more than innocent bystanders, obediently trying to meet the general public's tyrannical demands? Against the notion that our leaders are mere instruments of our desires, Žižek indicates how ideological fantasy teaches us how to desire. Put simply, through an ideological process of subjectivization, we are taught to desire through the big Other. But such ideological manipulation does not change the fact that we know things which we do not yet believe.

For example, we all know that for the sake of short-term profits (so the rich can get richer), the USA consistently blocks legislation which would improve the daily lives of the working poor. It is no secret that in September 2002, the USA blocked an international agreement which would have made prescription drugs less expensive. Similarly, in September 2003, the USA insisted on subsidies for cotton farmers, thus violating its own advice to the Third World to suspend subsidies and allow the so-called "free market" to work its magic (*Iraq*, pp. 21–2). Such inconsistencies in today's sociosymbolic order are truths which are "out there," and they indicate the workings of the Real of capital. Other indications that capital today functions as the disavowed Real (producing inconsistency in the sociosymbolic order) include the outsourcing of dirty jobs (such as torture) to Third World allies of the USA (p. 22).

Along these lines, in direct contradiction to the rhetoric about exporting democracy to the rest of the world, the USA ensures that countries like Saudi Arabia and Kuwait remain deeply conservative, repressive monarchies. The USA has a long history of supporting such blatantly undemocratic regimes. And in the case of Saudi Arabia and Kuwait, US support allows the USA to rely on these countries' oil reserves (*Iraq*, pp. 22–3). The truth behind the ideological manipulations of the USA is externalized in the inconsistencies of the symbolic register; these inconsistencies are plainly manifest to anyone who is not engaging in fetishistic disavowal. Again, far from being an Islamic fundamentalist stronghold, Saddam's Iraq was a *secular* socialist state (p. 23).

For such reasons, Žižek argues that the USA today is exporting its capitalist revolution around the world, meanwhile disingenuously claiming that US-style liberal "democracy" is God's gift to humanity (*Iraq*, p. 25). Thus anyone who opposes US policies is "rejecting God's noblest gift to humanity" (p. 26). This is how George W. Bush described the USA's "divine" mandate. Does fetishist disavowal prevent us from realizing that a president who was not democratically elected in 2000, but merely *appointed* by a majority of Supreme Court Justices, subsequently claimed the divine right to take "democracy" to Baghdad?

But surely we live in a "post-ideological" era? And is it not the case that the problem of racism has been resolved (witness the election of President Obama in the USA)? Žižek decisively does not agree with either of these two claims:

> Here I am inclined to bring in the old Marxist "humanist" opposition of "relations between things" and "relations between persons": in the much-celebrated free circulation opened up by global capitalism, it is "things" (commodities) which circulate freely, while the circulation of "persons" is more and more controlled. This new racism of the developed world is, in a way, much more brutal than the previous form: its implicit legitimization is neither naturalist (the "natural" superiority of the developed West) nor any longer culturalist (we in the West also want to preserve our cultural identity), but unabashed economic egotism – the fundamental divide is the one between those who are included in the sphere of (relative) economic prosperity and those who are excluded from it. (*Iraq*, pp. 34–5)

From Žižek's dialectical materialist perspective, the ethical potential of religion has been reduced to "a bargaining chip in political power conflicts" (p. 43). In addition, the capitalist ideology of liberal democracy involves a process of ideological foreclosure. For example, those acts that we label as "terrorism" are actually part of *a political project*, and should be treated as such. Such a stance in no way implies agreement with this political project (p. 45). The tragic events of September 11, 2001, brought an end to the spirit of the Clintonite 1990s, that is, the false capitalist "free-market" utopia. Since then, we have entered an era in which new walls and borders have been springing up around the world:

> between Israel and the West Bank, around the European Union, along the US-Mexican border. The prospect of a new global crisis is looming: economic crises, military and other catastrophes, states of emergency. … It was the very inflation of abstract ethical rhetoric in George W. Bush's public statements (of the type "Does the world have the courage to act against Evil or not?") which revealed the utter *ethical* misery of the US position – the function of ethical reference here is purely mystificatory; it merely serves to mask the true political stakes, which are not difficult to discern. (*Iraq*, pp. 51–2)

If we believe that we live in a democracy, then how do we reconcile this belief with the fact that the USA and the UK invaded Iraq *against the will of the majority of the citizens* of the USA and the UK, not to mention that the attack was contrary to the will of the international community (*Iraq*, p. 59). In light of such facts, Žižek raises the possibility that the so-called "war on terror" is actually a way of containing the anti-globalist movement, and distracting attention away from it (p. 61). If this suggestion seems paranoid, it is worth remembering that:

> In 1982, the State Department deleted Iraq from the list of states which supports terrorism. In 1986, in the UN Security Council, the USA vetoed the condemnation of Iraq for its use of poisonous gases, against Iranian soldiers. The USA (Dow Chemical) was delivering poisonous gases, unofficially claiming that while their use against civilians was not acceptable, their use against Iranian soldiers was justified, since the survival of Iraq was at stake. No wonder, then, that when, in December 2002, Iraq delivered its 11,800 page report on its WMDs to the Security Council, the report was first filtered by the USA, and thousands of pages disappeared in the version that reached the UN – pages which documented the USA's collaboration with Iraq! (*Iraq*, p. 65)

It is in such ways that Žižek shows in *Iraq: The Borrowed Kettle* why justice only has meaning if, in relating to others, it also relates to oneself.

20

How to Read Lacan

Žižek shows the relevance of psychoanalysis today by clarifying Lacan's "return to Freud." Lacan's interpretation of Freudian theory elaborates a fundamental core of psychoanalytic insights in light of twentieth-century developments in linguistics, mathematics, and the sciences. Žižek demonstrates that Lacan kept Freudian theory alive by *reinventing* it, and shows how Lacan elaborates implications of which Freud was unaware. Moreover, in this book Žižek indicates how he himself performs a similar, sectarian split from the main body of Lacanian theory and practice. Finally, Žižek indicates how Lacan's own emphasis on the Real and the logic of feminine sexuation run contrary to Lacan's liberal tendencies.

> *Nothing forces anyone to enjoy except the superego. The superego is the imperative of* jouissance – *Enjoy!*
> —Jacques Lacan, *On Feminine Sexuality, Seminar XX: Encore*

One of Žižek's most sustained engagements with the psychoanalytic theory of Jacques Lacan is *How to Read Lacan* (2006).[1] In this book (abbreviated *Lacan* below) Žižek elaborates the philosophical implications of the psychoanalytic theory of Jacques Lacan. Each chapter of this book confronts a passage from Lacan with a work (or an excerpt) from

[1]   Unless otherwise stated, page references for this work are to the following edition: *How to Read Lacan* (NewYork: Norton, 2007).

Žižek: A Reader's Guide, First Edition. Kelsey Wood.
© 2012 John Wiley & Sons, Inc. Published 2012 by John Wiley & Sons, Inc.

philosophy, art, popular culture, or ideology: Žižek further refines Lacanian theory by developing his own dialectical materialist interpretations of these works or excerpts. In *Lacan* – as in most of his works – Žižek focuses primarily on Lacan's later theory and re-inscribes key Lacanian concepts in order to analyze our current social and libidinal predicament from his own (unorthodox) Marxist perspective. These Lacanian concepts include (among others) the unconscious, the big Other, symbolic performatives, desire, anxiety, the Real, the forced choice, the fundamental fantasy, the lamella, superego, and *jouissance*.

Even though it is an introduction to Lacanian psychoanalytic theory, Žižek's *How to Read Lacan* is not an easy book to understand. But the thematic unity of the work is the law of desire as pointing toward an ethics of the Real. Žižek does not only explain the meaning of key Lacanian concepts, but also puts these concepts to work, using them to clarify today's "social and libidinal predicament" (*Lacan*, p. 6). As in all of his works, Žižek is careful to point out that he is not even attempting to offer an allegedly neutral, "objective" assessment of Lacanian theory. Instead, he engages in a thoroughly partisan reading, openly taking sides.

In the introduction to *Lacan*, Žižek argues that Lacanian psychoanalysis is more than a technique for the clinical treatment of psychic disturbances. It is also – like philosophy – a theoretical confrontation with the fundamental questions of human existence: "It does not show an individual the way to accommodate him- or herself to the demands of social reality; instead it explains how something like 'reality' constitutes itself in the first place. It does not merely enable a human being to accept the repressed truth about him- or herself; it explains how the dimension of truth emerges in human reality" (*Lacan*, p. 3). Succinctly put, Lacanian psychoanalysis leads the analysand to confront his or her *desire*. But desire, unlike a want or a wish, is unconscious. Again, what is the unconscious, according to Lacanian theory? In the first place, the unconscious obeys its own grammar and logic: in a sense, the unconscious talks and thinks. The unconscious is not the dark cellar of the mind, where wild drives are trapped before they are tamed by the ego. Instead, the unconscious is the externalized site where some traumatic truth speaks out. Žižek clarifies the Lacanian concept of the unconscious with reference to Freud:

> Therein lies Lacan's version of Freud's motto *Wo es war, soll ich werden* (Where it was, I am to become): not "The ego should conquer the id," the site of the unconscious drives, but "I should dare to approach the site of my truth." What awaits me "there" is not a deep Truth that I have to identify with, but an unbearable truth that I have to learn to live with. (*Lacan*, p. 3)

Žižek points out that Lacan's "return to Freud" was a *reinvention* of Freudian psychoanalysis, since most of Lacan's key concepts do *not* have counterparts in Freud's theory: "Freud never mentions the triad of Imaginary, Symbolic, and Real, he never talks about 'the big Other' as the symbolic order, he speaks of 'ego,' not of 'subject'" (*Lacan*, p. 4). Lacan imported these concepts from other disciplines in order to articulate a cluster of implications of which not even Freud was aware. For example, Lacan recognized that Freud was not fully aware of the role of speech and language in psychoanalytic theory. This is why Lacan developed the notion of speech in light of Saussurean linguistics, the theory of speech acts, and Hegelian dialectics (p. 4). And in spite of Lacan's occasional disparaging remarks about philosophy, his own theory is imbued with the spirit of Socratic intellectual modesty, insofar as "the most outstanding feature of his teaching is permanent self-questioning" (p. 5).

Before articulating the implications of the Real, Žižek prepares the way by clarifying the Lacanian concept of the big Other:

> The symbolic order, society's unwritten constitution, is the second nature of every speaking being: it is here, directing and controlling my acts; it is the sea I swim in, yet it remains ultimately impenetrable – I can never put it in front of me and grasp it. It is as if we, subjects of language, talk and interact like puppets, our speech and gestures dictated by some nameless all-pervasive agency. (*Lacan*, p. 8)

However, this does not mean that human subjects are mere pawns in a game of chess played by the intersubjective symbolic network of the big Other. Again, in opposition to the common misconception that psychoanalysis implies that human beings are determined by unconscious forces, Žižek affirms the subversive potential of human spontaneity, and the possibility of radical autonomy implicit to Freud's notion of death drive.

Žižek uses the game of chess to clarify the Lacanian symbolic, imaginary, and Real. The rules of chess signify its *symbolic* dimension. Thus the signifier "knight" is defined by the moves this figure is allowed by the rules to make, as distinguished from the other pieces. If the symbolic dimension of chess involves the public, shared rules of the game, the *imaginary* dimension is manifested in the shape, size, and color of the pieces, as well as their names: "it is easy to envision a game with the same rules, but with a different imaginary, in which this figure [the knight] would be called a 'messenger' or 'runner' or whatever" (*Lacan*, p. 8). The dimension of the *Real*, in this comparison to chess, is manifested in the entire complex of contingent circumstances which affect the game: for example, the players' training, intelligence, unforeseen distractions, etc. (p. 9).[2]

The rules of grammar and social conventions and prohibitions are symbolic. Thus when we speak, "the big Other must always be there" (*Lacan*, p. 9). However, the symbolic big Other is merely virtual; it is a presupposition of the subject in that it "exists" only insofar as subjects *behave as though it exists* (p. 10). The big Other cannot exist independently of the activity of subjects (p. 11). Nonetheless, the inherently reflexive nature of human subjectivity means that any act of communication "simultaneously symbolizes the fact of communication" (p. 12). This reflexivity is why Žižek asserts that, when a subject speaks, the big Other is "there," as a presupposition of the subject who behaves as if it were there (pp. 9–10). And, in addition to the public face of symbolic exchange (rules of grammar, etc.) communication also always involves *unwritten* rules and prohibitions, as well as the "empty gesture" of the forced choice:

> Belonging to a society involves a paradoxical point at which each of us is ordered to embrace freely, as a result of our choice, what is anyway imposed on us (we all *must* love our country, our parents, our religion). This paradox of willing (choosing freely) what is in any case compulsory, of pretending (maintaining the appearance) that there is a free choice although effectively there isn't one, is strictly co-dependent with the notion of an empty symbolic gesture, a gesture – an offer – that is meant to be rejected.[3]

This offer meant only to be rejected is the essence of all symbolic exchange, and it results in a pact of solidarity between the two parties involved (*Lacan*, p. 13).

But a sociopath – in contrast to a "normal" neurotic – cannot comprehend the fact that many human actions are performed simply for the sake of the symbolic interchange itself, and the gain for both parties – the pact of solidarity – which results from the empty gesture. Thus the sociopath merely uses language as an instrument; he is not "caught up in it." The sociopath's attitude toward morality is the same: he recognizes rules of morality and can behave so as to conform to them insofar as it suits his purpose, but he has no "gut feeling" of right and wrong.

---

[2] With reference to chess, Žižek also points out that *rocade* functions as the exception, the move that violates the fundamental logic of all other moves. See *The Ticklish Subject: The Absent Centre of Political Ontology* (London and New York: Verso, 1999), p. 99.

[3] Slavoj Žižek, "Tolerance as an Ideological Category," *Critical Inquiry*, Autumn 2007, available online at http://www.lacan.com/zizek-inquiry.html. Also in Slavoj Žižek, *How to Read Lacan* (New York: Norton, 2006), pp. 12–13.

(*Lacan*, pp. 13–14). But for most of us (neurotics), language is more than a mere instrument, insofar as it involves the performative dimension of choosing to identify with the written and unwritten rules of symbolic interchange.

One way to understand the Lacanian insight that the unconscious has its own grammar and logic involves recognizing that symbolic identification is always split. For example, a subject is alienated from himself at the moment he becomes a subject, insofar as he submits to the forced choice of the symbolic order. The neurotic *represses* Real trauma, and the repressed inevitably returns to disrupt his symbolic reality. For Lacan, anxiety is the only affect that does not lie, and anxiety indicates the proximity of the Real, that is, to the inconsistency of the symbolic order and the nonexistence of the big Other. A hero confronts such anxiety with courage and engages in the Lacanian act. An act reconfigures symbolic order by cutting into the Real of a situation. Thus a subject becomes a hero through the Lacanian act: the ethical act redefines – in a retroactive way – the entire symbolic coordinates of both reality and symbolic identity. In the experience of a psychotic, however, the prohibitions of the symbolic Father are *never* integrated into the symbolic universe; thus they are not repressed but foreclosed.

It cannot be repeated too often that Lacan and Žižek do *not* view the unconscious as determining human behavior in a mechanical way; the Lacanian concept of the unconscious in its relation to symbolic practice involves freedom. However, Žižek argues that freedom is unconscious: it is associated with the remainder of symbolization. Even the act of a hero is something that arises insofar as she simply cannot do otherwise. The "space" for freedom in this sense is indicated by the incompleteness of reality. The symbolic order is never consistent or unequivocal: there is no pure symbolic self-identity.

But, again, fantasy functions to mask symbolic inconsistency, and to shield us from repressed Real trauma or antagonism; fantasy is constitutive of symbolic reality insofar as fantasy teaches us how to desire: "while fantasy is the screen that protects us from the encounter with the Real, fantasy itself, at its most fundamental – what Freud called the 'fundamental fantasy,' which provides the most elementary coordinates of the subject's capacity to desire – cannot ever be subjectivized, and has to remain repressed in order to function" (*Lacan*, p. 59). Because of this repression, when we speak (no matter what we choose to say), in one way or another the unconscious speaks through us. The unconscious truth that is unbearable to us is "out there," all around us, in the inherent inconsistency of our symbolic practices:

Recall the everyday situation in which my (sexual, political, or financial) partner wants me to strike a deal; what he tells me is basically: "Please, I really love you. If we get it together here, I will be totally dedicated to you! But beware! If you reject me, I may lose control and make your life a misery!" The catch here, of course, is that I am not simply confronted with a clear choice: the second part of this message undermines the first part – somebody who is ready to damage me if I say no to him cannot really love me and be devoted to my happiness, as he claims. There is also a symmetrical hypocrisy, which consists in saying: "I love you and will accept whatever your choice will be; so even if (you know that) your refusal will ruin me, please choose what you really want, and do not take into consideration how it will affect me!"[4]

Such examples show why for Lacan and Žižek, the symbolic order cannot be understood as simply a pre-existing formal framework that limits human choices and practices (*Lacan*, p. 15).

On the contrary, like many Marxists (e.g. Georg Lukács), Lacan and Žižek emphasize how the process of symbolic identification is always thoroughly contextualized in historically contingent modes of collective practice (*Lacan*, p. 15). In short, the process of symbolic recognition/ identification is inherently reflexive, or *dialectical*:

> every utterance not only transmits some content, but, simultaneously, *conveys the way the subject relates to this content*. Even the most down-to-earth objects and activities always contain such a declarative dimension, which constitutes the ideology of everyday life. One should never forget that utility functions as a reflexive notion: it always involves the assertion of utility as meaning. A man who lives in a large city and owns a Land-Rover (for which he obviously has no use) doesn't simply lead a no-nonsense, down-to-earth life; rather, he owns such a car in order to *signal* that he leads his life under the sign of a no-nonsense, down-to-earth attitude.[5]

The implications of this declarative dimension of symbolic interaction are far-reaching and profound. For example, we are untroubled by certain things that we already know, so long as these things are not stated openly: in other words, so long as the intersubjective big Other remains ignorant of them.

---

[4] Slavoj Žižek, "How to Read Lacan," available online at http://www.lacan.com/zizciap. html. Also in Slavoj Žižek, *How to Read Lacan* (New York: Norton, 2006), p. 14.

[5] Slavoj Žižek, "How to Read Lacan," available online at http://www.scribd.com/ doc/23883523/How-to-Read-Lacan-Slavoj-Zizek. Also in Slavoj Žižek, *How to Read Lacan* (New York: Norton, 2006), p. 16.

This shows that there is an inherent split or gap between the enunciated content of speech and the act of enunciation itself (*Lacan*, p. 18). Along these same lines, the simple act of *not* mentioning something can sometimes reveal the very truth we hoped to conceal. In other words, the repressed, Real returns in our symbolic practices, not only in spite of, but sometimes precisely *because of*, our efforts to prevent this. Žižek shows this by means of an example on pages 19–20 of *Lacan*:

> When, in February 2003, Colin Powell addressed the UN assembly in order to advocate the attack on Iraq, the US delegation asked for the large reproduction of Picasso's *Guernica* on the wall behind the speaker's podium to be covered with a different visual ornament. Although the official explanation was that *Guernica* did not provide the right visual background for the televised transmission of Powell's speech, it was clear to everyone what the US delegation was afraid of: that *Guernica*, the painting that commemorates the catastrophic results of the German aerial bombing of the Spanish city during the civil war, would give rise to the "wrong kind of associations" if it were to serve as the background to Powell advocating the bombing of Iraq by the far superior US air force. This is what Lacan means when he claims that repression and the return of the repressed are one and the same process: if the US delegation had refrained from demanding its concealment, probably no one would associate Powell's speech with the painting displayed behind him – it was this very gesture that drew attention to the association and confirmed its truth.[6]

On page 48, Žižek formulates the question of the Other's desire as: "You're saying this, but *what is it that you actually want by saying it?*" Fantasy provides an answer to the question of the desire of the Other (*Lacan*, pp. 48–9). However, the fundamental fantasy that forms the core of my own existence is inaccessible to me. Contrary to the standard view – which regards the locus of personal identity to be the self-experience of the individual – Lacanian theory holds that I am alienated from my most intimate subjective experience. This means that I cannot consciously experience "the way things really seem to me," because the fundamental fantasy that constitutes the core of my existence is inaccessible to me (p. 53). The standard view of subjectivity is that a subject shows signs of inner life, a direct experience of self that cannot be reduced to external behavior (pp. 53–4). For Lacan, however, what characterizes the subject is the gap that separates "inner life" from external behavior:

---

[6] Slavoj Žižek, "How to Read Lacan," available online at http://www.lacan.com/zizciap. html. Also in Slavoj Žižek, *How to Read Lacan* (New York: Norton, 2006), pp. 19–20.

We thus obtain a relationship that totally subverts the standard notion of the subject who directly experiences himself via his inner states: a strange relationship between the empty, non-phenomenal subject and the phenomena that remain inaccessible to the subject. In other words, psychoanalysis allows us to formulate a paradoxical phenomenology without a subject – phenomena arise that are not phenomena *of* a subject, appearing *to* a subject. This does not mean that the subject is not involved here – it is but precisely in the mode of *exclusion*, as divided, as the agency that is not able to assume the very core of his or her inner experience.[7]

Thus fantasy is ambiguous: while fantasy can serve as a screen to protect us from the encounter with the Real, fantasy – at its most fundamental – provides the coordinates of the subject's desire, and, again, this fundamental fantasy must remain repressed in order to function (p. 59). The ambiguity of fantasy arises at the intersection of the imaginary register and the Real.

Lacan's concept of the lamella (*hommelette*, or "manlet") indicates this intersection of imaginary and Real: "it stands for the Real in its most terrifying imaginary dimension, as the primordial abyss that swallows everything, dissolving all identities" (*Lacan*, p. 64). But, significantly, in contrast to the lamella as the imaginary/Real, Žižek distinguishes another, scientific dimension of the Lacanian Real:

> This Real of the lamella is to be opposed to the scientific mode of the Real. For those used to dismissing Lacan as just another "postmodern" relativist, this may come as a surprise. Lacan is resolutely anti-postmodern, opposed to any notion of science as just another story we are telling ourselves about ourselves, a narrative whose apparent supremacy over other – mythic, artistic – narratives is grounded only in the historically contingent Western "regime of truth" (to use a term rendered popular by Michel Foucault).[8]

This shows that the Lacanian Real does not refer to some reality which exists apart from our perceptions and thoughts: the Real does not "exist." It is not some transcendent thing that resists symbolization; rather, the Real is the gap or fissure immanent to any symbolic network (*Lacan*, p. 73). Žižek further clarifies the concept of the Real in a way to emphasize the affinity between Lacanian theory and science: "in a way that

---

[7] Slavoj Žižek, "How to Read Lacan," available online at http://www.lacan.com/zizciap. html. Also in Slavoj Žižek, *How to Read Lacan* (New York: Norton, 2006), p. 54.

[8] Slavoj Žižek, "How to Read Lacan," available online at http://www.lacan.com/zizciap. html. Also in Slavoj Žižek, *How to Read Lacan* (New York: Norton, 2006), p. 64.

echoes Einstein, for Lacan the Real – the Thing – is not so much the inert presence that curves symbolic space (introducing gaps and inconsistencies in it), but, rather, an effect of those gaps and inconsistencies" (p. 74). Again, the Lacanian Real manifests as the inconsistency of symbolic order and symbolic identity, and the Real is constituted retroactively, as the remainder of symbolization.

Yet another aspect of the repressed Real is *jouissance*, usually translated as "enjoyment." *Jouissance* is surplus enjoyment (pleasure-in-pain) and as such it is excessive and intrusive (*Lacan*, p. 79). For Lacan, there is a kind of "equation between *jouissance* and superego" (p. 79). Put simply, this means that superego functions in Lacanian theory as the agency that places impossible demands on the subject to indulge in ever more enjoyment: "to enjoy is not a matter of following one's spontaneous tendencies; it is rather something we do as a kind of weird and twisted ethical duty" (p. 79). Insofar as it enjoins us to idiotic *jouissance*, for Lacan and for Žižek the superego is "anti-ethical" (p. 80). Žižek indicates concisely how Lacan revises Freud, how several key Lacanian concepts are defined in relation to one another, and how psychoanalysis can aid the critique of ideology. In Lacanian theory:

> "ideal ego" stands for the idealized self-image of the subject (the way I would like to be, the way I would like others to see me); Ego-Ideal is the agency whose gaze I try to impress with my ego image, the big Other who watches over me and impels me to give my best, the ideal I try to follow and actualize; and superego is this same agency in its vengeful, sadistic, punishing aspect. The underlying structuring principle of these three terms is clearly Lacan's triad Imaginary-Symbolic-Real: ideal ego is imaginary, what Lacan calls the "small other," the idealized mirror-image of my ego; Ego-Ideal is symbolic, the point of my symbolic identification, the point in the big Other from which I observe (and judge) myself; superego is real, the cruel and insatiable agency that bombards me with impossible demands and then mocks my botched attempts to meet them [...]. The cynical old Stalinist motto about the accused at show trials who professed their innocence ("The more innocent they are, the more they deserve to be shot") is superego at its purest. (*Lacan*, p. 80)

Žižek's focus in this book involves what Lacan sometimes referred to as "the law of desire," which indicates the agency that tells a subject to act in conformity with her desire. The repressed Real is inscribed into the core of symbolic subjectivity as the object-cause of desire; this is why Žižek's focus on the law of desire enables him to articulate an ethics of the Real, as opposed to an ethics that remains within the confines of the symbolic register: "At its most fundamental, authentic belief does not concern facts, but gives expression to an unconditional ethical commitment" (*Lacan*, p. 117). Regarding an ethics of the Real, it should be noted that Žižek not only begins *How to Read Lacan* with a quotation from Lacan's *The Ethics of Psychoanalysis* (*Seminar VII*, 1959–60), but also refers to *The Ethics of Psychoanalysis* throughout. The Lacanian *act* is "ethical" insofar as it involves an encounter with the Real, not insofar as it conforms to some symbolic order. This indicates the significance of Lacan's famous assertion that "The only thing of which one can be guilty is having given ground relative to one's desire."

Žižek ends the book with a true story of a Lacanian ethical act, an act which contributed to the neutralizing and eventual overcoming of Stalinist ideology. The hero of the story is Dr Sophia Karpai, head of the cardiographic unit of the Kremlin Hospital in the late 1940s (only a few years before Stalin's death). To summarize the relevant facts, if Sophia Karpai had lied and confessed to something of which she was innocent, Stalin's alleged "doctor's plot" would have been confirmed in the minds of those conducting the investigation, leading to the death of hundreds of thousands of Soviet citizens and perhaps even providing Stalin an excuse to attack Western Europe. But Karpai endured the torture without confessing, Stalin slipped into a coma, and the trumped-up case of the doctor's plot was dropped (*Lacan*, p. 119).[9]

In *How to Read Lacan*, as in most of his other works, Žižek indicates the crucial role of the logic of feminine sexuation in relation to the ethical act. The feminine logic of sexuation involves the Real as the universal dimension of subjectivity – *not* as some objective set of positive properties – but as the very *impossibility* of compiling such a set. The subject as such is feminine in this sense: subjectivity is the very split or impossibility that is more original than any positive attempts to cover it over. Subjectivity as such (as feminine) underlies the subsequent process of ideological "subjectivization." In such ways, Žižek shows that the subject as such – if she does not compromise her desire – is free to twist out of ideological manipulations, and to reinvent a new symbolic order through the act. It is along these lines that Žižek's philosophical reinterpretation of Lacanian psychoanalytic theory makes possible not only a radically new account of human nature, but also a critique of ideology.

---

[9] Also see Jonathan Brent and Vladimir P. Naumov, *Stalin's Last Crime* (New York: Harper Collins, 2003), p. 297.

21

The Parallax View

The "parallax gap" shows up in neurobiology as the gap between the human world of meaning versus the stacks of brain-meat inside our skulls. Žižek develops the implications of the fact that no deterministic account of human behavior can account for our ability to act *against* a spontaneous inclination, or for our ability to go against our own self-interest. In philosophy, the parallax of the ontological difference discloses the incommensurability between the ontic life world and its a priori, transcendental conditions of possibility (its ontological horizon). Because of this difference or gap, "transcendental constitution" is not the actual creation of what exists: in short, we cannot deduce the ontic domain (the world) from its ontological horizon (our understanding of reality). Along these lines, in Lacanian psychoanalysis, there is a parallax of the Real, insofar as the Real has no substantial consistency. The Real eludes symbolization, but nevertheless, it is impossible to get rid of the Real. If the Real is what is left out of symbolic reality, nonetheless reality is inherently inconsistent, and this inconsistency results from the repression of the Real. In *The Parallax View*, Žižek further develops his concept of the subject as Real, in other words, the subject as parallax gap. Whereas the imaginary *ego* functions as a fantasy of unity, the subject as Real is the *gap* of being. The subject in this sense (the subject as the question) is the empty place in the symbolic structure; this is why the subject as parallax gap is distinct from the process of symbolic subjectivization and ideological indoctrination. That is to say, the subject as the question is Real, and the Real is the "beyond" of the symbolic order. Thus the Real of the subject provokes the critique of ideology. But the success of global capitalism is based on the imaginary ego, and on the competitiveness and aggression that accompanies the artificial object character of the ego as a fantasy of wholeness. Before emancipation can be achieved, we need to recognize that the

Žižek: A Reader's Guide, First Edition. Kelsey Wood.
© 2012 John Wiley & Sons, Inc. Published 2012 by John Wiley & Sons, Inc.

symbolic order and public Law conceal an obscene superego injunction. For example, the superego injunction of capitalism today is "Enjoy!" But what would happen if we took the initial step toward liberation by refusing to participate in the injunction to enjoy? Žižek argues that such a formal gesture of refusal opens up new possibilities, possibilities that are outside both the hegemonic position as well as the simple negation of this position. If we participate in such a gesture of refusal, we may recognize the possibility for a decisive political act that would lead to substantial change (as opposed to merely reactive countermeasures that ultimately change nothing). Subsequently, if we work together to realize what seems impossible, a revolutionary collective of subjects may transform the very coordinates of an entire sociopolitical order.

That is the crucial insight of Freudian metapsychology emphasized by Lacan: the function of Prohibition is not to introduce disturbance into the previous repose of paradisiacal innocence, but, on the contrary, to resolve some terrifying deadlock.

—Slavoj Žižek, *The Parallax View*, p. 89

The Parallax View (2006)[1] is clearly one of Žižek's most important works. In *The Parallax View*, Žižek reads philosophical, scientific, and political theories in light of fundamental Hegelian and Lacanian insights. To put it succinctly, he deploys dialectical thinking and psychoanalytic categories to analyze contemporary culture and to reinvigorate a Marxist critique of capitalist globalism. Žižek discloses the functioning of an ineradicable negativity, and shows how the recognition of this gap (for example, between the enunciated content and the *act* of enunciation) may enable us, on the one hand, to reflectively distance ourselves from the ideological manipulations of late capitalism while, on the other, avoiding the deadlock of a globalized suspicion.

What then is "parallax"? Parallax refers to the apparent displacement in an object when viewed from different perspectives, especially a celestial body as viewed from two lines of sight. Žižek's usage gives the term a philosophical twist:

> The philosophical twist to be added, of course, is that the observed difference is not simply "subjective," due to the fact that the same object which exists "out there" is seen from two different stances, or points of view. It is rather that, as Hegel would have put it, subject and object are

---

[1] Unless otherwise stated, page references for this work are to the following edition: *The Parallax View* (Cambridge, MA: MIT Press, 2006).

inherently "mediated," so that an "epistemological" shift in the subject's point of view always reflects an "ontological" shift in the object itself. Or – to put it in Lacanese – the subject's gaze is always-already inscribed into the perceived object itself, in the guise of its "blind spot," that which is "in the object more than the object itself," the point from which the object itself returns the gaze. "Sure, the picture is in my eye, but I am also in the picture": the first part of Lacan's statement designates subjectivization, the dependence of reality on its subjective constitution; while the second part provides a materialist supplement, reinscribing the subject into its own image in the guise of a stain (the objectivized splinter in its eye). Materialism is not the direct assertion of my inclusion in objective reality (such an assertion presupposes that my position of enunciation is that of an external observer who can grasp the whole of reality); rather, it resides in the reflexive twist by means of which I myself am included in the picture constituted by me – it is this reflexive short circuit, this necessary redoubling of myself as standing both outside and inside my picture, that bears witness to my "material existence." Materialism means that the reality I see is never "whole" – not because a large part of it eludes me, but because it contains a stain, a blind spot, which indicates my inclusion in it.[2]

As this passage indicates, in Žižek's usage, parallax indicates a displacement which does not simply result from the current limits of knowledge. Even as knowledge is gained, the fissure that is the parallax gap still cuts through all of symbolic reality. This inconsistency of reality does not arise simply because there are regions that are not yet known. Instead, the parallax gap is irreducible insofar as any possible symbolic reality is constitutively split. In other words, the expansion of knowledge cannot overcome the parallax gap because this disjoint or lack of fit is constitutive of what we experience as reality. In short, the basic ontological insight of *The Parallax View* is that reality is unfinished and never whole; reality is indeterminate and never fully constituted. This is another way of saying that the big Other does not exist.

In *The Parallax View*, Žižek further develops the triad of imaginary-symbolic-Real, and contrasts what he calls "the parallax Real" with the standard Lacanian Real:

This means that, ultimately, the status of the Real is purely parallactic and, as such, nonsubstantial: it has no substantial density in itself, it is just a gap between two points of perspective, perceptible only in the shift from the one to the other. The parallax Real is thus opposed to the standard

[2] See Slavoj Žižek, "The Parallax View," available online at http://www.lacan.com/ zizparallax.htm. Also in Slavoj Žižek, *The Parallax View* (Cambridge, MA: MIT Press, 2006), p. 17.

(Lacanian) notion of the Real as that which "always returns to its place" – as that which remains the same in all possible (symbolic) universes: the parallax Real is, rather, that which accounts for the very *multiplicity* of appearances of the same underlying Real – it is not the hard core which persists as the Same, but the hard bone of contention which pulverizes the sameness into the multitude of appearances. In a first move, the Real is the impossible hard core which we cannot confront directly, but only through the lenses of a multitude of symbolic fictions, virtual formations. In a second move, this very hard core is purely virtual, actually nonexistent, an X which can be reconstructed only retroactively, from the multitude of symbolic formations which are "all that there actually is."[3]

The parallax Real is the ineradicable displacement or splitting that disrupts what we experience as reality. Because of this irreducible asymmetry or void, symbolic reality – any universe of meaning – is ruptured from within. As a result, there can be no common denominator between various universes of discourse; ultimately there is no shared metalanguage between levels of meaning: "The parallax is not symmetrical, composed of two incompatible perspectives on the same X: there is an irreducible asymmetry between the two perspectives, a minimal reflexive twist. We do not have two perspectives, we have a perspective and what eludes it, and the other perspective fills in the void of what we could not see from the first perspective" (*The Parallax View*, p. 29).

Žižek confronts a remarkable variety of these related but incompatible symbolic "worlds" or fields of reality. But the three main sections of the book focus on how the parallax gap delimits the discourses of philosophy, contemporary science, and politics. Žižek investigates this inherent tension or void as it functions between – and *within* – philosophical, scientific, and political discourses. In philosophical ontology, the parallax gap functions as the differentiation that is essential for the disclosure of any existence. In cognitivist brain science the parallax gap divorces causal explanations from experiences such as acting *against* one's spontaneous inclination. Finally, in political philosophy, the gap functions as the irreducible social antagonism that informs the very activity of critique as it emerges at the interstices between communities.

In such ways, *The Parallax View* shows why there can be no consistent overarching ontology that unifies particular modes of disclosure such as quantum physics, neurobiology, philosophy, and psychoanalysis. Any

---

[3] See Slavoj Žižek, "The Parallax View," available online at http://www.lacan.com/zizparallax.htm. Also in Slavoj Žižek, *The Parallax View* (Cambridge, MA: MIT Press, 2006), p. 26.

discourse implicitly involves processes of abstraction as well as the intentional effort to reduce to a comprehensible unity aspects of reality that are in fact utterly disparate. The basic idea of the parallax view is that such bracketing produces its own object. Because of reductions, refusals of awareness, and bracketing, any universe of meaning always contains a stain or incommensurability, a blind spot on the world-picture that signals the subject's inclusion in it. Does this mean that the "unfathomable X," the parallax object that causes the parallax gap is something in the subject himself?

The Parallax View is the companion to Žižek's earlier *The Ticklish Subject: The Absent Centre of Political Ontology* (1999). *The Ticklish Subject* clarified Žižek's notion of subjectivity by differentiating it from Heideggerianism, contemporary French political philosophy, and feminist deconstructionism. Žižek argued against these philosophical orientations by showing the inadequacy of a presumption they all share, namely a notion of Cartesian subjectivity as a positive, substantial identity. Because all three of these approaches overlook the subversive implications of Descartes' effort to erase the entirety of reality and to start with a clean slate, they miss the most radical dimension of subjectivity. In *The Ticklish Subject*, Žižek showed the functional role of the Cartesian *cogito* ("I think, therefore I exist") within the broader project of methodic doubt and developed Lacan's insight that the subject of psychoanalysis is none other than Descartes' *cogito*. Žižek disclosed the "empty place" of Lacanian subjectivity as a pure structural function that emerges only through a *withdrawal* from one's substantial identity. This means that true subjectivity arises only through encountering the Real, and through the subsequent disintegration of the self that had been constituted within a communal universe of meaning. In other words, as opposed to the "self" produced by the process of ideological subjectivization, the subject as such involves the hysterical *questioning* of the feminine subject. To summarize, *The Ticklish Subject* articulated and clarified Lacan's account of subjectivity in order to assert the emancipatory potential of the subject against capitalist ideology.

In describing the relation between these two companion works, Žižek said that it is the parallax object that tickles the ticklish subject. The parallax gap is a difference or opposition that cannot be grounded in positive properties, because it is ontologically prior to the disclosures between which it is a difference. The parallax gap is not only a shift between (or juxtaposition of) two perspectives; more fundamentally, it is the pure, minimal difference or incommensurability that even divides one perspective or one object *from itself*. Reality is dialectical in the sense that there is no pure self-identity: the identity or reality of anything involves what it is not (its Other). Žižek discloses this one that is noncoincident with itself – the parallax object – as *objet petit a*. The *objet petit a* is not *what* we desire; on the contrary, it is what sets desire into motion. Desire is metonymical; it slides from one signifier to another. But throughout these displacements, desire retains a minimal consistency. The *objet petit a* is both that which provides this formal frame of consistency and that which moves desire to slide from one object to another. Žižek argues that the *objet petit a* – as the object cause of desire – is the "unfathomable X" that causes the parallax gap:

> *L'objet petit a* is therefore close to the Kantian transcendental object, since it stands for the unknown X, the noumenal core of the object beyond appearances, for what is "in you more than yourself." *L'objet petit a* can thus be defined as a pure parallax object: it is not only that its contours change with the shift of the subject; it *exists – its presence can be discerned – only when the landscape is viewed from a certain perspective.* More precisely, *objet petit a* is the very cause of the parallax gap, that unfathomable X which forever eludes the symbolic grasp, and thus causes the multiplicity of symbolic perspectives.[4]

In order to articulate the parallax Real as the reflexive asymmetry or incommensurability inherent to any world picture, Žižek addresses the Hegelian theme of negativity. Dialectical consciousness is always ruptured from within by some nonrational element that undermines the complete, consistent understanding (or existence) of any whole. Any totality – or symbolic reality – is inconsistent/incomplete because unification (totalization or conceptual synthesis) is always implicitly disjointed by an indefinable void (the Real), which ultimately proves to be essential to the very totality which it undermines:

> The synthesis has to rely on an irreducibly external element, as in Kant, where being is not a predicate (that is, cannot be reduced to a conceptual predicate of an entity), or as in Saul Kripke's *Naming and Necessity*, in which the reference of a name to an object cannot be grounded in the content of this name, in the properties it designates. (*The Parallax View*, p. 51)

---

4 See Slavoj Žižek, "The Parallax View," available online at http://www.lacan.com/zizparallax.htm. Also in Slavoj Žižek, *The Parallax View* (Cambridge, MA: MIT Press, 2006), p. 18.

By making thematic this "irreducibly external element," Žižek shows how this implicit dimension of negativity within Hegelian dialectic prefigures both the materialism of Marx and the Freudian notion of the death drive:

> Here, however, we should avoid a key misunderstanding about Hegel's dialectics: its wager is not to adopt toward the present the "point of view of finality," viewing it as if it were already past, but, precisely, to *reintroduce the openness of the future into the past*, to *grasp that-which-was in its process of becoming*, to see the contingent process which generated existing necessity. Is this not why we have to conceive the Absolute "not only as Substance, but also as Subject"? This is why German Idealism explodes the coordinates of the standard Aristotelian ontology which is structured around the vector running from possibility to actuality. In contrast to the idea that every possibility strives fully to actualize itself, we should conceive of "progress" as a move of *restoring the dimension of potentiality to mere actuality*, of unearthing, at the very heart of actuality, a secret striving toward potentiality.[5]

The Parallax View focuses on this irrepressible, "secret striving toward potentiality" in order to reveal how the operations of the imagination – by camouflaging the parallax gap – produce an imaginary sense of wholeness that prevents any encounter with the Real. This is crucial since ideological manipulations rely on such fantasies. The only way to open the possibility of reinventing a new symbolic order is first to encounter the Real and then to traverse the fantasy through the political act. To facilitate this, Žižek articulates a version of dialectical materialism that emphasizes the limits and the negativity of the dialectical process. He argues that there is no universal law underlying the contingent play of appearances. On the contrary, the universe itself is inconsistent, incomplete, and irreducibly contingent (*The Parallax View*, p. 79). Žižek argues that the effort to think the negativity of the parallax gap is necessary in order to actualize the unfulfilled potential of dialectical materialism: "It is the wager of this book that, far from posing an irreducible obstacle to dialectics, the notion of the parallax gap provides the key which enables us to discern its subversive core. To theorize this

---

[5] See Slavoj Žižek, "The Parallax View," available online at http://www.lacan.com/zizparallax.htm. Also in Slavoj Žižek, *The Parallax View* (Cambridge, MA: MIT Press, 2006), p. 78.

parallax gap properly is the necessary first step in the rehabilitation of the philosophy of *dialectical materialism*" (p. 4).

However, as is already clear from the preceding remarks, Žižek's dialectical materialism does not involve the claim that there is a neutral reality "out there" which is then distorted by our various (mis) representations of it; nor does he assume that there is some neutral standpoint from which reality may simply be observed and described. Because any totality is incomplete and inconsistent, Žižek does not try to *overcome* the incompleteness/inconsistency of symbolic reality, but to think the parallax gap itself, without introducing any imaginary sense of completeness. All of this indicates why Žižek examines two opposed alternatives and, instead of reconciling the thesis and antithesis in a "higher" synthesis, points out something that both sides overlook. Žižek undermines traditional problems of philosophy by showing how both alternatives in a dilemma are wrong; both sides presuppose something and thus fail to recognize a more basic problem. An example of this is his critique of Ernesto Laclau in *The Parallax View*. Žižek argues that Laclau's logic relies on two positively existing, externally opposed poles:

> From a Hegelian standpoint, however, this logic continues to rely on the two externally opposed poles – the fact that each of the opposites, in its abstraction from the other (that is, brought to the extreme at which it no longer needs its opposite), falls into this other, merely demonstrates their mutual reliance. What we need to do is to take a step further from this external opposition (or mutual reliance) into direct internalized overlapping, which means: not only does one pole, when abstracted from the other and thus brought to the extreme, coincide with its opposite, but *there is no "primordial" duality of poles in the first place, only the inherent gap of the One*. Equivalence is primordially not the opposite of difference; equivalence emerges only because no system of differences can ever complete itself, it "is" a structural effect of this incompleteness.[6]

What does this mean? Put succinctly, Laclau neglects the inconsistency that is an effect of the Real, and lapses into an imaginary sense of completeness. But according to Žižek's dialectical materialism, any one, any totality, any symbolic reality – and any dualistic system of opposites – is inconsistent *with itself*. Moreover, this radical "noncoincidence of the

---

[6] See Slavoj Žižek, "The Parallax View," available online at http://www.lacan.com/zizparallax.htm. Also in Slavoj Žižek, *The Parallax View* (Cambridge, MA: MIT Press, 2006), p. 36.

Same with itself" (*The Parallax View*, p. 36) is a condition of possibility of all thought. And because any system of differences is incomplete, opposites are never neutralized in a system of mutual dependence. Instead, the difference is maintained and posited as such. In sum, Žižek's dialectical materialism emphasizes difference and inconsistency and undermines all imaginary unity, including the unity implicit to the notion of an allegedly complete system of differences, or a supposedly primordial dualism of opposite poles.

To put this in terms of Žižek's earlier works, by displacing the difference between the universal and the particular *into the particular itself,* Žižek shows that the only mediator of particular and universal is the splitting that runs through both of them.[7] *The Parallax View* refines the logic of dialectical materialism in a way that clarifies Žižek's negative version of universality. By analyzing closely linked but incommensurable universes of discourse, Žižek articulates a universality that involves pure differentiation as such. The parallax gap is related to the Real as that which suspends the instant of identity implicit to "ordinary" logic. For such reasons, Žižek never attempts to bridge this parallax gap between universes of meaning: once we confront the parallax gap "we should assert antinomy as irreducible, and conceive the point of radical critique not as a certain determinate position as opposed to another position, but as the irreducible gap between the positions itself, the purely structural interstice between them" (*The Parallax View*, p. 20).

Again, the notion that any consistent whole or totality (or complete synthesis) is possible is based on fantasy. Any symbolic system or reality is finite; there is no all-inclusive perspective. For this reason, if we try to comprehend the whole, we comprehend nothing: "And of course, the trap to be avoided here is precisely that of trying to formulate the totality parts of which are democratic ideology, the exercise of power, and the process of economic (re)production: if we try to keep them all in view, we end up seeing nothing; the contours disappear" (*The Parallax View*, p. 56).

In such ways, Žižek indicates how fantasy constructions unify (and hence make possible) our symbolic reality: even in order to be perceived, reality has to always already fit our "phantasmatic space." The element of fantasy implicit to the process of ideological subjectivization teaches us

---

[7] Cf. *Tarrying with the Negative: Kant, Hegel, and the Critique of Ideology* (Durham, NC: Duke University Press, 1993), p. 30.

how to desire: fantasy constitutes desire by providing its coordinates. Any subject's experience, any social system, and any regime or culture is given a minimum of consistency by fantasy; fantasy projections that are externalized as unreflective behaviors serve to mask the inconsistency of symbolic reality. But insofar as the imaginary is constitutive of what we experience as reality, fantasy functions in an invisible way, filling in the blind spot in our field of vision.

In ideology, the Master-Signifier is related to a fantasy construction which pins down or fixes our field of social practices. In a successful ideology, adherents behave as if the indefinable Master-Signifier actually names some transcendent thing: the very indefinability of the Master-Signifier enables believers to assume the validity of the system. The paradox is that these indefinable central terms imply a point of reference outside any possible universe of discourse. The void at the heart of any ideology allows subjects to interact with some degree of consistency; ideology offers us the social reality itself as an escape from some antagonism or trauma.

Paradoxically, that which is in one way most intimate to our existence proves to be in another way utterly foreign: it is our "extimate" core. The efficacy of ideology proves to reside so close to us as to be virtually invisible, namely, in the "unknown knowns" that condition our behavior. These are things that we know, but don't yet know that we know, because to fully realize them would be too traumatic and shattering. We "know" them, insofar as they are efficacious in our actions, and yet we do not know them to the point of consciously recognizing them. The danger is that these unknown knowns – things that we know but don't know that we know – control us; we do not control them.

Such analyses undermine the postmodern claim that we now live in a post-ideological world. Against this, Žižek shows how a belief or ideology functions in a *virtual* way; even if no one effectively believes, it is enough that the assumption persists that someone else believes. This implicit reference to "the subject supposed to believe" structures our choices and daily interactions. If ideological fantasy constitutes our reality by configuring the realm of human interactions, how can we free ourselves from ideology? One of Žižek's primary aims in *The Parallax View* is to articulate the sense in which subjects are capable of radical ethical autonomy. This is why his analyses of the brain sciences in this book are not some sort of digression or aside. Recent developments in scientific studies of the brain reveal that the brain's structure is open to plasticity. The very structure of the brain changes and develops:

This development is not prescribed in advance by our genes; what genes do is precisely the opposite: they account for the structure of the brain, which is open to plasticity, so that some parts of it develop more if they are used more; if they are disabled, other parts can take over their function, and so on. What we are dealing with here is not only differentiation but trans-differentiation, "changing the difference." Learning and memory play a key role in reinforcing or suspending synaptic links: neurons "remember" their stimulations, actively structure them, and so forth. Vulgar materialism and idealism join forces against this plasticity: idealism, to prove that the brain is just matter, a relay machine which has to be animated from the outside, not the site of activity; materialism, to sustain its mechanical determinist vision of reality. This explains the strange belief which, although it is now empirically refuted, persists: the brain, in contrast to other organs, does not grow and regenerate; its cells just gradually die out. This view ignores the fact that our mind does not only reflect the world, it is part of a transformative exchange with the world, it "reflects" the possibilities of transformation, it sees the world through possible "projects," and this transformation is also self-transformation, this exchange also modifies the brain as the biological "site" of the mind (*The Parallax View*, p. 209).

In sum, Žižek's arguments for the radical autonomy (freedom) of the subject are thus in accord with the latest developments in the scientific study of the brain insofar as the structure of the brain is open to plasticity.

Žižek approaches the subject as the void or split inherent to any symbolization. His dialectical materialism involves the formulation of subjectivity as a paradoxical relation between an empty, "nonphenomenal" subject and certain phenomena (e.g., the fundamental fantasy) that remain inaccessible to the subject (*The Parallax View*, p. 172). The symbolic order is a system of differences, and the Lacanian act is an intervention in the symbolic that can change the difference, in other words, provide a new system of coordinates that reinvents a new symbolic identity and a new symbolic reality. The act involves an encounter with the Real, and, as the source of ontological difference, the Real is both that which limits any symbolic reality/identity, and that which facilitates the reinvention of a new symbolic reality/identity.

Žižek's remarkable achievement in *The Parallax View* is that he reveals the inadequacy of previous philosophers' accounts of the conditions of possibility for truth. In doing so, he also opens up the possibility of a new starting point for the political left: "What if the domain of politics is inherently 'sterile,' a theatre of shadows, but nonetheless crucial in transforming reality? So, although economy is the real site and politics is a theatre of shadows, the main fight is to be fought in politics and ideology" (p. 315). In such ways, *The Parallax View* shows that the success of capitalist globalism is based on the imaginary object character of the ego (cf. Lacan on "the mirror phase"). In political life, imaginary ego identifications function so as to mask irreducible social antagonisms. To achieve emancipation, we must recognize that any Master-Signifier conceals not only the nonrational moment of inconsistency implicit to public Law, but also the superego injunction to transgress. The injunction of late capitalism is to "Enjoy!" But truly saying "No" to this obscene superego injunction does not consist in any form of protest that is parasitic on what it negates.

In *The Parallax View* Žižek calls each of us to take the initial step toward liberation by simply refusing to participate in both the injunction to enjoy and any ultimately futile, reactive countermeasures. Such a formal gesture of refusal, he contends, "opens up a new space outside the hegemonic position *and* its negation" (pp. 382–3). When we move to the other side of the political parallax gap, we shift from "the 'Bartleby' attitude of withdrawal" to directly engaging with social antagonism. The Lacanian act then takes the form of collective social action. A singular subject can directly participate in the universal by identifying with a collective that is, in principle, accessible to everyone (p. 10). And in the revolutionary act of a political collective, subjects may change the very coordinates of a situation and actualize what Žižek has more recently described as "a politics *between* fear and trembling."

22

In Defense of Lost Causes

In this book, Žižek rehabilitates the public use of reason, and isolates a subversive core in an assortment of "lost Causes." Against the cynical postmodern refrain that any commitment to great ideas (such as truth and justice) inevitably succumbs to the totalitarian temptation, Žižek argues wholeheartedly for universal emancipation. He reconsiders whether there might have been some emancipatory potential in, for example, Heidegger's politics, Stalinism, the dictatorship of the proletariat, and revolutionary terror from Robespierre to Mao. From these examples it is clear that one of Žižek's primary aims is to provoke liberals to reconsider the implications of their own rhetoric. In other words, the aim of *In Defense of Lost Causes* is not simply to defend, for example, revolutionary terror as such, but rather to demonstrate why liberal-democratic compromises with capitalism are not a viable option for the future. Since human beings make their own history, but not in circumstances of their own choosing, Žižek does not presume to offer a detailed plan for action. This would be to adopt the guise of the (nonexistent) Lacanian big Other. Instead, Žižek documents at great length the flaws within current thinking about – and responses to – the crises of late capitalism.

Constant revolutionizing of production, uninterrupted disturbance of all social relations, everlasting uncertainty and agitation distinguish the bourgeois epoch from all earlier ones. All fixed, fast-frozen relations, with their train of ancient and venerable prejudices and opinions are swept away, all new-formed ones become antiquated before they can ossify. All

Žižek: A Reader's Guide, First Edition. Kelsey Wood.
© 2012 John Wiley & Sons, Inc. Published 2012 by John Wiley & Sons, Inc.

that is solid melts into air, all that is holy is profaned, and man is at last compelled to face with sober senses his real conditions of life, and his relations with his kind. [...] In place of the old local and national seclusion and self-sufficiency, we have intercourse in every direction, universal inter-dependence of nations. And as in material, so also in intellectual production. The intellectual creations of individual nations become common property. National one-sidedness and narrow-mindedness become more and more impossible, and from the numerous national and local literatures, there arises a world literature.

—Karl Marx and Friedrich Engels, *Communist Manifesto*

Žižek includes the above quotation in his final chapter of *In Defense of Lost Causes* (2008),[1] arguing that the insights of Marx and Engels are more relevant now than ever (p. 434). In this book (abbreviated *Defense* below) Žižek's aim is "not to defend Stalinist terror, and so on, as such, but to render problematic the all-too-easy liberal-democratic alternative" (p. 6). Throughout, Žižek provokes liberal pseudo-leftist academics to realize that in intellectual production: "The ruling class (whose ideas are those of the ruling class) is represented by spontaneous ideology, while the dominated class has to fight its way through intense conceptual work" (p. 381). The spontaneous ideology of the ruling class is not only manifested in intellectual production, but even at the level of ordinary "common sense." For common sense, it appears as if there is no viable alternative to capitalism. The blind spot of this common sense view is that today, the excesses of global capitalism have undermined capitalism's own conditions of possibility. Capitalism depends on symbolic trust, and on individuals accepting the basic fairness of the system. But today, in a time of crises and ruptures, we must risk a leap of faith (p. 2).

Thus the problem for the left today is the problem of *fidelity*: how can leftists realize the emancipatory potential that was missed in the failed revolutionary events of the past? If we are to realize this emancipatory potential, we must avoid the twin pitfalls "of nostalgic attachment to the past and of all-too-slick accommodation to 'new circumstances'" (*Defense*, p. 3). Žižek argues that the only way to achieve our aim is to forget the liberal-democratic notion of universality as a neutral, "objective" space for pragmatic compromise. The truth arises only through engagement in the *struggle* for truth: "Not by running after

---

[1] Unless otherwise stated, page references for this work are to the following edition: *In Defense of Lost Causes* (London and New York: Verso, 2008).

'objective' truth, but by holding onto the truth about the position from which one speaks" (p. 3). But, Žižek observes, today's complacent liberal academics view any serious questioning of the status quo as "totalitarian" (pp. 3–4). Because complacent postmodern intellectuals have adopted the ideology of the ruling class, they view any serious political thought today as a dangerously radical, violent return to totalitarianism. Against the cynical postmodern refrain that the commitment to great causes and ideas inevitably leads to totalitarianism, Žižek aligns himself solidly on the side of universal emancipation, and specifically the communist hypothesis of the French philosopher, Alain Badiou:

> Our proposal is to turn this perspective around: as Badiou himself might put it in his unique Platonic way, true ideas are eternal, they are indestructible, they always return every time they are proclaimed dead. It is enough for Badiou to *state* these ideas again clearly, and anti-totalitarian thought appears in all its misery as what it really is, a worthless sophistic exercise, a pseudo-theorization of the lowest opportunist survivalist fears and instincts, a way of thinking which is not only reactionary but also profoundly *reactive* in Nietzsche's sense of the term. (*Defense*, p. 4)

In addition to this reference to Badiou in the introduction to *Defense*, Žižek also ends the book with a reference to Badiou. Moreover, Žižek even devotes an entire chapter to Badiou's thinking; in fact, explicit and implicit references to Badiou occur throughout *In Defense of Lost Causes*. Showing that the notion of totalitarianism functions as a stopgap to prevent thinking, Žižek argues for Badiou's idea of communism, and against liberal democracy. Liberal democracy functions today as the spontaneous ideology of global capitalism. But Žižek demonstrates in a variety of ways why the liberal-democratic compromise with capitalism is no longer a viable option. He calls instead for the reinvention of a new sociosymbolic order, an order that would facilitate universal emancipation. To ensure that liberals do not mistake him for some kind of "closet fascist," Žižek carefully distinguishes between communist and fascist violence:

> Nazism was not radical enough, it did not dare to disturb the basic structure of the modern capitalist social space (which is why it had to focus on destroying an invented external enemy, Jews). [...] Hitler did *not* "have the courage" to really change things; he did *not* really act, all his actions were fundamentally *reactions*, that is, he acted so that nothing would really change, he staged a great spectacle of Revolution so that the capitalist order could survive. (*Defense*, p. 151)

251

Žižek urges that true radicals, as opposed to both fascists and liberals, will not shirk from "the terror needed" to achieve aims such as equality, human rights, and freedom (*Defense*, p. 158). Žižek associates revolutionary terror with *justice*, and this makes terror an emanation of virtue (p. 159). Moreover, he argues that such terror – emanating from virtue – has a "rational kernel" (p. 160). By contrast, the democratic political order is inherently *susceptible to corruption* (*Welcome to the Desert of the Real*, p. 79). To support this, Žižek quotes Badiou's reference to Louis de Saint-Just (1767–1794), a radical Jacobin leader during the French Revolution: "For, as Saint-Just asked: 'What do those who want neither Virtue nor Terror want?' His answer is well known: they want corruption – another name for the subject's defeat" (*Defense*, p. 160). Along these same lines, Žižek argues that the French revolutionary terror of 1792–1794 was an example of what Walter Benjamin calls "divine violence" (p. 161).

To distance himself from the liberal pseudo-leftist's "dream of a 'pure' event which never really takes place," Žižek gives a clear and unambiguous example of divine violence: namely the establishment of the Paris Commune of 1871 and the dictatorship of the proletariat which it enforced (*Defense*, p. 161). And on the next page, Žižek argues that the Red Terror of 1919 was also an example of divine violence, and explains why:

> When those outside the structured social field strike "blindly," demanding *and* enacting immediate justice/vengeance, this is "divine violence" – recall, a decade or so ago, the panic in Rio de Janeiro when crowds descended from the favelas into the wealthy part of the city and started looting and burning supermarkets – *this* was "divine violence" ... Like Biblical locusts, divine punishment for men's sinful ways, it strikes from out of nowhere, a means without an end [...]. The "dictatorship of the proletariat" is thus another name for Benjaminian "divine violence" which is outside the law, a violence exerted as brutal revenge/justice – but why "divine"? "Divine" points towards the dimension of the "inhuman"; one should thus posit a double equation: divine violence = inhuman terror = dictatorship of the proletariat. (*Defense*, p. 162)

Žižek clearly distinguishes himself from pseudo-leftist "beautiful souls" who dream of "revolution without revolution" (*Defense*, p. 163). But significantly, Žižek also distances himself from Stalinism, precisely because Stalin's use of terror was part of an implicitly *humanist* project, "engendering the New Man" (pp. 164–5). Stalinist terror was carried out "as a kind of wager on the future," a bright Communist future which (allegedly) would retroactively justify Stalin's crimes (p. 224).

Arguing against *all forms* of humanism, Žižek refers to Lacanian psychoanalytic theory in order to indicate how "Lacan accomplishes the passage from theoretical to practical *anti-humanism*" (*Defense*, p. 166). This indicates the implications of the Lacanian ethics of the Real: the Real as irreducible antagonism separates a thing even from itself. As the remainder of symbolization, the Real is manifest in what symbolization cannot represent, namely the inconsistency of symbolization itself. Žižek even further radicalizes the Lacanian concept of the Real with his own concept of "the parallax Real" (the theme of his *The Parallax View* of 2006):

> The parallax Real is thus opposed to the standard (Lacanian) notion of the Real as that which "always returns to its place," namely, as that which remains the same in all possible (symbolic) universes: the parallax Real is rather that which accounts for the very *multiplicity* of appearances of the same underlying Real – it is not the hard core which persists as the Same, but the hard bone of contention which pulverizes the sameness into a multitude of appearances. In a first move, the Real is the impossible hard core which we cannot confront directly, but only through the lenses of a multitude of symbolic fictions, virtual formations. In a second move, this very hard core is purely virtual, actually non-existing, an X which can be reconstructed only retroactively, from the multitude of symbolic formations which are "all that there actually is." (*Defense*, p. 127)

Thus an ethics of the Real involves an act of fully identifying with those who have no place in "all that there actually is," the excluded ones who have fallen through the cracks of reality, the outcasts of the sociosymbolic order, society's "excremental remainder" (slum dwellers, the homeless, etc.). This explains why Žižek argues that not only right-wingers *but also moderates* are thoroughly complicit in the injustice of global capitalism today: "there are no innocent bystanders in the crucial moments of revolutionary decision, because in such moments, innocence itself – exempting oneself from the decision, going on as if the struggle I am witnessing does not really concern me – *is* the highest treason" (*Defense*, p. 167).

Only in light of this "anti-humanist" ethics of the Real can we understand Žižek's statements about proletarian divine violence, as opposed to the violence of capitalists and imperialists. Žižek illustrates the difference with a reference to Mao Zedong's message of courage regarding the prospect of an atomic world war (*Defense*, p. 168). Žižek argues that Mao's message was not empty posturing, because: "imperialists are Nietzschean slaves, they need wars, but are afraid to lose their possessions to which they are attached, while the proletarians are the true aristocratic Masters who do not want war (they do not need it), but are not afraid of it, because they have nothing to lose" (p. 169). Žižek contrasts the true leftist ethics of the Real on the one hand, with the postmodern, liberal emphasis on a normalized, neutralized Other. Žižek concisely exposes the hypocrisy of this liberal emphasis with a reference to Levinas' racist remarks about the "yellow peril" (p. 177). Žižek argues that revolutionary figures (e.g. Robespierre, John Brown, Lenin, Trotsky, Mao, Che Guevara), are *inhuman* in their fidelity to an ethics of the Real. Succinctly put, this means that true love of the Neighbor involves recognition of – and engagement with – a dimension of *inhuman* Otherness. Žižek also distinguishes the properly *leftist* orientation toward the radical "Otherness of the Other to itself" from *fascist* invocations of alterity: see his reference to Heidegger's insistent warnings about the "Asiatic" threat (*Defense*, p. 177). In light of his remarks about Levinas (the "yellow peril") and Heidegger (the "Asiatic" threat), it is crucial to bear in mind that Žižek is extremely critical of China's so-called "Communist" regime. In a lecture given in Athens in 2007, Žižek recounts how, during a visit to China, he questioned a Communist Party official about a project to reinvigorate Chinese Socialism. After learning that the goal of this project was social cohesion (the masking of Real social antagonism), Žižek retorted: "In the West, we just call that fascism."[2]

Leftists – in contrast to liberals and to fascists – identify with the inherent gap in the symbolic order. Simply put, because they fully identify with those who are excluded and disenfranchised by the sociosymbolic order, revolutionary heroes are willing to reject the forced choice implicit to the symbolic order, even when this rejection entails the loss of something precious, for example, family life – or even life itself: "Such an 'inhuman' position of absolute freedom (in my loneliness, I am free to do whatever I want, nobody has any hold over me) coinciding with an absolute subjection to a Task (the only purpose of my life is to enact vengeance) is what, perhaps, characterizes the revolutionary subject at its innermost" (*Defense*, p. 171).

Žižek states unequivocally that the task today is "to reinvent emancipatory terror" (*Defense*, p. 174). But we must go to the end, and be willing to disturb the very fundamentals of the capitalist economic order (p. 174). Žižek's extraordinarily nuanced, Hegelian-Lacanian version of

[2] Žižek's lecture, "The Liberal Utopia," was delivered in Athens on October 4, 2007. It is available online (in eight video segments) at http://www.youtube.com/watch?v=pMp8P3C_J7I.

dialectical materialism provides grounds for him to criticize the very revolutionaries that he also praises: for example, in *Defense*, Žižek criticizes Marx, Lenin, Mao, etc. In spite of the title's reference to "lost causes," there is nothing naive about Žižek's leftist political stance: for example, he even identifies a moment of emancipatory potential in Heidegger's political thought and in Stalinism, though he is also extremely critical of both Heidegger and Stalin.

The guiding concept that leads the careful reader through the mainstream of Žižek's arguments is the Lacanian ethical *act*. Žižek explains on page 309 of *Defense*: "I am systematically opposing true activity (fidelity to the act proper) and false activity (which merely reproduces the existing constellation – *plus ça change, plus ça reste le même*, we are active all the time to make sure that nothing will change)." The act proper in no way reproduces the existing sociosymbolic order, but rather reconfigures it in unforeseen ways. Such acts are possible at any given moment, because any symbolic order is inherently inconsistent. Simply put, this means that reality itself is incomplete and inconsistent; for example, the symbolic identity of the subject itself is split and inconsistent, and this gap signifies the very freedom of the subject to reinvent herself and her reality. The act of a true revolutionary collective today would break the grip of global capitalist liberalism *by dynamically inventing a new majority*: "An act proper is not just a strategic intervention into a situation, bound by its conditions – it retroactively creates its own conditions" (p. 311).

In contrast with the act proper, the violent outbursts of terrorist fundamentalists shows that *they lack true conviction*: "How fragile the belief of a Muslim must be, if he feels threatened by a stupid caricature in a low-circulation Danish newspaper" (*Defense*, p. 332). But liberals also lack true conviction; liberal "tolerance" and even egalitarianism should never be accepted at face value:

> Far from being opposed to the spirit of sacrifice, Evil is thus the very spirit of sacrifice itself, ready to ignore one's own wellbeing – if, through my sacrifice, I can deprive the Other of his *jouissance* ... And do we not encounter the same negative passion also in politically correct multicultural liberalism? Is its inquisitorial pursuit of the traces of racism and sexism in the details of personal behavior not in itself an indication of the passion of resentment? Fundamentalism's passion is a false one, while anemic liberal tolerance relies on a disavowed perverse passion. The distinction between fundamentalism and liberalism is sustained by a shared underlying feature: they are both permeated by the negative passion of resentment. (*Defense*, p. 333)

What then, is the task for the political left today? Žižek argues that science and technology have now developed to the point of being able create new life and to transform "human nature." This means that our task today involves not abandoning, but *reinventing* new notions of freedom, autonomy, and ethical responsibility (*Defense*, p. 436). To reinvent a true dialectical materialist position for today, the political left must avoid the mystical, fascist tendencies of "faith in Nature" (as in the inherently reactionary academic fashion of deep ecology). Instead, we must begin and end with the recognition that nature itself is a "meaningless chaotic manifold" (p. 444). Thus, according to Žižek's dialectical materialism, we are free, we are not "imprisoned" by determinism. The reason for this is that the subject – along with its striving against "external reality" – *is a part of reality*. This means that the conflict between our free striving and that which resists us "is a conflict inherent to reality itself" (p. 447).

To conclude: in *Defense*, Žižek shows that the limitations of our "common sense" today prevent us from realizing the extent to which "the flow of everyday reality can be upset" (p. 455). The intersubjective, symbolic network of the big Other is inconsistent with itself; it is split and divided to the point that ultimately the big Other does not exist. This means that the intersubjective symbolic network is inadequate; the symbolic order cannot fill up the lack that results from the primordial renunciation of Real enjoyment. This is why, rather than adopting the guise of the nonexistent big Other and offering a detailed plan for revolutionary action, Žižek instead documents the inconsistencies within current thinking about the crises of late capitalism. But, in the absence of a detailed plan, how are we to counter the crises of late capitalism: ecological catastrophe, imbalances within the economic system, biogenetic manipulation of human nature, and new forms of apartheid? Here Žižek again refers to the thought of Alain Badiou, arguing that what is demanded is, firstly "strict egalitarian justice," meaning that everyone pays the same price when it comes to inevitable impositions of worldwide norms limiting consumption. Secondly, we must ruthlessly punish those who violate these norms and limitations. Thirdly, we must engage in "large-scale collective decisions which run counter to the 'spontaneous' immanent logic of capitalist development." And, finally, we must trust in the true majority of the people (e.g. the millions who live in the Third World), as opposed to those elite few (mainly in Western so-called "democracies") who currently benefit from the capitalist order. This trust in the people will involve, for example, lauding as public heroes the insiders and whistleblowers who inform the authorities about violations of public law. In sum, we must reinvent the "eternal Idea" of revolutionary-egalitarian terror (*Defense*, p. 461).

23

Violence

By stepping back to gain critical distance from the horrifying lure of violence, Žižek formulates a crucial distinction between subjective violence and objective violence. *Subjective* violence (crime, terror) is perceived as a disturbance of the "normal" nonviolent state of things. However, *objective* violence (such as the implicit racism and discrimination that is embodied in language and symbolic practices) can be invisible: such objective violence is the relatively hidden counterpart to the highly visible subjective violence. There are two kinds of objective violence: namely, symbolic violence and systemic violence. Symbolic violence is embodied in forms of language, modes of symbolization. Systemic violence follows from the smooth functioning of economic and political systems. Systemic violence is hidden in the sense that critique of political economy is required to reveal the link between this smooth functioning and its (often catastrophic) consequences. For example, it is the absence of political-economic analysis that leads relatively privileged citizens (in countries like the USA) to ask "Why do they hate us?" after some highly visible outburst of violence. Such systemic violence must be taken into consideration in order to explain the apparently inexplicable outbursts of subjective violence. This distinction is the first step in Žižek's spirited exposure of the hypocrisy of those who voice concern about subjective violence while they themselves *contribute* to systemic violence.

Today's predominant mode of politics is post-political bio-politics – *an awesome example of theoretical jargon which, however, can easily be unpacked: "post-political" is a politics which claims to leave behind old*

Žižek: A Reader's Guide, First Edition. Kelsey Wood.
© 2012 John Wiley & Sons, Inc. Published 2012 by John Wiley & Sons, Inc.

> *ideological struggles and instead focus on expert management and administration, while "bio-politics" designates the regulation of the security and welfare of human lives as its primary goal.*
>
> —Žižek, *Violence*, p. 40

In *Violence* (2008),[1] Žižek analyzes three modes of violence that permeate the media: "irrational" youth outbursts, terrorist attacks, and the kind of chaos that allegedly followed in the wake of Hurricane Katrina, and delineates what he calls "the antinomies of tolerant reason."[2] These antinomies indicate the inconsistency of the hegemonic ideology of capitalism, namely liberal-democratic multiculturalism. Analysis of the inconsistencies of today's hegemonic ideology points us toward the Real, and one way in which the Real disrupts symbolic reality is through "divine violence." The notion of divine violence was developed by the German Marxist literary critic Walter Benjamin (1892–1940) in his essay "The Critique of Violence."[3] In this essay, Benjamin distinguished state violence – violence that founds the law and violence that conserves the law – from divine violence, which breaks the circle of state violence.

Against typical leftist commentators, who merely flirt with a "decaffeinated" version of Walter Benjamin, Žižek bluntly clarifies "divine violence" by citing examples (the French revolutionary terror of 1792–1794, the Red terror of 1919). Žižek's analyses reveal the emancipatory potential of such encounters with the Real, and force the

---

[1] Unless otherwise stated, page references for this work are to the following edition: *Violence* (London and New York: Picador, 2008).

[2] Žižek discusses racist fantasies about the aftermath of Hurricane Katrina: "We all remember the reports on the disintegration of public order, the explosion of black violence, rape and looting. However, later inquiries demonstrated that, in the large majority of cases, these alleged orgies of violence *did not occur*: non-verified rumors were simply reported as facts by the media. For example, on September 3, the Superintendent of the New Orleans Police Department told the *New York Times* about conditions at the Convention Center: 'The tourists are walking around there, and as soon as these individuals see them, they're being preyed upon. They are beating, they are raping them in the streets.' In an interview just weeks later, he conceded that some of his most shocking statements turned out to be untrue: 'We have no official reports to document any murder. Not one official report of rape or sexual assault.'" See Slavoj Žižek, "The Subject Supposed to Loot and Rape," *In These Times*, October 20, 2005, available online at http://www.inthese-times.com/article/2361/.

[3] See Walter Benjamin, "Critique of Violence," in *Selected Writings*, vol. 1, 1913–1926 (Cambridge, MA: Harvard University Press, 1996).

reader to confront his own complicity with capitalism's systemic violence. In sum, if we are manipulated by horrifying media images of subjective violence, our responses will take the form of merely localized acts which actually function to *sustain* the systemic violence of capitalism. The horror and fascination of highly visible incidents of violence (e.g. crime, terror, riots, and wars) prevents us from discerning another kind of hidden violence: "a violence that sustains our very efforts to fight violence and to promote tolerance" (*Violence*, p. 1).

Žižek begins his analysis of violence by distinguishing between subjective and objective violence. Subjective violence is the most visible kind of violence; examples include crime and terror. And subjective violence is performed by an easily recognized agent, such as a criminal or a terrorist. But objective violence is more pervasive, even though it is less visible and more subtle. Examples of objective violence include racism, hate-speech, and discrimination. Žižek further distinguishes two types of objective violence, *symbolic* violence and *systemic* violence. Although the primary cause of violence is the fear of the Neighbor, Žižek argues that symbolic violence is inherent to language itself; therefore it permeates our very speech and communicative practice. Symbolic violence includes not only relations of domination that are reproduced in our speech habits, it also involves "a more fundamental form of violence still that pertains to language as such, to its imposition of a certain universe of meaning" (*Violence*, p. 2). Discourse, is, in itself, "authoritarian." Every symbolic order is founded on some "violent" ethico-political decision. This is why, in Lacan's matrix of the four discourses, the discourse of the Master is the founding discourse.[4] Moreover, the word is the murder of the thing, in that the very symbolic representation of a thing mortifies it, as Hegel already recognized. Humans are capable of more violence than animals because we speak (p. 61). Thus it is language that constitutes human desire as inherently transgressive (p. 65). When we witness a scene of a raging crowd burning and lynching, it is the words on the signs they carry that sustain the violence (p. 67). Language is both that which forever separates me from the "abyss of the Neighbour" and "simultaneously that which opens up and sustains this abyss" (p. 73). Moreover, because symbolic violence is intrinsic to language, it is implicit to the very medium through which we try to overcome direct violence (p. 206).

---

[4] Slavoj Žižek, *Enjoy Your Symptom! Jacques Lacan in Hollywood and Out*, rev. edn. (New York and London: Routledge, 2001), p. 102.

The second kind of objective violence – systemic violence – involves "the often catastrophic consequences of the smooth functioning of our economic and political systems" (*Violence*, p. 2). The systemic violence of capitalism is the focus of this book. Subjective violence (crime, terror) is experienced as a disturbance of the normal, nonviolent state of things. However, Žižek argues that objective violence (symbolic and systemic) is the invisible violence that is inherent to the allegedly nonviolent, "normal" state of things (p. 2). This indicates the main thrust of Žižek's argument in *Violence*. Žižek argues that systemic violence – violence linked to our capitalist political-economic system – must be considered if we are to make sense of the otherwise inexplicable eruptions of subjective violence (p. 2). This is why he decisively rejects the hypocritical anti-violence of those who combat subjective violence even while they themselves engage in practices which sustain the systemic violence of capitalism: "In a superego blackmail of gigantic proportions, the developed countries 'help' the undeveloped with aid, credits, and so on, and thereby avoid the key issue, namely their complicity in and co-responsibility for the miserable situation of the undeveloped" (p. 22). Such symbolic inconsistencies are symptomatic of ideological mystification. That the ideology of liberal-democratic multiculturalism is irreducibly inconsistent indicates the workings of the repressed Real of capital:

> it is the self-propelling metaphysical dance of capital that runs the show, that provides the key to real-life developments and catastrophes. Therein resides the fundamental violence of capitalism, much more uncanny than any direct pre-capitalist socio-ideological violence: this violence is no longer attributable to concrete individuals and their "evil" intentions, but is purely "objective," systemic, anonymous. Here we encounter the Lacanian difference between reality and the Real: "reality" is the social reality of the actual people involved in interaction and in the productive processes, while the Real is the inexorable "abstract," spectral logic of capital that determines what goes on in social reality. (*Violence*, pp. 12–13)

Unlike the crimes of communists such as Stalin (which are clearly attributable to individuals who did wrong), typical academics today are blind to the millions who have died because of capitalist globalization, from Mexico in the 1500s to the Belgian Congo in the 1800s (*Violence*, p. 14). Though Žižek does not single them out, it is significant that highly paid, tenured professors of Political Science in the USA are some of the most ideologically mystified. We in the West *benefit* from the suffering of millions in the Third World, so it is no wonder that we remain unaware of the systemic violence of capitalism. But capitalism can adapt itself to any civilization from West to East. Capitalism "detotalises meaning: it is not global at the level of meaning" (p. 79). Capitalism's global dimension involves "truth-without-meaning, as the 'Real' of the global market mechanism" (p. 80). Žižek links the Real of capital to the violence which erupted in New Orleans after Hurricane Katrina:

> More fundamentally, what if the tension that led to the explosion in New Orleans was not the tension between "human nature" and the force of civilisation that keeps it in check, but the tension between the two aspects of our civilisation itself? What if, in endeavoring to control explosions like the one in New Orleans, the forces of law and order were confronted with the very nature of capitalism at its purest, the logic of individual competition, of ruthless self-assertion, generated by capitalist dynamics, a "nature" much more threatening and violent than all the hurricanes and earthquakes?[5]

This indicates that the fundamental gap in our capitalist symbolic system "is one between those included in the sphere of (relative) economic prosperity and those excluded from it" (p. 102). The only true solution to the systemic violence of capitalism is to tear down this socio-economic barrier (p. 104).

Regarding violence (allegedly) carried out in the name of religion, Žižek suggests that we should not renounce violence as such (*Violence*, p. 134). Rather, we should renounce any religion (or any ideology like Stalinism) that promotes the idea that the big Other actually exists:

> When confronted with an event like the Holocaust or the death of millions in the Congo over these last years, is it not obscene to claim that these stains have a deeper meaning through which they contribute to the harmony of the whole? Is there a whole which can teleologically justify and thus redeem or sublate an event such as the Holocaust? Christ's death on the cross surely means one should unreservedly drop the notion of God as a transcendent caretaker who guarantees the happy outcome of our acts, i.e., who enforces historical teleology. Christ's death on the cross is in itself the death of this *protecting* God.[6]

---

[5] See Slavoj Žižek, "Some Politically Incorrect Reflections on Violence in France and Related Matters," available online at http://www.lacan.com/zizfrance2.htm. Also see Slavoj Žižek, *Violence* (New York: Picador, 2008), pp. 95–6.

[6] See Slavoj Žižek, "Censorship Today: Violence, or Ecology as a New Opium for the Masses," available online at http://www.lacan.com/zizecology2.htm. Also see Slavoj Žižek, *Violence* (New York: Picador, 2008), pp. 180–81.

Thus we should resolutely refuse to "normalise" crimes like the Holocaust (p. 189). This indicates the atheistic moment of Žižek's Christian-materialism. Succinctly put, Žižek argues that only an atheist – anyone who recognizes the *nonexistence* of the big Other – can truly believe. And the uniqueness of the modern European legacy is that "atheism is a fully legitimate option" (p. 139).

One of the ways we can discern the inconsistency of liberal-democratic multiculturalism is by considering the way liberals misperceive actual political struggles as nothing more than religious and/or ethnic conflicts. Along the same lines, liberalism's emphasis on freedom of choice is *biased* towards modern Western culture, the liberal idea of free choice always leads to a conceptual impasse: "It is intolerant when individuals of other cultures are not given freedom of choice [...]. However, it ignores the tremendous pressure which, for example, compels women in our liberal society to undergo such procedures as plastic surgery, cosmetic implants, and Botox injections in order to remain competitive in the sex market" (*Violence*, pp. 144–5).

Liberal multiculturalist "tolerance" is hypocritical: liberalism is not tolerant of the Neighbor in her abyssal Otherness. Liberal-democratic multiculturalism can only tolerate a bland and homogenized Other, one who does not intrude too much on our Western sensibilities (e.g. she must bathe frequently and use deodorant). Before the subject is to be allowed our so-called "freedom of choice," we first violently tear her out of her life world, and cut her off from her roots (*Violence*, p. 146). In order to enjoy the benefits of our "freedom of choice" and our "tolerance," the Other must not, for example, choose to wear the burqa, or do any of the other things that we do not tolerate. This violent tearing away from the life world indicates the abstraction implicit to the liberal-democratic notion of human rights. In our Western societies, where commodity exchange predominates, before we can experience ourselves as subjects of human rights, we must first be reduced to "contingent embodiments of abstract-universal notions" (p. 149).

But to the extent that capitalism is multicultural; it is capable of adapting itself to the mores of all civilizations in order to maximize profits wherever it can. Where then, is the possibility for change?

> The formula of revolutionary solidarity is not "let us tolerate our differences," it is not a pact of civilizations, but a pact of struggles which cut across civilizations, a pact between what, in each civilization, undermines its identity from within, fights against its oppressive kernel. What unites us is the same struggle. A better formula would thus be: in spite of our differences, we can

identify the basic antagonism or antagonistic struggle, in which we are both caught; so let us share our intolerance, and join forces in the same struggle. In other words, in the emancipatory struggle, it is not the cultures in their identity which join hands, it is the repressed, the exploited and suffering, the "parts of no-part" of every culture which come together in a shared struggle. Such universality remains "concrete" in the precise sense that, once formulated, its persistence is not guaranteed: every historical epoch has to find its own specific way to accomplish the breakthrough to universality [...]. This universality which emerges/explodes out of a violent breakthrough is not the awareness of the universal as the neutral frame which unites us all ("in spite of our differences, we are basically all human ..."); it is the universality which becomes for-itself in the violent experience of the subject who becomes aware that he is not fully himself (coinciding with his particular form of existence), that he is marked by a profound split.[7]

Žižek insists that such a miracle of ethical universality (the revolutionary struggle of the exploited ones) cannot be reduced to any "distorted effect of 'lower' libidinal processes" (*Violence*, p. 194). On the contrary, the ethico-political act – as our refusal to compromise our desire – cannot be grounded in any personal interest or motivation (p. 195).

Žižek cites Walter Benjamin's "Critique of Violence" in order to clarify the distinction between *mythic* violence and *divine* violence (*Violence*, pp. 197–8). The following is an excerpt from the long passage quoted by Žižek:

> If mythic violence is law-making, divine violence is law-destroying; if the former sets boundaries, the latter boundlessly destroys them; if mythic violence brings at once guilt and retribution, divine power only expiates; if the former threatens, the latter strikes; if the former is bloody, the latter is lethal without spilling blood. [...] For blood is the symbol of mere life. The dissolution of legal violence stems [...] from the guilt of mere natural life, which consigns the living, innocent, and unhappy, to a retribution that "expiates" the guilt of mere life – and doubtless also purifies the guilty, not of guilt, however, but of law. For with mere life, the rule of law over the living ceases. Mythical violence is bloody power over mere life for its own sake, divine violence is pure power over all life for the sake of the living.[8]

---

[7]   See Slavoj Žižek, "Tolerance as an Ideological Category," in *Critical Inquiry*, Autumn 2007, available online at http://www.lacan.com/zizek-inquiry.html.

[8]   Cf. Walter Benjamin, "Critique of Violence," in *Selected Writings*, vol. 1, 1913–1926 (Cambridge, MA: Harvard University Press, 1996), pp. 249–51. Žižek quotes this passage in *Violence* (New York: Picador, 2008), on p. 197.

Mythic violence demands sacrifice, and mythic violence is "a means to establish the rule of Law" (*Violence*, p. 199). But precisely how does Žižek interpret Benjamin's understanding of "divine violence"? In the first place, divine violence "has nothing to do with the terrorist violence executed by today's religious fundamentalists who pretend they are acting on behalf of God" (p. 185). Moreover, divine violence is *not* "a means of the state power" (p. 199). In fact, if state terror is employed to preempt the direct, "divine" violence of the people themselves, then this is *perverse*, as in the claim: "we are doing it as mere instruments of the People's Will" (p. 202). And unlike *mythic* violence, which establishes law and social order, divine violence "serves no means" (p. 199).

Žižek is unequivocally clear on the point that there is no all-knowing, all-powerful big Other who guarantees the meaning of divine violence (*Violence*, p. 199). On the contrary, divine violence signifies the big Other's (God's) impotence (p. 201). Divine violence "is the heroic assumption of the solitude of sovereign decision. It is a decision (to kill, to risk or lose one's own life) made in absolute solitude, with no cover in the big Other. Žižek asserts that divine violence is the radically subjective, "*work of love*" and refers to Che Guevara to clarify this claim (p. 203). Che Guevara argued that the true revolutionary is guided both by love and by relentless hatred (p. 203). The true revolutionary is tough and hardened, but also tender (p. 204). Žižek acknowledges that this implies an underlying paradox:

> love without cruelty is powerless; cruelty without love is blind, a short-lived passion which loses its persistent edge. The underlying paradox is that what makes love angelic, what elevates it over mere unstable and pathetic sentimentality, is its cruelty itself – it is this link which raises it "over and beyond the natural limitations of man" and thus transforms it into an unconditional drive. (*Violence*, p. 204)

It is significant that Žižek ends this final chapter of *Violence* with reference to his Christian-materialism. What does it mean to "love with hatred"? Žižek refers here to the Christian philosopher Kierkegaard, and to Kierkegaard's reading of the ethical injunction to *love one's enemy* as a kind of madness which fulfills the law, so that "the Christian shall, if it be demanded, be capable of hating his father and mother and sister and beloved" (*Violence*, p. 204). Žižek closes the chapter with a reference to St Paul: "The notion of love here should be given all its Paulinian weight: *the domain of pure violence*, the domain outside law (legal power), the domain of the violence which is neither law-founding nor law-sustaining, *is the domain of love*" (p. 205).

In his epilogue, Žižek condenses the lesson of *Violence* into three main points. First, Žižek argues that those who condemn *all* violence have been ideologically mystified: "to chastise violence outright, to condemn it as 'bad,' is an ideological mystification which collaborates in rendering invisible the fundamental forms of social violence" (*Violence*, p. 206). The second lesson is that, while it may sometimes be easy to lose control, it is not easy to engage in any form of violence which effectively disturbs the parameters of the sociosymbolic system: "an authentic political gesture is *active*, it imposes, enforces a vision, while outbursts of impotent violence are fundamentally *reactive*, a reaction to some disturbing intruder" (pp. 212–13). The third and final lesson involves the relation between subjective violence and systemic violence. Žižek argues that violence is not simply a property of particular actions, "but is distributed between acts and their contexts, between activity and inactivity" (p. 213). Thus, true leftists today should resist the fake urgency to just do *something*, and, instead, be willing to engage in thorough critical analyses (p. 7). And we should avoid any actions that sustain the systemic violence of global capitalism (p. 216). This is why even refusing to vote can be a true political act, insofar as "it forcefully confronts us with the vacuity of today's democracies" (p. 217). In certain situations, the most violent thing one can do is to do nothing (p. 217).

However, it must be added that Žižek also argues that in other circumstances, revolutionary violence is fully justified:

Advising the CIA on how to undermine the democratically elected Chilean government of Salvador Allende, Henry Kissinger put it succinctly: "Make the economy scream." Senior US representatives openly admit that today the same strategy is being pursued in Venezuela. As former US Secretary of State Lawrence Eagleburger said on Fox News:

[Chávez's appeal] only works so long as the population of Venezuela sees some ability for a better standard of living. If at some point the economy really gets bad, Chávez's popularity within the country will certainly decrease and it's the one weapon we have against him to begin with and which we should be using, namely the economic tools of trying to make the economy even worse so that his appeal in the country and the region goes down [...] Anything we can do to make their economy more difficult for them at this moment is a good thing, but let's do it in ways that do not get us into direct conflict with Venezuela if we can get away with it.

The least one can say is that such statements give credibility to the suspicion that the economic difficulties faced by the Chávez government are not simply the result of its own inept policy making.[9]

Žižek argues that when the intelligence agencies of a powerful state (in collaboration with this state's wealthy elite) engage in a calculated strategy to undermine the economy of a small nation – in order to depose its leftist leader – the exercise of revolutionary violence is justified as a defensive counter-measure.

[9] See Slavoj Žižek, "The Jacobin Spirit." At the time of this writing, this new afterward to *Living in the End Times* is only available online in *Jacobin* at http://jacobinmag.com/archive/issue3/zizek.html.

24

First as Tragedy, then as Farce

Žižek's *First as Tragedy, then as Farce* is a masterpiece as an intervention. The tragedy referred to in the title is September 11, 2001; the farce is the financial meltdown of 2008. If it is inevitable that with the passage of time, scholars will become less aware of its "timeliness," nonetheless, the theoretical power of Žižek's dialectical materialism (the philosophy that underlies this acute critique of liberal-democratic ideology) will not be easily ignored. But although Žižek's dialectical materialist fusion of Hegel and Lacan is implicit to the argumentation of this book, the theoretical underpinnings are not emphasized to the point that the general reader will miss the aim of the analyses. Even those readers who are intimidated by some of Žižek's more theoretical works should find this text both accessible and convincing in its analysis of the antagonisms that reveal the limits of global capitalism.

The title of this book is intended as an elementary IQ test for the reader: if the first association it generates is the vulgar anti-communist cliché – "You are right, after the tragedy of twentieth-century totalitarianism, all the talk about a return to communism can only be farcical!" – then I sincerely advise you to stop here. Indeed, the book should be forcibly confiscated from you, since it deals with an entirely different tragedy and farce, namely, the two events which mark the beginning and the end of the first decade of the twenty-first century: the attacks of September 11, 2001 and the financial meltdown of 2008.
—Žižek, *First as Tragedy, then as Farce*, p. 1

Žižek: A Reader's Guide, First Edition. Kelsey Wood.
© 2012 John Wiley & Sons, Inc. Published 2012 by John Wiley & Sons, Inc.

As the above quotation indicates, in *First as Tragedy, then as Farce* (2009),[1] Žižek pulls no punches; he strikes with full force. The book is small in size, but large in scope, and so powerful that its arguments at times seem to crackle with energy. On the first page of his introduction, Žižek refers to the beginning of Marx's *Eighteenth Brumaire*, where Marx famously claims that "Hegel remarks somewhere that all great events and characters of world history occur, so to speak, twice. He forgot to add: the first time as tragedy, the second time as farce."[2] Žižek then argues that the ideological fantasy of a liberal-democratic, global capitalist utopia died its first (tragic) death on September 11, 2001; then it died its second (farcical) death with the financial meltdown of 2008. Today, the liberal-democratic, capitalist ideological fantasy is dead, it just doesn't know that it is dead yet. But if liberal democracy is dead, what can possibly replace it? Are we headed toward something like China's authoritarian, state-run capitalism? Or is it possible today to reinvent the idea of communism?

The tragedy of September 11, 2001, began an era in which new borders and walls are arising around the world: not only between nations (around the European Union, between Israel and the West Bank, the USA and Mexico), but significantly, within nations – *between the rich and the poor* – even in China. Gated communities and the members-only phenomenon are evidence that the rich live in fear, the fear of disease, crime, and other "dangers of mingling with ordinary people" (*Tragedy*, pp. 3–5). The introduction also includes this synopsis, in which Žižek lays his cards on the table. It is not any form of socialism, but communism which must supplant liberal democracy: "The first chapter offers a diagnosis of our predicament, outlining the utopian core of the capitalist ideology which determined both the crisis itself and our perceptions of and reactions to it. The second chapter endeavors to locate aspects of our situation which open up the space for new forms of communist praxis" (p. 5).

In asserting his allegiance to the idea of communism, Žižek refers to his dialectical materialist concept of truth as struggle: "What the book offers is not a neutral analysis but an engaged and extremely 'partial'

---

[1] Unless otherwise stated, page references for this work (abbreviated *Tragedy* below) are to the following edition: *First as Tragedy, then as Farce* (London and New York: Verso, 2009).

[2] Karl Marx, "The Eighteenth Brumaire of Louis Bonaparte," in *Surveys from Exile*, edited and introduced by David Fernbach (Harmondsworth: Penguin, 1973), p. 146.

one – *for truth is partial*, accessible only when one takes sides, and is no less universal for this reason. The side taken here is, of course, that of communism" (*Tragedy*, p. 6). Throughout his works, Žižek argues that the Hegelian concept of concrete universality is not the reduction of the universal to the particular. Rather, concrete universality involves the "surplus" of the universal. No single universal can totalize the entire field of the particular, because each particular *is itself* a "perspective" on the entire field. This is why he claims that concrete universality implies that what is eternal in the communist idea is not some particular content or set of features that are present in every historical instance of communism. On the contrary, the communist idea is eternal in the sense that "it has to be re-invented in each new historical situation" (p. 6). Our task as leftists is not merely to reveal the corruption of those in power; the real point is to render them impotent (p. 7). The time has come again for fully engaging in communism, and for acting in fidelity to the communist idea (p. 7). The days of anemic liberal compromise and moralizing are over. The left no longer needs to apologize, while "the other side had better start soon" (p. 8).

Žižek's chapter 1 is called "It's Ideology, Stupid!" He begins by pointing out that the 2008 financial meltdown was known to be imminent for years. In spite of the widely believed falsehood that markets were taken by surprise, Žižek reminds us that at meetings of the International Monetary Fund and the World Bank, protesters regularly warned that: "the banks were creating the illusion of growth by playing with fictional money, and how this would all have to end in a crash" (*Tragedy*, p. 9). Economists like Joseph Stiglitz and Paul Krugman also warned that promises of continuous growth belied the facts of what was going on (p. 9). Demonstrators in Washington in 2004 who were concerned about the imminent crash were tear-gassed, clubbed, and arrested:

> so many people demonstrated about the danger of a financial collapse that the police had to mobilise 8,000 additional local policemen and bring in a further 6,000 from Maryland and Virginia. What ensued was tear-gassing, clubbing and mass arrests – so many that police had to use buses for transport. The message was loud and clear, and the police were used literally to stifle the truth. (*Tragedy*, p. 9)

In a sense, this kind of abuse of power *is the message*. What are the authorities in the USA so afraid of? The smooth functioning of the economy relies on consumer confidence. Markets are based on beliefs, and even on beliefs about what other people believe (*Tragedy*, pp. 9–10). This is why the bail-out may help even though it is not only ruthless blackmail, but even economically misguided. At any rate, it is usually easier to just do something, anything, rather than to carefully analyze a problem: "Such as throwing $700 billion at a problem instead of reflecting on how it arose in the first place" (p. 11). So Wall Street's pain was foisted onto the taxpayers (p. 12). This shows that our capitalist society *is* one of choice and risk: the wealthy elite do the choosing, while the workers take the risks (p. 13). Was the bail-out a "socialist" measure? What kind of socialism is it "whose primary aim is not to help the poor, but the rich, not those who borrow, but those who lend" (p. 13)? Note the contradiction here: on the one hand, we are told constantly in the USA that socialism is a very bad thing; on the other hand, "socializing" the banking system is acceptable because it helps to sustain capitalism. Žižek notes the homology here between the USA and today's China: "in the same way, the Chinese Communists use capitalism to enforce their 'Socialist' regime" (p. 13). Again, note the contradiction: countless workers in China earn pennies a day for sweatshop labor, while others are paid far more even though their work is much easier. Is this "Socialism"?

During a lecture in Athens in 2007, Žižek recounted his questioning of a Chinese Communist Party official about a project to reinvigorate Chinese "Socialism." Upon learning that the goal of this project was *social cohesion*, Žižek replied: "In the West, we just call that fascism."[3] The Chinese regime today is nothing like Žižek's (and Badiou's) idea of communism. China provides much of the sweatshop labor that helps to sustain global capitalism. Around the world (even in China), the rich seem to be getting richer while the poor are getting poorer. And around the world – as a vulgar joke puts it – ideology turns ordinary working citizens into "mushrooms," kept in the dark and fed shit.

Does all of this imply that we should accept the populist refrain, and "Save Main Street, not Wall Street"? Žižek argues that this would be a disaster: "what keeps Main Street going under capitalism *is* Wall Street! Tear *that* wall down and Main Street will be flooded with panic and inflation" (*Tragedy*, p. 14). As long as we remain capitalist, then "kicking at Wall Street really *will* hit ordinary workers" (p. 15). Against the populist claim that state intervention harms working people, Žižek asserts on

---

[3] Žižek's lecture, "The Liberal Utopia," was delivered in Athens on October 4, 2007. It is available online (in eight video segments) at http://www.youtube.com/watch?v=pMp8P3C_J7I.

page 16 that "The true dilemma is thus not 'Should the state intervene?' but 'What kind of intervention is necessary?" And this is a properly *political* issue; in other words, there is no neutral, "objective" answer to be had from any so-called expert. Now, more than ever, Žižek urges us to stop and think for ourselves, in a radically new way. For example, although many of us are angered by events such as the bail-out plan,

> we should bear in mind that since this is actually a form of blackmail we must resist the populist temptation to act out our anger and thus wound ourselves. Instead of such impotent acting-out, we should control our fury and transform it into an icy determination to think – to think things through in a really radical way, and to ask what kind of a society it is that renders such blackmail possible. (*Tragedy*, p. 17)

The question as to the function of the state is a question regarding which "one just has to take one side or the other, politically" (*Tragedy*, p. 16). And the choice is between capitalism and communism. The most likely result of the economic crisis will not be the rise of a radical-emancipatory movement, but, on the contrary: "the rise of racist populism, further wars, increased poverty in the poorest Third World countries, and greater divisions between the rich and the poor within all societies" (p. 17). Financial speculators have no rational reason to change their practices, now that they have proof positive that the state will intervene in such a way that ordinary working people will suffer the consequences of irresponsible behavior: "It is not the creative geniuses who are now helping out lazy ordinary people, it is rather the ordinary taxpayers who are helping out the failed 'creative geniuses'" (p. 31). Žižek argues that state regulation is necessary: "the populist conservatives are literally *voting themselves into economic ruin*. Less taxation and deregulation means more freedom for the big companies who are driving impoverished farmers out of business; less state intervention means less federal help for small businessmen and entrepreneurs" (p. 33).

But even with state intervention, as long as we live under capitalism, Žižek argues that the Real of Capital controls us, we do not control it. Žižek refers to the Real dimension of Capital in several works, including this one. Simply put, the Real of Capital is the drive to continuously expand its sphere of circulation.[4] This is why Žižek argues that Bernard

---

[4] There is a homology here between Žižek's analysis of the functioning of Capital and Heidegger's account of technology as a mode of Being. Cf. Martin Heidegger, *The Question Concerning Technology* (New York: Harper and Row, 1982). But it is absolutely crucial to realize the extent to which Žižek *distances* himself from Heidegger. Succinctly put, Žižek's

Madoff's Ponzi scheme, or "pyramid" scheme, is a pure example of what causes the inevitable crises of capitalism:

> the temptation to "morph" legitimate business into a pyramid scheme is part of the very nature of the capitalist circulation process. [...] the very dynamic of capitalism blurs the frontier between "legitimate" investment and "wild" speculation, because capitalist investment is, at its very core, a risky wager that a scheme will turn out to be profitable, an act of borrowing from the future. (*Tragedy*, p. 36)

As long as we live in a capitalist sociosymbolic order, the Real dimension of Capital (its self-propelling drive towards ever-expanding circulation) will be constitutive of our symbolic reality and even *our very identity*. Symbolic reality/identity is inconsistent, and this inconsistency arises from the Real. In the global capitalist symbolic order, ideological fantasy masks the symbolic inconsistency produced by the Real of Capital. This is why, even if we know that late capitalism is headed toward inevitable collapse, we behave as though we do not know this. As Žižek puts it,

> It is one big fetishistic denial: "I know very well the risks I am courting, even the inevitability of final collapse, but nonetheless … [I can put off the collapse a little bit longer, take on a little bit more risk, and so on indefinitely]." It is a self-blinding "irrationality" strictly correlative to the "irrationality" of the lower classes voting against their own interests, and yet another proof of the material power of ideology. (*Tragedy*, p. 37)

Where then, is the possibility for change? Žižek argues that the possibility for change lies in the inherent antagonisms of global capitalism. The inconsistency of a symbolic order marks the Lacanian Real, the void that ruptures reality and a subject's symbolic identity. The Real permeates – and is constitutive of – symbolic order. Symbolic order is *reaction* against the trauma or antagonism of the Real. But as an attempt to resolve the irresolvable, symbolic order is inherently antagonistic *toward itself*. In several of his more recent works, Žižek has emphasized that there are four antagonisms which point toward the (Real) limits of the global capitalist symbolic order. In the following passage, he discusses these irresolvable, Real antagonisms, and indicates how a

---

anti-essentialist reading of Hegel, and his emphasis on the Lacanian Real, enables him to avoid Heidegger's "closed" notion of the event of appropriation.

properly communist perspective reveals the kind of response that these antagonisms call for:

> There are (at least) four such antagonisms: the looming threat of *ecological* catastrophe; the inappropriateness of *private property* rights for so-called "intellectual property"; the socio-ethical implications of *new techno-scientific developments* (especially in biogenetics); and, last but not least, *new forms of apartheid*, in the form of new walls and slums.
>
> The first three antagonisms concern the domains of what political theorists Michael Hardt and Toni Negri call "commons" – the shared substance of our social being whose privatization is a violent act that should be resisted with violent means, if necessary (violence against private property, that is).
>
> *The commons of external nature* are threatened by pollution and exploitation (from oil to forests and natural habitat itself); *the commons of internal nature* (the biogenetic inheritance of humanity) are threatened by technological interference; and *the commons of culture* – the socialized forms of "cognitive" capital, primarily language, our means of communication and education, but also the shared infrastructure of public transport, electricity, post, etc. – are privatized for profit. (If Bill Gates were to be allowed a monopoly, we would have reached the absurd situation in which a private individual would have owned the software texture of our basic network of communication.)
>
> We are gradually becoming aware of the destructive potential, up to the self-annihilation of humanity itself, that could be unleashed if the capitalist logic of enclosing these commons is allowed a free run.
>
> Economist Nicholas Stern rightly characterized the climate crisis as "the greatest market failure in human history."
>
> There is an increasing awareness that we need global environmental citizenship, a political space to address climate change as a matter of common concern of all humanity.
>
> One should give weight to the terms "global citizenship" and "common concern." Doesn't this desire to establish a global political organization and engagement that will neutralize and channel market forces mean that we are in need of a properly communist perspective? The need to protect the "commons" justifies the resuscitation of the notion of Communism: It enables us to see the ongoing "enclosure" of our commons as a process of proletarization of those who are thereby excluded from their own substance.[5]

---

[5] Slavoj Žižek, "The Ambiguous Legacy of '68," *In These Times*, June 20, 2008. The essay is available online at http://www.inthesetimes.com/article/3751/the_ambiguous_legacy_of_68/. Also in *First as Tragedy, then as Farce* (London and New York: Verso, 2009), pp. 90–91.

Along these lines, in *First as Tragedy, then as Farce* Žižek directs his fire primarily against liberal, pseudo-leftist compromises with global capitalism. He aligns himself with the French communist philosopher Alain Badiou against liberal academics (e.g. followers of Foucault). In one passage Žižek both clarifies a difficult point from Badiou's thought, and exposes a crucial limitation of the Foucauldian approach:

> in the Foucauldian notion of productive power, a power which works not in an exclusionary way, but in an enabling/regulatory way, there is no room for Badiou's notion of the point of inconsistency (or the "symptomal torsion") of a situation, that element of a situation for which there is no proper place (with)in the situation – not for accidental reasons but because its dislocation/exclusion is constitutive of the situation itself. Take the case of the proletariat: of course, the working class is "visible" in multiple ways within the capitalist world (as those who freely sell their labor-power on the market; as a potential rabble; as faithful and disciplined servants of capitalist managers, etc.). However, none of these modes of visibility covers up the symptomal role of the proletariat as the "part of no-part" of the capitalist universe. Badiou's "invisibility" is thus the obverse of visibility within the hegemonic ideological space, it is what has to remain invisible so that the visible may be visible. Or, to put it in another, more traditional way: what the Foucauldian approach cannot grasp is the notion of a two-faced symptomal element, whose one face is a marginal accident of a situation, and whose other face is (to stand for) the truth of this same situation. In the same way, the "excluded" are, of course, visible, in the precise sense that, paradoxically, *their exclusion itself is the mode of their inclusion*: their "proper place" in the social body is that of exclusion (from the public sphere).[6]

And, as already indicated, Žižek and Badiou have an understanding of universality derived from Hegel and Lacan. For Badiou and Žižek, there is no single, all-encompassing universality. On the contrary, the universal truth is *partial*; in other words, the universal is "concrete" in the sense that each particular has its own perspective on the universal. In this sense, Žižek's dialectical materialism may be thought of as a kind of "universal perspectivism." Thus, although there can be no neutral and "objective" universality, nonetheless in any symbolic order there is an element

---

[6] Slavoj Žižek, *First as Tragedy, then as Farce*, online at http://www.scribd.com/doc/21688744/Slavoj-Zizek-First-as-Tragedy-Then-as-Farce. Also in Slavoj Žižek, *First as Tragedy, then as Farce* (London and New York: Verso, 2009), pp. 101–2.

or part that has no proper place; any symbolic system is incomplete, and what renders it incomplete is a "nothing" that has no proper place in the system. Any social hierarchy excludes someone, and if the mode of exclusion is symptomatic of the way the sociosymbolic order functions, then – in a kind of short-circuit – these excluded ones occupy the position of *singular universality*, the direct embodiment of the truth of the entire social field. In several works, Žižek argues that in Hitler's Germany it was primarily the Jews who had access to the "truth" of Nazi ideology, precisely because *they were the living embodiments* of the symbolic order's mode of exclusion. In *First as Tragedy, then as Farce*, Žižek develops this analysis in terms of the fetish and the symptom:

> How is this appearance of ideology as its own opposite, as non-ideology, possible? It hinges on a shift in the predominant mode of ideology: in our allegedly "post-ideological" era, ideology functions more and more in a *fetishistic* mode as opposed to its traditional *symptomal* mode. In the latter mode, the ideological lie which structures our perception of reality is threatened by symptoms *qua* "returns of the repressed" – cracks in the fabric of the ideological lie – while the fetish is effectively a kind of *envers* of the symptom. That is to say, the symptom is the exception which disturbs the surface of the false appearance, the point at which the repressed Other Scene erupts, while the fetish is the embodiment of the Lie which enables us to sustain the unbearable truth.[7]

In the ideology of liberal democracy, limitations on freedom and equality function as *symptoms* (the repressed Real that always returns). In anti-Semitic fascism, however, the "Jew" functions as a fetish that allows anti-Semitic fascism to disavow the Real of class struggle (*Tragedy*, p. 67). This racist fantasy is implicated in the systematic exclusion of the Jew from the fascist symbolic order.

No doubt advocates of liberal democracy realize that the global capitalist order excludes millions of slum dwellers in the Third World. What Žižek shows is that the "proletarian" position today is the position of universality embodied by these excluded ones. Moreover, Žižek argues that with the rise of new forms of apartheid – new walls and borders between the rich and the rest of us – we are all of us, more and more, being "proletarianized." And the answer to this most fundamental

[7] Slavoj Žižek, *First as Tragedy, then as Farce*, online at http://www.scribd.com/doc/21688744/Slavoj-Zizek-First-as-Tragedy-Then-as-Farce. Also in Slavoj Žižek, *First as Tragedy, then as Farce* (London and New York: Verso, 2009), p. 65.

limit of capitalism is not liberal compromise, but the dictatorship of the proletariat:

> Liberals who acknowledge the problems of those excluded from the socio-political process formulate their goal as being the inclusion of those whose voices are not heard: all positions should be listened to, all interests taken into account, the human rights of everyone guaranteed, all ways of life, cultures and practises [sic] respected, and so on. The obsession of this democratic discourse is the protection of all kinds of minorities: cultural, religious, sexual, *e tutti quanti*. The formula of democracy is patient negotiation and compromise. What gets lost here is the proletarian position, the position of universality embodied in the Excluded. This is why, upon a closer look, it becomes clear that what Hugo Chavez has begun doing in Venezuela differs markedly from the standard liberal form of inclusion: Chavez is not including the excluded in a pre-existing liberal-democratic framework; he is, on the contrary, taking the "excluded" dwellers of favelas as his *base* and then reorganizing political space and political forms of organization so that the latter will "fit" the excluded. Pedantic and abstract as it may appear, this difference – between "bourgeois democracy" and "dictatorship of the proletariat" – is crucial.[8]

And finally, Žižek argues that it is not liberal democracy, right-wing populism, or socialism – but *only communism* which acknowledges the paradox of singular universality – communism acknowledges the paradox "of a singular subject who, in a kind of short-circuit, bypassing the mediation of the particular, directly participates in the Universal" (*Tragedy*, p. 104). What does this mean? Žižek articulates the paradox of singular universality with reference to Kant's concept of the public use of reason, and compares the profound implications of this concept to the vacuity of the liberal preoccupation with identity politics:

> The paradox of Kant's formula "Think freely, but obey!" [...] is thus that one participates in the universal dimension of the "public" sphere precisely as a singular individual extracted from, or even opposed to, one's substantial communal identification – one is truly universal only when radically singular, in the interstices of communal identities. It is Kant who should be read here as the critic of Rorty. In his vision of public space characterized by the unconstrained exercise of Reason, he invokes a dimension of emancipatory universality *outside* the confines of one's social identity, of

---

[8] Slavoj Žižek, *First as Tragedy, then as Farce*, online at http://www.scribd.com/doc/21688744/Slavoj-Zizek-First-as-Tragedy-Then-as-Farce. Also in Slavoj Žižek, *First as Tragedy, then as Farce* (London and New York: Verso, 2009), p. 102.

one's position within the order of (social) being – precisely the dimension so crucially missing in Rorty.

This space of singular universality is what, within Christianity, appears as the "Holy Spirit" – the space of a collective of believers *subtracted* from the field of organic communities, or of particular life-worlds ("neither Greeks nor Jews"). [...] The Paulinian collective of believers is a proto-model of the Kantian "world-civil-society," and the domain of the state itself is thus in its own way "private": private in the precise Kantian sense of the "private use of Reason" in the State administrative and ideological apparatuses.[9]

Žižek argues elsewhere that democratic procedures can play a positive role in communism. But the problem today is that in our so-called "democracy," solutions are sought through mechanisms that are themselves part of the state apparatuses that sustain the undisturbed reproduction of capital. The inherent susceptibility of democracy to corruption has now led to a situation which prevents any transformation of capitalist relations. This is the "private use of Reason" in our state administrative and ideological apparatuses. What gets lost here is the proletarian position, the position of universality embodied in the outcasts, those excluded by global capitalism. To put it in the simplest possible terms, when the rights of corporations as legal "persons" outweigh the rights of actual human beings, then the only alternative for the left (as a revolutionary collective) is to make changes *outside the sphere of legal rights.*

Thus what Žižek calls the paradox of singular universality is the link between his dialectical materialist ontology and his controversial rehabilitation of the concept of the dictatorship of the proletariat.

[9] Slavoj Žižek, *First as Tragedy, then as Farce,* available online at http://www.scribd.com/doc/21688744/Slavoj-Zizek-First-as-Tragedy-Then-as-Farce. Also in Slavoj Žižek, *First as Tragedy, then as Farce* (London and New York: Verso, 2009), pp. 105–6.

25

Living in the End Times

In *Living in the End Times*, Žižek sees four signs of the imminent collapse of global capitalism: ecological crisis, consequences of the biogenetic revolution, imbalances within the system itself, and the growth of social divisions (*Living in the End Times*, p. x). Žižek predicts that our social consciousness will be transformed by the coming crises in a way which follows the five stages of grief outlined by Elisabeth Kübler Ross: denial, anger, bargaining, depression, and finally, acceptance.

The question is whether every ethical universality is necessarily based on the exclusion of the abyss of the neighbor, or whether, to the contrary, there might be a universality which does not *exclude the neighbor. Our answer affirms the latter: namely, the universality grounded in the "part-of-no-part," the singular universality exemplified in those who are "out of place" in it and as such directly stand for the universal dimension.*
—Slavoj Žižek, *Living in the End Times*, p. 124

Introduction

Žižek's *Living in the End Times* (2010)[1] boldly predicts the imminent demise of global capitalism. In his introduction, Žižek begins by disturbing our liberal complacency: he reminds us that a few years after the fall

[1] Unless otherwise stated, page references for this work (abbreviated *Living* below) are to the following edition: *Living in the End Times* (London and New York: Verso, 2010).

Žižek: A Reader's Guide, First Edition. Kelsey Wood.
© 2012 John Wiley & Sons, Inc. Published 2012 by John Wiley & Sons, Inc.

of the Berlin Wall there were numerous ex-Communist leaders who were returned to power through democratic elections. He also points out that the collapse of Communism was *not* the intention of the very demonstrators who made it happen: "among the people protesting against the Communist regimes in Eastern Europe, a large majority of them were not demanding a capitalist society" (*Living*, p. viii). Instead, these protesters were inspired by *socialist* ideals; they were not demonstrating for capitalism but for "Socialism with a human face" (p. viii).

But if – contrary to the intentions of the demonstrators – Communist regimes "collapsed like a house of cards," why do so many of us feel secure in our belief that the global capitalist order is here to stay? Demonstrations by radical right-wing groups, for example, are occurring in the USA at the time of this writing. What if *our* sense of security is a fantasy? To drive his point home, Žižek summarily states the main premise of *Living in the End Times*: "the global capitalist system is approaching an apocalyptic zero-point. Its 'four riders of the apocalypse' are comprised by the ecological crisis, the consequences of the biogenetic revolution, imbalances within the system itself (problems with intellectual property; forthcoming struggles over raw materials, food and water), and the explosive growth of social divisions and exclusions" (*Living*, p. x).

Žižek predicts that our "social consciousness" will be transformed by the coming crises of global capitalism in a way which follows the famous five stages of grief, outlined by Elisabeth Kübler Ross:

> The following five chapters refer to these five stances. Chapter 1 – *denial* – analyzes the predominant modes of ideological obfuscation, from the latest Hollywood blockbusters up to false (displaced) apocalyptism (New Age obscurantism, and so forth). Chapter 2 – *anger* – looks at violent protests against the global system, and the rise of religious fundamentalism in particular. Chapter 3 – *bargaining* – focuses on the critique of political economy, with a plea for the renewal of this central ingredient of Marxist theory. Chapter 4 – *depression* – considers the impact of the forthcoming collapse in its less familiar aspects, such as the rise of new subjective pathology (the "post-traumatic" subject). Finally, Chapter 5 – *acceptance* – discerns the signs of an emerging emancipatory subjectivity, isolating the germs of a communist culture in all its diverse forms, including in literary and other utopias (from Kafka's community of mice to the collective of freak outcasts in the TV series *Heroes*).[2]

[2] Slavoj Žižek, *Living in the End Times*, available online at http://www.scribd.com/doc/51736113/LIVING-IN-THE-END-TIMES-Slavoy-Zizek. Also in Slavoj Žižek, *Living in the End Times* (London and New York: Verso, 2010), p. xii.

If it is true that the capitalist system is tottering, then what are we to do? If we are not simply "dumb determinists" (*Living*, p. 86), then we believe that through the act, a subject – or collective of subjects – can redefine the parameters of the possible. But how can we prevent the kind of horrifying decline that followed the end of the Roman Empire? How should leftists today engage with the current rise of nationalistic, religious, and ethnic violence?

Žižek's analysis begins by homing in on the notion of "objectivity." In the first place, there can be no emancipatory movement if the traumatic truth (of imminent crisis) is merely recognized and accepted in a disengaged way. Emancipation will be possible only if the truth "is fully lived" (*Living*, p. xii). And because the symbolic dimension of human subjectivity is *social* consciousness, living the traumatic truth must take the form of a shared struggle, not some withdrawn and private, inner meditative experience (p. xii). Because the unreflective state of daily life is *to live a lie*, the way to break out of the lie we are living is through continuous struggle. Žižek follows Karl Marx's lead and argues that the starting point – for breaking out of this lived lie – is "to become terrified by oneself" (p. xii). He cites Marx's "Contribution to the Critique of Hegel's *Philosophy of Right*" in order to indicate how today's shameless cynics must be "put in *terror* of themselves" before they will achieve courage (pp. xii–xiii).

And, as Žižek repeatedly emphasizes throughout his works (because the point bears repeating): "The truth we are dealing with here is not 'objective' truth, but the self-relating truth about one's own subjective position; as such, it is an engaged truth, measured not by its factual accuracy but by the way it affects the subjective position of enunciation" (*Living*, p. xiii). This means that whether or not Marxist theory proves to be true will be determined by "the truth-effect it unleashes in its address-ees (the proletarians), in transforming them into revolutionary subjects" (p. xiii). Žižek argues that truth, as opposed to knowledge, is only discerned by the gaze of one who is engaged in the struggle for truth, and thus already believes in what is disclosed to him. In this respect, he claims, truth is like love: unless we are actively engaged in it, "mere descriptions of the state of things, no matter how accurate, fail to generate emancipatory effects" (p. xiv). Žižek expresses the point concisely: "every 'objective' social fact is already 'mediated' by struggling subjectivity" (p. 182). This is why truth arises only through the struggle for truth. It is also why "one does not wait for the 'ripe' objective circumstances to make a revolution, circumstances become 'ripe' for revolution through the political struggle itself" (p. 182). Žižek ends his introduction with a translation from

St Paul (Ephesians 6:12), and segues from this Biblical reference into a quotation from the French communist philosopher Alain Badiou:

> "Our struggle is not against actual corrupt individuals, but against those in power in general, against their authority, against the global order and the ideological mystification which sustains it." To engage in this struggle means to endorse Badiou's formula *mieux vaut un désastre qu'un désêtre*: better to take the risk and engage in fidelity to a Truth-Event, even if it ends in catastrophe, than to vegetate in the eventless utilitarian-hedonist survival of what Nietzsche called the "last men." What Badiou rejects is thus the liberal ideology of victimhood, with its reduction of politics to a program of avoiding the worst, to renouncing all positive projects and pursuing the least bad option. Not least since, as Arthur Feldmann, a Viennese Jewish writer, bitterly noted: the price we usually pay for survival is our lives.[3]

Like many passages in *Living in the End Times*, this quotation functions as a kind of litmus test to distinguish pseudo-leftists from the genuine article: it is inspiring for those who are "engaged in the Truth-Event," but appears utterly insane to those who are not.

Chapter 1: Denial

In order to explain what ideology is, Žižek contrasts the imaginary-symbolic "reality" with the Lacanian Real. If the human face belongs to reality, nonetheless the Other, in the Real dimension of her subjectivity, evokes "the horror of the Neighbor-Thing" (*Living*, p. 2). And insofar as the Real as such is impossible, the Christian injunction, "Love thy neighbor!" literally asks the impossible. Thus love is an "impossible" miracle, which sometimes occurs. But as Real, the desire of the Other belongs to a monstrous, de-subjectivized subject: "This is why, in psychoanalytic treatment, the patient does not sit face to face with the analyst: they both stare at a third point, since it is only this suspension of the face which opens up the space for the proper dimension of the Neighbor" (p. 3). Žižek articulates an ethics of the Real, which enjoins us to reinvent the symbolic order through the Lacanian *act*. The act is enabled by an encounter with the impossible-Real.

[3] Slavoj Žižek, *Living in the End Times*, available online at http://www.scribd.com/doc/51736113/LIVING-IN-THE-END-TIMES-Slavoy-Zizek. Also in Slavoj Žižek, *Living in the End Times* (London and New York: Verso, 2010), p. xv.

Ideology, by contrast, introduces a distance between us and the trauma/ antagonism of the Real, thereby rendering it "livable" (*Living*, p. 3). Ideology renders Real *jouissance* livable by means of a split between the public face of law and its obscene superego supplement:

> Take military ideology for instance: it becomes "livable" only against the background of the obscene unwritten rules and rituals (marching chants, fragging, sexual innuendo …) in which it is embedded. Which is why, if there is an ideological experience at its purest, at its zero-level, then it occurs the moment we adopt an attitude of ironic distance, laughing at the follies in which we are ready to believe – it is at this moment of liberating laughter, when we look down on the absurdity of our faith, that we become pure subjects of ideology, that ideology exerts its strongest hold over us. (*Living*, p. 3)

This means that postmodern cynics are *pure subjects of ideology*. Ideology renders Real *jouissance* livable by enabling a distantiation from the barbarian violence that sustains the public face of law. This explains why many so-called "leftist" academics (especially in the USA) want to pose as revolutionaries, while retaining their privileges and job security. But the circumstances today are more and more forcing all of us to take a stand:

> The "interesting times" we are entering undermine such security. In a psychoanalytic treatment, one learns to clarify one's desires: do I really want what I think I want? Take the proverbial case of a husband engaged in a passionate extra-marital affair, dreaming all the time about the moment when his wife will disappear (die, divorce him, or whatever), so that he will then be able to fully live with his mistress – when this finally happens, all his world breaks down, he discovers that he also doesn't want his mistress. As the old proverb says: there is one thing worst [sic] than not getting what one wants – to really get it. Leftist academics are now approaching such a moment of truth: you wanted real change – now you can have it![4]

Insofar as we cynically refrain from the critique of ideology, we are perpetuating the systemic violence of global capitalism, its barbarism. But any civilization that disavows its own barbarian potential has already surrendered to barbarism (p. 6).

---

[4] Slavoj Žižek, "Welcome to the Interesting Times," Fifth International Marx Congress, September 2010, *Plenum d'ouverture*, available online at: actuelmarx.u-paris10.fr/cm6/com/ MI6_Plenum_Zizek.doc.

By way of a brief reference to Hegelian dialectics – specifically, the relationship between time and the enunciation of truth (*Living*, pp. 25–6) – Žižek argues that the French Revolutionary Terror was a deadlock through which it was necessary to pass in order to arrive at the modern rational state (p. 27). What does this mean? Žižek is claiming that the fact that the French Revolution failed to fully actualize its guiding Idea shows, on the one hand, the limitation of this utopian Idea. But, on the other hand, Žižek also argues that this failure can point out the falsity of the new historical reality, its *"inadequacy to its own Notion."*[5] In other words, Žižek acknowledges that the French Revolution devolved into utilitarian, bourgeois reality. But the flipside of this acknowledgment is Žižek's insistence that the failure of the Revolutionary Idea also reveals the limitation of what followed it, namely utilitarian bourgeois reality. Similarly, the limitations of the present reality – global capitalism – become visible if we view this present historical reality in light of the *failure* of the moment that preceded it.

Žižek insists that we must maintain a kind of double perspective – a parallax view – and recognize that the failure of Communism does not only signal the implicit deadlock of the Soviet version of communism. In other words, Soviet Communism's deadlock and failure imply the *unrealized potentiality* of the communist idea today. Žižek argues that it is this unrealized potential – e.g. what Lenin tried and failed to achieve – that should be endorsed today: "Even if, in this way, we do not get what we wanted and/or expected, we nonetheless change the coordinates of what appears as 'possible' and give birth to something new" (p. 38, note 40).

But will the failure of capitalism imply that it has unrealized potentiality too? Žižek reminds his readers frequently of capitalism's ability to adapt: "With regard to today's global social dynamic, there is thus a conclusion which cannot be avoided: today, it is capitalism which is properly revolutionary – it changed our entire landscape in the last decades, from technology to ideology, while conservatives as well as social democrats were mostly reacting to these changes, desperately trying to maintain old gains."[6]

The main thrust of Žižek's argument in *Living in the End Times* is that – in light of the Real antagonisms which limit global capitalism today – our adherence to liberal democracy is little more than ideological fantasy. But before leftists find the courage for the revolutionary act, we must first recognize the degree to which we participate in the obscene

---

[5]   Slavoj Žižek, *In Defense of Lost Causes* (London and New York: Verso, 2008), p. 209.

[6]   Slavoj Žižek, "Welcome to the Interesting Times," Fifth International Marx Congress, September 2010, *Plenum d'ouverture*, available online at: actuelmarx.u-paris10.fr/cm6/com/MI6_Plenum_Zizek.doc.

underside of the public law. Žižek shows that the true power of the law lies not its public face (e.g. explicit prohibitions), but in the way the law allows – but *regulates* – the violations of prohibitions: "the law silently accepts that the basic prohibitions are violated (or even discretely solicits us to violate them), and then, once we find ourselves in this position of guilt, it tells us how to reconcile the violation with the law by violating the prohibition in a regulated way" (*Living*, p. 19). Democracy is inherently susceptible to this corruption; we find ever new ways to violate the public law in our submission to the obscene superego injunction to transgressive enjoyment: "How, then, does psychoanalysis stand with regard to enjoyment [*jouissance*]? Its great task is to break the hold over us of the superego injunction to enjoy, that is, to help us include in the freedom *to* enjoy also the freedom *not* to enjoy, the freedom *from* enjoyment" (p. 74).

Even our liberal concern for suffering Third World "victims" is a manifestation of *jouissance*. It is no accident that our sympathetic concern for those excluded by the capitalist system (e.g. slum dwellers) is expressed in a way that *sustains* our privileged position. On page 124, Žižek refers to Thoreau in order to drive this point home: "In the summer of 1846, Thoreau was arrested for refusing to pay taxes (raised to finance the Mexican War). When Emerson visited him in jail and asked "What are you doing in here?" Thoreau answered: "What are you doing out there?" This is the proper radical answer to the liberal's sympathetic concern for the excluded: "How come that they are out there, excluded from public space?" – "How come that you are in here, included in it?"[7]

We are also complicit in the injustices of our global capitalist system insofar as we remain unaware of the inconsistencies of our own ideology. How is the ideology of liberalism inconsistent?

> Today, the meaning of "liberalism" moves between two opposed poles: economic liberalism (free market individualism, opposition to strong state regulation, etc.) and political liberalism (with an accent on equality, social solidarity, permissiveness, etc.). In the US, Republicans are more liberal in the first sense and Democrats in the second. The point, of course, is that while one cannot decide through closer analysis which is the "true" liberalism, one also cannot resolve the deadlock by proposing a kind of "higher" dialectical synthesis, or "avoid the confusion" by making a clear distinction between the two senses of the term. The tension between the two meanings is inherent to the very content that "liberalism" endeavors to

[7] Slavoj Žižek, *Living in the End Times*, available online at http://www.scribd.com/doc/51736113/LIVING-IN-THE-END-TIMES-Slavoy-Zizek. Also in Slavoj Žižek, *Living in the End Times* (London and New York: Verso, 2010), p. 124.

designate, it is constitutive of the notion itself, so that this ambiguity, far from signaling a limitation of our knowledge, signals the innermost "truth" of the notion of liberalism.[8]

This inconsistency inherent to liberalism explains why we are tolerant only of an Other who is non-threatening to our Western bourgeois sensibilities. We grant the privilege of free choice only to those who will choose what we want them to choose. As Žižek points out, our tolerance and our freedom of choice are revealed in their inconsistency when we cannot tolerate a Muslim woman who chooses to wear the burqa.

Chapter 2: Anger

In this chapter, Žižek argues that it is ultimately because our postmodernist era perceives itself to be "post-ideological" that we are witnessing the rise of religious and ethnic violence (*Living*, p. 97). Against the rising tide of religious fundamentalism, Žižek articulates his materialistic version of Christianity, arguing that Christian love is an inherently violent passion to introduce a difference in the symbolic order, to privilege the object of love at the expense of some other (p. 99). Žižek argues that Christian love (*agape*) is a form of political love "that enjoins us to 'unplug' from the organic community into which we were born" (p. 106). *Agape* enjoins us to love the outcast, the excluded Other, the Neighbor in all her Otherness. To support this, he quotes several of Christ's statements from the Bible which make clear how hatred and violence are implicit to Christian love (e.g. Matthew 10:34–9; Luke 12:49–53; Luke 14:26; etc.). Žižek argues that *agape* as political love is not hierarchical, but is, rather, "an unconditional egalitarian love for the Neighbor" (p. 117). Only against this Christian background can we understand Che Guevara's statements on revolutionary love (p. 108). As Žižek puts it:

> when one confronts the choice between love and duty, duty should prevail. [...] Perhaps there is no greater love than that of a revolutionary couple, where each of the two lovers is ready to abandon the other at any moment should the revolution demand it. They do not love each other less than the amorous couple bent on suspending all their terrestrial links and obligations

---

[8] Slavoj Žižek, *Living in the End Times*, available online at http://www.scribd.com/ doc/51736113/LIVING-IN-THE-END-TIMES-Slavoy-Zizek. Also in Slavoj Žižek, *Living in the End Times* (London and New York: Verso, 2010), p. 37.

in order to burn out in a night of unconstrained passion – if anything, they love each other more.[9]

In sum, the point is not simply to avoid or stifle anger, but instead to direct our anger against our common political enemy. Žižek analyzes concrete examples of recent violence (e.g. in the Congo) in order to show that "Beneath the façade of ethnic warfare, we discern the workings of global capitalism" (p. 163). The cause of such conflicts is not the clash of cultures; the cause is the systemic violence of global capitalism. Žižek argues that the unemployed and the working poor, slum dwellers and stateless persons, all the outcasts of the capitalist symbolic order are today's proletarians. As a response to this systemic violence, his Christian-materialism enjoins us to *agape* as political love for the excluded Other, a form of revolutionary love that also involves hatred – not of the ethnic or religious Other – but of our common political enemy.

Chapter 3: Bargaining

Žižek begins this chapter by analyzing the thought of his friend and rival Alain Badiou, and discerns a moment of "hidden Kantianism" in Badiou's thinking (*Living*, p. 185). Against Badiou, Žižek argues for an unorthodox version of Marxist historical materialism, and asserts that: "A resuscitation of the 'critique of political economy' is the *sine qua non* of contemporary communist politics" (p. 185). Žižek refers to the work of Moishe Postone in order to articulate a "non-Marxist Marx."[10] Žižek's criticisms of Badiou and Postone are subtle; but one way to get a sense of his main point is to say that Žižek discerns – in the later Marx – insights that anticipate Lacan's distinction between the three dimensions of imaginary, symbolic, and Real. Simply put, Žižek, like the later Marx, views class struggle (social antagonism) as Real and therefore inherent to any sociosymbolic order. Thus Žižek argues that Postone: "fails to see how class struggle is not a positive social phenomenon, an ontic component of objective social reality; it designates the very limit of social objectivity, the point at which subjective engagement co-determines what appears as social reality" (p. 198). Along the same lines, Žižek argues that

---

[9] Slavoj Žižek, *Living in the End Times*, available online at http://www.scribd.com/doc/51736113/LIVING-IN-THE-END-TIMES-Slavoy-Zizek. Also in Slavoj Žižek, *Living in the End Times* (London and New York: Verso, 2010), p. 109.

[10] Cf. Moishe Postone's "Rethinking Marx (in a Post-Marxist World)," online at http://platypus1917.home.comcast.net.

Badiou "reduces classes to parts of a social body, forgetting the lesson of Louis Althusser, namely that 'class struggle' paradoxically precedes classes as determinate social groups, that is, that every class position and determination is already an effect of the 'class struggle'" (p. 198).

To comprehend Žižek's argument, it must be kept in mind that his dialectical materialism is a fusion of Hegel and Lacan that bears a strong affinity to the Enlightenment project of scientific rationality and universal emancipation. For example, Žižek's view of the dialectical relationship between subject and object involves *both* the predictability allowed by science *and* the "impossibility" of the Lacanian Real (class struggle is Real). In the opposition between human subjects and nature, external obstacles configure subjects' options, and collectivities of subjects respond by altering their environment (e.g., with technology). Subsequently, this new, altered reality reconfigures social consciousness and, in turn, new obstacles arise. In response, subjects transform productive processes and develop yet another symbolic reality. This dialectical opposition between humans and nature is mirrored *within society*, in the antagonism between productive workers who are dominated by capitalists:

> Human subordination of nature is thus reflected in the split within humankind itself, where the relation is inverted: the general productive relationship between humankind and nature is that between subject and object (humanity as a collective subject asserts its domination over nature through its transformation and exploitation in the productive process); within humankind itself, however, productive workers as the living force of domination over nature are themselves subordinated to those who are the agents of, or stand-ins for, subordinated objectivity. This paradox was clearly perceived already by Adorno and Horkheimer in their *Dialectic of Enlightenment*, where they show how domination over nature necessarily entails the class domination of people over other people. The question to be raised here concerns the classical Marxian notion of proletarian revolution: is it not all too subjectivist, conceiving communism as the final victory of subject over substance? This does not mean that we have to accept the necessity of social domination; we should, rather, accept the "primacy of the objective" (Adorno): the way to rid ourselves of our masters is not for humankind itself to become a collective master over nature, but to recognize the imposture in the very notion of the Master.[11]

---

[11] Slavoj Žižek, *Living in the End Times*, available online at http://www.scribd.com/ doc/51736113/LIVING-IN-THE-END-TIMES-Slavoy-Zizek. Also in Slavoj Žižek, *Living in the End Times* (London and New York: Verso, 2010), pp. 242–3.

The point is not that social domination is a necessary feature of human existence. But Žižek argues that we will not recognize the imposture of our political masters without a renewal of the critique of political economy. The goal of this critique – as we will see – is to first recognize the limitations of "formal freedom," our freedom to choose from within the existing parameters (e.g., power relations). Secondly we must realize our "actual freedom" as the possibility of reconfiguring the very parameters of choice (*Living*, p. 358).

Chapter 4: Depression

In this chapter, Žižek considers the consequences of the coming collapse of global capitalism for subjectivity: "If the twentieth century was the Freudian century, so that even its worst nightmares were read as (sado-masochistic) vicissitudes of the libido, will the twenty-first be the century of the post-traumatic disengaged subject, whose first emblematic figure, that of the Muselmann, is multiplying in the guise of refugees, terror victims, survivors of natural disasters or of family violence?"[12] Žižek's psychoanalytic analyses are extended and sophisticated, but to summarize the main thrust of his arguments: we human subjects are being deprived of our substance and "proletarianized" by the enclosures of global capitalism.

This deprivation of substance is manifested in the first place through the privatization (or enclosure) of the commons of *external nature*, as productive workers are exploited and their products are taken away from them. But moreover, privatization/enclosure deprives us of the commons of our symbolic and intersubjective *second nature*. While the shared, symbolic commons is being enclosed, we grow more dependent on our "daily infusion of the media-drug" (*Living*, pp. 363–4). Many of us spend hours each day, immersed in virtual reality, all the while oblivious to the "ideological mechanism of (mis)recognition which overdetermines our everyday perceptions and interactions" (p. 338). Finally, the enclosure of our *inner nature* is already becoming manifest: the crises of late capitalism are reducing us to the "post-traumatic subject."

---

[12] Slavoj Žižek, *Living in the End Times*, available online at http://www.scribd.com/doc/51736113/LIVING-IN-THE-END-TIMES-Slavoy-Zizek. Also in Slavoj Žižek, *Living in the End Times* (London and New York: Verso, 2010), p. 294.

Chapter 5: Acceptance

Some hasty critics of Žižek claim that he never criticizes Lacan. But a close reading of Žižek's works reveals that he exposes and resolves deadlocks in Lacan's thinking. Sheila Kunkle gives an example:

> In carefully tracing Žižek's contribution to the ethical debate of Kant and Sade we find him ending up on neither side (that is, he sees neither the Kantian in Sade nor the Sadean in Kant); what we find instead is Žižek's conclusion that Sade is the symptom of Kant's failure to take his own discovery to its ultimate and paradoxical end. Žižek takes us further into the analysis by overcoming a deadlock that Lacan confronted when he considered whether Sade's acts were or were not in accord with the jouissance of transgressing a Law. The dilemma is nicely stated by Lorenzo Chiesa as either: the Jouissance of the Law (Kant) or the Law of Jouissance (Sade); however, what Žižek presents is the realization that the law is already excessive and not itself a universal.[13]

In *Living in the End Times*, Žižek argues that Lacan did not recognize the political implications of his own growing emphasis on the Real in his later theory. As opposed to Lacan's liberal, individualistic response to what Žižek calls "the glorious events of May '68," Žižek argues that a collective political act can involve an encounter with the Real:

> Lacan's thesis is effectively liberal, in the precise sense that it obliterates the Real which one encounters at the collective level. The political as such is here devalued as a domain of imaginary and symbolic identifications; by definition, it involves a misrecognition. The basic premise of liberalism is the nominalism of truth: truth is individual, the social can only provide a neutral frame for the interaction and self-realization of individuals. What if, however, the collective is not merely the level of imaginary and symbolic identifications? What if, in it, we encounter the Real of antagonisms?[14]

Against liberal appropriations of Lacanian theory, Žižek shows how the ideals of May 1968 were co-opted and transformed by capitalism. The hierarchical, Fordist production process was gradually replaced by a network-based organization that relied on employee autonomy and initiative in the workplace (*Living*, pp. 355–6). Then, in the 1980s and

---

[13] Sheila Kunkle, "Embracing the Paradox: Žižek's Illogical Logic," *International Journal of Žižek Studies*, vol. 2, number 4 (2008), p. 8.

[14] Slavoj Žižek, *Living in the End Times*, available online at http://www.scribd.com/doc/51736113/LIVING-IN-THE-END-TIMES-Slavoy-Zizek. Also in Slavoj Žižek, *Living in the End Times* (London and New York: Verso, 2010), p. 355.

1990s another shift took place, a shift that is apparent if one considers the advertisements of the time. Žižek calls the result of this shift the first phase of cultural capitalism, in which "it was the direct reference to personal authenticity or quality of experience that predominated" (p. 356). In the second (current) phase of cultural capitalism "one can note the increasing mobilization of socio-ideological motifs (ecology, social solidarity): the experience referred to here is that of being part of a larger collective movement, of caring for nature and for the ill, the poor and the deprived, of doing something to help" (p. 356). Žižek characterizes this as *ethical capitalism*, and shows how "the very act of participating in consumerist activity is simultaneously presented as a participation in the struggle against the evils ultimately caused by capitalist consumerism" (p. 356). Žižek shows how certain aspects of the 1968 struggle are mobilized today by liberals and right-wingers in support of global capitalism's ideology of choice, and against what is called "Socialism," such as President Obama's proposed healthcare reforms in the USA (p. 358).

But what liberals and right-wingers *both* ignore is the distinction between formal and actual freedom. As Žižek puts it: " 'formal freedom' is that freedom to choose *within* the coordinates of the existing power relations, while 'actual' freedom grows when we can change the very coordinates of our choices" (*Living*, p. 358). Freedom of choice is meaningless except against a background of regulations (legal, educational, ethical, economic, etc.) that serve to make the freedom to choose actual and effective (p. 359). Žižek points to countries such as Norway as a counterexample to the liberal and right-wing ideology of choice: "although all the main agents respect a basic social agreement and ambitious social projects are enacted in a spirit of solidarity, productivity and dynamism remain at extraordinarily high levels, flatly denying the common wisdom that such a society ought to be stagnating" (p. 359).

Along the same lines, Žižek discerns signs from the future, signs of the possibility for realizing some of the latent potential of the communist idea. He refers to Franz Kafka's last story, "Josephine the Singer, or the Mouse Folk,"[15] in order to indicate the character of a radically egalitarian community:

Note how Josephine is treated as a celebrity, but *not* fetishized – her admirers are well aware that there is nothing special about her, that she is just one of them. To paraphrase Marx, she thinks people admire her

[15] See Franz Kafka, "Josefine the Singer, or the Mouse Folk," in *The Basic Kafka* (New York: Pocket Books, 1984), p. 128; available online at fortunecity.com.

because she is an artist, but in reality she is an artist only because people treat her as such. Here we get an example of how, in a communist society, the Master-Signifier is still operative, but deprived of its fetishistic effects – Josephine's belief in herself is perceived by the people as harmless and rather ridiculous narcissism which should be gently, but ironically, tolerated and sustained. This is how artists should be treated in a communist society – they should be praised and flattered, but they should not be given any material privileges like exemption from work or special food rations."[16]

But is an egalitarian community a realistic option? Again, it will become a realistic option if leftists mobilize and work together to make it happen. Today there are almost seven billion human beings on the planet, and about four billion of these people live in extreme poverty. If leftists are to achieve the courage required for the revolutionary act, they will overcome liberalism's ineffectual and hypocritical sympathy for "victims," since this concern ultimately functions in such a way so as to sustain the systemic violence of global capitalism.

In a new afterword to the paperback edition of *Living in the End Times*, Žižek refers to "the democratic illusion":

> Marx's key insight remains valid, perhaps more than ever: for Marx, the question of freedom should not be located primarily in the political sphere proper (Does a country have free elections? Are its judges independent? Is its press free from hidden pressures? Does it respect human rights?). Rather, the key to actual freedom resides in the "apolitical" network of social relations, from the market to the family. Here the change required is not political reform but a transformation of the social relations of production – which entails precisely revolutionary class struggle rather than democratic elections or any other "political" measure in the narrow sense of the term. We do not vote on who owns what, or about relations in the factory, and so on – such matters remain outside the sphere of the political, and it is illusory to expect that one will effectively change things by "extending" democracy into the economic sphere (by, say, reorganizing the banks to place them under popular control). Radical changes in this domain need to be made outside the sphere of legal "rights." In "democratic" procedures (which, of course, can have a positive role to play), no matter how radical our anti-capitalism, solutions are sought solely through those democratic mechanisms which themselves form part of the apparatuses of the "bourgeois" state that guarantees the undisturbed reproduction of capital.

---

[16] Slavoj Žižek, *Living in the End Times*, available online at http://www.scribd.com/doc/51736113/LIVING-IN-THE-END-TIMES-Slavoy-Zizek. Also in Slavoj Žižek, *Living in the End Times* (London and New York: Verso, 2010), pp. 370–71.

In this precise sense, Badiou was right to claim that today the name of the ultimate enemy is not capitalism, empire, exploitation, or anything similar, but democracy itself. It is the "democratic illusion," the acceptance of democratic mechanisms as providing the only framework for all possible change, which prevents any radical transformation of capitalist relations.[17]

If we have to work from within capitalism in order to dispel the democratic illusion, nonetheless, we cannot stop short and resort to partial measures that really change nothing. Instead of the spirit of liberal compromise, *agape* as political love of the neighbor – and hatred of the common political enemy – is required to reinvent our sociosymbolic order.

It might be argued that Žižek is even more faithful to the Marxist notion of class struggle than is Badiou, insofar as Žižek never forgets that so-called "peaceful" social life is always sustained by state violence. There is no "normal" functioning of the state, because social life itself is an effect of the predominance of the wealthy elite over the proletariat:

> In other words, one cannot separate violence from the state conceived as an apparatus of class domination: from the standpoint of the oppressed, the very existence of a state is a violent fact (in the same sense in which Robespierre claimed there was no need to prove that the king had committed any crime, since the very existence of the king was a crime in itself, an offense against the freedom of the people). In this sense, every act of violence against the state on the part of the oppressed is ultimately "defensive." Not to concede this point is, *nolens volens*, to "normalize" the state and accept that its own acts of violence are merely contingent excesses to be dealt with through democratic reforms. This is why the standard liberal motto – that violence is never legitimate, even though it may sometimes be necessary to resort to it – is insufficient. From a radical emancipatory perspective, this formula should be reversed: for the oppressed, violence is always legitimate (since their very status is the result of the violence they are exposed to), but never necessary (it will always be a matter of strategy whether or not use violence against the enemy).[18]

But how do we form a collectivity that is not based on the market or state bureaucracy? What would a radically egalitarian community look like? Žižek argues that, in the first place, a communist culture would involve "a shamelessly total form of immersion into the social body, a shared

---

[17] Žižek's new afterword to *Living in the End Times*, "The Jacobin Spirit," available online in *Jacobin* at http://jacobinmag.com/archive/issue3/zizek.html.

[18] Slavoj Žižek, "The Jacobin Spirit," online in *Jacobin* at http://jacobinmag.com/archive/issue3/zizek.html.

ritualistic performance that would send all good liberals into shock with its 'totalitarian' intensity" (*Living*, p. 371). Secondly, communist culture involves the passionate immersion in a disciplined collective that brings about the dissolution of individuality and the "normal" rational ego, along with the reign of the instinct for survival (p. 373). A third element of communist culture is that personal idiosyncrasy is subordinated to the social consciousness in order to clear the way for "the cold universal space of rational thought" (p. 374).

This brief summary of Žižek's *Living in the End Times* does not convey the careful distinctions he makes at every stage of his analysis in order to ensure that his message is not co-opted and neutralized by New Age obscurantists, right-wingers, liberals, or proponents of "total democracy." In a time like today, when the state fails even in its proper function of "servicing the goods," who are the true patriots? Žižek argues that fidelity to the idea of communism means recognizing that those who say "No!" to despotism are the true patriots, *even when their views are opposed to the opinion of the majority*:

When *la patrie est en danger*, Robespierre said, one should fearlessly state the fact that "the nation is betrayed. This truth is now known to all Frenchmen"; "Lawgivers, the danger is imminent; the reign of truth has to begin: we are courageous enough to tell you this; be courageous enough to hear it." In such a situation, there can be no room for those taking a neutral third position. In his speech celebrating the dead of August 10, 1792, *abbé* Grégoire declared: "there are people who are so good that they are worthless; and in a revolution which engages in the struggle of freedom against despotism, a neutral man is a pervert who, without any doubt, waits for how the battle will turn out to decide which side to take." Before we dismiss these lines as "totalitarian," let us recall a later time when the French *patrie* was again *en danger*, in 1940, when none other than General de Gaulle, in his famous radio address from London, announced to the French people the "strong truth": France is defeated, but the war is not over; against the Pétainist collaborators, the struggle goes on. The exact conditions of this statement are worth recalling: even Jacques Duclos, second in command of the French Communist Party, admitted in a private conversation that, had free elections been held at the time, Marshal Pétain would have won with 90 percent of the votes. When de Gaulle, in his historic address, refused to capitulate and pledged his continued resistance, he claimed that only he, not the Vichy regime, could speak on behalf of the true France (that is: on behalf of France as such, not only on behalf of the "majority of the French"!). What he asserted was deeply true, even if, "democratically speaking," it not only lacked legitimacy, but was clearly opposed to the opinion of the majority of the French people. (The same goes for Germany: those who stood for Germany were the tiny minority who actively resisted Hitler, not the Nazis or the undecided opportunists.)[19]

Another key point Žižek emphasizes in *Living in the End Times* is that regulation and discipline are essential to actual freedom. It is important to realize that Žižek's association of freedom with discipline and regulation derives from a venerable tradition in Western philosophy: a homologous view of freedom's two aspects informs the philosophy of St Augustine, who derived it from the Platonic tradition.[20]

But the sheer power of Žižek's formulation arises from the way he fuses Christian-materialist *agape* (as the political transfiguration of narcissistic – i.e. imaginary – modes of love) with both the Lacanian act and the concept of actual freedom. As Žižek writes in his introduction:

> When, in 1948, Sartre saw that he was likely to be maligned by both sides in the Cold War, he wrote: "if that were to happen, it would prove only one thing: either that I am very clumsy, or that I am on the right road." As it happens, this is often how I also feel: I am attacked for being anti-Semitic *and* for spreading Zionist lies, for being a covert Slovene nationalist *and* an unpatriotic traitor to my nation, for being a crypto-Stalinist defending terror *and* for spreading bourgeois lies about Communism ... So maybe, just maybe, I am on the right path, the path of fidelity to freedom. (*Living*, p. xiv)

---

[19] Slavoj Žižek, "The Jacobin Spirit," online in *Jacobin* at http://jacobinmag.com/archive/issue3/zizek.html.

[20] Along the same lines, Alain Badiou suggests that the origins of the idea of communism may be located in Plato's critique of democracy. See *The Idea of Communism*, ed. Costas Douzinas and Slavoj Žižek (London and New York: Verso), pp. 1, 12.

26

Conclusion

Žižek's position is Hegelian in philosophy, Lacanian in psychoanalysis, Christian-materialist in religion, and communist in politics. This chapter develops some implications of Žižek's methodology in order to indicate the significance of his reinvention of dialectical materialism. We will look again at Žižek's re-inscriptions of Hegel, Marx, and Lacan, especially relating to Hegelian Absolute Knowledge, the Other, the split subject, fantasy, enjoyment, ideology, belief, death drive, desire, sexual difference, and what is meant by an ethics of the Real. Finally we will consider the paradox of singular universality. Singular universality functions as a link between dialectical materialist ontology, an ethics of the Real, and the ethico-political act. Understanding the subtractive "space" of singular universality is crucial if we are to understand Žižek's controversial endorsement of the dictatorship of the proletariat.

His conclusion – to begin from the beginning – makes it clear that he is not talking about merely slowing down and fortifying what has already been achieved, but about descending back to the starting point: one should begin from the beginning, not from the place that one succeeded in reaching in the previous effort. In Kierkegaard's terms, a revolutionary process is not a gradual progress but a repetitive movement, a movement of repeating the beginning, again and again.
—Žižek, "How to Begin from the Beginning," *New Left Review*, no. 57, pp. 43–55, May–June 2009

Don't Just Do Something; Think!

What is most innovative about Žižek's dialectical materialist methodology and most significant about his results? In various works, Žižek concisely traces the origins of dialectical materialism back through Marx and the German Idealists to Plato's *Parmenides*. Žižek argues that, because of the inherent inconsistency of any symbolic system, any dichotomy that presents us with an either/or decision proves to leave alternatives out. Kant, Schelling, and Hegel developed this insight into the incompleteness (non-All) of any conceptual synthesis. Žižek's books contain many passages in which he refers to the German Idealists in order to show how both poles of a dichotomy fail to consider something, such as a presupposition that both alternatives share.

Žižek usually articulates his examples in terms of standard problems in philosophy, such as the problem of personal identity, the mind-body problem, and the nature of consciousness and the unconscious. One way Žižek subverts traditional approaches to these philosophical problems is to utilize Kant's distinction between negating a predicate (negative judgment) as opposed to affirming a non-predicate (infinite judgment). For example, to negate the predicate "dead" in reference to someone simply means that person is alive. But to affirm the non-predicate "undead" is to open a third domain that subverts the distinction between living and dead. This subversive excess is neither alive nor dead. Moreover, this excess is *neither nature nor culture*: an animal that does not speak (an ape for example) is, in this sense, part of nature. And culture can never domesticate or "dialectically mediate" the subversive and undead excess inherent to subjectivity. Žižek argues that this nonrational, "immortal" excess is the proper way to interpret the Freudian death drive. Another name for this uncanny domain is the absolute negativity of freedom in the Hegelian dialectic, which Žižek links to the radical autonomy of the subject in the Lacanian ethico-political act.

Again, it is this excessive and nonrational domain that distinguishes speaking subjects from animals. On the one hand, apes do not do differential calculus. But, on the other hand, an ape does *not* demonstrate the excessive "madness" of the autonomous act, which Žižek associates with the death drive. In this respect, an ape is more rational than a speaking subject. Thus it is neither utility nor "instrumental reason" that leads to the creation of things like differential calculus. Instead, Žižek argues, the free, creative act involved in mathematical (or any other) innovation indicates the domain of radical autonomy anticipated by

Hegelian negativity and the Freudian death drive. The incompleteness and inconsistency of the existing symbolic order (reality), is simultaneously the potential for the invention of a new symbolic order, a new reality. As the German Idealists already recognized, freedom is more "primordial" than either nature or culture. Progress and cultural developments do not arise from some "natural" substratum. Rather, once we are "in" culture, we retroactively "de-naturalize" nature: for example, the animal instinct to reproduce becomes permeated by signifiers. Lipstick, high heels, and diamond wedding rings function as signifiers. In sum, cultural development involves the excessive domain of autonomy (death drive), and the retroactive de-naturalization of nature.

Along the same lines, freedom is unconscious. And, again, the subject's "unconscious" is the discourse of the symbolic big Other. Put simply, this means that the unconscious is constituted by signifiers. However, the Other is split by the "pre-ontological" Real:

> when I assert about a thought that "it *is* unconscious," this is quite different from asserting that such a thought "*is not* conscious." In the latter case – when I negate the predicate "conscious" – the (logical) subject is simply located in the domain of the non-psychic (of biology, and so on – in short, in the vast domain of all that goes on in our body beyond the reach of our consciousness). However, when I affirm a non-predicate and assert that the thought is unconscious, I thereby open up a third, uncanny domain that subverts the very distinction between psychic-conscious and somatic, a domain that has no place in the ontological-phenomenological distinction between psychic and somatic, and whose status is for that reason, as Lacan puts it in *Seminar XI*, "pre-ontological."[1]

On the one hand, the Real as absolute negativity is this uncanny, "pre-ontological" domain. On the other hand, there is no symbolic "reality" apart from alienation in the signifier. In sum, once the subject is alienated in the pre-existing, intersubjective symbolic network, we can never completely and unambiguously isolate the thing from its symbolization. For both Lacan and Žižek, this means that the subject's symbolic identity is "outside of" the individual.

Sheila Kunkle concisely summarizes some of the implications of the disavowed Real for the subject and for reality:

---

[1]   Slavoj Žižek, *The Metastases of Enjoyment: On Women and Causality* (London and New York: Verso, 2005), p. 43.

Žižek's articulation of ontology, then, begins with a Hegelian commitment to reversing the standard notion of Reason, of detecting the madness that inheres at its core, and he envisions the Real as "the disavowed X on account of which our vision of reality is anamorphically distorted [...] it has no substantial density in itself, it is just a gap between two points of perspective" [...] It is through a parallax view of phenomena that Žižek aspires to reveal that there is no untainted reality that escapes a kind of enframing; indeed, the two points of perspective mentioned above really unfold as a perspective and what eludes it, and this bears on his notion of ontology. By changing (reframing) the view of an X, one also changes the ontology of that X, or in Žižek's words, "Once introduced, the gap between reality and appearance is thus immediately complicated, reflected-into-itself: once we get a glimpse, through the Frame, of the Other Dimension, *reality itself turns into appearance.* In other words, things do not simply appear, they *appear to appear.*[2]

The parallax Real disrupts what we experience as reality. Because of this disavowed X, any subject is split, and any symbolic reality is ruptured from within. As Kunkle indicates in her essay, Žižek's theoretical work revolves around the analysis of how we – as subjects – orient ourselves in relation to the Real that makes any identity or reality inherently paradoxical.

All of this can help us to understand why, according to Žižek's dialectical materialism, there can be no "depoliticized" analysis of the individual; the diagnosis of the individual is always already a sociosymbolic (collective) diagnostic. This is why psychoanalysis can legitimately move back and forth between analysis of the individual and analysis of the sociosymbolic order: *there is no firm distinction between the individual and the collective.* In other words, we cannot understand symbolic reality without reference to symbolic identity (the barred subject) and vice versa. Thus the libidinal economy of the individual – the economy of *jouissance* – cannot be analyzed in abstraction, apart from the critique of political economy. However, the "mediation" between the individual and the collective is not some positive characteristic or set of predicates, but rather the same Real split that runs through both of them. The particular (subject) and the universal (collectivity) are "reconciled" by the very splitting that cuts through both.

Dialectical materialism involves fidelity to the Real as the inconsistency inherent to symbolic order. The symbolic dimension is a network of

---

[2] See Sheila Kunkle, "Embracing the Paradox: Žižek's Illogical Logic," in *International Journal of Žižek Studies*, vol. 2, number 4 (2008), p. 3. In the quotation above, Kunkle's references are to Žižek's *The Parallax View* (Cambridge, MA: MIT Press, 2006), pp. 26, 29.

signifiers defined by relations of difference with one another. In short, shared practices such as language cannot constitute a coherent identity, because subjectivity also involves the Real as the *failure* or inconsistency of symbolic systems. In a homologous way, symbolic reality (the universe), is incomplete and ruptured into dimensions that are inconsistent with one another. The symbolic order is never *the same* as itself. Thus the big Other exists only insofar as we behave as though it exists. Fantasy allows us to behave as if symbolic identity and symbolic reality actually exist as whole, consistent entities.

Because the subject of desire is alienated or externalized in the signifier, only speaking animals desire. Unlike a want or a wish, desire is unconscious; it exists "outside" of consciousness, in the distortion and inconsistency of the metonymical sliding of signifiers that is the symbolic order. Žižek elaborates Lacan's claim that the unconscious is the discourse of the big Other by showing that the intersubjective symbolic network is the *beyond* in which desire is disclosed. Desire "exists" only in the distortions, repetitions, and inconsistencies of signification. But the essential life substance is *jouissance*, and enjoyment is Real. This means that symbolic desire is opposed to Real *jouissance*. Nonetheless, Žižek asserts that the Real as drive is the driving force of desire. Again, Žižek sharply distinguishes drive from a biological urge or "instinct," and asserts that "*the status of the drive itself is inherently ethical.*"[3] The essence of trauma is that it cannot be remembered, cannot be integrated into our symbolic universe. Thus drive involves the ethical imperative to mark repeatedly, by means of some empty symbolic gesture, the trauma in its very impossibility.[4]

Thus the intersubjective, symbolic network (the big Other) is structured around a void, a traumatic cut or primordial repression: the symbolic order stands in for a void that comes to be through repressing Real trauma/ antagonism. Žižek links this primordial repression (and process of substitution) to the dual character of the superego: the symbolic side of superego is the prohibitions of the public law, but the obscene underside of superego is the injunction to *transgress* these very prohibitions. So prohibition incites the desire to transgress, but insofar as the law also regulates pleasures, prohibition can also *free us* from the obscene superego injunction to enjoyment which dominates daily life in capitalist societies. The obscene

---

[3] Slavoj Žižek, *For They Know Not What They Do: Enjoyment as a Political Factor* (London and New York: Verso, 2002), p. 272.

[4] Slavoj Žižek, *For They Know Not What They Do: Enjoyment as a Political Factor* (London and New York: Verso, 2002), p. 272.

superego imperative of capitalism is the transgressive command "Enjoy!" However this capitalist injunction to enjoy involves an ambiguous relation to Real *jouissance*, and therefore undermines itself.

On the one hand, the injunction to enjoyment conflicts with the public law. On the other hand, full access to *jouissance* is a fantasy; and the more we try to realize this fantasy, the more we confront the opposition between idiotic, masturbatory *jouissance* as opposed to fidelity to desire:

> In his "Kant with Sade," Lacan does not try to make the usual "reductionist" point that every ethical act, pure and disinterested as it may appear, is always grounded in some "pathological" motivation (the agent's own long-term interest, the admiration of his peers, right up to the "negative" satisfaction provided by the suffering and extortion often demanded by ethical acts); the focus of Lacan's interest, rather, resides in the paradoxical reversal by means of which desire itself (i.e., acting upon one's desire, not compromising it) can no longer be grounded in any "pathological" interest or motivations, and thus meets the criteria of the Kantian ethical act, so that "following one's desire" overlaps with "doing one's duty." The opposition is thus not between the egotist search for pleasures and ethical care for others, but between unconditional fidelity to the "law of desire" beyond the pleasure principle (which can assume the form of fidelity to a sexual Truth Event of love, the form of fidelity to an ethico-political Idea, the form of fidelity to one's artistic or scientific engagement ...) and the betrayal of this "law of desire" on behalf of some pathological "goods."[5]

Fidelity to desire here does not refer to the transgressive desire generated by the prohibitory law. Instead, the Lacanian "Do not give way on your desire" refers to fidelity to desire as elevated to the level of ethical duty. For Lacan, desire is a defense against going beyond a certain limit in *jouissance*. Once we recognize that full access to enjoyment is not desirable, we are in a position to traverse the fantasy that induces us to remain within the vicious cycle of prohibitory law and transgressive desire.

Democracy as Fetishist Disavowal

Because of its ambiguous relation to Real *jouissance*, the ideology of late capitalism – liberal, politically correct, and (allegedly) tolerant multiculturalism – proves to be self-undermining. Žižek shows, for

---

[5] Slavoj Žižek, "Dialectical Clarity versus the Misty Conceit of Paradox," in Slavoj Žižek and John Milbank, *The Monstrosity of Christ: Paradox or Dialectic?*, ed. Creston Davis (Cambridge, MA: MIT Press, 2009), p. 239.

example, how in postcommunist Eastern Europe, the upheaval caused by capitalism after the fall of Communism resulted in the formation of the fantasy of a harmonious, "organic" body politic, undisturbed by (allegedly) unnatural social antagonism. Instead of the realization that it is global capitalism that increases social division, the fantasy arose of a national enemy, an ethnic Other who disrupts social stability.

In the West, the anti-Enlightenment, relativist tendency of postmodernism is a symptom of our alienation. One of the ways this alienation manifests is as the externalization of belief. Belief is not some inner state of mind; belief is radically exterior: thus even postmodern cynics still believe, but they believe the way we all tend to believe and to desire, namely, *through the Other*. For example, we may be cynical about our corrupt and dysfunctional "democracy," but we nonetheless believe that someone, somewhere still believes in democracy. This externalization of belief sustains the status quo and undermines postmodernist claims that we live in a "post-ideological" condition. As Žižek's analyses of postmodern culture demonstrate, today's cynical late-capitalist subjects believe more than ever, but belief is externalized in the Other, in the subject supposed to believe. Postmodern cynicism sustains global capitalist ideology by enabling us to conform (to unreflectively accept that capitalism is here to stay) even while we displace our belief in the system onto some Other, and thus fantasize that we are not influenced by any pressure to submit or conform. This is the fetishist disavowal that characterizes the ideology of liberal democracy: "I know very well, but nevertheless ..."

Thus instead of Marx's "they do not know it, but they are doing it," Žižek shows how our social reality involves fetishistic inversion. Insofar as a fetish fills in the empty space in the symbolic – the space of the primordial repression – the fetish-object is the "positivization of an impossibility."[6] Again, the network of signifiers – the intersubjective big Other – is inherently lacking, since the signifying network is articulated in the void opened up by primary repression of Real trauma or antagonism. The fetish serves as a fantasy of unity to cover over the inherent inconsistency and lack that constitutes the network of symbolic signification. Whereas Marx interprets the fetishism of commodities as concealing the "positive" network of social relations, Žižek argues that a fetish conceals the *void* around which symbolic networks revolve. Thus de-fetishization is the experience of encountering, not some positive

[6]   Slavoj Žižek, *Did Somebody Say Totalitarianism? Five Interventions in the (Mis)use of a Notion* (London and New York: Verso, 2002), p. 80.

matrix, but the constitutive lack in the symbolic order. According to Žižek's re-inscription of Hegel, the point is not to resolve antagonism in reality, but to enact the parallax shift that allows us to recognize antagonism as such. The fatal limitation of the liberal-democratic ideology of global capitalism is its failure to encounter the Real functioning of Capital; this is the primordially repressed void in our late-capitalist symbolic order.

The attempt to fill this constitutive void (the place of the primordial repression) leads to the hegemony of the phallic Master-Signifier. Adherents of any successful ideology behave as though the Master-Signifier (e.g., Democracy) actually names some transcendent thing, or some consistent formal procedure:

> The impossible fullness at the level of meaning (of the signified) is sustained by the void (the castrating dimension) at the level of the signifier; we encounter the "meaning of phallus" when, apropos some notion, we enthusiastically feel that "this is IT, the true thing, the true meaning," although we are never able to explicate WHAT, precisely, this meaning IS.[7]

The mythic unity around which ideologies revolve proves to be a rupture that is "positivized" so as to camouflage antagonisms within the sociosymbolic order. For example, the capitalist Master is an imposter; he would be nothing without those whom he exploits: he exists as a Master only insofar as we continue to treat him as such.

But the obverse of this is that without the Master-Signifier, there would be no ambiguity, and no multitude. Even an equivocation revolves around a "One." Without the One, there would just be an undifferentiated indefiniteness. However, it must be added that the Master-Signifier – the One – is an empty inconsistency: "In Lacanian terms we can also say that the One is always already ex-timate with regard to what it unifies. The One totalizes the field it unifies by way of 'condensing' in itself the very excess that threatens this field."[8] The *dialectical* aspect of dialectical materialism implies that there can be no multiplicity, no plurality, no many, except through relations of difference with some One. This dialectical insight, which may be traced in the history of philosophy back

---

[7] Slavoj Žižek, "An Answer to Two Questions," in Adrian Johnston, *Badiou, Žižek, and Political Transformations: The Cadence of Change* (Evanston: Northwestern University Press, 2009), p. 191.

[8] See Markus Gabriel and Slavoj Žižek, *Mythology, Madness and Laughter: Subjectivity in German Idealism* (London and New York: Continuum, 2009), p. 8.

through the German Idealists (especially Hegel) to Plato's dialogue *Parmenides*, may help postmodern proponents of "radical democracy," "total democracy," and "multitude," to understand why Žižek's and Badiou's critiques of democracy resonate so powerfully with philosophers who are already familiar with Plato's critique of democracy. Žižek indicates this homology between Plato's *Parmenides*, Hegelian dialectic, and the feminine logic of "non-All":

> Hegel effectively denies that there is a Real external to the network of notional representations (which is why he is regularly misread as an "absolute idealist" in the sense of the self-enclosed circle of the totality of the Notion). However, the Real does not disappear here in the global self-relating play of symbolic representations; it returns with a vengeance as the immanent gap or obstacle on account of which representations cannot ever totalize themselves, on account of which they are "non-All." (At the very outset of philosophy, Plato also approached this non-All of the field of logos in his *Parmenides*. This is why *Parmenides* occupies a unique place between early and late Plato: a gap becomes visible here which Plato desperately tries to fill in in his late dialogues. *Parmenides* is a proto-version of Hegel's logic. Its eight [or nine] hypotheses are the first version of the complete [AND non-All – complete in the sense of "no exceptions"] set of categories, and, as in Hegel's logic, it is meaningless to ask which hypothesis is "true" – "true" is the conclusion [nothing exists ...] which throws us back into the entire movement.)[9]

What prevents the pure self-identity of the One is not the multitude that subverts unity, but the primordially repressed Real as the immanent obstacle to totalization. The One (the Master-Signifier) unifies a multitude by inscribing into this multitude its own inherent emptiness. This means that any One implies a moment of self-reference; the empty Master-Signifier is the tautological point at which the signifier collapses into its signified. Thus inconsistency, at the most fundamental ontological level, is always the inconsistency of some One with itself. The Lacanian Master-Signifier is this One that signifies the impossibility of pure oneness.

Many proponents of multitude, total democracy, or radical democracy misperceive this dialectic as involving a "binary" logic. But from the perspective of dialectical materialism, the key point is the inconsistency of the One with itself. The reason Žižek refers so often to the Moebius

---

[9] Slavoj Žižek, "An Answer to Two Questions," in Adrian Johnston, *Badiou, Žižek, and Political Transformations: The Cadence of Change*, (Evanston: Northwestern University Press, 2009), p. 205.

strip is that it is an illustrative example of what he means by the "self-referential loop." The Moebius strip is one continuous looping surface, even though at any given point it is apparently dualistic ("binary"). Žižek (like Hegel and Plato before him) shows that multitude is not some fundamental ontological "presence." There is multitude insofar as the One does not coincide with itself. The originary division is not between One and Other (multitude), but between the One and itself. *It is thus the lack of a binary signifier that spawns truth as the struggle for the truth*: the multitude emerges from the inconsistency of the One with itself, as the effort to "fill in the gap of the missing binary signifier."[10] Dialectical materialism does not involve the reconciliation of binary "opposites" in some third term. There is no emphasis on a binary opposition between two polar concepts; again, the most fundamental inconsistency is *inherent* to the One. The fundamental difference (inherent to the Master-Signifier) is the split between the signifier and the empty "place" of its inscription: the Master-Signifier functions not only as a "quilting point," but also as the signifier of the *impossibility* of signifying something. The One in its inherent inconsistency evokes the very zero-point of signification. The Master-Signifier is thus the empty nonsense that pins down and thereby generates the realm of what makes sense. This realm (symbolic reality) is never as coherent as it seems: it always involves the struggle for hegemony between competing and antagonistic realities:

> If one translates the moral of this story into the language of philosophy, it becomes evident that the One, the master-signifier which is supposed to constitute the "divine gift" of intelligibility, is not exempt from the process of totalization. The obvious problem is that there are various simulacra of the One, various totalizing opportunities, which are inherently destabilized because they are only maintained by the fantasy of an original One. In other words, the Hegelian "true infinite" is the infinity generated by the self-relating of a totality, by the short-circuit which makes totality an element of itself (or, rather, which makes a genus its own species), which makes re-presentation part of presence itself.[11]

The obverse of the Master-Signifier is *objet petit a*, the object of fantasy. *Objet a* is the remainder of repressed enjoyment that is the underside of

---

[10]   Slavoj Žižek, "An Answer to Two Questions," in Adrian Johnston's *Badiou, Žižek, and Political Transformations: The Cadence of Change*, (Evanston: Northwestern University Press, 2009), p. 195.

[11]   See Markus Gabriel and Slavoj Žižek, *Mythology, Madness and Laughter: Subjectivity in German Idealism* (London and New York: Continuum, 2009), p. 10.

the big Other, the symbolic register. Initially, social reality is made possible by the illusion of consistency allowed by ideological fantasy. However, though fantasy constructions mask the Real, such efforts are doomed from the outset. The repressed Real always returns in the form of some traumatic intrusion, and reveals the inherent inconsistency of the Master-Signifier.

Paradoxically, the masculine subject supports the symbolic order precisely by maintaining a (false) distance from the big Other. The masculine subject indulges in – and unconsciously identifies with – a fantasy, a mythical exception to the universal phallic function, e.g., the primordial father, or the capitalist Master who ignores public law and (allegedly) enjoys completely. Along the same lines, Žižek argues that nationalistic mobilizations – and the masculine logic that underlies them – are sustained by an obscene superego injunction, the dark side of the public law. This superego injunction is the imperative to enjoy in and through the mythical exception, e.g., the mythical father of unrestrained *jouissance*. Similarly, nationalist mobilizations involve a relationship toward a phantasmatic Thing, which represents the incarnation of enjoyment. Nationalist movements today are privileged portals for enjoyment because of the obscene "nightly law" – the superego injunction to enjoy – that sustains global capitalism. But the liberal-democratic ideology of multiculturalism is complicit in the rise of nationalism because of liberalism's accommodation with capitalism. Insofar as the ideology of liberal democracy sustains capitalism, democracy is impotent in the face of nationalism, ethnic violence, and fundamentalism: democratic movements will always be co-opted by nationalist populism.

For such reasons, Žižek argues that the liberal-democratic notion of universality as a neutral space for compromise is misguided. Universality is the engaged struggle for truth; truth arises through the identification with the symbolic order's point of exclusion (e.g., those who are made abject and excluded by the hegemonic ideology).

An Ethics of the Real

Dialectical materialism points toward the Real by highlighting the inconsistency of imaginary-symbolic reality. But the inevitable return of the Real shows the sense in which there is no big Other: any symbolic universe is incomplete and inconsistent. In other words, because reality itself is "unfinished," there can be no all-encompassing metalanguage.

Along these lines, material reality (the universe) is incomplete; it is non-All. This, Žižek argues, is *the true formula of materialism*: material reality is non-All. There is no complete notional determination of material reality.

This recognition (that the big Other does not exist) signifies the moment of atheism in Žižek's Christian-materialism: "This is the kind of God an authentic left needs: a God who wholly 'became man' – a comrade among us, crucified together with two social outcasts – and who not only 'doesn't exist' but also himself knows this, accepting his erasure, entirely passing over into the love that binds members of the Holy Ghost (the party, the emancipatory collective)."[12] In sum, the Master-Signifier is an imposture that conceals a void.

By acknowledging this void at the heart of the law and traversing the fantasy through the act, the subject annuls herself as subject, accepts her destitution, and transforms fantasy, desire, and the economy of enjoyment in ways that cannot be determined in advance. In any actual set of circumstances, external obstacles configure the subject's options. The subject must let go of excuses and exploit the given circumstances in order to deploy the potentials which are configured by the external obstacles. When the decision takes the form of a heroic confrontation with the Real as the return of the repressed, such an act may transform the very parameters of meaning. Through the act, subjects intervene in the symbolic order and re-inscribe the Real into a new symbolic texture that was not foreseeable from within the original coordinates of the situation. In this respect, the act can be both a form of symbolic suicide and of symbolic rebirth. Žižek shows throughout his works that it is precisely this utopian leap that develops subjectivity. In itself, the subject is the self-reflexive negativity evoked in Hegelian dialectic, but in the political act, subjectivity is enacted and the only true "utopia" is realized, *as the act itself.*

An ethics of the imaginary is grounded in some notion of the supreme good. An ethics of the symbolic is grounded in some set of moral norms or principles, and might also be called an ethics of the word. By contrast, an ethics of the Real means that the subject cannot rely on any external, symbolic support of, or justification for decisions. Such an ethics of the Real involves encountering – by traversing the fantasy through the act – the "impossibility" around which symbolic order is constructed. Thus an ethics of the Real cannot be grounded in any calculus of pleasure or utility, because such an ethics involves fidelity to the Real as the crack or gap in symbolic reality.

---

[12] See Slavoj Žižek, "The Soul of the Party," in *New Statesman* (April 1, 2010), available online at http://www.newstatesman.com/religion/2010/04/god-order-wisdom-paul-love.

How is Hegelian dialectic relevant to an ethics of the Real? On Žižek's reading, Hegel's Absolute Knowledge anticipates the Lacanian recognition that there is no big Other, that the symbolic order is irreducibly inconsistent. Again, the big Other does not exist insofar as the symbolic order is an inadequate attempt to fill out the empty space of the primordial renunciation of "impossible" Real enjoyment. Along the same lines, according to Žižek's reading of Hegel, the point of dialectic is not to resolve antagonisms, but to enact a parallax shift between two antagonistic perspectives. In this sense, Hegelian Absolute Knowledge is homologous to the final moment in the psychoanalytic process, the *passe*, as an encounter with the lack (parallax gap) inherent to symbolic reality. Thus the implicit negativity of Hegelian dialectic anticipates Lacan's concept of traversing the fantasy, that is, experiencing the lack in the symbolic big Other. In traversing the fantasy, the analysand achieves the pure desire of the analyst, a desire which is not for any particular end or object of goal, but is non-pathological, in the sense that it is not linked to any phantasmatic object, but is instead oriented toward the lack in the symbolic register. In assuming the place of the analyst, the analysand effectively embodies the Hegelian Absolute Knowledge as the experience of the irremediable loss inherent to the symbolic order.

Again, Žižek discerns in Hegel an anticipation of Lacan's feminine logic of sexuation as non-All: "the Hegelian truth is precisely without the external limitation/exception that would serve as its measure-standard, which is why its criterion is absolutely immanent: one compares a statement with itself, with its own process of enunciation." Because there is no external standard of truth, Hegelian totality is an inconsistent totality, infinite in the sense that there is no exception to serve as an external limit. Hegelian totality is thus homologous to the feminine logic of non-All.[13] Žižek argues that insofar as any symbolic identity or reality is inconsistent/incomplete (non-All), the subject has the potential to be radically autonomous, or free.

Žižek emphasizes the link between Hegel's constitutive "madness of reason" and Lacan's interpretation of the Freudian death drive as an ineradicable moment of unreason that is inherent to subjectivity as such. Drive is the driving force of desire, and drive as such is death drive. The death drive indicates the radical autonomy or freedom of the subject, and the possibility of traversing the fantasy and encountering the Real

---

[13] Slavoj Žižek, in *Hegel & the Infinite: Religion, Politics, and Dialectic*, ed. Slavoj Žižek, Clayton Crockett, and Creston Davis, (New York: Columbia University Press, 2011), pp. 226–7.

through the ethico-political act of a feminine subject. By traversing the fantasy through the act, a feminine subject achieves an ethics of the Real: the goal is to apprehend the proximity of the Real and then refuse to give way on our desire. In the act, the subject renounces the support of the symbolic big Other. The feminine subject undermines the universality of the phallic function; she sees through the posturing display and false allure of the fascinating "presence" of the phallic signifier. She discerns in the Master-Signifier the doomed attempt to fill out the inconsistency of the symbolic, big Other.

The feminine subject position is inherently subversive because it does not rely on any phantasmatic exception to the phallic economy and the public law. Through her unreserved identification with the symbolic order, the feminine subject forces the confrontation with the inconsistency in the big Other. The feminine subject embodies revolutionary, subversive potential precisely because she is *fully immersed* (without exception) in the symbolic order. In other words, insofar as a masculine subject enjoins submission to the public law while secretly indulging in the transgression of it, he actually supports the status quo (the vicious cycle of law and its transgression). It can be the full submission to the public law that most effectively undermines a sociosymbolic order or regime; thus sometimes the most *violent* act can be to do nothing. The feminine subject recognizes the mythical character of the exception that is implicit to the rule of phallic universality. She rejects the imposture of the exceptional master, and her very identification with the public law serves to bring into relief the masculine strategy of public compliance and secret transgression.

Again, the symbolic order is a response to the originary repression or exclusion of the Real, but the repressed Real always returns. This is one reason why Žižek argues in *Metastases* (and several other works) that the universal is not conceptual: the universal is the *struggle* for conceptualization. The truth is not revealed in the intersubjective, sociosymbolic network. On the contrary, the universal (partisan) truth of an entire situation is accessible only from the position of those who are excluded. Their exclusion is yet another mark of the inconsistency of the sociosymbolic big Other; thus the "truth" of the entire social field (the big Other) is located in the experiences of those who are systematically excluded and made abject by the hegemonic ideology. In sum, *universal* truth is only revealed in and through a *contingent* locus in the social system.

Žižek's dialectical materialism embraces the "chanciness" of this contingency. Regarding a particular action, there may be no reliable indicators – no horizon of meaning – that allow us to recognize the ethico-political act proper, and to distinguish it from hysterical acting out and from the impotent *passage à l'acte*. In other words, even if we can distinguish in theory between hysterical acting out, the passage to act, and the act proper, I may not know whether my particular behavior on a specific occasion is acting out, or whether it is the passage to act, or whether it is the act proper. But the act proper involves the radical reinvention of the subject's symbolic reality and her symbolic identity: the act proper has an affinity with the impossible Real, as does the subject as such who "exists only through his own impossibility."[14] Along these lines, radical contingency implies that reality is an inconsistent multiplicity that cannot be unified or totalized (again, this is what it means to say that the big Other does not exist).

Because Capital functions today as the Real that disrupts the imaginary and the symbolic registers, there is no purely formal democracy: democratic procedures are inherently corrupted so as to favor the wealthy and to further disenfranchise the poor. Efforts to make democratic procedures more inclusive respect national boundaries even when global capitalism does not. The expansion of networks of communication has proved to further – not democratic inclusiveness – but the social antagonism, disruption, and violence inherent to world market globalization. The Real of Capital functions so as to ensure that, around the world, the difference that makes a difference is the division between the rich, privileged few and billions of excluded poor. Thus the task for the left today involves politicizing the economy, and traversing the fantasy of democracy through an act that will reinvent a new sociosymbolic order. This is possible due to the subversive potential of the feminine subject.

Dialectical materialism's critique of capitalist ideology can free the subject from the obscene superego injunction to enjoy. This means that you can still enjoy, but you are also free to *not* enjoy. Traversing the fantasy through the Lacanian act reinvents the symbolic universe, and transfigures Real *jouissance*. It is thus possible to overcome ideology insofar as interventions in the symbolic can produce changes in the Real. In ideological discourse, any antithesis presupposes the same general *form* (the same symbolic reality) as the thesis, but involves a transfiguration of the *content* of the thesis within the limits of this formal-symbolic dimension. The synthesis – as the negation of negation – marks the failure of the formal system (understanding of reality) that is implicit to both the thesis and the antithesis. The universal *is this failure*; the universal is not some determinate

---

[14] Slavoj Žižek, *On Belief* (London and New York: Routledge, 2004), p. 89.

form or some specific content. Rather, the universal is the Real as the negativity that undermines our understanding of reality. The universal is the return of the repressed Real, an "impossible" event that nonetheless sometimes actually occurs (as in "miracles" like love or political revolution). Repression of the Real serves to configure a determinate, symbolic order, but the repressed Real inevitably returns as the impossibility that undermines symbolic order. Just as the inevitable return of the repressed undermines the fantasy of unity that is the ego, so also does the return of the Real highlight the inadequacy of capitalist ideology, which revolves around the imaginary object that is the ego. Moreover, the return of the Real as traumatic intrusion (e.g., economic and ecological crises), reveals the masturbatory idiocy implicit to global capitalism's injunction to ever more enjoyment.

The free act of a subject eludes symbolization and thus bears an affinity to the Real. Žižek shows how the act reactualizes subversive potentiality that was repressed by the pre-existing symbolic order. Through the act, subjects can re-inscribe this revolutionary potential into present circumstances. In the political act of a revolutionary collective – if we act as if the choice is not forced and choose the impossible – a community of believers in a cause, by acting together, may reinvent the very parameters of meaning. The Real is the point of (im)possibility that is the only universality that always returns, because it both constitutes and undermines any symbolic order. But because a symbolic order is constituted through the repression of the traumatic, intrusive Real, the Real is a *negative* form of universality.

The Paradox of Singular Universality

Žižek argues that the dictatorship of the proletariat is just such a "direct intrusion of universality into the political field."[15] The most basic meaning of the "dictatorship of the proletariat" is that moment in which a sociosymbolic order is suspended through the act of a revolutionary collective. The leftist revolutionary collective embodies the position of *singular universality* by speaking and acting from identification with the gap in the symbolic order, not from the perspective of some particular national, cultural, or ethnic identification.

Particularity has to do with my national, social, or communal identity. But universal singularity involves a subject who is subtracted from any particular life-world. The paradox is the "short circuit" through which a

---

[15]   Slavoj Žižek, *In Defense of Lost Causes* (London and New York: Verso, 2008), p. 415.

singular subject bypasses the particularity of substantial identifications (national, communal, etc.) and instead directly identifies with the universal:

> This identification with the Universal is not the identification with an all-encompassing global Substance ("humanity"), but the identification with a universal ethico-political principle – a universal religious collective, a scientific collective, a global revolutionary organization, all of which are in principle accessible to everyone. [...] The paradox is thus that one participates in the universal dimension of the "public" sphere precisely as a singular individual extracted from or even opposed to one's substantial communal identification – one is truly universal only as radically singular, in the interstices of communal identities.[16]

Singular universality – as an identification with the gap in the global capitalist symbolic order – is what distinguishes communism from both liberal democracy and from socialism. Žižek refers (in *First as Tragedy, then as Farce*) to Frantz Fanon as an example of a leftist revolutionary who embodied and articulated the position of singular universality. Here is the quotation from Fanon that indicates the subtractive "space" of singular universality:

> I am a man, and what I have to recapture is the whole past of the world. I am not responsible solely for the slave revolt in Santo Domingo. Every time a man has contributed to the victory of the dignity of the spirit, every time a man has said no to an attempt to subjugate his fellows, I have felt solidarity with his act. In no way does my basic vocation have to be drawn from the past of peoples of color. In no way do I have to dedicate myself to reviving a black civilization unjustly ignored. I will not make myself the man of any past [...] My black skin is not a repository for specific values [...] Haven't I got better things to do on this earth than avenge the Blacks of the seventeenth century? [...] I as a man of color do not have the right to hope that in the white man there will be a crystallization of guilt toward the past of my race. I as a man of color do not have the right to seek ways of stamping down the pride of my former master. I have neither the right nor the duty to demand reparations for my subjugated ancestors. There is no black mission; there is no white burden [...] I find myself one day in the world and I acknowledge one right for myself: the right to demand human behavior from the other [...] I do not want to be the victim of the Ruse of a black world [...] Am I going to ask today's white men to answer for the slave traders of the seventeenth century? Am I going to try by every means available to cause guilt to burgeon

16 Slavoj Žižek, *The Parallax View* (Cambridge, MA: MIT Press, 2006), p. 10.

311

in their souls? [...] I am not a slave to slavery that dehumanized my ancestors [...] it would be of enormous interest to discover a black literature or architecture from the third century before Christ. We would be overjoyed to learn of the existence of a correspondence between some black philosopher and Plato. But we can absolutely not see how this fact would change the lives of eight-year-old kids working in the cane fields of Martinique or Guadeloupe.[17]

Singular universality is the link between Žižek's dialectical materialist ontology and his rehabilitation of the concept of the dictatorship of the proletariat. But how, precisely, are we to understand what Žižek means by "the proletariat"?

Žižek contrasts the masculine universality of "the people" (used as a Master-Signifier), with the feminine universality implicit to "the proletariat": *"The people is inclusive, the proletariat is exclusive; the people fights intruders, parasites, those who obstruct its full self-assertion, the proletariat fights a struggle which divides the people at its very core. The people wants to assert itself, the proletariat wants to abolish itself"*.[18] But how, today, could the dictatorship be established?

Žižek insists that we must be realists, and demand the impossible. Since "impossible" miracles like love and political revolution sometimes occur, one of the first steps toward realizing the impossible is to recognize the extent to which today we are all subjects who are being deprived of our substance; in other words, more and more we are all proletarians:

It is as if the three components of the production process – intellectual planning and marketing, material production, the providing of material resources – are more and more autonomized, emerging as three separate spheres. In its social consequences, this separation appears in the guise of the "three main classes" of today's developed societies, which are precisely *not* classes but three fractions of the working class: intellectual labourers, the old manual working class, and the outcasts (unemployed, or living in slums and other interstices of the public space). The working class is thus split into three, each part with its own "way of life" and ideology: the enlightened hedonism and liberal multiculturalism of the intellectual class, the populist fundamentalism of the working class, and the more extreme, singular forms of the outcast fraction. In

---

[17] This quotation from Frantz Fanon is in Žižek's *First as Tragedy, then as Farce* pp. 117–18. The quotation here has been slightly altered in order to conform more closely to the most recent translation of Fanon's *Peau noire, masques blancs*. See *Black Skin, White Masks*, trans. Richard Philcox (New York: Grove Press 2008), pp. 201–5.

[18] Slavoj Žižek, *In Defense of Lost Causes* (London and New York: Verso, 2008), p. 415.

Hegelese, this triad is clearly the triad of the universal (intellectual workers), particular (manual workers), and singular (outcasts). The outcome of this process is the gradual disintegration of social life proper, of a public space in which all three fractions could meet – and "identity" politics in all its forms is a supplement for this loss. Identity politics acquires a specific form in each of the three fractions: postmodern multicultural identity politics in the intellectual class, regressive populist fundamentalism in the working class, half-illegal initiatic groups (criminal gangs, religious sects, etc.) among the outcasts. What they all share is recourse to a particular identity as a substitute for the missing universal public space.

The proletariat is thus divided into three, each part played off against the others: intellectual labourers full of cultural prejudices against the "redneck" workers; workers who display a populist hatred of intellectuals and outcasts; outcasts who are antagonistic to society as such. The old call "Proletarians, unite!" is thus more pertinent than ever: in the new conditions of "post-industrial" capitalism, the unity of the three fractions of the working class *is* already their victory."[19]

Utopias emerge through the act, when we cannot do otherwise. And today, from around the world, there are leftists who realize that global capitalism is leading the world to catastrophe. These revolutionaries, disappointed by failure of twentieth-century Communism, are ready to "begin from the beginning" and reinvent the idea of communism on a new foundation. These leftists are those "who have really awakened from the utopian dream which holds most of us under its sway. They, not those nostalgics for twentieth-century 'Really Existing Socialism,' are our only hope."[20]

There is No Blueprint for the Future

What then is to be done, if we are to reinvent the idea of communism for today? Today we are witnessing the increasing privatization of the commons: the commons are being enclosed by the wealthy elite at the expense of the majority of the world's citizens. But it is crucial to realize that the utopian moment of the ethico-political act is *only the beginning*. The true work of revolution begins the morning after, when a new way of life and a new symbolic reality must be invented:

---

[19] See *The Idea of Communism*, ed. Costas Douzinas and Slavoj Žižek, (London and New York: Verso, 2010), pp. 225–6.

[20] Slavoj Žižek, *First as Tragedy, then as Farce* (London: Verso, 2009), pp. 156–7.

In a genuine revolutionary breakthrough, the utopian future is neither simply fully realized, present, nor simply evoked as a distant promise which justified present violence – it is rather as if, in a unique suspension of temporality, in the short-circuit between the present and the future, we are – as if by Grace – for a brief time allowed to act *as if* the utopian future is (not yet fully here, but) already at hand, just there to be seized. Revolution is experienced not as a present hardship we have to endure for the happiness and freedom of future generations, but as the present hardship over which this future happiness and freedom already cast their shadow – in it, we are already free even as we fight for freedom; we are already happy even as we fight for happiness, no matter how difficult the circumstances.[21]

However, Žižek emphasizes throughout his works that the tragedy of human existence is that we cannot determine any blueprint in advance. It is only through participating in the movement and engaging in the struggle for truth that we learn. We cannot know where history is going; we make history under conditions we do not choose, and the future is an abyss.

But even though the future is an abyss, nonetheless it is likely that Žižek will prove to be the twenty-first century's definitive philosopher. Žižek's fusion of Hegel and Lacan enables a new approach to the problem of truth. Unlike some previous dialectical philosophers, Žižek clearly indicates the limit of dialectic: namely, the Real as fundamental negativity or "parallax gap." He avoids pretensions to completeness by stressing throughout his works that any totality is inherently inconsistent, and it is this dialectical materialist approach that enables his Marxist-style critique of ideology. For such reasons, the next innovative philosophical orientation will have to define itself through a critical relation toward Žižek's dialectical materialism.

---

[21] Slavoj Žižek, "Afterword: Lenin's Choice," in *Revolution at the Gates: Žižek on Lenin, the 1917 Writings*, ed. Slavoj Žižek (London: Verso, 2002), pp. 259–60.

Further Reading

Adam, Barbara, Ulrich Beck, and Joost van Loon (eds.). *The Risk Society and Beyond: Critical Issues for Social Theory*. London: SAGE Publications, 2000.

Adorno, Theodor, and Max Horkheimer. *Dialectic of Enlightenment*, trans. John Cumming. London and New York: Verso, 1997.

Agamben, Giorgio. *Homo Sacer: Sovereign Power and Bare Life*. Stanford: Stanford University Press, 1998.

Althusser, Louis. *Lenin and Philosophy, and Other Essays*. London: New Left Books, 1971.

Althusser, Louis. "Ideology and Ideological State Apparatuses (Notes Towards an Investigation)," in Slavoj Žižek (ed.) *Mapping Ideology*. London and New York: Verso, 1994, pp. 100–40.

Badiou, Alain. *Saint Paul: la fondation de l'universalisme*. Paris: Presses universitaires de France, 1997.

Badiou, Alain. *Being and Event*, trans. Oliver Feltham. London and New York: Continuum, 2005.

Badiou, Alain. *Logics of Worlds (Being and Event, 2)*. London and New York: Continuum, 2009.

Badiou, Alain. *Pocket Pantheon*, trans. David Macey. London and New York: Verso, 2009.

Benjamin, Walter. *Illuminations: Essays and Reflections*, ed. with an introduction by Hannah Arendt. New York: Schocken Books, 1969.

Bordwell, David, and Noël Carroll (eds.). *Post-Theory*. Madison, WI: University of Wisconsin Press, 1996.

Boucher, Geoff, Jason Glynos, and Matthew Sharpe. *Traversing the Fantasy*. Aldershot, UK: Ashgate, 2005.

Žižek: A Reader's Guide, First Edition. Kelsey Wood.
© 2012 John Wiley & Sons, Inc. Published 2012 by John Wiley & Sons, Inc.

Bowman, Paul, and Richard Stamp. *The Truth of Žižek*. London and New York: Continuum, 2007.

Burbidge, John. *The Logic of Hegel's* Logic. Ontario: Broadview Press, 2006.

Butler, Judith. *Gender Trouble: Feminism and the Subversion of Identity*. London and New York: Routledge, 1990.

Butler, Judith. *Bodies that Matter: On the Discursive Limits of Sex*. London and New York: Routledge, 1993.

Butler, Judith, Ernesto Laclau, and Slavoj Žižek. *Contingency, Hegemony, Universality: Contemporary Dialogues on the Left*. London and New York: Verso, 2000.

Butler, Rex. *Slavoj Žižek: Live Theory*. London and New York: Continuum, 2005.

Chion, Michel. "The Impossible Embodiment," in Slavoj Žižek (ed.) *Everything You Always Wanted to Know about Lacan (But Were Afraid to Ask Hitchcock)*. London and New York: Verso, 1992, pp. 195–207.

Chion, Michel. *David Lynch*, trans. Robert Julian. London: British Film Institute, 1995. First published, Paris: Editions de l'Etoile/*Cahiers du cinema*, 1992.

Clemens, Justin, and Russell Grigg. *Jacques Lacan and the Other Side of Psychoanalysis: Reflections on* Seminar XVII. Durham, NC, and London: Duke University Press, 2006.

Copjec, Joan. *Supposing the Subject*. Cambridge, MA: MIT Press, 1994.

Copjec, Joan. *Read My Desire: Lacan Against the Historicists*. Cambridge, MA: MIT Press, 1996.

Copjec, Joan. *Imagine There's No Woman: Ethics and Sublimation*. Cambridge, MA: MIT Press, 2004.

Copjec, Joan (ed.). *Radical Evil*. London and New York: Verso, 1996.

Daly, Glyn. "Ideology and its Paradoxes: Dimensions of Fantasy and Enjoyment," *Journal of Political Ideologies*, vol. 4/2, 1999, pp. 219–38.

Dean, Jodi. *Žižek's Politics*. London and New York: Routledge, 2006.

Deleuze, Gilles. *Sacher Masoch: An Interpretation. Together with the Entire Text of "Venus in Furs,"* trans. Jean McNeil. London: Faber and Faber, 1971.

Deleuze, Gilles. *Difference and Repetition*, trans. Paul Patton. New York: Columbia University Press, 1990.

Deleuze, Gilles. *The Logic of Sense*. New York: Columbia University Press, 1995.

Deleuze, Gilles, and Felix Guattari. *Anti-Oedipus: Capitalism and Schizophrenia*, trans. Robert Hurley, Mark Seem, and Helen Lane. Minneapolis: University of Minnesota Press, 1983.

Derrida, Jacques. *The Post Card: From Socrates to Freud and Beyond*, trans. Alan Bass. Chicago: University of Chicago Press, 1993.

Derrida, Jacques. *Spectres of Marx: The State of the Debt, the Work of Mourning, and the New International*. London and New York: Routledge, 1994.

Descartes, René. *Meditations on First Philosophy with Selections from the Objections and Replies*, trans. John Cottingham. Cambridge: Cambridge University Press, 1996.

Descombes, Vincent. *Modern French Philosophy*, trans. L. Scott-Fox and J. M. Harding. Cambridge: Cambridge University Press, 1981.

Further Reading

Dolar, Mladen. "Hitchcock's Objects," in Slavoj Žižek (ed.) *Everything You Always Wanted to Know about Lacan (But Were Afraid to Ask Hitchcock)*. London and New York: Verso, 1992, pp. 31–46.

Dolar, Mladen. "Beyond Interpellation," *Qui Parle*, vol. 6, 1993, pp. 73–96.

Dolar, Mladen. "Cogito as the Subject of the Unconscious," in Slavoj Žižek (ed.) *Cogito and the Unconscious*. Durham, NC: Duke University Press, 1998, pp. 11–40.

Dolar, Mladen, and Slavoj Žižek. *Opera's Second Death*. London and New York: Routledge, 2002.

Douzinas, Costas, and Slavoj Žižek. *The Idea of Communism*. London and New York: Verso, 2010.

Eagleton, Terry. "Enjoy!" *Paragraph*, vol. 24, 2001, pp. 40–52.

Evans, Dylan. *An Introductory Dictionary of Lacanian Psychoanalysis*. London and New York: Routledge, 1996.

Fink, Bruce. *The Lacanian Subject: Between Language and Jouissance*. Princeton, NJ: Princeton University Press, 1995.

Fink, Bruce. *A Clinical Introduction to Lacanian Psychoanalysis: Theory and Technique*. Cambridge, MA: Harvard University Press, 1997.

Fink, Bruce. *Lacan to the Letter*. Minneapolis: University of Minnesota Press, 2004.

Freud, Sigmund. *The Standard Edition of the Complete Psychological Works of Sigmund Freud, Volume V* (1900–1). London: Hogarth Press, 1953.

Freud, Sigmund. *The Standard Edition of the Complete Psychological Works of Sigmund Freud, Volume VII* (1901–5). London: Hogarth Press, 1953.

Freud, Sigmund. *The Standard Edition of the Complete Psychological Works of Sigmund Freud, Volume X* (1909). London: Hogarth Press, 1955.

Freud, Sigmund. *The Standard Edition of the Complete Psychological Works of Sigmund Freud, Volume XXI* (1927–31). London: Hogarth Press, 1964.

Freud, Sigmund. *The Standard Edition of the Complete Psychological Works of Sigmund Freud, Volume XXII* (1932–6). London: Hogarth Press, 1964.

Freud, Sigmund. *The Standard Edition of the Complete Psychological Works of Sigmund Freud, Volume XXIII* (1937–9). London: Hogarth Press, 1964.

Gabriel, Markus, and Slavoj Žižek. *Mythology, Madness, and Laughter: Subjectivity in German Idealism*, London and New York: Continuum, 2009.

Gould, Stephen Jay. "Phyletic Size Decrease in Hershey Bars," in *Hen's Teeth and Horse's Toes*. London and New York: Norton, 1983, pp. 313–19.

Hardt, Michael, and Antonio Negri. *Empire*. Cambridge, MA: Harvard University Press, 2000.

Harvey, David. *A Companion to Marx's* Capital. London and New York: Verso, 2010.

Hegel, Georg Wilhelm Friedrich. *Philosophy of Right*, trans. T. M. Knox. Oxford: Clarendon Press, 1942.

Hegel, Georg Wilhelm Friedrich. *The Science of Logic*, trans. A. V. Miller. London: Allen and Unwin, 1969.

Hegel, Georg Wilhelm Friedrich. *Phenomenology of Spirit*, trans. A. V. Miller, analysis and forward by J. N. Findlay. Oxford: Oxford University Press, 1977.

Hegel, Georg Wilhelm Friedrich. *The Encyclopedia Logic*, trans. T. F. Geraets, W. A. Suchting, and H. S. Harris. Indianapolis: Hackett, 1991.

Heidegger, Martin. *Being and Time*, trans. John Macquarrie and Edward Robinson. Oxford: Blackwell, 1978.

Homer, Sean. *Jacques Lacan*. London and New York: Routledge, 2005.

Jameson, Fredric. *The Prison-House of Language: A Critical Account of Structuralism and Russian Formalism*. Princeton, NJ: Princeton University Press, 1972.

Johnston, Adrian. *Žižek's Ontology: A Transcendental Materialist Theory of Subjectivity*. Evanston: Northwest University Press, 2008.

Johnston, Adrian. *Badiou, Žižek, and Political Transformations: The Cadence of Change*. Evanston: Northwest University Press, 2009.

Kant, Immanuel. *Critique of Pure Reason*, trans. Norman Kemp Smith. New York: St Martin's Press, 1965.

Kant, Immanuel. *Grounding for the Metaphysics of Morals* (3rd edn.), trans. James Ellington. Indianapolis: Hackett, 1993.

Kant, Immanuel. *Critique of Practical Reason*, ed. Mary Gregor, introduction by Andrews Reath. Cambridge: Cambridge University Press, 1997.

Kant, Immanuel. "An Answer to the Question: What is Enlightenment?" http://www.english.upenn.edu/~mgamer/Etexts/kant.html (accessed August 2, 2010).

Kay, Sarah. *Žižek: A Critical Introduction*. Cambridge: Polity Press, 2003.

Kierkegaard, Søren. *Fear and Trembling; Repetition*, ed. and trans. with introduction and notes by Howard Hong and Edna Hong. Princeton, NJ: Princeton University Press, 1983.

Kieślowski, Krzysztof. *Kieślowski on Kieślowski*. London: Faber and Faber, 1993.

Kojève, Alexandre. *Introduction to the Reading of Hegel*. New York: Basic Books, 1969.

Lacan, Jacques. *The Four Fundamental Concepts of Psychoanalysis, The Seminar of Jacques Lacan, Book XI*, ed. Jacques-Alain Miller, trans. Alan Sheridan. New York: Norton, 1981/1998.

Lacan, Jacques. *Freud's Papers on Technique, 1953–1954, The Seminar of Jacques Lacan, Book I*, ed. Jacques-Alain Miller, trans. with notes by John Forrester. New York: Norton, 1988.

Lacan, Jacques. *The Ego in Freud's Theory and in the Technique of Psychoanalysis, 1954–1955, The Seminar of Jacques Lacan, Book II*, ed. Jacques-Alain Miller, trans. Sylvana Tomaselli, with notes by John Forrester. New York: Norton, 1988.

Lacan, Jacques. *The Ethics of Psychoanalysis, 1959–1960, The Seminar of Jacques Lacan, Book VIII*, ed. Jacques-Alain Miller, trans. with notes by Dennis Porter. New York: Norton, 1992.

Lacan, Jacques. *The Psychoses, 1955–1956, The Seminar of Jacques Lacan, Book III*, ed. Jacques-Alain Miller, trans. with notes by Russell Grigg. New York: Norton, 1993.

Lacan, Jacques. *On Feminine Sexuality, The Limits of Love and Knowledge, 1972–1973: Encore, The Seminar of Jacques Lacan, Book XX*, trans. with notes by Bruce Fink. New York: Norton, 1998.

Lacan, Jacques. *Écrits*, trans. Bruce Fink. New York: Norton, 2002/2006.

Lacan, Jacques. *The Other Side of Psychoanalysis, The Seminar of Jacques Lacan, Book VII*, trans. Russell Grigg. New York: Norton, 2007.

Laclau, Ernesto. *New Reflections on The Revolution of Our Time*. London and New York: Verso, 1990.

Laclau, Ernesto, and Chantal Mouffe. *Hegemony and Socialist Strategy*. London and New York: Verso, 1985.

Leader, Darien, and Judy Groves. *Lacan for Beginners*. Cambridge: Icon Books, 1995.

Marx, Karl, and Friedrich Engels. *The Marx-Engels Reader* (2nd edn.), ed. Robert C. Tucker. New York: Norton, 1978.

McCumber, John. *The Company of Words: Hegel, Language, and Systematic Philosophy*. Evanston: Northwestern University Press, 1993.

Myers, Tony. *Slavoj Žižek*. London and New York: Routledge, 2003.

Parker, Ian. *Slavoj Žižek: A Critical Introduction*. London: Pluto Press, 2004.

Pascal, Blaise. *Pensées*, trans. with an introduction by A. J. Krailsheimer. Harmondsworth: Penguin, 1966.

Pound, Marcus. *Žižek: A (Very) Critical Introduction*. Grand Rapids, MI, and Cambridge: Wm B. Eerdmans Publishing Co., 2008.

Reinhard, Kenneth. "Coming to America: Psychoanalytic Criticism in the Age of Žižek," *Paragraph*, vol. 24/2, 2001, p. 162.

Salecl, Renata, and Slavoj Žižek (eds.). *Gaze and Voice as Love Objects*. Durham, NC: Duke University Press, 1996.

Santner, Eric L. *My Own Private Germany: Daniel Paul Schreber's Secret History of Modernity*. Princeton, NJ: Princeton University Press, 1996.

Saussure, Ferdinand de. *Course in General Linguistics*, trans. Wade Baskin. Glasgow: Fontana/Collins, 1974.

Schelling, F. W. J. *Philosophical Inquiries into the Nature of Human Freedom*. La Salle, IL: Open Court, 1992.

Sharpe, Matthew. *Slavoj Žižek: A Little Piece of the Real*. Aldershot, UK: Ashgate, 2004.

Sloterdiijk, Peter. *Critique of Cynical Reason*. London and New York: Verso, 1988.

Stok, Danusia (ed.). *Kieślowski on Kieślowski*. London: Faber and Faber, 1993.

Wood, Kelsey. *Troubling Play: Meaning and Entity in Plato's* Parmenides. Albany: State University of New York Press, 2005.

Wood, Kelsey. *Plato's Later Dialectic and Continental Philosophy*. Amsterdam and New York: Rodopi, 2012.

Wright, Elizabeth. *Feminism and Psychoanalysis: A Critical Dictionary*. Oxford: Blackwell, 1992.

Wright, Elizabeth. *Lacan and Postfeminism*. Duxford, UK: Icon Books, and Lanham, MD: Totem Books, 2000.

Wright, Elizabeth, and Edmond Wright (eds.). *The Žižek Reader*. Malden, MA, and Oxford: Blackwell, 1999.

Žižek, Slavoj. *The Sublime Object of Ideology*. London and New York: Verso, 1989.

Žižek, Slavoj. *For They Know Not What They Do: Enjoyment as a Political Factor.* London and New York: Verso, 1991.

Žižek, Slavoj. *Looking Awry: An Introduction to Jacques Lacan through Popular Culture* Cambridge, MA, and London: MIT Press, 1991.

Žižek, Slavoj. *Enjoy Your Symptom! Jacques Lacan in Hollywood and Out.* New York and London: Routledge, 1992.

Žižek, Slavoj. *Tarrying With The Negative: Kant, Hegel, and the Critique of Ideology.* Durham, NC: Duke University Press, 1993.

Žižek, Slavoj. *The Metastases of Enjoyment: On Women and Causality.* London and New York: Verso, 1994.

Žižek, Slavoj. *The Indivisible Remainder: On Schelling and Related Matters.* London and New York: Verso, 1996.

Žižek, Slavoj. *The Plague of Fantasies.* London and New York: Verso, 1997.

Žižek, Slavoj. *The Ticklish Subject: The Absent Centre of Political Ontology.* London and New York: Verso. 1999.

Žižek, Slavoj. "When the Party Commits Suicide," *New Left Review,* 238, 1999, pp. 26–47.

Žižek, Slavoj. *The Art of the Ridiculous Sublime: On David Lynch's Lost Highway.* Seattle: The Walter Chapin Simpson Center for the Humanities, University of Washington, 2000.

Žižek, Slavoj. *The Fragile Absolute: or, Why is the Christian Legacy Worth Fighting For?* London and New York: Verso, 2000.

Žižek, Slavoj. *Did Somebody Say Totalitarianism? Five Interventions in the (Mis)use of a Notion.* London and New York: Verso, 2001.

Žižek, Slavoj. *On Belief.* London and New York: Routledge, 2001.

Žižek, Slavoj. *The Fright of Real Tears: Krzysztof Kieslowski between Theory and Post-Theory.* London: British Film Institute, 2001.

Žižek, Slavoj. "The Real of Sexual Difference," in Suzanne Barnard and Bruce Fink (eds.) *Reading Seminar XX: Lacan's Major Work on Love, Knowledge, and Feminine Sexuality.* Albany: State University of New York Press, 2002.

Žižek, Slavoj. *The Puppet and the Dwarf: The Perverse Core of Christianity.* Cambridge, MA: MIT Press, 2003.

Žižek, Slavoj. *Welcome to the Desert of the Real.* London and New York: Verso, 2002.

Žižek, Slavoj. *Organs without Bodies: On Deleuze and Consequences.* London and New York: Routledge, 2004.

Žižek, Slavoj. *Iraq: The Borrowed Kettle.* London and New York: Verso, 2004.

Žižek, Slavoj. *How to Read Lacan.* New York: Norton, 2006.

Žižek, Slavoj. *The Parallax View.* Cambridge, MA: MIT Press. 2006.

Žižek, Slavoj. *Violence.* New York: Picador, 2008.

Žižek, Slavoj. *In Defense of Lost Causes.* London and New York: Verso, 2008.

Žižek, Slavoj. *First as Tragedy, then as Farce.* London and New York: Verso, 2009.

Žižek, Slavoj. *Living in the End Times.* London and New York: Verso, 2010.

Žižek, Slavoj (ed.). *Everything You Always Wanted to Know about Lacan (But Were Afraid to Ask Hitchcock).* London and New York: Verso, 1992.

Žižek, Slavoj (ed.). *Mapping Ideology*. London and New York: Verso, 1994.

Žižek, Slavoj (ed.). Cogito *and the Unconscious*. Durham, NC: Duke University Press, 1998.

Žižek, Slavoj (ed.). *Revolution at the Gates: A Selection of Writings from February to October 1917: V. I. Lenin*. London and New York: Verso, 2002.

Žižek, Slavoj (ed.). *Lacan: The Silent Partners*. London and New York: Verso, 2006.

Žižek, Slavoj, Clayton Crockett, and Creston Davis (eds.). *Hegel & the Infinite: Religion, Politics, and Dialectic*. New York: Columbia University Press, 2011.

Žižek, Slavoj, and Glyn Daly. *Conversations with Žižek*. Cambridge: Polity Press, 2004.

Žižek, Slavoj, and John Milbank. *The Monstrosity of Christ: Paradox or Dialectic?*, ed. Creston Davis. Cambridge, MA: MIT Press, 2008.

Žižek, Slavoj, and F. W. J. von Schelling. *The Abyss of Freedom / Ages of the World*. Schelling's *Die Weltalter*, trans. Judith Norman. Ann Arbor, MI: Michigan University Press, 1997.

Zupančič, Alenka. *Ethics of the Real: Kant, Lacan*. London and New York: Verso, 2000.

Index

Note: Pages references followed by 'n', refer to entry only to be found in the Footnotes.

'Absolute Knowledge' 29, 33, 48, 83, 94, 307
abstract negativity 31, 87
abstraction 49
acceptance 289–94
Adorno, Theodor 142, 287
    Dialectic of Enlightenment (and Horkheimer) 165, 287
Afghanistan war 223
agape (Christian love) 285
alienation 18, 46, 77, 115–24
Allende, Salvador 265
Althusser, Louis 2, 43, 79, 287
anger 285–6
antidescriptivism 7, 8–9
anti-emancipatory project 166
anti-Semitism 275
anxiety 228
apartheid 273, 276
Aquinas, Thomas 33
Aristotle 185
Artificial Intelligence 165

atheism 262
Aufhebung (sublation) (Hegel) 94, 216–17
Augustine, St 294
Austin, J.L. 14

Badiou, Alain 2, 14, 38, 43, 64, 188, 139–40, 206, 218, 251, 252, 256, 274, 281, 286, 287, 292, 303
bargaining 286–8
Beck, Ulrich 63
becoming, concept of (Kierkegaard) 204
belief 51
Benjamin, Walter 202, 203, 204, 252, 264
    'Critique of Violence, The' 258, 263
    'Theses on the Philosophy of History' 196
Bergson, Henri 213

Žižek: A Reader's Guide, First Edition. Kelsey Wood.
© 2012 John Wiley & Sons, Inc. Published 2012 by John Wiley & Sons, Inc.

big Other 48, 51, 53, 59–61, 64, 77, 80, 87, 92, 101, 105, 106, 111–12, 122–3, 126, 128, 133, 144, 182, 184, 186–7, 188, 201–2, 207, 210, 218, 222, 224, 228, 229, 230, 232, 239, 249, 256, 261–2, 264, 297, 299, 301, 305, 308
Bin Laden, Osama 198
Bordwell, David 171, 174, 175
Bosnian war 108, 109–10, 112, 114
Boss, Medard 4
Brecht, Bertholdt: *Mother* 5n
Brown, John 254
Buddhism 167, 205
  Western 164, 165
Bush, George W. 198, 224, 225
Butler, Judith 37, 38, 95, 139
Butler, Rex 12

capitalism 58, 250, 260–1, 289–90
Carroll, Noel 171, 174
Cartesianism 32, 137
Casablanca (film) 147–8
Chávez, Hugo 265–6, 276
chess, imaginary and symbolic register and 20–1
Chesterton, G.K. 205
Chiesa, Lorenzo 289
Chinese communism 270
Christian fundamentalists 169
Christianity 155–62, 163–70
  revolutionary potential 201–211
Christian-materialism 184, 203, 204–9
cogito (Descartes) 38, 82, 136, 137, 138, 241
cogito ergo sum 32, 98
coincidence of opposites 18
Colours (film) 172
commodities 49, 52
commodity fetishism (Marx) 49, 50, 52
'commons' 273

communication, failure of 31
communism 166, 268–9, 276, 283
  collapse of 58
Communist Manifesto, The (Marx and Engels) 58, 59, 249–50
concrete universality 43, 175, 269
Copjec, Joan 100, 175
cultural capitalism 290
cyberspace 166, 190, 192, 194

Daly, Glyn 57, 63
death drive (Freud) 40–1, 42, 94, 103, 138, 139, 229. 296, 297, 307
Decalogue (film) 172
Deleuze, Gilles 43, 182, 212–19
  Anti-Oedipus 212, 217
  Difference and Repetition 212
  Logic of Sense, The 212, 218
  Mille Plateaux 213k
democracy 8, 9, 18, 53–4, 56, 62, 73–4, 102, 193–4, 199, 221, 223, 224–5, 256, 265, 277, 284, 291–2, 300–5
denial 281–5
depression 288
Derrida, Jacques 2, 37, 43, 75, 95, 176
Descartes 38, 98, 99, 136, 137, 138, 241
  Meditations 82
descriptivism 7, 8
desire 22–3, 26, 59, 80, 85, 126, 167, 168, 184, 228, 242
dialectical materialism 6, 10–13, 17, 18, 30, 39, 42–3, 44, 45, and *passim*
différance (Derrida) 176
discourses as social linkage 25
divine violence 258, 263–4
Doctor Zhivago (film) 212
documentation of trauma 65
Double Life of Veronique, The (film) 172, 179

Index

Dow Chemical 223, 226
drive 40–1, 65
    death 40–1, 42, 94, 103, 138, 139,
        229, 296, 297, 307
Duclos, Jacques 293

Eagleburger, Lawrence 265
ecological catastrophe 273
ego, formation in mirror phase
    19–20
Einstein, Alfred 235
emancipatory project 166
Emerson, Ralph Waldo 284
Engels, Friedrich 250
    Communist Manifesto, The (and
        Marx) 58, 59, 249–50
enjoyment 108–14
    see also jouissance
Essential, the 35
Eternity, notion of 160
ethical capitalism 290
ethical courage 199
exchange value 49–50
extension 7

falsification, ego as agent of 20
Fanon, Frantz 311
fantasy 23–4, 26, 52, 126, 195, 299
    concealment of antagonism through
        narrative 129
    empty gesture 133–5
    fall into symbolic castration and
        Law 131–2
    fundamental 228, 231
    ideological 26, 55, 60
    intersubjective 129
    Law is transgressive and
        violent 133
    staged for gaze of the Other 132–3
    transcendental schematism 127–8
    traversing 307
fascism 166
Feldmann, Arthur 281
feminine logic 84–5

feminine sexuation (Lacan) 210, 216,
    236
feminine subject position 31, 111–12
femme fatale 149–50
fetish 166
fetishism 18, 26–7, 46, 126
fetishist disavowal 128, 222, 224, 301
fetishization 27
Fichte 41, 116
fidelity 250
film noir 149
Fink, Bruce: *Lacan to the Letter* 79
forced choice 228
Foucault, Michel 213, 274
'framing' 174
French Revolution 252, 258, 283
Freud, Sigmund 2, 40–1, 138, 221,
    227, 229–30
    Interpretation of Dreams, The 57n,
        220
    Totem and Taboo 111
fundamental fantasy 228, 231

Gabriel, Markus 12
Gates, Bill 273
Gaulle, Charles de 31, 293
'gaze', concept of 51, 126, 178, 239
German Idealism 3, 10, 14, 24, 32,
    39, 40, 61, 94, 96, 98, 116, 139,
    296, 297, 303
global citizenship 273
Gnosticism 164
Gödel, Kurt 39
Goering, Herman 221
Grégoire, Abbé 293
grief, five stages of 278, 279
Guattari, Felix 212, 213–14, 217–18
Guevara, Che 254, 264, 285

Hardt, Michael 273
Hawking, Stephen 29
Hegel, G.F.W. 2, 3, 10, 29, 31, 32,
    83, 116, 138, 163, 205, 214, 215,
    259

Lectures on the Philosophy of Religion 101
'Logic of Essence' 103–5
Phenomenology of Spirit 37
Realphilosophie manuscripts 104
Science of Logic 104–5, 173
Heidegger, Martin 2, 4, 38, 43, 45, 139, 166, 176, 249, 254, 255
historical contingency 32–3
historicism 182
Hitler, Adolf 190, 251, 275, 294
Mein Kampf 191
Hollywood, terrorism and 195
Holocaust 166, 181, 261, 262
Homer 173
Horkheimer, Max 142, 165
Dialectic of Enlightenment (and Adorno) 165, 287
Hume, David 82–3, 95, 213
humor, sense of 4
Hurricane Katrina 258, 261
Hussein, Saddam 223, 224
Husserl, Edmund 99
hysteria 21–2

identity politics 33, 139, 313
ideological fantasy 26, 55, 60
ideology, Marxian definition 51
Id-Evil 153
imaginary ego 117, 127
imaginary register 20, 23, 76, 126
impossible subjectivity, concept of 172, 177, 178
Inessential, the 35
intellectual property 273
intension 7
interface 178
International Monetary Fund 197, 269
intervention 6
Iraq, US invasion of 220–6

Jameson, Fredric 62, 119, 188, 214
Johnson, Barbara 79

jouissance 4, 6, 13, 23, 24, 26, 27, 41, 55, 57, 59, 60, 62, 63, 77, 85, 86, 87, 92, 112, 119, 122, 123, 125–8, 130, 165, 166, 167, 207, 208, 228, 235, 282, 284, 299–300
Judaism 161–2
Judeo-Christian tradition 167

Kafka, Franz: 'Josephine the Singer, of the Mouse Folk' 290–1
Kant, Immanuel 32, 39, 41, 94–5, 83, 96–7, 99–100, 138, 213, 276, 277
Critique of Pure Reason 96, 100
Karpai, Dr Sophia 236
Kierkegaard, Søren 53, 88, 204, 264
Kieślowski, Krzysztof 171, 172, 173, 174, 178, 179
Kissinger, Henry 265
Kripke, Saul 7
Naming and Necessity 242
Krugman, Paul 269
Kunkle, Sheila 11, 289, 297–8

Lacan, Jacques 1, 2, 5, 32, 35, 47, 116, 117, 184, 206, 207, 214, 217, 221
Ethics of Psychoanalysis, The 236
'Logic of Sexuation', in *Seminar XX: Encore* 218
On Feminine Sexuality, Seminar XX: Encore 227
Seminar XX: Encore 149, 165
Lacanian Real 6, 17, 27, 28
Laclau, Ernesto 102n, 219, 243
lamella (Lacan) 228, 234
language, acquisition of 20, 21, 77
Lean, David 212
Leibniz, Gottfried 213
Lenin, Vladimir 170, 187, 204, 254, 255
letter, agency of 78–81
Levinas, Emmanuel 254

liberal democracy 43, 106, 109, 114, 138, 148–9, 181–3, 188, 194, 199, 218–19, 225, 249–51, 258, 262, 268, 275–6, 283, 301–2, 305, 311
liberal multiculturalism 262
liberalism 284–5
'living in Christ' 163–70
Locke, John 82
logic of sexuation 81
logocentrism 31, 75, 76
Lost Highway (film) 150–1
Lukács, Georg 232
Lynch, David 150, 151, 152, 154
Lyotard, Jean-François 95

Madoff, Bernard 271–2
Malabou, Catherine 214
Mallarmé, Stéfan: *Un coup de dés* 123
Mao Zedong 249, 253, 254, 255
Marx, Karl 2, 38, 46, 49 138, 143, 158, 159, 173, 184, 250, 255, 280, 286, 291
  Capital 46–7
  Communist Manifesto, The (and Engels) 58, 59, 249–50
  'Contribution to the Critique of Hegel's *Philosophy of Right*' 280
  Eighteenth Brumaire 268
  Grundrisse manuscripts 215
Marxism 163, 164, 165
masculine logic 84
masculine sexuation 209
masculine subject position 111, 112
Master-Signifier 8, 9, 13, 14, 15, 25, 30, 37, 46, 48, 52, 53, 75, 85, 87, 95, 96, 106, 112, 123, 143, 159, 161, 246, 248, 274, 302, 303–4
metaphor 78
metonymy 78
Microsoft 192
'mirror phase', Lacan's theory of 19–20, 117, 248
Moebius strip 303–4

Mouffe, Chantal 102n
multiculturalism 18, 33, 143–4
multiple reality 90–3
Mulvey, Laura 171
Muslim fundamentalism 223
Myers, Tony 87
myth 165
mythic violence 263–4

Name/No of the Father (*le nom du père*) 89–90, 91–2, 126
names as objects 7–9
nationalism 105–7
Nazism 139, 166, 186, 189–90, 191, 197, 251, 275
negation of negation 61–2
negativity of the Real 34
Negri, Toni 273
neoliberalism 97
neurosis 21, 24
New Age spiritualism 155, 156, 163, 164, 166
Nietzsche, Friedrich 206, 213, 251, 253, 281
nominalism 6–7, 141–2
non-All, notion of 303
Notion (*Begriff*; Hegel) 105, 215–16
noumena (Kant) 83, 139

Obama, Barack 225, 290
objective reality 14
objective violence 257, 259, 260
objectivity 280
objet petit a 9, 13, 14, 25, 82, 96, 102, 112, 126,129, 153, 242, 304
obsessional neurosis 21
Oedipus complex 217
ontological difference (Heidegger) 176
'Other of the Other' 59
Other, the 20
  see also big Other

panlogicism 33
parallax 112
parallax gap 6, 17, 38–9, 41, 42, 237–48, 314
parallax Real 39, 253, 298
parallax view 17
Parker, Ian 3, 6, 156
particularity 173
Pascal, Blaise 166
passage à l'acte 92, 144, 168, 309
Pécheux, Michel 79
père-version 115
performative gesture 9
perversion 207
Pétain, Philippe 31
Pfaller, Robert 202
phallic function 81
phenomena (Kant) 83, 140
Picasso, Pablo: *Guernica* 233
Plato 3, 39, 41, 94, 95
 Eleatic dialogues 14
 Parmenides 14, 296, 303
 Sophist 14
point de capiton 15, 37
political parallax 38
Popper, Karl 175
postmodern racism 144
postmodern relativism 39
postmodernism 35, 36, 52–3
Postone, Moishe 286
post-secular thought 155
Post-Theory 171–9
Powell, Colin 233
pragmatic utilitarianism 200
'Pre-Theory' 174
private property rights 273
problem-deadlock 13
prohibition, universalization of 59
proto-Fascism 191
psychoanalysis 42, 164, 165, 167, 186, 229, 298

racism 113–14, 155–6
Real of Capital 159, 271–2

Real, the 19, 22, 23–4, 26–9, 30, 31, 40, 41–2 and *passim*
realism 6, 7, 141
reflexive asymmetry 60–1
relativism 32–3
repetition 87–9, 50, 170
res cogitans 98, 99
Robespierre 249, 254, 292, 293
Rorty, Richard 33, 95, 277
Ross, Elisabeth Kübler 278, 279

Sade, Marquis de 289
Saint-Just, Louis de 60, 252
Santner, Eric 36, 196
Sartre, Jean-Paul 294
Schelling, F.W.J. 2, 24, 32, 41, 218
 Weltalter, Die (The Ages of the World) 115, 119
scientific parallax 38
Searle, John 7
self-consciousness 100
self-identity 120
self-reference, paradox of 16–17
self-reflexive negativity 40
self-transparency 100
Sense-Event 218
September 11, 2001 193–200, 268
set theory 61
sexuation 100
signified 78
signifier 15, 78–9
Silverman, Kaja 171
singular universality 275–7, 310–13
sinthome 13, 92
social antagonism 55–6
social linkage 25
sociopath 230
Socrates 4
Sohn-Rethel, Alfred 49, 50
speech 77
Spinoza, 213
Stalin, Josef 191, 236, 249, 255, 260
Stalinism 185, 186, 187–8, 189–91, 207, 249, 252, 255, 261

Stalinist Socialism 166
Stavrakakis, Yannis 86n, 102n
Stern, Nicholas 273
Stiglitz, Joseph 269
Stoicism 173
straw man fallacy 28
subject-object distinction 13–14
subjective destitution 53
subjective violence 257, 259, 260
subjectivization 21–2
sublation (*Aufhebung*) (Hegel) 94,
    216–17
'sublime', the 36
superego 30, 63, 90, 228, 235
suture 13, 177, 178
Suzuki, D.T. 205
symbolic castration 21, 81, 90, 126,
    127, 131–2
symbolic identity 17
symbolic Law 196, 198, 208–10
symbolic order 101, 272
symbolic performatives 228
symbolic phallus 81–2, 89
symbolic reality 17
symbolic register 20, 23, 24, 36, 77,
    94, 117, 174, 221, 224, 305
symbolic subjectivization 26
symbolic suicide 30
symbolic violence 257, 259, 260
symptom 165
systemic violence 257, 259, 260, 261,
    265

'tarrying with the negative' 37
techno-scientific developments 273
terrorism 225
Third Culture 174
Third Way ideology 166
Thoreau, Henry 284
totalitarianism 166, 180–92
transcendental constitution 237
transcendental empiricism 219
'trans-cultural universal' 175, 176
transference 5

trauma 65
Trotsky, Leon 254
truth as struggle 268–9

UK invasion of Iraq 225–6
unconscious (Freud) 50, 126, 228
universal perspectivism 12–13
universality 173, 175, 176
university discourse (Lacan) 25–6
USA, invasion of Iraq 220–6

vanishing mediator, notion of
    (Jameson) 62, 101, 119
violence 64, 257–66

war on terror 195, 220–6
Wieczorek, Marek 3, 146
Wolfowitz, Paul 221, 222
woman, as symptom of man 81–7
World Bank 269
World Trade Organization 197

Zeitgeist 32
Zen Buddhism 205
Žižek, Slavoj
    on 'dialectic' 6–19
    major contribution 32–9
    philosophical re-inscription of
        Lacanian Theory 19–31
    primary aim 39–45
    Works:
    *Art of the Ridiculous Sublime, The: On
        David Lynch's Lost Highway*
        146–55
    *Did Somebody Say Totalitarianism?
        Five Interventions in the (Mis)use
        of a Notion* 180–92
    *Enjoy Your Symptom! Jacques Lacan
        in Hollywood and Out* 39, 75–93
    First as Tragedy, then as Farce
        267–77, 311
    *For They Know Not What They Do:
        Enjoyment as a Political Factor* 9,
        54, 55–65, 180

Fragile Absolute, The: or, Why is the Christian Legacy Worth Fighting For? 155–62, 163, 185

Fright of Real Tears, The: Krzysztof Kieślowski between Theory and Post-Theory 171–9, 191

How to Read Lacan 227–36

In Defence of Lost Causes 249–56

Indivisible Remainder, The: On Schelling and Related Matters 115–24

Iraq: The Borrowed Kettle 220–6

Living in the End Times 278–94

Looking Awry: An Introduction to Jacques Lacan 66–74, 92, 93

'Matrix, or Two Sides of Perversion, The' 130–1

Metastases of Enjoyment, The: On Women and Causality 108–14, 308

On Belief 163–70

Organs without Bodies: On Deleuze and Consequences 212–19

Parallax View, The 36, 38–9, 237–48, 253

Plague of Fantasies, The 125–35

Puppet and the Dwarf, The: The Perverse Core of Christianity 201–11

'Return of the Natives' 126

Sublime Object of Ideology, The 3, 9, 36–7, 46–54, 56–7, 61, 67, 217

Tarrying with the Negative: Kant, Hegel, and the Critique of Ideology 36, 37, 94–107

Ticklish Subject, The: The Absent Centre of Political Ontology 36, 38, 136–45, 241

'Two Totalitarianisms, The' 189

Violence 64, 257–66

Welcome to the Desert of the Real 193–200, 220

Žižek! (documentary film) 32, 32n, 36

329